T0295799

Investing in Cryptocurrencies and Digital Assets

Investing in Cryptocurrencies and Digital Assets

A Guide to Understanding Technologies, Business Models, Due Diligence, and Valuation

KEITH BLACK

WILEY

Published by John Wiley & Sons, Inc., Hoboken, New Jersey.
Published simultaneously in Canada.

For general information on our other products and services or for technical support, please
contact our Customer Care Department within the United States at (800) 762-2974, outside
the United States at (317) 572-3993 or fax (317) 572-4002.

Wiley also publishes its books in a variety of electronic formats. Some content that appears in
print may not be available in electronic formats. For more information about Wiley products,
visit our website at www.wiley.com.

Library of Congress Cataloging-in-Publication Data is Available:

ISBN 9781394268627 (Cloth)
ISBN 9781394268641 (ePub)
ISBN 9781394268658 (ePDF)

Cover Design: Wiley
Cover Image: © InfiniteStudio/Adobe Stock Photos
Author Photo: Courtesy of Keith Black

Printed and bound by CPI Group (UK) Ltd, Croydon, CR0 4YY

C9781394268627_160824

For Melissa, Trish, and Parker.

Contents

Preface

Cryptocurrencies and digital assets are exciting, innovative, and potentially lucrative investments. Similar to the internet of the late 1990s, blockchain technology may fundamentally transform the ways many industries conduct business. Much of the conversation to date has focused on speculative investments that have provided rags-to-riches and riches-to-rags stories, as well as the potential of crypto-based protocols to upset the current world order of financial markets and sovereign borders.

However, many investors in cryptocurrencies and digital assets may not have explored the characteristics of assets that may rise or decline in value. This book offers a balanced view, embracing the potential to profit and democratize markets while tempering the unbridled optimism that has tempted some to invest their entire net worth in a single, highly speculative crypto asset. While the market capitalization of some crypto protocols may one day exceed the valuation of today's largest tech stocks, most crypto assets today are likely to lose value in the coming years.

This book provides an in-depth exploration of cryptocurrencies and digital assets from the point of view of experienced investors in traditional financial markets. While the technology backing blockchains and digital assets has developed rapidly since 2008, venture capital and stock market investing can provide important historical precedents on the outlook for digital asset investments. The venture capital model shows us that, while most startup companies never reach critical mass, disciplined investing in a portfolio of companies or digital assets can provide strong long-term profits. That is, a small number of massive winners can more than offset the losses from many unprofitable investments.

This book is designed to benefit readers with various goals. First, undergraduate and graduate students in business and computer science wishing to enter an exciting industry can study this volume to get up to speed quickly, demonstrating a breadth of knowledge derived from a full semester course. Second, this book can assist investors and financial advisors in understanding the investment implications of this new technology, including the asset allocation and portfolio construction implications of adding crypto assets to a traditional portfolio of stock and bond investments. Finally, corporate leaders seeking to future proof their business can search for applications of blockchain technology to their current operations.

Part 1 defines cryptocurrencies and digital assets. Chapters 1 to 15 provide a comprehensive introduction to proof-of-work blockchains, such as Bitcoin, and proof-of-stake blockchains, such as Ethereum. The discussion also delves into the characteristics of centralized finance, making a compelling case for adopting distributed ledgers, which can facilitate more transparent and global transactions.

This book also explores the revolutionary potential of smart contracts, paving the way for groundbreaking applications like decentralized finance and non-fungible tokens. Moreover, it highlights how stablecoins and central bank digital currencies could serve as catalysts for the widespread adoption of digital assets on a global scale, opening up new horizons for investors.

Part 2 provides considerations for investing in cryptocurrencies and digital assets. Chapters 16 to 25 describe ways to access digital asset investments, including holding crypto assets on centralized exchanges or in self-custody wallets, crypto-related stocks, venture capital, hedge funds, and derivative products, including futures, options, and perpetual swaps. The fundamental valuation models and due diligence processes that are discussed can be used to evaluate investment decisions carefully. Lessons learned from previous risk events can help investors keep their holdings safe and avoid losses due to overleverage, custody events, and counterparty and credit risk.

The long-term potential of blockchain technology may be most beneficial in tokenizing assets, using the transparency and security of distributed ledgers to provide ownership records for real-world assets, including automobiles, real estate, and event tickets. Distributed ledger and blockchain technology promise to make the world smaller and more equitable, allowing global peer-to-peer transactions while bringing property rights and financial services to the world's 1.4 billion unbanked citizens.

DISCLAIMER

This book is for educational purposes only and does not provide legal, tax, regulatory, or investment advice. The author may have an economic interest in the stocks, cryptocurrencies, and digital assets discussed in this book. Efforts were made to ensure this book's accuracy when the manuscript was drafted. However, taxes, regulations, and the specifics of crypto protocols can and will change over time.

One

Defining Cryptocurrencies and Digital Assets

The first 15 chapters define the landscape of cryptocurrencies and digital assets, including the differing technologies and asset types.

Chapter 1 discusses money, banking, and inflation. The rationale for creating the digital assets industry arose from dissatisfaction with current institutions, especially regarding bank failures and the debasement of the value of fiat currencies through inflation.

Chapter 2 explains the institutions involved in the centralized finance (CeFi) and traditional finance (TradFi) markets. The crypto universe seeks to recreate, replace, or disintermediate many traditional institutions, including central banks, securities exchanges, and commercial banks.

Chapter 3 introduces the concepts of blockchains and distributed ledgers. As investors move away from reliance on centralized counterparties, information is securely stored by thousands of global recordkeepers.

Chapter 4 discusses the revolutionary concept of Bitcoin, including the process of mining in a proof-of-work protocol. Miners earn block rewards for approving transactions and securing the Bitcoin blockchain.

Chapter 5 continues with the evolution of digital assets by discussing the 2014 launch of smart contract technology. The Ethereum blockchain remains a leader in smart contract distributed applications to this day.

Chapter 6 provides a list of alternatives to Ethereum-based smart contracts. Proof-of-stake protocols such as Binance, Avalanche, and Solana seek to provide faster and cheaper access to smart contract-based distributed applications.

Chapter 7 discusses the need to increase the scalability of blockchains, especially Ethereum, which relies on layer 2 solutions such as Polygon, Optimism, and Arbitrum to speed transactions and reduce gas fees.

Chapter 8 introduces stablecoins, which seek to provide a store of value linked to the value of gold, euros, or US dollars. Stablecoins issued by governments are termed central bank digital currencies (CBDCs).

Chapter 9 expands on the use cases of digital assets by explaining oracles and insurance. Oracles provide the price and data feeds required for the smooth operation of smart contracts. Smart contract–enabled insurance policies may revolutionize the cost and speed of insurance operations.

Chapter 10 explains that while the Bitcoin and Ethereum blockchains are designed to be transparent, privacy tokens seek to keep transactions private. The regulatory risks of obscuring transactions are also discussed.

Chapter 11 introduces what could be the most important innovation in the digital assets universe: the creation of a parallel financial system in which decentralized finance (DeFi) seeks to replace the role of banks and securities exchanges.

Chapter 12 explains how smart contract ecosystems can be combined using the concepts of composability and the stacking of distributed applications (DApps) to work together like "money Legos" to accomplish DeFi's goals.

Chapter 13 lists various uses of blockchain applications beyond financial markets, where blockchain technology may revolutionize supply chain management and ticketing for concerts and sporting events.

Chapter 14 explores the exciting impact that blockchain technology may have on popular culture. While initially focused on art, music, and gaming, non-fungible tokens may provide the entry point for consumers to access the metaverse and Web 3.0 using a single wallet as their portable digital identity.

Finally, Chapter 15 explains how the corporate governance structure may be replaced by distributed autonomous organizations (DAOs) that can manage businesses remotely in a much flatter hierarchy than traditional corporations.

CHAPTER 1

Money, Banking, and Inflation

Cryptocurrencies are one portion of the digital asset universe. Digital assets include cryptocurrencies and tokenized assets, including real estate, tickets, art, music, equities, and others that can be viewed as money. Let's discuss some very traditional money and banking economics that describe the current banking system. Later, we will see how cryptocurrencies and digital assets have the potential to improve today's global banking system.

Our discussion starts with fiat currencies and the history of money.

Thousands of years ago, trade relied on the barter system, which did not build the most efficient economy. Those who worked as farmers produced meat, milk, eggs, or grains as their contribution to the economy. Under the barter system, farmers needing clothing must find another participant in the economy willing to trade clothing for the farmer's produce. This barter system has a significant search cost, as participants couldn't always find someone who wanted to take the goods or services they were offering in exchange for the goods or services that they needed.

These high search costs caused many farmers to also chop wood and make clothing, and perhaps some clothing makers to grow their own food. People who weren't able to trade for everything they needed would produce those needed goods or services on their own. This was a relatively inefficient way to trade.

Eventually, market participants agreed on a definition of money, as it was easier to sell the food for money and use the money to purchase the clothing. This reduced the time it took to search for the person willing to trade for whatever goods or services you had to offer. Marketplaces grew with each merchant selling their goods or services for money in a common location, dramatically increasing economic efficiency and allowing market participants to specialize in the good or service where they exhibited the most skill or enjoyment.

The first form of money was based on commodities such as seashells, gold, silver, corn, or tobacco. Of course, once the form of money was defined in an economy, some market participants stopped making food or clothing and set out in search of gold or seashells. Ideally, the commodity money was relatively scarce, but not too scarce that there was not enough money supply to support the desired level of economic activity.

Money is defined as whatever is generally accepted in exchange for goods, services, and debts. Today, fiat money is currencies defined and produced by governments, such as US dollars, Japanese yen, or Euros. While gold or corn may have some intrinsic value, or use beyond exchanging for the goods and services consumers need, fiat currencies have no intrinsic value. The banknotes and coins only have value because the government says they have value.

Efficiencies increase as an economy moves from the barter system into a commodity money system, and increase again as the economy moves from commodity money to fiat money. Consumers don't spend time searching for barter partners, and workers can specialize in the goods they produce most efficiently. As specialization increases, productivity increases, and the economy has a greater quantity and quality of all goods and services available.

There are three characteristics of money. Money is a medium of exchange, a store of value, and a unit of account. A medium of exchange is the characteristic of being able to use money to buy goods and services. When consumers arrive at the market, prices are denominated and listed in money: gold, silver, seashells, or US dollars. Consumers with sufficient money can trade it for whatever goods and services can be procured within their budget. Transactions become more straightforward, and the economy benefits from the division of labor.

Money as a store of value allows producers to save the proceeds of their labor and transfer purchasing power from one time period to another. This is easier with fiat currency and commodities such as gold, but harder with perishable commodity money such as food or tobacco. Those who don't spend their gold or dollars today will be able to buy goods and services at a future date rather than spending all of their income in the current period. Holding commodity money or fiat currency in the form of banknotes does not allow savers to earn interest.

Money is also a unit of account. The listed prices for goods or services are the number of monetary units that the seller will accept for their produce. Consumers have to choose which goods and services to purchase while keeping to their current holdings of money. Producers must determine the price that will be charged for their goods or services in the marketplace. Comparing prices and reducing costs brings economic efficiency into the market.

Once prices are listed in monetary units, economists can track those prices over time. If the price level of goods and services rises over time, there is inflation in the economy and consumers are encouraged to spend their money quickly because rising prices will reduce the future level of goods and services that can be purchased.

Bankers arose to pay interest to savers while lending money to borrowers. Savers were being paid to wait to consume while borrowers were paying more to consume today. Ideally, savers can earn enough interest to offset the decline in purchasing power through inflation, while bankers can earn a positive net interest margin by charging borrowers a higher interest rate and paying depositors a lower interest rate.

Historically, precious stones, gold, silver, seashells, corn, fish, and other foods were used as commodity forms of money. The US was on the gold standard from 1934 to 1971.[1] During this period of time, US dollars were convertible into gold at a fixed price of $35 per ounce. The US did not print dollar bills unless there was sufficient gold in the vaults to guarantee this conversion. From 1934 to 1971, dollars could be exchanged for gold at $35 per ounce, as the dollar was a gold-backed currency. Dollars were inherently worth something because they could be traded for ounces of gold.

This limited ability to print money kept the rate of inflation low but also capped potential economic activity. The gold supply was relatively fixed over time, while the demand for economic activity continued to increase. In 1971, as inflation started to increase, President Richard Nixon ended the gold standard. Without its direct convertibility into gold, the US dollar became a fiat currency unbacked by any store of value. Inflation skyrocketed to more than 11% by 1974 and to more than 13% in 1980. Gold moved away from its fixed price regime and was allowed to trade at a floating price. With gold priced at more than $2,000 per ounce in 2024, the US dollar has lost more than 98% of its value as denominated in gold in just 53 years. The price of most other goods and services in the US also rose sharply over the last 50 years, reducing the purchasing power of a single US dollar. Each dollar now buys less milk, fewer eggs, fewer gallons of gas, and less value in the housing market. Each dollar is worth less as the economy-wide level of prices continues to rise.

The paper dollar bills that consumers have in their wallets or bank accounts are not backed by any physical asset. There's nothing to back those dollars except for the full faith and credit of the US government. The US construct is that dollars are legal tender, meaning that dollars are accepted for US tax payments and for all goods and services sold in the US. Legal tender means that US dollars are required to settle all trades in the US.

Therefore, a vital focus of the cryptocurrency and digital asset community is avoiding inflation or the debasement of fiat currencies. Ideally, this new type of digital money will not have this type of inflation. Cryptocurrencies and digital assets can potentially serve as a stronger store of value than a fiat currency subject to substantial value debasement through the accumulated effects of price inflation over time.

Fiat currencies, such as dollars, euros, and yen, are exchangeable for valuable goods and services because the respective governments declare them to be valuable. It costs governments very little to print currencies, as printing presses can continually crank out $100 bills or 500 euro notes. The ability of governments to print money without limit is mocked by crypto memes, such as "Money printer go Brrr."

Fortunately for US consumers and investors, the US has a relatively strong financial system. The dollar serves as a hard currency or a safe haven given its history of strong global demand during economic crises. Relatively few currencies serve this role, including dollars, euros, Swiss francs, and British pounds. Even though the dollar has been deemed a strong currency, its value has fallen by more than 97% over the last 50 years due to inflation. Investors need to earn 2% to 3% per year on their savings to maintain the current level of purchasing power over time.

While an average annual inflation rate of 2% or 3% in the US or Europe debases the value of currencies over long periods of time, countries with excess inflation and weak currencies can see purchasing power decline much more quickly. In some emerging markets, governments seek to repay debts or increase spending by increasing the money supply quickly and printing fiat currency without limit. With inflation compounding at more than 600% per year in Zimbabwe or totaling more than 50,000,000% from 2016 to 2019 in Venezuela, people lose trust in the value of the fiat currency. Currency is printed in ever-increasing denominations, such as the 10-trillion-dollar bill issued by Zimbabwe, which is worth less than $1 US dollar. I own one in my personal collection, as it sounds fun to say that I have $10 trillion in cash.

People are paid daily, hopefully at a new wage each day. The pay must be spent immediately because the prices of goods will be even higher next week. When grocery shopping requires wheelbarrows of bolivars or dollar bills, the currency has effectively become worthless. Consumers seek to abandon the use of fiat currencies and search for other stores of value, whether it be dollars, euros, bitcoin, stablecoins, or even move back to commodity money such as gold or precious stones.

Access to hard currencies or cryptocurrencies can be an economic lifeline for consumers in countries with weak currencies or failing banking systems. Rather than going back to the barter economy in Venezuela with consumers trying to buy any goods possible to maintain the value of their assets, it can be easier to store value in cryptocurrencies and digital assets.

While bitcoin or Ether tokens have volatile prices, the value of stablecoins is linked to the value of one dollar or one euro. When moving into blockchain-based wallets, the assets of consumers are no longer linked to the value of their home country's currency or subject to the risks of the local banking system.

Money is valuable because demand exceeds supply. If it's hard to find money, then that money is going to be valuable. The faster the government prints money, the faster the value of that money declines. Prices rise when the money supply grows faster than real GDP. When too much money is chasing too few goods, price levels tend to quickly increase. For example, during the COVID-induced supply chain shortages, the US government was distributing $1,400 stimulus checks to US consumers regardless of their financial need or whether their income had declined. As goods were scarce and money was not scarce, prices rose quickly, such as the 40% increase in used car prices in less than two years after the start of the pandemic.[2]

Hopefully, you've learned as a finance or economics student that personal prosperity requires spending less money than is earned as income. Once you get your first job, you should open a 401(k) plan, save 5% to 10% of your salary and receive your employer's matching contribution. If you can live on 80% to 90% of your income today, eventually you'll be able to retire. You invest those retirement account contributions into stocks and bonds. If stocks and bonds have a higher return than inflation over time, the purchasing power of your assets can increase. By saving money today, you can increase the level of your future consumption.

The US national debt rose from $5 trillion in 1996 to $15 trillion in 2012 and to more than $33 trillion as of the third quarter of 2023.[3] This was the equivalent of 65% of GDP in 1996, 100% of GDP in 2012, and more than 132% of GDP at its peak in the second quarter of 2020, with the debt per capita approaching $100,000. As a percentage of GDP, the US national debt more than doubled from 1996 to 2020. This demonstrates continued borrowings as the US regularly engages in deficit spending whether the economy is strong or in recession. This ever-growing national debt increases the portion of the US budget needed to service the debt, which may require future tax increases or spending cuts.

The US money supply is tracked through the M1 and M2 measures. M1 includes currency and the value of checking accounts, while M2 includes M1 and the value of savings accounts, certificates of deposit, and money market funds. M1 balances are available for immediate spending needs, while M2 can quickly be converted to use for immediate spending needs. Consumers may spend most or all of their M1 balances in any given month, while the savings portion of M2 is designed to be a store of value that is not spent in the current month. Balances held in investment accounts, such as stocks, bonds, or cryptocurrencies are not counted in the US money supply.

Inflation, economic growth, and money supply growth are closely linked. Between 2000 and 2019, US M2 money supply growth averaged 5.8% while inflation averaged 2.2%. In the three years ending September 2022, US M2 money supply growth exploded to an annualized average rate of 12.4% due to COVID-era stimulus policies as well as the continued easy monetary policy of the Federal Reserve. After CPI inflation reached a low of 0.1% in May 2020, inflation exploded to reach a peak of 9.1% by June 2022, a direct result of the increased money supply growth rate on top of supply chain issues that made goods and services less available. When inflation was just 1% in July 2020, theories of money supply growth could be used to forecast future inflation. In "Socially Distant Inflation," CPI inflation was predicted to reach 5% to 15% due to this growth in money supply and scarcity of goods.[4] With the annual inflation rate having been 2.9% or less since 2012, prices increased by 5.4% in the year ending July 2021 and 9.1% in the year ending June 2022.

US short-term interest rates were near zero from 2009 to 2016 before the Fed tightened to reach 2.4% by mid-2019. By April 2020, the Fed again reduced rates to near zero as a result of the COVID-induced slowdown in the economy. In 2022 and 2023, once it was clear that inflation had reached uncomfortably high levels, the Fed quickly increased rates to more than 5.25%. When economic growth is slow, the Fed might reduce interest rates in order to facilitate economic activity, and when interest rates are rising, the Fed is trying to tighten monetary conditions and reduce inflation.

Money can also be created through fractional reserves, which allow banks to loan more money than they have in deposits. The required reserve ratio is the percentage of deposits that banks must hold as reserves. For banks with assets below $47.8 million in checking account deposits, reserve requirements are set at 3%. Larger banks have reserve requirements of 10%. No reserves are required on M2 categories such as savings accounts or certificates of deposit.

Any deposits in excess of the required reserves are excess reserves that can be lent out as new loans. As excess reserves become loans, the money supply increases. The Fed sets and enforces reserve requirements, but they are rarely changed, as this would be extremely disruptive. Increasing the reserve requirement would tighten credit availability and shrink the money supply while reducing reserve requirements can increase the money supply as loans become more plentiful.

Money is created through an interaction between the Federal Reserve and the banks. Banks extend loans based on customer deposits, which are tracked through the M1 and M2 money supply measures. The excess of deposits over reserve requirements can be lent to consumers through mortgages, credit cards, car loans, and businesses through commercial loans. Money supply growth accelerates as loan growth increases and the proceeds of the loans are spent more quickly. The monetary base is the amount of bank reserves plus circulating currency. Open market operations, the most frequently used tool of the Fed, change the money supply by about twice their size.

When the Fed is easing monetary policy, it creates money by buying bonds from banks and introducing more cash into the system. When the Fed is tightening, it is selling bonds to take cash out of the system. These open market operations are the most frequently used tool of the Fed. The balance sheet of the US Federal Reserve Bank increased from $4.2 trillion in February 2020 to nearly $9 trillion in the second quarter of 2022. Liquidity at US banks increased by nearly $5 trillion in two years as the Fed bought bonds and injected cash into the US banking system, some of which was recently printed. As the Fed tightened interest rates and sold bonds or allowed them to mature from the second quarter of 2022 to the end of 2023, the Fed's balance sheet declined from nearly $9 trillion to around $7.8 trillion, taking $1.2 trillion out of the banking system. The Fed's decade-long stimulus started at the beginning of the GFC in 2008, as the Fed balance sheet moved from less than $1 trillion in September 2008 to nearly $3 trillion at the end of 2011.

The Fed directly controls short-term interest rates, but less directly influences long-term interest rates. While the Federal funds rate rose from 0% to 5.5%, the 10-year Treasury rate has risen from 2% to 4.25%.

According to Milton Friedman and the monetary school of economists, the money supply primarily influences output in the short run. Easy monetary policy and stimulative fiscal policy can temporarily positively influence GDP growth. The COVID-era stimulus was largely spent by the end of 2023, which kept the US economy out of a recession. However, an increase in the money supply increases prices more than economic growth in the long run. That is, an economy can't simply grow GDP by printing money. Empirically, the more money is printed, the greater the increase in the price level. Fluctuations in real GDP and inflation come primarily from volatility in money supply growth.

The equation of exchange is $P * Y = M * V = GDP$. Price * output = money * velocity. This quantity theory of money implies that only prices are affected by the growth of the money supply. Output growth is impacted by productivity, labor force size, education, and resource availability. Velocity measures how quickly money is spent.

There's a strong log-linear relationship between inflation and money supply growth. Inflation occurs whenever the money supply grows faster than GDP. For example, 5% money supply growth in a country with 2% real GDP growth is likely to lead to an inflation rate of 3%. Slower money supply growth is less correlated to inflation. Money supply growth of 2% to 3% might not have a direct correlation to GDP growth or inflation.

The fastest GDP growth experienced in emerging markets can be 5% to 10%. Money supply growth in excess of 10% annually, even in emerging markets with the strongest GDP growth, is likely to lead to inflation. The rates of hyperinflation seen in Venezuela and Zimbabwe come from the government printing money and increasing the money supply by more than 100% annually.

From 2002 to 2019, M2 growth in the US averaged 5.8% while inflation averaged 2.1%, very close to the Fed's target inflation rate of 2%.[5] Besides the global financial crisis of 2008 and 2009, US GDP tended to grow steadily during this period. From 2020 to 2022, M2 growth averaged 11.6%, far above US GDP growth. In 2020, monetary policy was easy, interest rates were near zero, homeowners quickly refinanced mortgages to rates under 3%, and credit was widely available. In addition to stimulative monetary policy, fiscal policy was also stimulative with multiple rounds of $1,400 checks provided to the majority of US taxpayers. With M2 growth of 11.6%, inflation averaged 4.8% from 2020 to 2022, reaching a peak of 9.1% in June 2022, an inflation rate not seen in the US since the 1970s. The US dollar lost more than 15% of its purchasing power as inflation compounded at a 4.8% rate over three years. By the third quarter of 2022, the Fed quickly moved to raise rates from zero to more than 5% in just one year to combat inflation.

The decline in the value of fiat currencies gave digital currency adherents ammunition to say fiat currencies are inherently unstable and untrustworthy. Because the central bank can be stimulative and debase the value of a currency so quickly, it can be difficult to find a store of value.

It is difficult for a central bank to know when to ease and tighten monetary policy, as monetary policy and fiscal policy are implemented with a lag. The effect on employment and output may take 12 to 18 months, while the impact on prices may take two years or longer. The record levels of monetary and fiscal policy stimulus in 2020 resulted in the highest inflation rate in more than 40 years in 2022. The stimulus payments received by consumers were fully spent, but it took until the end of 2023 to work off those levels of excess savings.

The goal of monetary and fiscal policy is to be expansionary below full employment in times of slow GDP growth and recessions. If the Fed could know exactly when the economy will experience a period of slow growth, the economy can improve if the Fed is stimulative during that time. Central banks also want to be restrictive in times of excess growth. Once the economy is growing too quickly, the goal is to slow growth and reduce potential inflation.

The difficulty is that when decisions are made regarding monetary and fiscal policy, the central bank doesn't know what economic conditions will be one to two years from now when those policies will eventually impact the economy. There is a potential for stimulative policies to impact the economy during a time of growth, which can accelerate inflationary pressures. There is also the potential for restrictive policy to impact the economy during a time of slowing growth, perhaps deepening a recession.

In 2022 and 2023, it was probably too late for the Fed to increase interest rates and too late to slow that money supply growth. In 2022, the Fed is starting to implement restrictive monetary policy while fiscal policy is becoming more restrictive as stimulus programs are ending. While both monetary and fiscal policy are simultaneously restrictive, the Fed's balance sheet is also shrinking. Interest rates have risen from zero to more than 5% in an attempt to slow the economy, but the timing of how this will impact the economy is unknown as policy changes impact the economy with a lag.

It is unknown if the interest rate increases implemented in the second half of 2022 will move the US economy into recession in 2024. The interest rate increases implemented in 2022 aren't immediately impacting the economy in 2022, but can impact the economy in 2023 and 2024. The Fed doesn't know exactly how tight monetary policy should be because the impact is going to be felt in the economy with a lag. It makes sense for a pause in any easing or tightening cycle to observe the impact on employment and output.

Unfortunately, a central bank may be stimulative for too long, leading to excess growth and inflation, or restrictive for too long, perhaps pushing the economy into recession. Rather than attempting to time the economy by being stimulative during times of slow growth and restrictive during times of strong growth and inflationary pressures, some economists would prefer that central banks simply implement a stable money supply growth policy.

If the central bank believes that maximum long-term GDP growth is 2% to 3%, inflation can remain under control with a policy of targeting a stable money supply growth rate of 4%. When money supply growth is 4% and GDP growth averages 2%, the central bank may reach a target of an average annual inflation rate of 2%. With stable money supply growth, businesses can plan for relatively stable inflation rates of around 2%.

With a stable money supply growth rate, the central bank isn't trying to predict when to stimulate a weak economy or when to restrict a strong economy. The stable money supply growth rate will automatically be stimulative in a weak economy and automatically restrictive in a strong economy. Whenever GDP growth exceeds 4%, 4% money supply growth is automatically restrictive. The slower the economy becomes, the more stimulative the money supply growth becomes. Another benefit of stable money supply growth is that business owners and central bankers don't have to predict when monetary policy is going to be stimulative or restrictive, so the economy will automatically react to the stable policy.

It is important to understand real interest rates and nominal interest rates. Fixed-rate bonds and bank deposits earn a nominal interest rate. In early 2024, nominal rates were 5% on short-term Treasury bills and 4% on 10-year Treasury notes. Consumers were able to earn more than 4% on carefully chosen checking accounts or certificates of deposits. Nominal rates equal real rates plus expected inflation.

Expected inflation can be observed as the difference between nominal Treasury notes and Treasury Inflation-Protected Securities (TIPS), which pay a real yield. In early 2024, the five-year Treasury had a nominal yield of 4.0% while the 5-year TIPS had a real yield of 1.6%, making expected inflation 2.4%.[6] Consumers investing at rates of 4% have a positive real yield, meaning that their purchasing power increases over time as the interest earned exceeds the inflation rate. Those holding assets in cash or bank accounts earning yields near zero will experience declines in purchasing power close to the annual inflation rate.

Investors are not encouraged to compare nominal rates across countries, as the main source of the difference in interest rates around the world is inflation rates. Real rates are relatively stable around the world. For example, the US has nominal yields of around 4% and real yields of around 1.6%. Investors may be tempted to buy Brazilian government bonds at 10% yields, but they are likely to lose more than 8% to inflation, leaving real rates near 2%. While the difference in nominal rates between the US and Brazil is 6%, the difference in real rates is less than 1%. Investors seek to invest in countries with the highest real interest rates, not countries with the highest nominal interest rates, as real rates measure the ability to preserve purchasing power over time.

The US inflation rate is based on the annual change in the consumer price index (CPI). Compiled by the US government, the CPI regularly measures the cost of a typical bundle of goods purchased by households. The CPI basket is about 33% housing; about 20% goes into food and energy, including groceries, restaurants, heating bills, electric bills, and gasoline. Housing, food, and energy make up 53% of the CPI basket, with another 15% on education and medical care, 9% on new and used cars, and 23% on all other consumer goods and services.

The government regularly surveys the prices of goods and services to determine the inflation rate and the change in the consumer price index year over year. A 6% inflation rate is experienced when the cost of goods and services in the consumer price index has risen by 6% from last year to this year, meaning that the basket of goods and services consumed by the average

American is 6% more expensive than it was last year. The higher the inflation rate, the weaker the value of the dollar.

Currencies exist in a global market. The dollar is worth whatever basket of goods and services consumers could buy with it. We can also measure the value of the dollar relative to the Brazilian real or the euro. The value of each currency is calculated relative to another.

A key determinant of the currency's value is the difference in inflation rates from one country to another. If Brazil has a higher inflation rate than the US, the Brazilian currency is expected to devalue or weaken relative to the dollar. Inflation rates also influence exports and imports. If prices in a country are increasing relative to other countries, that country is likely to purchase more imported goods at lower prices and export fewer goods at higher prices. These dynamics mean there is excess selling of the currency to pay for imports, which drives the currency's price lower. Countries with lower relative inflation rates are likely to experience greater exports and fewer imports. Higher exports create demand for the currency, which leads to higher prices.

Nominal rates are equal to real rates plus expected inflation. Higher real interest rates cause a currency to appreciate over long periods of time, as money from around the world flows into that country's investment markets.

From its low in 2008 until early 2024, the US dollar appreciated 40% relative to a basket of large global currencies. The strong dollar was driven by real interest rates and strong stock prices that attracted capital from around the world.

This has been an overview of the traditional money and banking system. We've defined monetary policy and how the Fed sets interest rates. We've defined fiscal policy as the government's taxing and spending policies. When monetary and fiscal policies are stimulative, the economy may experience rising inflation and faster GDP growth. Restrictive policies are designed to slow inflation and economic growth.

The cryptocurrency community views a number of weaknesses in this TradFi system, as they seek to build a parallel monetary system that can reduce the impact of inflation and excessive money supply growth on the debasement of fiat currencies.

CHAPTER 2

Centralized Finance (CeFi) and Traditional Finance (TradFi) Markets

In Chapter 1, we explored traditional methods of money and banking and the impact of inflation on the long-term purchasing power of fiat currencies. In this chapter, we will discuss how blockchain-based markets seek to improve on the inefficiencies of the centralized finance (CeFi) and traditional finance (TradFi) markets.

The digital asset market facilitated by blockchain will change many of the industries in today's economy. One of the first areas of innovation is moving functions from traditional and centralized financial markets into a parallel financial market facilitated by blockchain technology.

Once we understand these different financial systems, we'll move to the Bitcoin and Ethereum blockchains to see how this new financial technology may one day replace many existing financial systems.

Our financial system has a variety of goals including price discovery, asset liquidity, facilitating payments, and efficiently bringing savers and borrowers together.

Price discovery allows investors to know exactly what an asset is worth at any point in time, while liquidity allows investors to sell an asset quickly for close to the expected price. The insurance industry and derivative products, such as futures and options, are among the largest businesses in the financial sector. Facilitating payments and purchases allows consumers in an economy to efficiently interact without resorting to barter.

Savers have excess capital with a desire to earn a return, ideally a yield that is higher than inflation, so their savings can have greater purchasing power in the future than in the present. There is also a need for individuals and corporations to borrow. In many cases, older individuals are savers and younger individuals are borrowers. Younger companies need to access capital to grow while more mature companies may have excess capital to invest.

Bringing borrowers and savers together allows money to move through the economy, while the capital markets help the economy grow jobs and make investments. An economy can develop a shared prosperity when the savings of the savers are used to lend to the borrowers, and hopefully, the borrowers will put that money to good use, perhaps starting a business, buying a house, or earning a college degree.

Cryptocurrencies, digital assets, and blockchain technology have the ability to transplant or reinvent many of the areas of the CeFi industry. Centralized means that there is one specific institution that's in charge. It might be a bank, a securities exchange, a governmental regulator, or a central bank. Other centralized counterparties include credit card payment processors, remittance facilitators, and insurance companies. Many of these large financial institutions are now seeing competitors in the blockchain space.

Banks bring together savers and borrowers. Savers deposit their money into the bank to earn a yield to maintain or grow the future purchasing power of their cash. Banks loan those deposits to borrowers who consume or invest today and repay the loans in the future. Ideally, the investments made with the borrowed funds have a higher return than the loan's interest cost, allowing the borrower's wealth to grow. Banks allow borrowers to spend now, and savers to store and increase their assets for future spending.

Many institutions have relatively similar functions, such as banks, credit unions, and savings and loans. In the US, deposits are insured up to $250,000 per individual per institution by Federal government institutions such as the Federal Deposit Insurance Corporation (FDIC) and the National Credit Union Administration (NCUA). While US banks insure a portion of deposits, deposit insurance is not available in every country and certainly not widely available in the cryptocurrency and digital asset industry.

It is important to understand the assets and liabilities of these depository institutions. A bank's assets are the customers' liabilities, and the bank's liabilities are the customers' assets. Banks borrow money from their customers' deposits into checking accounts, savings accounts, and certificates of deposit. Many of those deposits bear interest, which comprises the bank's borrowing costs. In addition to customer deposits, banks may borrow money through short-term credit facilities or by issuing long-term bonds.

Assets (Often Long Term)	Liabilities (Often Short Term)
Loans	Checking accounts
Cash	Savings accounts
Central bank reserves	Certificates of deposit
Bonds and investments	Bank borrowings

The liabilities of bank customers, such as loans, are the key assets of a bank. Banks can also keep cash reserves in their vault or on deposit with the central bank. Banks can also purchase bonds and make other investments.

The goal of a bank is to earn a positive net interest margin, which is the income on loans and other assets relative to the costs of the bank's deposit base and borrowings. For example, if the bank offers a corporate loan at 8% and pays a 3% yield on a checking account, the bank's net interest margin is 5%. The bank earns a profit when the net interest margin exceeds the cost of their operations, employees, buildings, and losses on loan defaults and bad investments.

The goal is to borrow at a lower rate and lend at a higher rate. The net interest margin is the difference between a lower borrowing rate and a higher lending rate. Banking is difficult when the duration of the assets differs from the duration of the liabilities. An asset-liability mismatch is created when bank deposits can be withdrawn at any time, while the bank uses the volatile deposit base to lend to homeowners in the form of 30-year fixed-rate mortgages. Banks naturally tend to have short-term liabilities and long-term assets. If not carefully managed and hedged, times of rising rates can be especially challenging for banks.

In centralized finance, investors are concerned about the potential failure of a key institution. In the great financial crisis (GFC) of 2008, a number of significant players in the financial industry failed, including Bear Stearns and Lehman Brothers. When banks fail, depositors are concerned about when, and if, they will receive the return of their assets.

There's a concern that banks exhibit censorship when some types of consumers are denied service. Denials of service may be due to a consumer's income or credit quality, country of citizenship, or even discrimination based on race or other issues. A key goal of the cryptocurrency industry is to provide a level playing field for consumers around the world. Consumers are free to interact with any blockchain-based protocol as long as they meet the financial requirements.

Many countries, especially those in emerging markets, have strict regulations or a lack of access to financial services. If the services are available, they may be expensive or difficult to access.

Finally, centralized counterparties, whether banks or social media providers, tend to operate as walled gardens. While the assets or social media connections are the consumer's property, centralized businesses make it difficult to transfer across platforms. In order to transfer an account from one US bank or brokerage firm to another, it may take several days or even weeks to fully close one account, open another account, and transfer assets to the new account. It is even more difficult to transfer US dollar–denominated assets from a US bank to euro-denominated assets at the European bank.

While transferring assets from one firm to another is time-consuming, it is extraordinarily difficult to transfer liabilities, such as a home mortgage, from one bank to another. That process typically involves refinancing, borrowing a new mortgage at today's current rate, and using the proceeds to retire the original mortgage. This is beneficial during declining interest rates, but infeasible and expensive during times of rising mortgage rates.

Similarly, there is no portability of a user's followers, friend list, or connections between Twitter/X, Facebook, or LinkedIn platforms.

The goal of the blockchain and cryptocurrency community is to use a decentralized, peer-to-peer system to disintermediate banks, reduce costs, and make it easier for consumers to access financial services worldwide.

Banks fail for a variety of reasons, especially credit losses, investment losses, and asset-liability mismatches. A recipe for bank failure is when the bank's assets are long term and illiquid, and the liabilities are called immediately. A moral hazard is created if the banks receive the profit or reward for taking risks while the losses from taking those risks are insured by the government or the taxpayers. In fact, taking greater risks by lending to more risky borrowers is expected to have a higher net interest margin, but the riskiest borrowers also have the highest probability of defaulting on the loan and not repaying principal and interest as scheduled.

What are the mechanics of a bank failure? Consider the market in 2021, where savers were earning near-zero interest rates while borrowers were able to lock in 30-year mortgages at 3%. Banks expected to earn a net interest margin of 3%. However, after the Fed tightened rates aggressively in 2022 and 2023, savers sought to earn 5% yields on Treasury bills, money markets, and even checking accounts. Banks paying zero interest rates were forced to either increase the interest rates they offered to maintain their deposit base or see their deposits depart for higher-yielding accounts in other institutions. Banks paying 5% on deposits while earning 3% income on 30-year mortgages face a negative net interest margin that can threaten the profitability and stability of the bank.

In March 2023, Silicon Valley Bank (SVB) experienced the largest bank failure in 15 years and second only to the 2008 demise of Washington Mutual as the largest bank failure in US history. As SVB's assets increased from $71 billion in 2019 to $211 billion in 2022, the bank was unable to increase loan growth as quickly as asset growth, so a substantial amount of bonds was purchased.

As short-term interest rates increased rapidly, SVB's portfolio of long-term Treasury bonds was losing value. After mark-to-market losses of more than $15 billion combined with a bank run of rapid customer withdrawals, the bank failed and its operations were sold to First Citizens Bancshares.

SVB noted that its available-for-sale bond portfolio held $21 billion in US Treasury and agency securities, yielding 1.79% with an average duration of 3.6 years.[1] As interest rates rise, bond prices decline at a rate of the duration multiplied by the change in yield.

$$\text{Bond Losses} = \text{Yield Change} * \text{Portfolio Size} * (-\text{Duration})$$
$$\$2.26\,\text{billion} = 3\% * \$21\,\text{billion} * (-3.6)$$

If rates rose to 4.79% during the Fed's tightening cycle, SVB would lose $2.26 billion, which is the 3% yield change multiplied by the $21 billion position size and the 3.6-year duration of the bond portfolio. Notice that this loss was 10.8% of the bond portfolio's value or more than 6 years of interest on the portfolio at a yield of 1.79%. With total assets of $211 billion at the end of 2022 and total equity of $16 billion, a loss of just 7.6% of assets was sufficient to wipe out the bank's equity base. The bank was widely criticized for its lack of interest rate hedges, as a short position in Treasury note futures would have profited from a decline in Treasury prices and a rise in Treasury yields and offset the decline in the value of the bank's assets caused by a sharp increase in interest rates.

A similar asset-liability mismatch led to the failure of the Federal Savings and Loan Insurance Corporation (FSLIC) in 1989, which could not fully insure the one-third of US savings and loans that failed between 1986 and 1995. As discussed in Chapter 1, inflation exploded after the US abandoned the gold standard in 1971. In August 1971, the US ended backing the US dollar with gold, with the 10-Year Treasury yielding around 6.3%. By September 1981, 10-Year Treasury rates exceeded 15.8%.

Over this same time period, mortgage rates rose from 9% to more than 17%. The savings and yields originated 9% mortgages in the 1960s when CD yields were often around 6%, for an expected net interest margin of 3%. Thirty-year mortgages originated in 1970 allowed consumers to repay their loans over time to as late as the year 2000. As Treasury yields spiked and CDs matured, savers withdrew their funds in search of higher yields than the S&Ls were allowed to pay by government regulation. Banks invested in junk bonds and risky real estate projects to increase returns, but many of those investments soured. With mortgages locked in for the long run at 9%, the increases in interest rates combined with losses on risky investments wiped out the capital of the S&L industry. The FSLIC insurance fund was decimated, even after receiving two taxpayer-funded infusions.

Many of the participants in the cryptocurrency and digital asset space have a libertarian view that banks and insurance companies are being paid too much for the services that they offer and that governments and taxpayers should not be subsidizing their losses with bailouts. One goal of digital assets is to disintermediate the banks or reduce the fees to the intermediary. In terms of banking, this would have the effect of paying higher rates to savers and charging lower rates to borrowers. By reducing the size of the net interest margin, banks earn a lower share of the national income, which leaves more income for consumers and businesses. With savers lending directly to borrowers, the function of a bank is eliminated. This is the global and peer-to-peer vision of the proponents of cryptocurrencies and digital assets.

The goal of the Federal Reserve Bank is to have a stable value of the dollar with inflation at 2% or lower, stable employment, and a safe banking system. As discussed in Chapter 1, the central bank's monetary policy sets the level of short-term interest rates, while the government sets fiscal policies of taxing and spending. The Fed and other US banking regulators require solvency and a limit on the risk-taking of banks.

After governments worldwide bailed out banks due to the losses on real estate and mortgage investments in the GFC, regulations were passed to reduce the risk-taking of banks. The Dodd-Frank regulations in the US and the Basel III regulations in Europe set up stress tests and risk-based capital requirements for banks. As a result, over the ensuing decade, banks largely abandoned proprietary trading businesses while sharply reducing the size of the bond dealer inventory and loans to small businesses. Banks with greater asset risks, either in bond holdings or loans, are required to hold greater loss reserves.

Central banks in developed markets, such as the US, Canada, Australia, and Europe, are well-run and have generally done a good job of keeping their currencies and economies stable. Other countries that don't have strong banking systems or financial regulations may attract risky banks and financial activities that are not allowed in developed markets with strong regulations. For example, crypto trading platforms offering trading at up to 100 times leverage and highly speculative coins are not available to US residents.

Some countries substantially restrict capital flow, such as the limit on Chinese citizens moving more than 100,000 RMB ($15,000) per year out of the country. A global cryptocurrency market seeks to remove such limits from investors regardless of their country of origin.

Other key players in the TradFi system are stock and derivatives exchanges. In the US, these include the CME Group and the New York Stock Exchange, while key European exchanges include Euronext, London Stock Exchange, and Deutsche Borse. Stock exchanges facilitate trades in equity markets, while derivatives exchanges offer access to futures and options trading.

Despite technology advances, US stock markets are still on a T-plus-1 settlement schedule, where the exchange of stock and cash is completed one full business day after the trade is made. Trades made on Monday are settled on Tuesday, while trades executed on Friday are not completed until Monday. Blockchain-based financial markets can bring efficiencies to the settlement process, with most transfers of digital assets confirmed and settled in hours if not minutes. The US Depository Trust and Clearing

Corporation (DTCC) has been moving to settle repurchase and credit default swaps on the day of the trade using blockchain and distributed ledger technology.[2] Shorter times to settlement may decrease the risk to the financial system by reducing the potential for and the cost of trades that fail to settle.

Under Regulation T, the US Federal Reserve Bank regulates the amount of leverage that can be used in the equity market. Stock market investors can borrow a maximum of 50% of the purchase price, or two-to-one leverage. The maximum borrowing allowed on a $5,000 purchase of stock would be $2,500.

Derivatives exchanges, such as the CME Group (Chicago Mercantile Exchange) and Cboe (Chicago Board Options Exchange) facilitate trades in options and futures markets. Cboe focuses on equity options, allowing investors to trade put or call options on the S&P 500 or on individual stocks. The CME Group focuses on financial and commodity futures, including interest rates, stock indices, gold, oil, bitcoin, Ether, and the value of the dollar versus a variety of foreign currencies.

Bitcoin (BTC) and Ether futures contracts trade at the CME, with each BTC futures contract denominated at the value of 5 bitcoin. With a notional value of 5 bitcoin multiplied by a price of $42,000, the value of each contract would be $210,000. In January 2024, the CME required a maintenance margin of $49,000 for each bitcoin futures contract held either long or short. Dividing the notional value by the maintenance margin ($210,000 / $49,000) shows the maximum available leverage of 4.3 times investor capital. Leverage in futures markets is higher than the two times leverage available to investors in the US equity market.

Futures exchanges guarantee investor performance through the use of margins and a clearing corporation. Gains and losses are settled on a daily basis. At the end of each trading day, investors are required to have assets in each account that meet or exceed the maintenance margin required for the sum of all positions. Traders with losses on a given day may be required to add additional funds to the account. If the trader is unable or unwilling to add funds to the account to meet the minimum margin requirements, positions are liquidated until the capital in the account is sufficient to support the remaining positions.

The CME Group facilitates trading in call and put options on listed futures markets, including bitcoin, Ether, gold, oil, Treasury bonds, and the S&P 500. Call options give the buyer the right, but not the obligation, to buy an asset at a stated strike price before a stated expiration date. If the price of the underlying asset doesn't rise above the strike price before expiration, the call option expires worthless, and the seller keeps the premium. The buyer of the call option wants the price of the underlying asset to rise, while the seller of the call option wants the price to fall.

Option buyers have access to substantial embedded leverage. For example, with gold trading at $2,037 per ounce, a 60-day call option with a strike price of $2,035 may cost just $25 per ounce at the CME. If the price of one ounce of gold is below $2,035 60 days after the call option is purchased, the option expires worthless and the buyer loses 100% of the $25 premium they paid for the option. However, if gold had an explosive move higher to $2,235, the option that was purchased for $25 would be worth $200 at expiration, as the gold price moved $200 above the strike price of $2,035. Buyers of options have losses limited to the price paid for the option while having potentially unlimited gains. Sellers of options have the opposite profit potential, with the maximum profit being the premium received if the option expires worthless, while the seller of call options faces potentially unlimited losses if the price of the underlying asset continues to move higher beyond the strike price. The option's expiration date works against the buyer of the option and for the seller of the option, as the passing of each day reduces the option's time value as fewer days remain for the underlying price to move beyond the strike price. Buying call options has a bullish price view while selling call options expresses a bearish price view.

Option prices increase with the underlying asset's price, the time remaining until the option's maturity, and the expected volatility of the underlying asset's price. Options on bitcoin and Ether are expected to be substantially more expensive than options on Treasury bonds or the S&P 500. This is due to the greater volatility, or the broader range of potential price moves, as the annualized standard deviation of bitcoin prices has been 80% over several years while the S&P 500 has recently experienced price volatility of less than 20%. Buyers of options tend to benefit when the volatility of price moves experienced during the life of the option is higher than the volatility implied in the purchase price of the option, while sellers benefit when price volatility declines after the option is sold.

Relative to the price change in the underlying asset, put options have the opposite characteristics of call options. Buyers of put options have the right, but not the obligation to sell the asset at a stated strike price until the option's expiration date. If the underlying asset's price doesn't fall below the strike price before expiration, the put option expires worthless, and the seller keeps the premium. Buyers of put options are expressing a bearish view, as they want the price of the underlying to decline below the strike price before the expiration date. Sellers of put options are expressing a bullish view, as they wish for the price of the underlying to rise above that strike price.

Call options and put options on the same asset, the same at-the-money strike price, and the same maturity tend to have similar prices. With gold at $2,037 per ounce, a 60-day put option with a $2,035 strike price recently cost $24. If the price of gold is above $2,035 in 60 days, the seller of the option keeps the entire $24 premium while the buyer of the put option experiences a 100% loss of the option price. However, if the price of gold crashed to $1,835 within 60 days, the put option buyer would own put options worth $200 for each ounce, a strong profit relative to the original $24 purchase price.

Most investors are familiar with long positions, where profits occur when the price of a stock rises above its purchase price. Short sales benefit from a decline in the price of the stock, futures, or options contract after it is sold. Taking a short position in a futures or options contract is relatively straightforward, as each trade requires one buyer and one seller. There is a long position for every short position. For every buyer of a futures or options contract, there is a seller of that same contract. Futures and options are a zero-sum game, as the combined gains/losses of the buyers equal the combined losses/gains of the sellers.

Short sales in the equity market are much more complicated, as all shares of stock are owned by the issuing company or an investor, while only 3% of the shares of the average stock in the S&P 500 have been sold short.[3] In a short sale, an equity investor borrows shares from another investor through a brokerage firm. After the borrow is completed, the short seller sells the shares and keeps the cash proceeds. The short seller hopes that the price of the stock will decline and the shares can be repurchased and returned to the lender at a price lower than when they were borrowed. This becomes complicated when a greater portion of the shares has been borrowed. The 10 stocks in the S&P 500 with the greatest short interest may have 30% of their shares sold short while small cap stocks may have more than 80% of their shares sold short. When short interest is very high relative to the number of outstanding shares, a short squeeze can occur when the short sellers compete with each other to buy back the stock as prices rise quickly. As short interest and trading volume increases, investors and their brokers may demand that short sellers return the stock that has been borrowed. If the short seller is unable to borrow the stock from another lender, they are forced to buy stock to return to the lender and their short position is closed. Short squeezes can inflict substantial losses on short sellers, such as when the price of GameStop Corp (GME), adjusted for stock splits, rose from $4.42 on January 4, 2021, to more than $120 the week of January 25, 2021.

Whenever we think about cryptocurrencies, digital assets, and blockchains, we must think of what business they're trying to dislocate. One of the largest businesses in the world is that of a credit card processor. Every time a credit card is used, Visa, Mastercard, Discover, or American Express charges the merchant more than 2% of the value of the transaction. The total 2022 revenue for Visa was $29.3 billion while Mastercard earned $22.2 billion.[4] As the world is becoming increasingly cashless, there is a greater usage of credit cards as well as smartphone app-based payments. Increasing use of credit cards and electronic payments reduces the demand for cash. Stored value cards, such as Starbucks gift cards, are big business, with consumers holding more than $1.6 billion in balances. These balances reduce the cost of credit card fees to Starbucks while the coffee chain can earn interest on the balances while consumers wait to redeem the value.

Responsible consumers can swipe their credit cards all month, earn points and cash back on each purchase, and then pay the balance in full at the end of each month with zero interest charges. While there will be multiple charges on the credit card, there will only be a single payment from the user's checking account, which will accrue interest until the payment is sent to the credit card company. A credit card that pays 1% cash back is simply sharing less than half of the more than 2% fee that the credit card issuer charges each merchant to facilitate payments.

Other payment processors include firms such as PayPal/Venmo and Stripe/CashApp. PayPal has more than $36 billion in customer accounts that earn interest for the payment processor and not for its users.

Cryptocurrencies, digital assets, and blockchain projects may disintermediate many of these banks and payment processors. Hopefully, they can make stock transactions clear more quickly. Hopefully, they'll reduce the need to keep $100 on your Starbucks card, and one of the key use cases is remittances.

A key part of the global economy is immigration. Many Latin American immigrants who now live in the US have come from El Salvador, Mexico, Ecuador, and other countries across Latin America. These immigrants may have family in El Salvador, while they might be working in Chicago or New York. One or two people from that family will come to the US to work, earning a substantially greater wage working in the US than in their home country. These workers send home a substantial portion of their earnings in order to support their families. El Salvador is not rich, making these remittances a key part of their economy. In 2022, these expatriate workers sent $7.8 billion to their families in El Salvador, 23.7% of GDP.[5] One of every $4 of income in El Salvador was earned by someone living and working in a foreign country and sending that money home. There are two million Salvadoreans who work in the US and send money home, comprising almost one-quarter of their entire GDP.

The TradFi sector that is likely the most vulnerable to the rise of digital assets is the remittance providers, such as Western Union and MoneyGram. Money transfer services such as Western Union or MoneyGram can be slow and expensive. Historically, remittances sent from the US cost more than 5% of the transaction amount and might take days to get there. While Western Union uses Ripple/XRP and MoneyGram uses Stellar to facilitate payments, these firms cannot sustain fees of more than 5% when consumers embrace blockchain technology to transfer payments themselves across countries. Within the crypto world, money can be sent across borders very quickly for a much lower cost, which is one of the key use cases of digital currencies.

Another large financial business is insurance, which has two key lines of business: property and casualty insurance, and life and longevity insurance. Property and casualty insurance has relatively short-term risks that are somewhat unpredictable. Homeowners who buy insurance against fires or floods or drivers who buy car insurance are protecting against relatively unpredictable events. They don't know when, or if, some accident will happen to their car or their home. While these events have a low probability, they have a high severity. If there is a loan on the car or the home, the lender typically requires the purchase of insurance to make sure the asset retains value or can be replaced after an accident. The property and casualty insurance business can experience very large and catastrophic losses in hours or days, as billions of dollars in damage can happen in a single week from a hurricane or a forest fire. The insurance company is taking highly correlated risks in a specific geography, so it is important for each insurance company to be geographically diversified.

The life and longevity insurance business is much more predictable, as mortality tables closely predict the range of ages at which people die. If an American man lives to the age of 60, he's expected to live another 20.47 years to a life expectancy of 80.47 years old.[6] Sixty-year-old women are expected to live to age 83.7, while newborn boys have a life expectancy of 74.1 years, and newborn girls have a life expectancy of 79.8 years. Mortality is relatively predictable for a very large pool of people. Mortality tables closely predict how long that average person will live, and how many deaths will occur in any given year.

Consumers buy life insurance to insure against the risk of a shorter-than-expected life. If a parent dies in their 30s or 40s, life insurance proceeds can provide assets to their spouse and children that can be used to replace their income and make sure the mortgage and other bills are paid to support their family. A non-smoking male aged 30 might be able to purchase 20 years of term life insurance with a $1 million death benefit for a premium under $600 per year. If the premiums are paid and the insured dies before age 50, the family would receive a death benefit of $1 million.

While younger people buy life insurance to insure the risk of dying young, older people may purchase annuities to hedge the risk of living longer. A 65-year-old retiree can buy a $1 million dollar annuity from an insurance company which will pay $80,000 for the rest of their life.

To prevent an asset-liability mismatch, the insurance company would like to have people on both sides of that equation. They'd like to have one million

65-year-old men with life insurance and one million 65-year-old men with annuities, which would balance the risk of longer versus shorter lives.

There are a number of concerns that the crypto space has about the CeFi market.

When governments implement exchange rate controls, citizens cannot freely move their assets around the world. This limits the amount of assets, especially cash, that can be exported from one country to another in any given year.

There is a concern that if you're participating in this banking system, you don't have complete freedom with how to invest or spend your money. There's a lack of portability across institutions, especially across borders. It's not easy to send your dollars from an American bank to a European bank in euros, without incurring fees and waiting days for the transfer.

Low-income consumers in the US, as well as in emerging markets, may lack access to basic banking services. Transactions are slow to settle. Intermediaries may charge excessive fees. Perhaps, most of all, crypto proponents are concerned about centralization, with power focused on governments, banks, and large companies that might not have the consumer's interest in mind.

The idea of a single point of failure is especially relevant in countries with hyperinflation or during times of war. Notice that three of the top ten countries ranked by the largest portion of the population owning cryptocurrencies include Iran, Ukraine, and Venezuela. Imagine the value added to a Venezuelan citizen who can hold assets in dollar-linked stablecoins that retain their value regardless of the local inflation rate. Similarly, Ukrainian citizens can protect themselves from a decline in the value of the Ukrainian hryvnia, which fell 30% in three years around the time the Russian invasion threatened the physical safety of the country's banking system.

		% of Population Owning Crypto
1	United Arab Emirates	27.7%
2	Vietnam	20.5%
3	Saudi Arabia	17.5%
4	Singapore	13.9%
5	Iran	13.5%
6	United States	13.2%
7	Philippines	13.0%
8	Ukraine	10.3%
9	Venezuela	10.3%
10	South Africa	10.0%

Source: Adapted from https://investingintheweb.com/crypto/crypto-ownership-by-country/ Last accessed: 22 April 2024.

A centralized point of failure could be the demise of a bank due to failed investments or the physical destruction of buildings and computer servers that can occur during acts of war.

Cryptocurrencies, digital assets, and blockchains are designed to work as distributed ledgers. Rather than placing faith in one government, one bank, or one currency, the blockchain economy distributes recordkeeping across thousands of computers in dozens of countries worldwide.

Countries may enact exchange rate controls that restrict or prohibit the export of a currency. The government might state an official value of the currency, which is often higher than the black-market rate for the currency, the price at which the currency trades outside of the government and the banking system. Buying the currency from the bank or the government takes place at the higher official rate, and transactions for goods and services may take place at a much lower price.

Some countries are seeking to ban cryptocurrencies because the tighter the controls on the exchange rate, the harder it is to access cash, and the harder it is to move cash from one country to another, the more exciting cryptocurrency becomes.

If the government in China, Russia, Egypt, Iraq, Qatar, Oman, Morocco, Algeria or another country has banned cryptocurrency, they're doing it to maintain control over their currency. Their citizens might not want to be controlled but would like the freedom to move their assets to a safer or more prosperous region of the world.

The promises of reinventing these CeFi systems in the decentralized finance (DeFi) world is that markets become faster, cheaper, and more global. Consumers are able to access peer-to-peer services at lower costs with fewer intermediaries. The hopes are to reduce the number of consumers in the world without a banking relationship.

While 5% of American families are not participating in the banking system, more than 1.4 billion adults globally are unbanked. This number is steadily improving from 1.7 billion in 2017. In just four years, the number of unbanked declined by 20%, with 300 million adults starting a banking relationship for the first time. The unbanked population tends to be higher in emerging markets countries, which often have higher inflation rates and lower incomes than in developed countries. Unbanked consumers may have greater exposure to inflation rates if they are unable to earn interest on their cash holdings. The World Bank reports that 40% of the global unbanked population lives in India, China, and Indonesia.[7]

Consumers with a banking relationship have their paycheck directly deposited into a bank account and have access to a credit card and bill pay services. Mortgage and utility payments are paid electronically, and everyday transactions are completed with credit cards or smartphone applications, which can earn points and cash back. Cash sitting in checking accounts can earn interest until the credit card payment is due. Assets held in banks reduce the risk that consumers have their money lost or stolen when held in cash.

The unbanked receive a paper paycheck that they will convert into cash by paying fees to a storefront check cashing service. It is also a security risk to keep your entire paycheck in cash. They also don't have the benefit of earning interest on that cash while it is in their wallet or earning cash back or rebates for spending on credit cards. The unbanked typically lack access to credit.

A success story about moving the unbanked into the financial system started with M-Pesa, a mobile phone payments company founded in Kenya in 2007. Over five years, more than 17 million accounts were opened, nearly all of which were from unbanked consumers. This was a fast and significant market penetration in a country with a population of under 40 million. Over the course of 10 years, transaction fees fell from more than 20% to just 1%.

As much as 50% of Kenyan GDP was soon using this system, with deposits, withdrawals, payments, credit, savings, and transfers accomplished without ever building or visiting a bank branch. As financial inclusion increased, poverty was reduced, especially for rural consumers. In addition, consumers carrying less cash became less likely to be robbery victims.

That's an overview of the world of centralized finance and traditional finance. The goal of cryptocurrencies, digital assets, and blockchain is to move into a decentralized peer-to-peer world. This moves power from banks and governments and into a global electronic peer-to-peer system. The promise of crypto is not necessarily for us to all make millions of dollars by trading these coins. The promise is to have a unit of account, a store of value, and a way to make payments across borders. American consumers are blessed with a relatively low inflation rate and a very strong banking system.

Imagine the promise of digital assets for consumers living in a country with high inflation rates or a weak banking system. Consumers in Venezuela, Zimbabwe, or Ukraine can use digital currencies to access a global banking system and a store of value in euro or US dollar–based stablecoins. Digital assets can hedge many of the financial risks of consumers in these high-risk countries who might otherwise turn to physical goods to serve as a store of value.

Imagine living in Ukraine or Venezuela and hoping to move your family to a safer country with a stronger economy. You transfer money from your bank to your crypto account. You can walk to another country with crypto assets on your phone or in a USB drive in your pocket. Rather than holding their assets in Venezuelan bolivars or Ukrainian hryvnia, their assets are held in bitcoin or stablecoins, which can serve as a store of value or less volatile currency than their home country. Once arriving in their new country, they can transfer the crypto into that country's banking system, and start their life over again without exposure to failing banks and currencies. The promise of cryptocurrencies and digital assets is to recreate the centralized and traditional financial systems, ideally making finance more equitable across the world with faster and lower-cost transactions. While digital assets can reduce financial risks when used properly, they also introduce new risks into the financial system.

CHAPTER 3

Uses of Blockchains and Distributed Ledgers

The discussion of blockchains and digital ledgers begins with Bitcoin, which was the first successful cryptocurrency. The first information written to the Bitcoin blockchain, the Genesis block, was created on 3 January 2009. The format of this information is designed to be machine-readable and not necessarily understandable upon visual inspection. The anonymous inventors of Bitcoin have a libertarian philosophy, as they are not necessarily excited about banks, central banks, governments, and even fiat currencies. Notice that part of the data written into this first block on the Bitcoin blockchain notes "Chancellor on brink of second bailout for banks." The very first thing that's written to the Bitcoin blockchain indicates worries about the instability in the traditional financial system, and the bank failures and bailouts experienced during the global financial crisis.

The goal of bitcoin is to build a global peer-to-peer currency that disintermediates governments and banks. Bitcoin gives investors the ability to send value to each other without their assets passing through governmental entities or the existing banking system.

As previously discussed, there are a number of concerns about the centralized finance system (CeFi). These concerns include slow transaction times and settlement times, such as the one-day settlement for US stock transactions and international wire transfers that can take longer.

There is also concern about the high cost of financial intermediaries, such as for international remittances that may cost between 2% to 7% or more. There's a lack of transparency regarding financial transactions and concerns about a single point of failure, such as the failure of Lehman Brothers and other banks in 2008 and 2009. Investors with assets on deposit in a failing bank or brokerage firm may have to wait to recover their assets, even if those assets were insured by the FDIC or the Securities Investor Protection Corporation (SIPC).

There is also a lack of interoperability across institutions, which makes it difficult to move assets from one bank or brokerage firm to another, especially across national borders. Many global consumers still do not have access to the centralized finance banking system, especially if they're low-income or live in an emerging markets country.

Investors are also worried about fiat currencies, both from the standpoint of excess inflation as well as the restrictions on capital flows across countries. The desire to invest in cryptocurrencies and digital assets is greatest in countries with inflation problems and restrictions on capital flows. If the government limits or prohibits citizens from exporting their assets out of the country, investors may turn to cryptocurrencies to gain freedom of movement for their wealth. There can be, however, issues of taxes and regulatory enforcement for investors availing themselves of this solution.

Central banks control money supply growth. Central banks that allow for very high growth rates of the money supply may cause substantial inflation in the economy, leading to the debasement in the value of the fiat currency and a loss of purchasing power. Consumers may face inflation rates of 20% to 70% per year in countries including Iran, Ethiopia, Liberia, South Sudan, Sudan, or Argentina, while inflation rates have exceeded 600% annually in Zimbabwe and thousands of percent per year in Venezuela. As inflation rises, the value of the fiat currency declines on a daily basis, making it difficult for the currency to serve as a store of value, where the purchasing power is relatively stable over time. Investors who forego consumption today benefit from a stable currency that would allow them to consume equal or greater amount of goods and services in the future.

Another concern about fiat currencies is the absence of a global currency. Travelers or those engaged in international businesses need to exchange currencies each time they transact in a new country. Each time one currency is exchanged for another, transaction fees are paid to an intermediary such as a bank or currency exchange, creating friction. With more than 180 currencies used in the member states of the United Nations, there are significant costs of transacting as a global business or as an investor.

The inventors of Bitcoin were frustrated with the banking system, the reliance on centralized counterparties, and the time and cost required to move currency from one country to another. Each centralized counterparty, whether a bank or a brokerage firm, maintains a ledger for each investor's account. This ledger contains the name of the investor, an account number, and a history of transactions over the life of the account. The account's current balance is simply the accumulated value of all prior transactions.

Ledgers in the CeFi world are centralized and permissioned. Centralized means that the ledger is maintained by a single bank or broker, where each investor's assets exist only in the computer systems of the bank or brokerage firm. These assets are vulnerable to the collapse of the value of the fiat currency, the failure of the bank or brokerage firm, or even a computer failure or a cybersecurity incident. There are many risks to doing business with a centralized counterparty. A bank or brokerage firm may give a client a credit limit or deny service to an individual for a variety of reasons. The bank or brokerage firm may fail due to risky loans, bad investments, or an inflationary decline in the value of the nation's fiat currency. Banks can also fail due to physical destruction from a war or a natural disaster. If an investor's assets are held by a bank or brokerage firm or in a currency degraded by inflation, this single point of failure can cause investors to lose all or part of their assets.

Permissioned means that the ledger is only available to the bank and the investor, with no transparency or access for third parties. Access is only available to the investor with the correct account number and password. This security can make it difficult for third parties to steal from an investor's account. However, this lack of transparency to the external financial system means that investors cannot evaluate the soundness of the counterparty in real time. Investors would prefer to be able to perform due diligence so their assets are only held at the banks and brokerage firms that are least likely to fail.

Distributed ledgers are decentralized, permissionless, and transparent. When interacting on a blockchain, investors are moving from the centralized CeFi system to the decentralized DeFi system. Rather than keeping their assets in a single ledger with a centralized counterparty subject to a single point of failure, their assets can now be secured in a decentralized ledger. This takes power away from single banks or a specific government, as assets are tracked and secured by hundreds of computers worldwide. Rather than being vulnerable to a single point of failure, investors have their ledgers backed up in multiple countries and on multiple computers. Distributed ledgers are permissionless and transparent, meaning that the health of the network can be evaluated in real time and viewed by all market participants.

Moving to a decentralized system alleviates investors' worries regarding the health of a single bank's balance sheet, its physical security, and vulnerabilities to hacks or data corruption. In the world of digital assets, redundant copies of this ledger are saved, meaning that the failure of a single counterparty is not likely to lead to the loss of investor assets.

Cryptocurrencies and digital assets typically provide transparency to the transaction activities on public blockchains. No password is needed to view the transaction activity on specific addresses on the Bitcoin or Ethereum blockchains. A visitor to Etherscan or a Bitcoin block explorer can view all of the transactions that have taken place simply by querying the activity of a specific blockchain account. All accounts have complete transparency, including the balances and transaction history. However, these account numbers or addresses are not directly linked to the names of the account owners.

The account number and transactions in each account are transparent, but the person or entity that controls the account is not disclosed.

Transactions on the Bitcoin and Ethereum blockchains are transparent because these are permissionless blockchains. Some CeFi institutions, such as banks or securities exchanges, are now using permissioned blockchains, which do not offer transparency to third parties without permission or passwords to view those balances and transactions. These private or permissioned blockchains tend to have a small number of participants, such as brokerage firms that may interact with a specific securities exchange.

The initial use cases for distributed ledgers that hold peer-to-peer electronic cash is to disintermediate or replace accounts at banks or brokerage firms. After a digital asset is viewed as a store of value, investors may seek deposit and lending accounts where they can earn a yield on their cryptocurrency or digital asset investment. Distributed ledgers can be used in securities and derivative exchanges to track transactions and holdings in options, futures, or stocks.

While storing information on assets typically held in banks or brokerage accounts was a key initial use case of blockchains and distributed ledger technology, any type of asset can be securely held on a globally distributed blockchain.

Supply chains can be a key use case of blockchain technology. It is important to track the chain of custody of goods, whether shipped by truck or shipping containers. Blockchains are already used to track fresh produce from each farm to each grocery store. Unfortunately, some produce items, such as romaine lettuce, can become tainted and dangerous to consume. Before tracking technologies, it was not possible to know where a specific case of romaine lettuce came from, what day it was picked, and how long it had taken to travel from the farm or to the grocery store. Previously, recalls that were enacted to protect consumers from dangerous food may have been too broad and discarded food that was safe to eat. With blockchain technology, the provenance of each case of food can be tracked and verified across the supply chain, verifying food supplies in real time.

Imagine a world where the chain of custody for food products is tracked throughout the supply chain. Every case of meat or vegetables could have a barcode or a crypto address. Each time it moves from the farm to the distributor, warehouse, and grocery store, it's scanned. Information is tracked on exactly which days the food spent in each location or shipping vehicle. In the event of a recall, we could determine exactly which farm the lettuce came from and only destroy the lettuce sourced from that specific farm. This would keep the supply chain safe for consumers and prevent unnecessary waste.

Fungible items, such as dollars or euros, bitcoin or Ether tokens, or a barrel of light sweet crude oil, are interchangeable. Physical commodities are frequently commingled, as the quantity matters, not the specific barrel or dollar received. In contrast, non-fungible tokens (NFTs) are not interchangeable. Each NFT is unique, either in its appearance, its function, or its history of ownership. NFTs and real-world assets (RWAs) may be the most important long-term applications of blockchain technology. While many people think of NFTs in terms of gaming items or digital art, their potential goes far beyond that.

This concept could be applied to a distributed ledger, where redundant copies of a record are kept around the world in an immutable place. Use cases for NFTs include academic credentials, health records, and tickets to sporting events or concerts. For example, verifying degrees becomes more challenging as more colleges and universities close their doors. That is, the university's failure as a centralized counterparty threatens to devalue or invalidate the educational credentials received by the institution's graduates. However, an NFT could immutably and permanently prove that a specific individual is a university graduate along with the details of their studies and degree. With an immutable record on a publicly accessible blockchain, graduates could immediately verify their credentials, while those seeking to fraudulently claim a degree will be immediately disproven.

Tickets would be easier to transfer when held as NFTs and it would become routine to distinguish legitimate from fraudulent tickets. In an emergency, verifying health records that are tracked in a publicly accessible blockchain could save lives, as traditional methods of accessing health records from a previous doctor or hospital visit may take too long.

Many in the asset management industry are intrigued by tokenized or fractionalized ownership of real-world assets. The title to any real-world asset could be tracked on a publicly accessible blockchain, providing a secure, transparent, and efficient way to manage and transfer ownership of assets, such as automobiles, houses, and other real estate, as well as art or collectibles. Typically, a specific car, house, or collectible is owned by one person or one family.

Tracking the ownership of larger assets through fractionalized tokenization opens up new investment possibilities. Historically, commercial real estate, such as hotels and office buildings, has been viewed as illiquid assets with ownership limited to the largest investors due to the cost of each asset. However, consider a $20 million office building that is tokenized into NFTs, each representing a fraction of the building's ownership. If each token is priced at $1,000, it becomes easier for the owner to sell a fraction of their ownership while allowing smaller investors access to a diversifying asset at a much lower cost. The fractionalized ownership of the property is recorded on the blockchain, providing a transparent and immutable record of ownership and liquidity of the token on a secondary market. Rather than waiting for the majority owner to sell the building, smaller investors can seek liquidity by selling their ownership token at any time.

Blockchain technology can facilitate insurance through smart contracts, which can verify external events, such as weather conditions or flight schedules. If a flight is delayed or canceled an insurance payout could be automatically triggered by the smart contract, reducing the need for manual claims processing.

Blockchains like Bitcoin and Ethereum have key features like transparency and auditability. All transactions are disclosed in real time and can be viewed by anyone, making each blockchain a transparent and immutable record of all transactions. This immutability is crucial in preventing double-spending, a problem where a digital asset (like a Bitcoin) could be spent more than once.

Compared to traditional financial systems, blockchains can offer faster settlement times, reduced costs of intermediaries, and a globally accessible peer-to-peer network. Regardless of location, race, religion, or age, anyone can participate as long as they have the necessary assets and code.

Cryptocurrencies like Bitcoin are far more traceable than cash. Every Bitcoin can be tracked from the moment it was mined, through every transaction, to its current owner. This level of traceability has even allowed authorities to track and recover stolen or misappropriated digital assets.

For instance, on the Ethereum blockchain, every transaction that has ever taken place can be viewed on Etherscan.io. This includes details such as the block number, the time at which the transaction took place, the addresses involved, and the assets exchanged.

For example, on 29 January 2022, a transaction took place where an Ethereum wallet with the address 0x00. . .1e35 swapped 0.3399 Ether on Uniswap, a decentralized exchange, and received 7 billion Google Metaverse tokens in return. The location of the Uniswap V3 smart contract is also tracked.

This level of transparency allows us to see exactly what happened in this account: the Ether sent, the Google Metaverse tokens received, and the addresses involved. However, it's important to note that while the transactions are transparent, the identities of the address owners remain anonymous unless revealed by the owners themselves.

Addresses on different blockchains have different formats. Addresses on the Ethereum blockchain start with "0x." Addresses on the Bitcoin blockchain don't have a specific starting character, but are clearly not Ethereum addresses that start with "0x." Each address on the Bitcoin blockchain represents a specific wallet and can be used to view the history of transactions involving that wallet.

For instance, the block explorer at blockchain.com records the transaction history of a bitcoin wallet with the address starting "39KD1." This wallet has been involved in 528 transactions, receiving a total of 0.384 Bitcoin and sending a total of 0.291 Bitcoin. The final balance in this account is 0.0933 Bitcoin, worth about $3,519 at the time the transaction was viewed.

This level of transparency allows anyone to view the transaction history and current balance of any public address on the blockchain. However, while the transactions are transparent, the identities of the individuals behind the addresses remain anonymous unless they choose to reveal themselves. This provides a level of privacy for users while maintaining transparency of transactions.

This transparency, combined with the immutability of blockchain transactions, is what makes blockchain technology so revolutionary. It allows for a level of trust and verification that is not possible with traditional financial systems. However, it also requires users to be very careful when conducting transactions, as mistakes can lead to the irreversible loss of assets. For instance, sending Ether to a Bitcoin address, or vice versa, could result in the loss of those funds. Therefore, it's crucial to always check the compatibility of tokens with each blockchain and ensure transactions only take place on compatible blockchains.

The immutability of blockchain transactions is a fundamental feature that provides security and trust in the system. Once a transaction is confirmed and added to the blockchain, it cannot be altered or deleted. This ensures that once a bitcoin has been sent or spent, that transaction cannot be reversed.

This immutability is achieved through the use of cryptographic hash functions in the blockchain's design. Each block in the blockchain contains a unique hash that depends on the contents of the block. If someone attempts to alter a transaction, the block's hash would change, making it immediately obvious that the block has been tampered with. This design makes the blockchain secure and resistant to fraud.

When sending money to another country, verifying that the recipient has received the funds is imperative. In traditional financial systems, this process can take several days. However, with blockchain technology, transactions can be settled in a matter of seconds or minutes, depending on the specific blockchain being used.

The process of mining on the Bitcoin blockchain involves validating transactions and adding them to a new block. Every 10 minutes, all the newly verified bitcoin transactions are included in a single block of transactions. Each transaction involves an address sending a certain amount of Bitcoin to another address. Validators, also known as miners, check all proposed transactions. They verify whether the sender has enough bitcoin to send and whether the sender actually owns the bitcoin they are trying to send.

Once all transactions for a 10-minute period have been validated, they are securely added to the blockchain. This record is immutable, meaning it cannot be changed. Each block in the blockchain is linked to the next block, creating a chain of blocks, hence the term "blockchain." Each block contains the hash of the previous block, linking them together. If anything changes in a single block, the chain between the blocks is broken. Validators notice this and restore the transaction to its previous state.

This process ensures the security and integrity of the blockchain, making it a reliable and efficient system for conducting and settling transactions. It's a revolutionary technology that has the potential to greatly speed up and simplify financial transactions, among many other applications.

One key advantage of blockchain technology is the faster settlement of transactions. Traditional financial systems, such as stock trades (T+2 days 1 day) or international wire transfers, can take days to settle transactions. In contrast, blockchains like Ethereum and Bitcoin can settle transactions in seconds or minutes.

This speed is achieved by having a network of validators (also known as miners) who validate the transactions proposed in a given time period (12 seconds for Ethereum, 10 minutes for Bitcoin) and add them to a new block in the blockchain. Once a transaction is included in a block and that block is added to the blockchain, the transaction is considered settled. The more blocks that are added after the block containing a specific transaction, the more confirmations a transaction has, the more likely the transaction is considered to be permanently settled.

Another advantage of blockchain technology is the potential reduction in intermediary costs. Traditional financial intermediaries, such as credit card processors or money transfer services, often charge fees ranging from 2% to 7% or more. In contrast, some blockchains offer costs of less than 0.1% of the transaction value.

Furthermore, blockchains provide a globally accessible, peer-to-peer network. This allows anyone, regardless of their location, race, religion, or age, to participate in the financial system. This inclusivity can help reduce economic inefficiency caused by censorship or discrimination and allows everyone in the world to participate in financial markets on an equal footing.

Property rights, such as having a bank account or owning a home, are the key to building wealth. These rights contribute to economic growth, and countries without strong property rights often struggle to experience sustained economic growth. Blockchain technology can help secure these rights by providing a transparent, immutable record of transactions and ownership.

Some countries, especially in Africa, the Middle East, and South America, restrict property rights and make it difficult to move assets out of a country. Some countries may not have the legal structures allowing legal title to a house or a secure bank account. The internationalpropertyrightsindex.org ranks countries on the freedom citizens have to keep a store of value that's globally portable and to grow their wealth.

Institutions may limit access due to age, race, religion, or perceived creditworthiness. In crypto networks, those who follow the code and have the assets should be able to participate, even if they are unable to access the traditional banking system in their country. Crypto may be the only way for citizens of some countries to safely store and title assets. If you're keeping your money in Zimbabwe dollars or Venezuelan bolivars, that's not a store of value. Investors who keep assets in Bitcoin, Ethereum, or stablecoins are able to protect their earnings and wealth in a far greater way than they could by keeping their assets in a weak fiat currency or failing banking system.

Advocates of cryptocurrencies and digital assets may have a utopian or a libertarian view of how the world could and should work. However, the world is complicated by different governments, regulations, computer systems, fiat currencies, and financial systems. While it may be attractive to envision a single global system to securely, cheaply, and quickly access currencies, futures, options, stocks, and banking services, this is a complicated system to build. While many smart engineers and economists are working to build these systems, it is difficult to be simultaneously secure, decentralized, and scalable.

Cryptocurrencies and digital assets are secured through a system of private keys and public keys. Similar to an email address, a public key can be disclosed. All public addresses on the Ethereum and Bitcoin blockchains are disclosed, such as the 0x001. . . address previously viewed on Etherscan.io. Anyone can send value or information to any email address or to any blockchain address. Both email addresses and blockchain addresses can receive information and value, but can also receive junk mail.

While it is safe to disclose the address of crypto wallets and blockchain addresses, doing so may allow others to link the address to the real-world identity of the owner of the contents of the address. Once an address is linked to a real-world person or entity, the assets and transactions of that person are visible. Just because a public address is transparent on a block explorer doesn't mean that the assets can be easily stolen from that wallet, as only the public key has been disclosed. Similarly, just because someone knows the email address of a person or entity doesn't mean that anyone can send email from that account. While email access requires a password, private keys are required to send information or value from a blockchain address or wallet.

Everyone should be exceedingly careful to guard both their email password and their private keys, as the security of each digital asset is paramount. A private key is needed to send value or content from each address. There is an extraordinarily important phrase: "Not your keys, not your crypto." If the private key for a wallet address for a Bitcoin or Ethereum (or any other blockchain) wallet is disclosed, anyone with access to the private key can use that information to move the assets out of the wallet. Anyone with access to the combination of the public and private keys can sign off on transactions and send whatever value is in that account to another address on that blockchain. Once the crypto assets are moved, transactions are immutable, and there is no centralized counterparty to reverse the transaction. It's extraordinarily important to keep private keys private.

There are a number of centralized exchanges that allow investors to trade cryptocurrencies and digital assets. Exchanges such as Binance, Kraken, Coinbase, Gemini, and others, allow the exchange of fiat currencies for cryptocurrencies. That is, investors send dollars or euros from their bank to the centralized exchange where those fiat currencies can be used to purchase bitcoin, Ether, or hundreds of other digital assets. This process will seem very familiar to investors who have traded stocks online, as centralized exchanges have websites, login credentials, beneficiary forms, and password reset functionality. However, it is imperative to realize that centralized exchanges keep custody of investors' crypto assets and their private keys. This is not 100% safe, as the employees of the digital currency exchange or potential hackers can access private keys and move funds away from the investors' accounts at the exchange. Chapter 25 will discuss the hacks, scams, thefts, and frauds of 2022, including how employees of the FTX centralized exchange used private keys to move client funds, which is obviously against the law. Chapter 21 will also discuss ways to keep crypto assets secure by maintaining personal custody of crypto assets and private keys.

The process that miners and validators undertake to process transactions on the Bitcoin and Ethereum blockchains provides a layer of security. Due to the high level of encryption involved, the Bitcoin blockchain has not been hacked. However, wallets holding bitcoin and Ether tokens have had assets stolen by exchange employees or by hackers that have tricked investors through a fake website or a phishing email. All of the usual caveats regarding phishing emails apply here. Coinbase does not require reverification of an investor's KYC information and Trust Wallet does not require investors to reenter their private keys in response to an email.

One key goal of investing in digital assets is the desire to be decentralized. Rather than remaining invested with a bank or brokerage firm that may be that single point of failure, investors can have their assets tracked and secured on a decentralized basis. If there are thousands of redundant copies of the ledger around the world, that ownership record will not be lost. That ownership record is duplicated thousands of times on different servers in different countries. The ownership records cannot be compromised due to the authority of a specific government. Even if a single country expels all of the Bitcoin miners, miners in dozens of other countries will still maintain that immutable nature of the value held in each wallet on the Bitcoin blockchain.

It is difficult to build a blockchain that is simultaneously secure, decentralized, and scalable. Most blockchains or CeFi systems typically accomplish two of these three goals. One of the key analogies we'll use for this global network is credit card processors such as Mastercard and Visa. These processors are highly secure and highly scalable, processing thousands of transactions per second worldwide. This scale allows them to handle substantial global spending in real time, but Mastercard and Visa are highly centralized. If something happens to one of these processors or their global network, their ability to process transactions is impaired. The Bitcoin and Ethereum networks are highly decentralized and secure, but they currently face challenges with scalability. Bitcoin, for instance, can process only about seven transactions per second globally. This limitation could potentially hinder Bitcoin's utility as a global currency.

Engineers and economists working in the cryptocurrency and digital asset space are actively seeking ways to increase the scalability of each blockchain. Concepts like proof-of-work, proof-of-stake, and layer 2 solutions are all part of this ongoing effort. The goal is to create a network that can process as many transactions per second as centralized finance networks like Mastercard and Visa.

Blockchains, when secure, are also immutable. Every transaction on the Bitcoin blockchain, for example, is permanent. Once a bitcoin is received, it cannot be taken away by hacking the blockchain. Once a bitcoin is spent, it's gone forever because double-spending is not possible. This reduces reliance on a single government, central bank, stock exchange, or bank.

As we enter the world of global finance, we must address issues such as security, regulations, and ways to keep digital assets safe. But the key issue now is scalability. The goal is to scale blockchains and distributed ledgers to a point where they can handle a large number of transactions to facilitate global commerce.

CHAPTER 4

Bitcoin Mining and Proof-of-Work Protocols

Cryptocurrencies get their name from "crypto" or cryptography, which is the science of making and breaking codes. Some blockchains have built and enforced very high levels of security due to the complexity of the codes and encryption deployed. Bitcoin mining is the process of securing the Bitcoin blockchain through cryptography as well as processing transactions and updating the globally distributed ledger.

While the Bitcoin blockchain was created in 2008, the history of cryptography and digital currencies goes back much further. Asymmetric encryption technology, or public key cryptography, was developed at Stanford in 1976.[1] The Diffie-Hellman key exchange is widely used by today's cryptocurrencies, with different codes used for the private keys and the public keys, which provide for secure and anonymous transactions. Hash functions add to the security of communications, with one-way encryption compressing information into a hash of standard length.

David Chaum from UC Berkeley invented a blinding formula demonstrating how to send and receive digital assets without a centralized authority.[2] Chaum was one of the first to release a cryptocurrency, with his company DigiCash launching eCash in the early 1990s.[3] While eCash and other digital assets failed in the 1990s and early 2000s, the research laid a path to the invention of Bitcoin in 2008. Computing power and cryptographic technology continued to evolve, with the US adopting the Advanced Encryption Standard (AES) as its first Federal encryption standard in 2002.[4]

Satoshi Nakamoto is one or more anonymous people who started this cryptocurrency revolution with the creation of the Bitcoin network. We don't know exactly who created Bitcoin, and it's probably for the best, because the entire idea of cryptocurrencies is to be decentralized. It's all about not knowing who's in charge because if one person is in charge, the whole network can get shut down, or they could have issues with a particular government depending on where they live. There were attempts at cryptocurrencies before Bitcoin. But Bitcoin is the first, and by far the most successful cryptocurrency in the world.

Satoshi Nakamoto wrote an 8-page paper, "Bitcoin: A Peer-to-Peer Electronic Cash System"[5] that changed the world as we know it. The paper was released on 31 October 2008, just 6 weeks after the failure of Lehman Brothers, with the very first block written to the Bitcoin blockchain including a note regarding bank bailouts. Those wishing to truly understand the Bitcoin network are highly encouraged to read this paper, which is generally understandable without significant technical knowledge. The paper designs an electronic payment system based on cryptographic proof rather than trust.

Those wishing to open a bank account or a brokerage account typically have to submit to a credit check and complete a Know Your Client process (KYC). These steps are required to build trust between counterparties with the goal of both counterparties being able to complete all transactions requested. The key innovation of the Bitcoin white paper is to build a trustless system by solving the double spending problem. Historically, any digital information has been easy to copy and paste. For money to be valuable, there must be scarcity. If money could be copied and pasted, it would have no value. The bitcoin mining process ensures the scarcity of bitcoin by guaranteeing that once a bitcoin is sent or spent, it is removed from the sender's account balance. Miners prevent double spending by timestamping all transactions, verifying balances before each transaction is completed, and preventing attempted transactions with insufficient balances. If a wallet contains 10 bitcoins and 6 of them are spent in a verified block that is written to the Bitcoin blockchain, the 6 bitcoins are deducted from the account, leaving just 4 bitcoins available for future transactions. Any subsequent attempts to send more than 4 bitcoins will be denied as an invalid transaction.

Miners are members of the Bitcoin community that are paid to validate transactions and maintain the distributed ledger known as the Bitcoin blockchain.

A number of advantages have led to bitcoin being the world's most valuable cryptocurrency. In February 2024, coingecko.com notes that the entire cryptocurrency sector of more than 12,000 coins was valued at $1.8 trillion. At the same date, Microsoft, Apple, Amazon, and Nvidia stocks were each valued at more than $2 trillion. Bitcoin dominance, or the percentage of the combined market capitalization of the cryptocurrency sector, was near 50%, while Ether, the token driving the Ethereum blockchain, was more than 16%. That is, bitcoin and Ether have a combined market capitalization of nearly two-thirds of the entire cryptocurrency market. Understanding both Bitcoin's proof-of-work algorithm and Ethereum's proof-of-stake process is critical for those engaged in the cryptocurrency ecosystem. After studying these two competing systems of verifying transactions, investors have the building blocks to understand the vast majority of what's going on in the cryptocurrency space.

The goal of Bitcoin is to be decentralized. In a decentralized system, no one person, bank, government, or central bank is in charge. The power to maintain the system is distributed across thousands of miners or validators in dozens of countries, reducing the probability of a single point of failure. Investors access cryptocurrencies to move away from weak banking systems, fiat currencies debased by inflation, and governments that seek to maintain assets in a specific country by restricting capital flows. Businesses wish to be able to move money across borders without the frictions of converting from one fiat currency to another.

Chapter 1 discussed how excessive growth in the money supply leads to inflation. The key advantage of Bitcoin is its known monetary policy. The Bitcoin algorithm has a hard-coded inflation rate that enforces its scarcity. In February 2024, there were 19.6 million bitcoins in circulation, with the code enforcing a maximum bitcoin supply of 21 million, which will be reached in the year 2140. The maximum supply of 21 million bitcoins is relatively small compared to the 24 million Americans or 47 million global citizens with a net worth exceeding \$1 million.[6] That is, there is not enough supply for each millionaire in the world to own just one bitcoin.

The code running the Bitcoin blockchain specifies the schedule by which new bitcoins are created. Bitcoin (BTC) is issued as block rewards to miners who solve cryptographic puzzles, secure, and update the distributed ledger. At the inception of the Bitcoin blockchain in 2009, one miner was awarded 50 bitcoins for solving the cryptographic puzzle and posting a new block of transactions every 10 minutes. Block rewards are cut in half approximately every four years or every 210,000 blocks written to the Bitcoin blockchain. Starting at 50 BTC per block in 2009, block rewards were reduced to 25 BTC in November 2012, to 12.5 BTC in July 2016, and 6.25 in May 2020. The next anticipated halving, or halvening, takes place when block number 840,000 is written to the Bitcoin blockchain. Each subsequent four years, the block reward will continue to be halved until all 21 million bitcoins have been issued in the year 2140. As the issuance rate of bitcoin declines, the scarcity increases, which investors hope will lead to increased prices.

Bitcoin block reward	Beginning date	Block number at halving
50 BTC	January 2009	
25 BTC	November 2012	210,000
12.5 BTC	July 2016	420,000
6.25 BTC	May 2020	630,000
3.125 BTC	April 2024	840,000

The inflation rate of the bitcoin money supply is lower than most fiat currencies, with an annual inflation rate of 1.7% from 2020 to 2024, and a rate of just 0.85% from 2024 to 2028. To many, this is the key attraction of bitcoin, with a known maximum supply of 21 million bitcoins and an inflation rate that is algorithmically designed to decline every four years.

Each user has an account number on the Bitcoin network, which can also be termed a public key, a public address, or a wallet. The main function of the Bitcoin network is for investors to own bitcoin as a store of value. Each bitcoin can be saved for as long as the investor chooses, or it can be spent by sending the coins to another user on the network.

Satoshi Nakamoto's Bitcoin white paper lists six steps to running the Bitcoin network.

The steps to run the network are as follows:

1. New transactions are broadcast to all nodes.
2. Each node collects new transactions into a block.
3. Each node works on finding a difficult proof-of-work for its block.
4. When a node finds a proof-of-work, it broadcasts the block to all nodes.
5. Nodes accept the block only if all transactions in it are valid and not already spent.
6. Nodes express their acceptance of the block by working on creating the next block in the chain, using the hash of the accepted block as the previous hash.[7]

The first step is to broadcast new transactions to all nodes. In every 10-minute period, all proposed transactions are broadcast to each node, where each miner will verify and build a block of transactions. The miner that solves a difficult proof-of-work problem writes the next block of transactions to the Bitcoin blockchain and collects their block reward. Thousands of Bitcoin miners around the world are applying computing power in a competition to solve this difficult proof-of-work cryptographic puzzle. The larger the computing power applied to solve this puzzle, the more secure the Bitcoin network becomes. The Bitcoin network is calibrated so that exactly one computer in the world can solve this problem in each 10-minute period. As more miners enter the network, the puzzle becomes more difficult, while exiting miners make the puzzle a bit easier. The difficulty of the network is continuously adjusted so that the average time to earn each block reward remains at 10 minutes.

Once a single miner has written a block of transactions to the Bitcoin blockchain, other miners need to validate that block of transactions. Each miner writing a subsequent block of transactions to the blockchain verifies that all prior blocks only contain valid transactions. The greater the number of blocks added beyond a specific transaction, the more final the transaction is considered. Many network participants believe that a bitcoin transaction is considered final in 30 minutes, the time it takes for two blocks to be confirmed after the block posting the original transaction.

The original design of the Bitcoin network was solely to support investors who wish to spend or send bitcoin tokens, the peer-to-peer electronic cash, or to save them securely in their wallet. In 2023, developers started adding additional functionality to the Bitcoin blockchain, such as using the block space to track ownership of other assets, such as ordinals, which are similar to the non-fungible tokens, or NFTs, tracked on proof-of-stake blockchains.

Bitcoin aspires to be a store of value, with some market participants comparing it to digital gold. Due to its speed and block size limitations, the Bitcoin network is not currently able to support global consumer spending. Bitcoin processes approximately seven transactions per second, far less than the 5,000 to 24,000 transactions that Mastercard and Visa process per second globally.[8]

Bitcoin is very secure and highly decentralized, but it hasn't yet scaled to the speed needed for consumers to regularly use it to purchase their daily coffee. In addition to the limited size of storage on the Bitcoin blockchain, it is also infeasible for in-person retail transactions, as each block of transactions on the Bitcoin blockchain is verified with a 10-minute block time. That is, waiting up to 10 minutes for a new block of transactions to be posted to the Bitcoin blockchain is slower than the seconds that it takes to approve transactions on the Mastercard or Visa network.

Functionality such as Taproot and the Lightning Network has been added to increase the speed and scalability of the Bitcoin blockchain. The standard Bitcoin network processes transactions one at a time, verifying each user's private key, public key, and account balance. This method of verifying transactions is transparent, as the sending address, the receiving address, and the transaction amount can all be seen using a block explorer.

It can be time-consuming to process transactions with multiple inputs, such as a transaction sending value from three wallets with the proceeds sent to two wallets. Bitcoin's Taproot upgrade aggregates signatures for validation as a batch of transactions. Rather than verifying and disclosing each individual address, Taproot considers the transaction as a whole, verifying the validity of all private keys and balances at once. While standard Bitcoin transactions are highly transparent and traceable, transactions with multiple addresses processed through Taproot can obscure the identity of sending addresses.

The Lightning Network works like a credit card by batching transactions between two parties for some period of time. Rather than clearing transactions as they happen, they are cleared at some specific interval, such as the end of each day or month. On the Lightning Network, two users agree to open a payment channel. Consider a university student who has the ability to charge meals or bookstore purchases to their student ID card. The transactions accumulate for an entire semester, at which point payment for all transactions is due at one time. The same approach is used in the Lightning Network, as two users accumulate transactions for some period of time before settling in a single, combined transaction that is written to the Bitcoin blockchain.

Each blockchain is governed by computer code and has a community of users, such as the miners who validate transactions on the Bitcoin blockchain. The code governing the Bitcoin blockchain has changed over time, such as the introduction of upgrades for Taproot and the Lightning Network. Given that no single person or entity is in charge of the Bitcoin blockchain, changes to the code are subject to a governance process. A change to the protocol's algorithm is proposed, debated, and debugged before being put to a vote by the community's stakeholders. Given that all miners run the same code to validate transactions on the Bitcoin blockchain, the code will not be modified unless the community approves it. When the code running a blockchain protocol is changed after being approved by a community vote, a soft fork occurs. That is, the code has changed (or forked) with the community's permission. All miners must update to the new version of the code before continuing to validate transactions.

When a codebase is forked, there has been a change or upgrade to the code governing a blockchain. In a soft fork, the community has agreed to, say, upgrade from version 2 to version 3 of the code to implement an agreed revision to the protocol. The code is updated when the community has agreed to a soft fork, while the blockchain and coins continue to run uninterrupted. A soft fork maintains the same coins and the same history of blockchain transactions while upgrading to a new operating system.

A hard fork, however, occurs when the community does not agree to upgrade the blockchain to the proposed protocol. As a result, two blockchains emerge, one with the original codebase and protocol design and a second with an updated codebase and protocol design. For instance, some participants in the Bitcoin community were concerned about the slow transaction times and small block sizes, which prevented bitcoin from being used for everyday transactions. A proposal was made to update the Bitcoin network protocol to larger block sizes, allowing for a larger capacity to process transactions.

After a failed vote in 2017, the Bitcoin blockchain experienced a hard fork, which led to the addition of the Bitcoin Cash blockchain. Users holding bitcoin balances before the fork continued to hold their bitcoin while also being awarded Bitcoin Cash tokens. This allowed the traditional Bitcoin blockchain to continue to run using the current protocol, with each block containing 1 megabyte of transaction information. A portion of the mining community arose to maintain the Bitcoin Cash blockchain with 32-megabyte block sizes.[9]

The term "cryptocurrency" comes from the cryptography used to encrypt and secure a blockchain network. Cryptography is the science of codes, encryption, and decryption. Bitcoin uses SHA-256, a 256-bit, 32-byte hash called the Secure Hash Algorithm. This is an extraordinarily secure algorithm because there are 2 to the 256 power possible inputs, which is an extraordinarily large number. This makes it virtually impossible for hackers to guess a private key by brute-force computing.

The encryption standard used in the Bitcoin network seeks to have hidden keys that are collision-free. Hiding a key means that knowing the hash output doesn't allow us to recreate the input. A user would not be able to use an encrypted version of a code to see what information was written to the blockchain. When encryption is collision-free, no two inputs create the same hash output. However, it is easy to verify that the input generates a specific hash output.

An online hash generator can be used to calculate hash outputs.[10] The information written to the Bitcoin blockchain includes all of the valid transactions from the last 10 minutes, including all the sending addresses, all the receiving addresses, all the amounts that were sent and the ending balances. Each block of transactions will be summarized and secured with a hash. Every time a single character of information in the block changes, the hash changes significantly.

Consider the hashes of three phrases. Notice how a slight change in the phrase produces a significant change in the hash.

Input	Hash
Goals of a blockchain	ec704997cfad61bde181c04528b6e5cdd328f2cb2fc-31da309ee25cfc7103a24
goals of a blockchain	6eaaad44154c41ad7ec7aabf036cde7da0343f71671977b-443297c865c44b1a0
Goals of the blockchain	22c4c267a16f5c53a3d552d012af553c154ffc54a8a5d76a8d-860968b9deef93

With hiding, the hash cannot be used to recreate the input. The hash size is consistent whether the input is four words, 10 minutes of blockchain transactions, or the entire dictionary. The hash changes radically if a single comma is removed from the entire dictionary.

Hashes are the key to understanding blockchain technology and how it is used to prevent double spending. The transaction information from

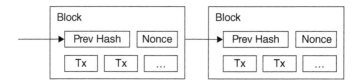

Source: Bitcoin: A Peer-to-Peer Electronic Cash System, https://bitcoin.org/
bitcoin.pdf.

the prior block is summarized with a hash. The prior block's hash is included with all of the transaction information in the subsequent block. That is, the hash of the output must match the hash of the input. When the hashed output of the prior block matches the hashed input into the subsequent block, miners and investors can be confident that nothing has been changed in the transaction information in the prior block. When the blocks are chained together with the proper hash, the immutability of the prior transaction information is guaranteed. In computer science terms, this is a linked list.

If an actor were to change transaction information in a prior block from sending 20 bitcoins to sending 2 bitcoins, the hash of the block's transaction information would change and the chain to the next block would be broken. Miners will see that the blockchain has been broken, and return the transaction information in the prior block to its original state.

Investors can disclose their public key, which is the address of their Bitcoin or Ethereum wallet. Just like an email address, anyone can send value or information to a blockchain wallet. It's crucial, however, for investors to keep their private key secure, as anyone with access to the private key will be able to send value out of the wallet. Just as someone doesn't want their email hacked and used to send spam, they also don't want their blockchain wallet hacked and the value in their accounts immutably sent to other wallets. As the saying goes, "Not your keys, not your crypto." If anyone, including a centralized exchange, has access to an investor's private keys, they are vulnerable to having the value in the wallet stolen. Chapter 21 will discuss the security of blockchain wallets, including hot wallets, cold wallets, and paper wallets.

Before processing a transaction, the miners validate that each account has sufficient bitcoin available to complete the proposed transaction. The miners evaluate the account balance as the sum of all transactions that have taken place since the wallet was opened. The miners verify that the proper private key was used to request the transaction and send the value. The miners can't see the private key, but are able to verify that the correct private key was used. Anyone can verify that the digital signature is valid, but only the private key owner can generate the digital signature needed to send value.

Each block written to the Bitcoin blockchain has information regarding each transaction verified during the 10-minute period. Information in the block includes the timestamp, the coinbase that creates the block reward that is distributed to the miner, inputs including the address(es) and amount of the sending account(s), outputs including the address(es) of the sending account, and verification of the digital signature using the private key of the sending account(s). An optional message can also be included.

One way to simplify the accounting is that all the bitcoin in a wallet is spent every time a transaction is requested. A private key holder with access to an account containing 20 bitcoins may wish to initiate a transaction to send 9.9 bitcoins to another wallet. The transaction would send all 20 bitcoins, with 9.9 bitcoins going to the designated receiving account, a transaction fee of less than 0.1 bitcoin is deducted, with the sending account receiving more than 10 bitcoins back into their account as change from the transaction. The key issue is to avoid double spending, where all transactions are verified to ensure that precisely one wallet owns each bitcoin and that each bitcoin is spent only once.

The blockchain's distributed nature is demonstrated by the fact that every miner has access to all of the proposed transactions and the history of all transactions since its inception. If a single miner's computer goes down or a country expels all bitcoin miners, the remaining miners are still available to ensure the continuous processing and verification of transactions.

Miners worldwide compete to verify transactions and earn the newly issued bitcoins that are awarded to the publisher of the next block. The publisher of the block is determined by a proof-of-work process, with the winner being the owner of the computer that is the first to solve the cryptographic puzzle proposed in each 10-minute period. Because there are thousands of miners worldwide, no single entity is going to be able to approve consecutive blocks of transactions. The larger the number of miners, the more decentralized and secure the network becomes, and the fewer consecutive blocks a single miner can write to the blockchain.

The difficulty of mining bitcoin is adjusted so that a new block is published approximately every 10 minutes. Only one of the computers in the world will be able to solve this complex proof-of-work problem in any given 10-minute period. The Bitcoin miners compete to discover the nonce, a hashed number that complies with the difficulty requirement. The winner of the block reward is the first to discover this secret number, which, when combined with the hash of the prior block and the proposed transactions for the new block, reaches a solution that is lower than the network's targeted difficulty. Thousands of computers worldwide try trillions of combinations; the first one every 10 minutes is the winner.

The difficulty of the proof-of-work algorithm ensures that the Bitcoin blockchain can't be hacked to send bitcoin from wallets without providing access to the private keys. The difficulty of mining Bitcoin continues to increase as more mining rigs are added to the network. As more computers are added to the Bitcoin mining network, the more secure the network becomes, and the harder it is to solve the nonce. As the hash rate increased from about 100 million terahashes per second in February of 2020 to more than 500 million in February 2024, the difficulty in mining Bitcoin has increased by five times over the last four years. Combined with the April 2024 halving that reduces the block reward by 50%, the average mining rig is far less profitable today than in 2020. It has never been more difficult to mine bitcoin than in late 2023 and early 2024.

The summer of 2021 saw a significant shift in the location of global Bitcoin mining. At that point, more than 40% of the world's Bitcoin mining rigs were located in China. However, the Chinese government expelled Bitcoin miners from the country due to concerns over energy usage. Over the course of about four months, the majority of China's Bitcoin mining capacity found homes elsewhere in the world.

The computing power of an individual computer or mining rig is based on its hash rate, which is the number of hashes that are calculated each second. Each mining company competes by constantly adding more computers and faster computers in search of the winning nonce. As individual mining firms add capacity at relatively equal rates, the network's security continues to increase, while each miner's market share remains relatively constant. As a mining firm doubles the number of rigs to maintain its share of the global hash rate, its cost of rigs and electricity doubles, while the number of expected bitcoins earned is relatively unchanged.

The earliest Bitcoin miners used graphics processing units (GPUs), similar to those found in high-end gaming computers. In fact, demand for GPUs for mining proof-of-work cryptocurrencies contributed to a global shortage of GPUs starting in 2017.[11] Exacerbated by supply chain shortages and increased computing demand during the COVID pandemic shutdown, GPU shortages lasted at least through 2021. With the rise of generative AI starting in 2023, chip shortages continue, driving up the stock prices of Nvidia and other suppliers of high-end computing components.

As Bitcoin mining became more globally competitive, generating the required hash rates using solely GPUs became more challenging. Today, mining is a large business with publicly traded mining companies deploying hundreds or thousands of specific mining rigs called application-specific integrated circuits (ASICs). These computers have chips designed specifically to mine

Bitcoin and will use less energy per hash than GPUs, as the sole function of ASICs is to find the nonce and verify proposed transactions on the Bitcoin blockchain. The ability to hash transactions using the SHA-256 is hard coded into the hardware of the mining rig.

A miner that operates 1% of global Bitcoin mining capacity is expected to earn a block reward approximately once every 1,000 minutes or 16.7 hours (which is dividing the average block time of one-sixth of an hour by the 1% market share of the miner). A miner controlling 0.01% of the global hash rate would be expected to solve one block every 69 days or just four to five blocks each year.

Block rewards are winner-take-all. The miner that solves the nonce and writes the block to the Bitcoin blockchain gets the entire block reward. In early 2024, with bitcoin priced at $45,000, a block reward of 6.25 BTC was valued at $281,250. Due to the substantial electricity required to run a Bitcoin mining operation, it is difficult to go weeks or months without solving a single block. As the size of the block reward is reduced to 3.125 bitcoins at April 2024 halving, miners are counting on an increase in the price of each bitcoin to offset a potential revenue decline of 50% while the cost of running the mining rigs continues unchanged.

Rather than operating as a solo miner, some miners have chosen to participate in a mining pool. When joining forces with other miners, the agreement is that a block reward earned by any miner in the pool is shared with all other miners based on their contribution to the total hash rate. That is, a miner controlling 10% of the hash rate in the pool will earn 10% of the block rewards earned by all cooperating miners regardless of the number of block rewards actually earned by that miner's rigs. Participating in a mining pool provides a more consistent earnings stream but a smaller cash flow each time a block is found by a pool member.

While the Bitcoin network is designed to be decentralized, mining pools have significant power. The Bitcoin network generates approximately 144 block rewards daily, with a total daily value of more than $40 million using the prior math. While not all miners join pools, the size of the largest pools leads to significant concentration with four pools earning 75% of pooled block rewards (Foundry USA, AntPool, F2Pool, ViaBTC).[11] If a single entity were able to control the majority of the mining capacity, it might be able to approve consecutive blocks, which could make the blockchain less secure. Cryptocurrency investors are concerned about this 51% attack, where miners with significant market power being able to approve consecutive blocks and impair the security of the network. Of course, doing so would make bitcoin less valuable, which offsets the incentive to earn dishonest short-term gains.

At a network speed of just seven transactions per second, some Bitcoin transactions may be delayed. Investors, such as arbitrage traders, may have such an urgency to settle transactions that they may offer a priority fee to the miners to ensure that their transaction is included in the current block. Miners can experience increased profitability when earning priority fees in addition to block rewards.

Miners of proof-of-work cryptocurrencies consumed 150 terawatt-hours of electricity in 2022, similar to those of entire countries such as Greece or Argentina.[13] Because of this substantial demand and political pressure, Bitcoin miners are sensitive to the cost and type of electricity used. Miners seek to locate their server farms and mining rigs in areas with low-cost electricity, often consuming renewable energy generated by solar, wind, hydroelectric, and even volcano-fired facilities.[14] Significant mining operations have been built to take advantage of flared natural gas and wind power in Texas or turbines run by steaming volcanoes in Iceland and El Salvador. Flare gas is a byproduct of oil and gas production where methane and natural gas are burned into the environment. Some Bitcoin mining rigs have been located in Texas oil fields, which can reduce pollution when flare gas is used to generate electricity rather than simply being burned as waste.

Some miners sign interruptible power contracts with electric companies that reduce the average cost of electricity if the miner agrees to shut down their rigs when the electric grid is approaching its maximum capacity.

While environmentalists are concerned about the carbon footprint of Bitcoin mining, Bitcoin proponents believe that mining provides a societal purpose of democratizing the global financial system. By maintaining a distributed ledger of financial transactions, the Bitcoin network is enhancing financial inclusion and ending financial discrimination, especially in emerging markets where fiat currencies are experiencing high inflation rates. The Bitcoin Mining Council reports that miners used nearly 60% sustainable energy in the first half of 2023.[15] In contrast, renewable electricity represents approximately 38% of the global generation mix,[16] showing the commitment of proof-of-work miners to use electricity generated by solar, wind, hydro, volcanoes, and nuclear facilities.

The profitability of a Bitcoin miner is based on the cost to buy the mining rigs, build or lease a data center, the cost of electricity, and the amount of electricity consumed relative to the income earned through block rewards and priority fees. Given the increasing competition between miners and the halving of block rewards every four years, the profitability of Bitcoin mining is not guaranteed. As California became crowded with miners in the gold rush of 1849, some entrepreneurs found it more profitable to sell supplies to the miners than to mine for gold themselves. The picks-and-shovels strategy seeks to sell gold mining supplies, such as picks, shovels, and Levi's jeans, to the ever-growing population of miners. As each new miner arrives, the profitability of selling mining supplies increases, and the profitability of gold mining declines. Applying the picks-and-shovels analogy to today's gold rush of cryptocurrency mining and artificial intelligence, selling GPUs, ASICs, data centers, and electricity may be more profitable than mining bitcoin. Just ask Nvidia.

This gives investors a variety of ways to invest in the cryptocurrency revolution. Investors could operate a mining operation, buy bitcoin or Ether tokens, or invest in stocks of crypto mining firms, computing companies such as Nvidia, real estate investment trusts (REITs) that own data centers, or financial companies such as Coinbase or CME Group. Investing in crypto-related equities may have less volatile returns than investing directly into cryptocurrencies.

In summary, Bitcoin can be decentralized and secure but not necessarily scalable. The proof-of-work mining process involves thousands of computers worldwide competing to solve the same problem. This makes the Bitcoin network highly secure but duplicates much effort. While some are concerned about the energy consumption of Bitcoin mining, the next chapter examines the Ethereum blockchain, which converted from proof-of-work to proof-of-stake mining in September 2022. As a result of this change, the Ethereum network now consumes 99% less electricity than Bitcoin mining by eliminating the redundant efforts of transaction validation.

CHAPTER 5

Ethereum Blockchain and Smart Contracts

When discussing cryptocurrencies and digital assets, we generally speak first about Bitcoin and then about Ethereum. Bitcoin started with the 2008 white paper and the first transactions in 2009. This was followed by the Ethereum white paper in 2014. While the creator or creators of Bitcoin are anonymous, the Ethereum team is known and is led by Vitalik Buterin. The Ethereum team had great interest in the Bitcoin network and had five or six years to study Bitcoin and its design before launching their own blockchain. The goal of Ethereum is to add the functionality they believed was missing from the Bitcoin blockchain.

Despite thousands of cryptocurrencies being launched on dozens of blockchains, bitcoin has maintained approximately 50% of the market capitalization of the entire cryptocurrency industry, while Ether has 16% dominance of the industry's market capitalization. The dominance of any cryptocurrency is defined as the market capitalization of a given cryptocurrency relative to the total market capitalization of the combined cryptocurrency universe. While dominance varies over time, bitcoin and Ether typically combine to account for between 60% and 70% of the value of the entire cryptocurrency ecosystem. Real-time calculations of the market capitalization of thousands of cryptocurrencies, including the dominance of bitcoin and Ether, can be seen at coinmarketcap.com, coingecko .com, and other sites that track the value of cryptocurrencies and digital assets.

Despite their shared beginnings, Bitcoin and Ethereum have very different goals and operations. Bitcoin has been called "digital gold," the globally decentralized currency that serves as a store of value and strives to be a medium of exchange. The design of the Bitcoin blockchain is relatively simple, as investors can either store or save their bitcoin. Ordinals on the Bitcoin blockchain, which started in 2023 and will be discussed in Chapter 14 on non-fungible tokens (NFTs), seek to extend the functionality of the Bitcoin blockchain. However, Bitcoin purists or maxis do not approve of ordinals and may wish that the Bitcoin blockchain stick to its roots as simply accounting for bitcoin transactions and securing the Bitcoin network.

Bitcoin miners who secure the network by solving cryptographic puzzles and tracking transactions on the distributed ledger participate in a proof-of-work (POW) system. In the POW system, thousands of miners simultaneously compete to write the next block to the Bitcoin blockchain. While the system is highly secure, the redundant computer operations consume a tremendous amount of electricity, which has led to criticisms of the impact that Bitcoin mining has on the environment. In September 2022, the Ethereum blockchain moved from a proof-of-work mining system to a proof-of-stake (POS) validation system, reducing its electricity consumption by more than 99%.

Ethereum has the same functionality as Bitcoin, where the value of Ether tokens saved or spent is tracked on the Ethereum blockchain. The designers of Ethereum added substantially greater functionality by having their blockchain store the output of programs run on the Ethereum Virtual Machine (EVM), a globally decentralized computer. Users can design smart contract computer programs that run on this network. The smart contracts submitted by the users of the EVM will be executed by one of the validators managing the Ethereum network. While Bitcoin could be compared to gold as a store of value, Ethereum is compared to oil as a system that facilitates commerce.

Beyond the addition of Taproot and the Lightning Network, the protocol governing the design of the Bitcoin blockchain is relatively unchanged since its 2008 inception. While there have been attempts to modify the protocol through soft forks, most proposals have failed or led to hard forks, such as Bitcoin Cash.

Ethereum is a living, breathing entity that is changing all of the time, with constant upgrades being made to the Ethereum network. Community members can submit an Ethereum Request for Comment (ERC) document that outlines a request to change how the code governing the Ethereum blockchain is designed. Once the ERC is debated, revised, and accepted, it graduates to an Ethereum Improvement Proposal (EIP). EIPs create the roadmap for future development projects to be implemented on the Ethereum blockchain. Soon after the 2014 launch of Ethereum, the ERC-20 token standard was adopted in 2015, which outlined the creation of smart contracts. Any participant in the global crypto community can choose to build a smart contract that will be executed on the EVM or launch a new currency or token that is secured and tracked on the Ethereum blockchain. Smart contracts and tokens must follow the technical rules of ERC-20 to be compatible with the Ethereum ecosystem. ERC-20 tokens are fungible tokens that can be held in Ethereum wallets and transferred on the Ethereum blockchain.

Assets that are fungible are interchangeable with no discernable difference in quality or ownership. Investors are indifferent to which dollar bill they receive, which barrel of light sweet crude oil, or which specific bitcoin or Ether token they own. Fungible assets are also divisible, as investors can easily trade or own half of one bitcoin or a half barrel of oil. Assets that are non-fungible are unique and not divisible, as each individual asset has a specific ownership, a specific provenance, or features that distinguish the specific asset from other similar assets.

Three years after fungible tokens were created under the ERC-20 standard, ERC-721 was introduced to support non-fungible tokens on the Ethereum blockchain. Starting in 2018, non-fungible tokens could be minted using smart contracts with ownership tracked on the Ethereum blockchain. The Ethereum blockchain records the ownership of the NFT, as well as the location where that NFT is stored.

Improvements to the Ethereum blockchain have continued from 2020 to 2024. Ethereum's transition from a proof-of-work to a proof-of-stake blockchain was approved under EIP-3675 in 2020 and implemented in September 2022. The transition to POS was termed the merge, as the Ethereum main network (mainnet) that was running as a POW blockchain merged into the Beacon chain that was testing the POS methodology.

To support the merge, EIP-1559 (London upgrade) and EIP-4895 (Shanghai upgrade) were implemented. In a POW protocol, miners are compensated with newly issued tokens for each verified block of transactions written to the blockchain. Under a POS protocol, block rewards are no longer necessary to compensate validators, as the electricity and computing resources expended are much lower. However, the validators are using their computing resources to execute the smart contracts and support the global operation of the Ethereum Virtual Machine. Users submitting smart contracts must pay "gas fees" for the computing time used on the EVM based on the complexity of the program's operation.

In the London upgrade, gas fees are assessed based on the congestion of the Ethereum blockchain. The more crowded Ethereum gets, the more expensive it becomes to execute transactions and smart contracts. Gas fees are denominated in gwei, with each Ether token containing 1 billion gwei. The London upgrade changes how validators are compensated when moving to the POS protocol.

The Ethereum blockchain operated as a POW system from its 2014 inception until September 2022, when it merged into the POS system. The POW system offered block rewards of 2 Ether tokens to a validator as a new block was written to the Ethereum blockchain every 12 seconds. In the POS system, validators earn the gas fees paid by network users. The London upgrade substantially slowed the increasing supply of Ether tokens by eliminating block rewards and by burning a portion of the Ether tokens that are used for transactions. Tokens that are burned are eliminated from the money supply by sending them to a wallet with no usable private keys, making it impossible for those tokens to be spent and returned to the circulating supply.

While the Ethereum blockchain was anticipating the merge, which transitioned the protocol from POW to POS, validators were required to stake, or lock up, 32 Ether tokens to show their commitment to the new POS protocol. The lockup period started in December 2020 and was of an unknown duration. After the merge was completed in September 2022, the lockup period expired in March 2023. Once the lockup period expired, validators could choose to remove their staked Ether from the protocol and stop their services as a validator. Approximately 14% of the outstanding Ether tokens were staked in the Beacon chain during this lockup period.[1]

There are a number of differences between POW mining and POS validation. In a POW protocol like Bitcoin, thousands of miners compete to write the next block and earn the block reward. This redundant effort makes the Bitcoin blockchain highly secure but also expends substantial computing effort. The financial resources committed to a POW mining operation are external to the blockchain and the token, with miners spending millions of dollars on electricity and mining rigs.

In a POS system, such as Ethereum post-September 2022, validators must lock up a financial stake in the blockchain. Validators commit more assets to Ether tokens than to the cost of electricity and mining rigs. That is, a POS protocol invests more money into the blockchain ecosystem and less into external vendors such as electric companies and computer chip suppliers.

Validators must stake a minimum of 32 Ether tokens to participate in the POS system. With a two-year lockup of tokens costing more than $50,000, this stake demonstrates each validator's financial investment in the ecosystem. Not only are these tokens locked in for an unknown period of time, but they are also at risk to the validator's performance. Validators must contribute positively to the network by providing reliable computing resources, approving valid transactions, and rejecting invalid transactions. Validators who provide unreliable computing uptime or approve invalid transactions may be fined by the network, where the size of their stake can be slashed.

Miners are chosen to write blocks to a POW blockchain by expending computing power to solve the nonce. This competition secures the network but is very expensive in terms of computing power and electricity consumption. Transitioning from a POW to a POS protocol reduced the electricity consumption of Ethereum validators by more than 99%. A POS protocol eliminates the competition between validators by randomly assigning a new validator for each block based on the size of their stake in the network. A validator that owns 1% of the staked Ether tokens has a 1% probability of being chosen to write the next block and earn the gas fees spent by the users of the blockchain.

Future upgrades to the Ethereum network will be used to increase scalability and reduce fees by redirecting the redundant resources deployed on a POW blockchain to distributed computing on the POS blockchain. That is, a POS blockchain could have 1,000 computers working on 1,000 different groups of transactions to scale the blockchain's speed and number of validated transactions, while the POW blockchain has 1,000 computers working on a single block of transactions.

Ethereum was running two blockchains in parallel for more than three years. The Beacon chain has been running proof-of-stake since 2020, while the Ethereum mainnet was running proof-of-work since its 2014 inception. Once the Ethereum team was satisfied with the performance of the validators in the POS system, the merge was completed in September 2022, and the Ethereum blockchain fully transitioned to POS.

In the Ethereum POS validation protocol, all of the proposed transactions enter the mempool, where forgers or validators verify and order the transactions. Miners on the POW Bitcoin blockchain simply verify the sending address, the receiving address, the transaction amount, and the sender's private keys. Validating Ethereum transactions is more complicated, as EVM network computers run smart contract computer programs. In addition to sending and saving Ether tokens, the output of all smart contract transactions is saved to the Ethereum blockchain.

Each validator node contributes to the global computing capacity to facilitate smart contract transactions. The proof-of-stake system rewards the forgers randomly with the ability to write the next block to the Ethereum blockchain, based on the number of Ether that is staked. While blocks are written to the Bitcoin blockchain every 10 minutes, the block time on the Ethereum blockchain is 12 seconds.

A validator can earn an annual return of between 5% and 8% on the value of their staked Ether in return for running a validator node. Validators must invest a stake of at least 32 Ether tokens, computing resources to run the EVM and write blocks to the Ethereum blockchain, and technical knowledge of how to consistently validate transactions without incurring slashing penalties.

A validator's Ether stake can be slashed when they are not contributing positively to the health of the network. Stakes can be slashed for violations such as computer downtime and the approval of inaccurate transactions.

Investors have the ability to earn financial rewards without running a validator node by staking their own Ether tokens with a validator. The investors contribute the financial capital of staked Ether without providing the computing resources or technical know-how required to run a validation node. While the validators can earn an annual yield of 5% to 8%, those delegating their stake to a validator can earn annual yields of 2% to 4%. Rewards for staking and validating transactions are paid in Ether tokens, not in cash. While investors or validators may have 2% to 8% more Ether tokens at the end of the year than at the beginning of the year, the financial return can be either positive or negative, as the value of Ether tokens can increase or decrease over time.

Lido, Coinbase, and Figment have the largest Ethereum staking pools, comprising more than half of the 29.1 million staked Ether tokens. With 120 million Ether tokens outstanding in early 2024, approximately 15% have been staked.[2] Investors can participate in the validation process and earn staking yields by exchanging Ether tokens for staked Ether tokens. These include Lido (st ETH), Coinbase (CB ETH), and RocketPool (RETH) staked Ether tokens.

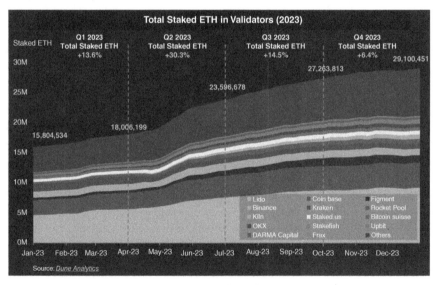

Source: https://www.coingecko.com/research/publications/2023-annual-crypto-report, Dune Analytics

Some of the largest staking platforms are operated by the centralized exchange operators: Coinbase, Binance, and Kraken. Registration as a securities offering may be required to legally operate a staking-as-a-service platform in the US. In February 2023, Kraken ceased staking for all US users, with the exchange paying a $30 million fine to the US Securities and Exchange Commission (SEC) for not registering the service. The official SEC statement notes, "Whether it's through staking-as-a-service, lending, or other means, crypto intermediaries, when offering investment contracts in exchange for investors' tokens, need to provide the proper disclosures and safeguards required by our securities laws."[3]

The Ethereum blockchain is significantly more complex than the Bitcoin blockchain, as the Bitcoin blockchain was initially designed to securely store and send bitcoin tokens as peer-to-peer digital cash. While functionalities such as Taproot, Lightning Network, and Ordinals have been added to the Bitcoin blockchain in recent years, there is no smart contract functionality similar to that deployed on the Ethereum blockchain.

Ethereum, then, serves as a base layer for fungible tokens built under the ERC-20 standard and non-fungible tokens complying with the ERC-721 standard. For example, the ERC-20 standard allows investors to hold Polygon tokens on the Ethereum blockchain, while the ERC-721 standard allows verifiable ownership of NFTs such as CryptoPunks.

The Ethereum blockchain is the settlement layer, often referred to as layer-zero, layer-one, or the base layer. The output of smart contract transactions is secured, cleared, and settled, with ownership tracked on the Ethereum blockchain. At the protocol layer, smart contracts and distributed applications (DApps) are added to the Ethereum ecosystem. These DApps may revolutionize global businesses by adding decentralized access to borrowing and lending platforms and exchanges for stocks, futures, options, and other derivative products.

There are a wide variety of DApps leveraging the security and functionality of the Ethereum blockchain, including NFTs, decentralized finance (DeFi), gaming and metaverse, decentralized exchanges (DEXes), oracles, information, and storage. Each of these DApp categories will be discussed at length later in this book.

NFTs	Decentralized Finance (DeFi)	Gaming and Metaverse	Oracles, Information, and Storage	Decentralized Exhanges (DEXes)
Open Sea	Compound	Decentraland	Chainlink	Uniswap
Rarible	Aave	Axie Infinity	Basic Attention Token	SushiSwap
CryptoPunks	Tether	Enjin	Storj	Kyber

Source: https://dappradar.com/rankings.

While coingecko.com tracks price information on more than 12,000 digital assets, centralized exchanges, such as Binance, Kraken, or Coinbase, may only provide US investors access to a few dozen cryptocurrencies.

Decentralized exchanges such as Uniswap or PancakeSwap may provide access to hundreds of tokens not available on centralized exchanges. Coingecko.com, coinmarketcap.com, and other websites list information on cryptocurrencies, including the price, number of tokens outstanding, market capitalization, and the centralized and decentralized exchanges offering access to each digital asset. Centralized exchanges allow investors to hold their tokens on exchange or transfer them to a personal wallet. In contrast, decentralized exchanges only exchange tokens. An investor would send Ether tokens from their personal wallet to a decentralized exchange with a request to exchange for Chainlink tokens. The DEX would swap the Ether tokens and send the Chainlink tokens back to the investor's personal wallet. DEXes are non-custodial, as they only execute token swaps and return tokens back to investors on their choice of custody platform.

Decentralized finance, or DeFi, seeks to recreate the financial system on-chain. DApps such as Compound and Aave facilitate the borrowing and lending of assets and stablecoins. While the Tether and USDC stablecoins are tied to the value of one US dollar, other stablecoins may track other real-world assets, such as one euro or one ounce of gold.

DeFi platforms require information to operate, such as the relative prices of Ether and Chainlink tokens on a decentralized exchange. Chainlink is an oracle that provides information to DeFi apps regarding the price of digital currencies and real-world assets. Oracles can link to any source of information required by a DApp, such as the weather, flight schedules, and the results of elections and sporting events. The Brave internet browser, which competes with Google Chrome, has built a privacy-first way to browse the internet. Brave users can earn Basic Attention Tokens for viewing online ads.

The fun side of digital assets includes NFTs, video games, and new worlds in the metaverse. OpenSea and Rarible are trading platforms for NFTs such as CryptoPunks and Bored Apes. While some video games are crypto-native, other games have crypto functionality where the ownership of in-game items such as swords, shields, clothes, and magic powers are stored on the Ethereum blockchain.

The Ethereum Virtual Machine runs smart contracts that are written in the Solidity computer code. The EVM is a Turing-complete system, meaning that it has the full capabilities of any computer system. Smart contracts execute code autonomously with the output stored on the Ethereum blockchain. Nick Szabo defines smart contracts as "a set of promises, specified in digital form, including protocols within which the parties perform on these promises."[4] When a user sends information or value to a smart contract, they agree to accept the results of whatever that smart contract is designed to do, including sending and receiving information and value. The code for the smart contracts is stored on a DApp or on the Ethereum blockchain.

The code is executed by sending information or value to the wallet address where the smart contract is located. The code executes automatically without any input from the user.

The Chamber of Digital Commerce provides 12 use cases for smart contracts in business and beyond as well as the anatomy of a smart contract.[5] There are six steps listed as the anatomy of a smart contract.

- Identify Agreement
- Set Conditions
- Code the Business Logic
- Encryption and Blockchain Technology
- Execution and Processing
- Network Updates

Smart contracts are simply an automation of an agreement that parties may choose to execute in real-world transactions or contracts. The parties first agree that they would like to reach a deal or an agreement, the conditions of the agreement, and the business logic backing the agreement. The first three steps of the smart contract should be familiar to any experienced business person and may differ little from real-world negotiations. The final three steps are technical, as the agreement is written into a computer program executed across distributed networks with the results of the transaction recorded onto a blockchain. Smart contracts coded in the Solidity programming language are compatible with the EVM and other smart contract blockchains such as Polygon, Arbitrum, Optimism, Avalanche, and Polkadot. The Solidity language was explicitly developed for blockchains and smart contracts, while the Solana blockchain runs programs written in Rust, a computer language originally developed outside of the cryptocurrency ecosystem.

Smart contracts should be designed to run efficiently, as users pay for the computing time consumed. The more complex the program becomes, the more expensive it becomes to run and the more error-prone it becomes. Smart contracts can be relatively straightforward to run if they simply rely on "if, then" statements.

- If you bought insurance, and your flight is delayed or canceled, then you get a refund.
- If you put enough money in a vending machine, then the selected product will be delivered to you.
- If you send Ether to a decentralized exchange, then you receive the other digital asset in return.
- If you correctly predict the outcome of a sporting event or an election, then you receive the proceeds of your bet.

- If you borrow money, then it must be paid back with interest.
- If you borrow too much in a collateralized loan, then your collateral will be liquidated when its value declines below a specified level.

The creators of smart contract blockchains envisioned a future where many real-world tasks could be accomplished in a secure, immutable, decentralized global network. Twelve key use cases for smart contracts include:[6]

- Digital Identity
- Records
- Securities
- Trade Finance
- Derivatives
- Financial Data Recording
- Mortgages
- Land Title Recording
- Supply Chain
- Auto Insurance
- Clinical Trials
- Cancer Research

An endless variety of tasks can be computed with the results stored on the secure, immutable, and transparent Ethereum blockchain. Property rights can be enhanced when ownership is documented on a transparent blockchain. Global health can be improved when researchers collaborate on a globally transparent platform that shares research results from clinical trials.

Some participants in the digital asset universe believe that code is law and that transactions should always be irreversible regardless of the outcome. Before interacting with a smart contract, users should understand the code and be willing to accept its output. The smart contracts will execute as they are written, for better or for worse. As a best practice, users may wish to wait before interacting with a new blockchain, digital asset, or smart contract protocol. If an obvious bug in the program can be exploited, it is likely to be found in the initial days or weeks after the code is first implemented. An exploit is a software bug or a vulnerability that can be used by someone other than the asset owner to withdraw assets from the protocol. The smart contract must be written in a secure way that prevents unintended uses that leave the protocol vulnerable to theft or misuse.

It becomes safer to interact with a protocol after the smart contract is aged beyond several weeks or months, several thousands of transactions, or millions of dollars of value locked into a smart contract protocol. Specialized consulting firms perform smart contract audits by reading and testing the code to make sure that no obvious ways to exploit the code are visible. Some users insist on only interacting with open-source protocols, where all of the code governing the protocol has been disclosed. Caution is well warranted, as there were 13 hacks and exploits during 2023, each costing users more than $20 million.[7]

Users pay gas fees proportional to the complexity and run time of the smart contract. Gas fees are enforced to make sure that global computing resources are used efficiently. Programs stop running when the wallet running the smart contract runs out of tokens used to pay for gas fees, which is necessary to prevent smart contracts from running as infinite loops and crashing the globally distributed computing platform. The Ethereum blockchain's gas fees for executing smart contracts are denominated and paid in Ether. The concept of gas in Ethereum is similar to the fuel for a car. You can't reach your destination if your car runs out of gas. Similarly, if a smart contract runs out of gas before it's completed, the user incurs the gas fees, but no transactions actually take place. This is because smart contracts are atomic, meaning they run in full or don't run at all. This is a safety feature for users of the smart contract. For instance, if an investor sends Ether tokens to Uniswap and requests another token in return, they want to make sure that the contract doesn't run out of gas after the Ether tokens are sent to the DEX and before the swap occurs and the desired tokens are returned. The safety feature of atomic contracts ensures that transactions are not halfway completed, causing one party to lose a substantial asset due to the failure of the smart contract to run to completion.

Computer scientists writing the Solidity code need to design the smart contract efficiently with an understanding of gas fees in mind. The Ethereum yellow paper discloses the gas fees for each type of computing operation.[8] There's a fee to start a transaction of 21,000 units of gas. Creating or deleting an account is around 30,000, adding non-zero data to storage is 20,000, transferring value (moving Ether from one wallet to another) costs 9,000, and so on. Gas fees are denominated in gwei, which is one-billionth of an Ether token.

Operation	Gas Consumed
Fee to start a transaction	21,000
Creating or deleting an account	24,000 to 32,000
Adding non-zero data to storage	20,000
Non-zero value transfer	9,000
Check account balance	400
Each non-zero byte of data or code	16
Add, subtract, multiply, divide, logic	2 to 8

Source: https://ethereum.github.io/yellowpaper/paper.pdf

The cost of gas varies over time and can be very expensive when the network is congested. For example, in 2020 and 2021, there were times when the Ethereum network was 100% full, making transactions very expensive. Gas fees tend to spike when there is significant urgency for immediate transactions, such as when trying to complete an arbitrage transaction, purchase an initial coin offering (ICO), or minting NFTs that are in short supply. Those seeking to complete these transactions as quickly as possible may offer extra gas fees to encourage the validators to include their transaction in the current block. The expected profit of an arbitrage trade or the purchase of an ICO or an NFT should include an estimation of gas fees. Users not involved in these urgent transactions are encouraged to delay their smart contract usage until the blockchain congestion has subsided and transaction fees have declined.

Gas can be understood in two ways: gallons and dollars per gallon. If a car gets 20 miles per gallon, a 20-gallon tank may allow for 400 miles of driving. Sometimes gas costs $2 per gallon and other times it is $5 per gallon, based on the weather, the cost of oil, and refinery conditions, etc. When the highway is congested, traffic will slow the journey and decrease the miles per gallon.

The Ethereum network has the same properties. The number of gas units consumed by a smart contract is constant over time as noted in the previous table. While the units of gas consumed are constant, the price of gas varies over time. The price of gas, denominated in gwei, is prominently displayed online on sites such as CoinMarketCap or CoinGecko. The gas prices for smart contract executions on the Ethereum blockchain can be as low as 10 gwei during quiet times and exceed 600 gwei during times of peak demand. This peak demand may last minutes or hours when an ICO is issued or an NFT is minted. Gas prices also tend to spike during times of peak trading volume, such as when millions of users are trading or moving tokens to evade a market crisis, such as moving tokens out of the FTX centralized exchange immediately before its demise.

Users must consider the gas price relative to their transaction's value. It might not make sense to pay $75 in gas fees to purchase a $10 NFT or trade $100 of value in a cryptocurrency. Users with larger and more urgent transactions may be aware of the elevated gas fees and still choose to interact with the blockchain during congestion due to their activity's higher expected profit.

In addition to being used to pay gas fees for smart contracts, Ether tokens can be saved as a store of value or used as collateral for transactions in the DeFi ecosystem. In Chapter 11, DApps such as Aave and Compound will be explained as platforms that allow for borrowing and lending of tokens using Ether as one of the methods of posting collateral. Ether is also a key source of collateral used by Maker DAO to support the value of the DAI stablecoin.

The Ethereum team has posted a roadmap of future blockchain upgrades and enhancements.[9]

- The Merge: upgrades relating to the switch from proof-of-work to proof-of-stake
- The Surge: upgrades related to scalability by rollups and data sharding
- The Scourge: upgrades related to censorship resistance, decentralization, and protocol risks from MEV
- The Verge: upgrades related to verifying blocks more easily
- The Purge: upgrades related to reducing the computational costs of running nodes and simplifying the protocol
- The Splurge: other upgrades that don't fit well into the previous categories.

The merge was accomplished in September 2022 when the Ethereum validation system moved from POW to POS. Work on later elements continues to be implemented, such as the March 2024 Dencun upgrade that accomplishes the goals of the surge related to reducing costs for layer 2 transactions.

The ultimate goal of the Ethereum blockchain is to increase to 100,000 transactions per second, to be as robust and scalable as the Visa or the Mastercard network. In early 2024, scaling transactions is accomplished through layer 2 blockchains and rollups, which will be discussed in later chapters. In order to avoid high gas fees and reduce reliance on the Ethereum blockchain and EVM, many users have taken to using layer 2 solutions, such as Optimism and Arbitrum. Smart contracts are executed on a layer 2 blockchain external to the EVM where gas fees are cheaper, and the result of the smart contract output is recorded on the layer 1 Ethereum blockchain.

One of the keys to upgrading Ethereum is sharding, which allows validators to process transactions more quickly by evaluating only a portion of the history of the Ethereum blockchain. Rather than working with the entire history of the Ethereum blockchain, which is a hardware-intensive large dataset, validators will only process a portion, or a shard, of the data. In effect, this is moving from serial transactions to parallel transactions. Instead of processing transactions one at a time (or one block at a time), validators will be freed up to each work on different transactions (or blocks) simultaneously, multiplying the speed and capacity to process transactions. Sharding allows smaller computers to participate in validating the Ethereum network, increasing the decentralization of the system.

The goal of the verge and the purge is to make it faster and cheaper to verify transactions by allowing validators to process only the most recent transactions in the database. By reducing the computing requirements of validators to feasibly run on a laptop or even a cell phone, the number of validators can increase. Ideally, this would scale the Ethereum network to a point where hundreds of thousands of transactions could be verified each second at a lower cost.

After that, there's the scourge. We're going to reduce the risk of maximal extractable value (MEV) and ensure credible and neutral transaction inclusion. MEV is the maximum amount of fees that a validator can earn by choosing the order in which transactions are or are not written to the blockchain. Validators have some choice as to which pending transactions will be added to the next block. Validators have been known to include or exclude transactions based on the gas fees or other value paid by the user proposing the transaction.[10] While MEV allows validators to increase their income, it increases the cost for users of the blockchain, potentially reducing the long-term attractiveness of Ethereum as a transaction venue. As such, the designers of Ethereum wish to reduce this flexibility for miners, which could result in lower and more consistent fees for users.

The final stage of the current roadmap for Ethereum upgrades is the splurge, where all of the desired features are added after Ethereum has met its goals to be faster, cheaper, more robust, and accessible. The splurge would seek to make the blockchain less inflationary and more energy efficient.

Until these Ethereum network upgrades are complete, the blockchain is still expensive and congested, and users will continue to rely on layer 2 scaling solutions or other layer 1 blockchains, such as Solana and Avalanche, which will be discussed in the next chapter. These alternative layer 1 POS blockchains are much faster and cheaper than Ethereum. The longer it takes the Ethereum network to scale, the greater the chance that Solana, Cosmos, Polygon, Cardano, Avalanche, or others can take market share from Ethereum, the blockchain that first introduced smart contracts.

CHAPTER 6

Proof-of-Stake Protocols and Other Layer 1 Blockchains

Ethereum was the first successful layer 1 blockchain and remains the most valuable when ranked by market capitalization. However, the Ethereum blockchain can be expensive and congested. In recent years, a number of other layer 1 blockchains have been created to compete with Ethereum by offering cheaper and faster transactions. The most prominent include Cardano, Solana, Avalanche, Cosmos, Tezos, Binance Smart Chain, Phantom, and Tron.

Layer 1 blockchains can be thought of as operating systems. Comparisons across blockchains may evoke comparisons between operating systems such as Android vs Apple iOS or Windows vs MacOS. Which blockchain will attract the most developers, the best developers, the most popular DApps, or the most total value locked? Total value locked is the amount of economic value that is interacting in a staking protocol or a DeFi protocol. Many of these blockchains will be developing their own ecosystems, including NFT marketplaces, decentralized exchanges, stablecoins and payments, and decentralized finance applications or DeFi.

Users of blockchains and DApps are searching for the best combination of speed, fees, security, decentralization, as well as functionality and user interfaces. Success of a blockchain can be measured in many ways, including market capitalization, total value locked, number of wallets, and the number of transactions.

Blockchain technology is frequently compared to the internet. Today's internet is termed Web 2.0, while blockchain-enabled networks are termed Web 3.0. The internet began in what is today termed Web 1.0, which was the beginning of email and web browsers. Web 1.0 was generally read-only, as large media companies posted static content, such as digital versions of leading newspapers. Web 2.0 is read-write, the interactive web where users can post content on social media platforms and easily build web pages.

Fat Protocol Thesis

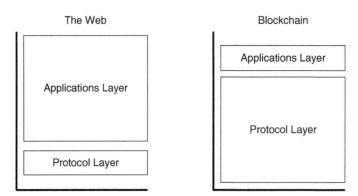

Source: Union Square Ventures.

The builders of the protocols for Web 1.0, such as HTTP, SMTP, TCP/IP, and other technologies that enable sending emails and viewing web pages, generally did not seek to monetize their contributions. Many of these protocols were built by universities and government agencies that chose not to charge a fraction of a cent for each web page viewed or each email sent. The fat protocol thesis developed by Union Square Ventures[1] notes that a very small portion of the value of the internet was captured by the builders of the protocols. This resulted in massive economic value flowing to the application layer of Web 2.0. If it is basically free to send emails and view web pages, companies such as Google, Amazon, Microsoft, and Facebook/Meta can build companies worth trillions of dollars by developing popular internet-based applications. Skeptics of Web 2.0 note that while products offered by Meta and Google are free to users, consumers give up their right to privacy, and their data is commercialized and used for marketing purposes. Consumers give up the ownership of the data and content they have created as a condition of using these applications for free.

While Web 2.0 was built on a thin protocol and fat application layer, the majority of the value in Web 3.0 is captured by the protocol layer. The miners and validators that are explicitly paid to process transactions capture the majority of the economics at the protocol layer. In the fat protocol thesis, the majority of the economics are paid to owners and operators of the protocols, while applications, to date, have accrued less of the value of the blockchain economy. It is notable that as consumers pay to use blockchain-based protocols and applications, they retain ownership of their data which is transferrable across platforms.

Total Cap ($ Billion)	$2,055		coingecko.com
Number of coins	12,768		2/18/2024

Coin	Market Capitalization Rank	Cap ($Billion)	Cumulative Weight
Bitcoin	1	$ 1,016.4	49.5%
Ethereum	2	$ 340.2	66.0%
Binance	3	$ 54.0	68.6%
Solana	5	$ 49.7	71.1%
Cardano	9	$ 21.8	72.1%
Avalanche	10	$ 14.8	72.8%
Tron	12	$ 11.8	73.4%
Polkadot	14	$ 10.3	73.9%
Polygon	15	$ 9.0	74.4%
Cosmos	26	$ 4.0	74.5%
Optimism	32	$ 3.5	74.7%
Arbitrum	43	$ 2.5	74.8%
Fantom	72	$ 1.1	74.9%
Tezos	85	$ 1.0	74.9%

Source: Adapted from CoinGecko.com

In February 2024, CoinGecko tracked more than 12,700 cryptocurrencies and digital assets with a combined market capitalization of $2.055 trillion. Bitcoin and Ethereum alone account for 66% of the total market capitalization of all digital assets tracked, while a dozen layer 1 and layer 2 protocols account for an additional 9% of the value of the crypto universe. This means that 75% of the total value of the blockchain economy, to date, has been captured by Bitcoin, layer 1 and layer 2 protocols. With 7% of the value accounted for in just the top four stablecoins, the remaining 18% of economics has flowed to the other 12,700 DApps and coins, including platforms for DeFi, NFTs, oracles, insurance, and other applications.

Beyond Bitcoin and Ethereum, the major layer 1 and layer 2 protocols have amassed a market capitalization exceeding $180 billion. How have these third-generation protocols evolved and what value do they add to the crypto ecosystem?

Bitcoin is the first-generation blockchain, with its white paper published in 2008 and the first block of transactions written in 2009. The Bitcoin network, which still comprises half of the value of the entire crypto ecosystem, is still proof-of-work. Two key reasons for the success of Bitcoin are that it was the first to solve the double spending problem and the known money supply that limits the long-term issuance to 21 million bitcoins.

Ethereum ushered in the second generation of blockchain technology in 2014, adding the innovation of smart contracts. Rather than being limited to saving and spending a cryptocurrency, the Ethereum blockchain and EVM enabled a new type of decentralized commerce. The Ethereum blockchain started as proof-of-work and merged into a proof-of-stake validation system in 2022.

The third generation of blockchains was introduced between 2017 and 2021. These blockchains implemented proof-of-stake years before Ethereum and were able to offer much greater speed and capacity than the Ethereum blockchain. While the design of Ethereum added functionality relative to that offered by the Bitcoin network, the third-generation blockchains learned from Ethereum and noticed that users were concerned about the cost, speed, and capacity of the Ethereum blockchain. There are concerns, however, that the reduced costs and increased speed of some third-generation blockchains come at the cost of reduced decentralization. Because these smart contract blockchains were expressly built to overcome the challenges facing the Ethereum network, many of these third-generation blockchains have been termed "Ethereum killers." The longer it takes for Ethereum to complete its improvement plans, the longer the Ethereum blockchain has limited capacity and high fees, the greater the potential for a third-generation blockchain to steal market share from Ethereum.

Bitcoin is the largest and most prominent proof-of-work blockchain. The Bitcoin blockchain is highly secure and decentralized, with thousands of miners around the world competing to write the next block to the blockchain. Both the Bitcoin and Ethereum networks are relatively expensive to maintain and have very limited capacity to process transactions. Visa, MasterCard, and some third-generation blockchains can process hundreds of times more transactions per second than the Bitcoin or Ethereum network. However, in early 2024, Bitcoin and Ethereum still combine to hold nearly two-thirds of the market capitalization of the digital asset ecosystem.

When comparing proof-of-stake and proof-of-work, it is noted that proof-of-work protocols reward miners who invest money that flows out of the digital asset ecosystem to providers of electricity and computing resources. Miners invest these resources in competition with other miners to earn the block rewards paid by the Bitcoin protocol every 10 minutes. With expenses denominated in fiat currencies and revenue from block rewards denominated in bitcoin, miners are forced to sell most or all of their earned bitcoin to pay their expenses.

In contrast, proof-of-stake networks reward those who invest in the crypto ecosystem. Approving transactions and maintaining transactions on a proof-of-stake network is accomplished by validators with the largest financial investment in a specific cryptocurrency. Those wishing to serve as a validator must invest in Ether tokens, Chainlink tokens, Phantom tokens, etc., and lock up those assets as a stake until they choose to cease their services as a validator. Rather than expending resources such as electricity and computing costs that flow out of the network, validators on proof-of-stake blockchains invest the majority of their assets directly into the token. By eliminating the requirement of the redundant computing required on a proof-of-work blockchain, proof-of-stake networks consume 99% less electricity than a proof-of-work network. Reducing the electricity consumption of a blockchain network serves to reduce the environmental impact, which may make proof-of-stake blockchain networks less of a target for politicians and environmentalists. There is a question of whether proof-of-stake blockchains sacrifice security or decentralization in order to deliver much faster, cheaper, and more scalable transaction volume relative to proof-of-work blockchains.

Proof-of-stake protocols reward those who invest in that crypto ecosystem. When you buy Ether tokens, when you buy Chainlink tokens, when you buy Phantom tokens, you're reinvesting that money into that specific blockchain that's used to grow the capacity. Rather than sending money outside of the crypto ecosystem, as you're doing in proof-of-work, that money stays within a proof-of-stake network. Staking occurs when validators lock their tokens into a protocol.

The size of the validator's stake is the economic value of their staked tokens. A validator that stakes 1% of all Ether tokens staked has a 1% chance of writing the next block and earning the fees for validating those transactions. Rather than competing with thousands of other miners or validators for these transactions, validators are randomly assigned to process transactions based on the size of their economic stake in the protocol.

Validators in a proof-of-stake blockchain are aligning themselves with the success of the blockchain. The larger the size of the stake and economic commitment to a specific blockchain, the more the validator wants or needs that blockchain to be successful. At a price of $2,812.50 per Ether token, validators staking a minimum of 32 Ether tokens have made at least a $90,000 commitment to the Ethereum ecosystem. These significant economic commitments serve to align incentives, as the largest investors are the ones most committed to the success of the blockchain.

In a proof-of-stake protocol, validators are rewarded for making the blockchain more successful by adding computing resources, staying online, continually processing valid transactions, and denying invalid transactions. Each of these contributions serves to make the blockchain more successful.

Validators who do not contribute to making the blockchain more successful may see the value of their stake in the network slashed. Slashing reduces the balance of staked tokens of validators who do not meet their commitment to the blockchain, such as by having extended network downtime or repeatedly approving invalid transactions.

The economics of proof-of-stake make sense, as those profiting the most from a blockchain protocol are the ones contributing the most capital, the most computing power, and the most stability to the network. It is also expensive to be a proof-of-work miner, but those investments are made predominately outside of the crypto ecosystem through the purchase of electricity and mining rigs. There are concerns, however, that both validators and miners are benefitting from wealth inequality, as the minimum investment to participate in building a blockchain network is often $90,000 and higher. Whether buying native tokens, buying electricity, or installing dozens of ASIC rigs, it is expensive to serve as a miner or a validator of transactions. While the original goals of blockchain technology included democratizing finance, decentralizing transactions, and disintermediating bankers and brokers, the mining and validation rewards are making the rich richer. This concerns some of the teams overseeing blockchain protocols, who are now moving to democratize how blockchains are run. If transactions can be validated using laptops or cell phones without a substantial economic stake, the rewards to validation can be more broadly distributed and the capacity of the blockchain network may substantially increase.

There are a number of metrics to track the growth of a blockchain network. These include transaction activity, total value locked, active addresses, and the number of validators.

Network	Avg Daily Transactions (30 days)	Avg Daily Active Addresses	Avg Daily New Addresses	Avg Tx Fee (USD)	Active Validator Operators
Ethereum	1.09M	328.13K	78.68K	$ 7.28	881.62K
BNB Chain	3.84M	829.12K	204.95K	$ 0.11	57
Solana	21.76M	164.73K	158.67K	$ 0.000015	1.99K
Polygon	5.4M	401.79K	382.95K	$ 0.01	105

Source: CoinMarketCap December 2023 Market Overview.

In December 2023, CoinMarketCap disclosed this information in a table explaining these metrics for Ethereum, BNB Chain, Solana, and Polygon.[2] BNB Chain and Solana are proof-of-stake layer 1 blockchains that will be discussed later in this chapter. Polygon is a layer 2 scaling solution that will be discussed in the next chapter.

Notice that the Ethereum blockchain had the lowest average daily transactions, 1.09 million, as well as the highest fees per transaction, at $7.28. The attractiveness of these other protocols is noted by the larger number of daily transactions, at 3.84 million for BNB Chain, 5.40 million for Polygon, and 21.76 million for Solana. Transaction fees on the BNB chain averaged 11 cents, Polygon fees averaged 1 cent, while more than 600 Solana transactions can be processed for less than 1 cent in combined transaction fees. It is notable that both Polygon and BNB Chain have a greater number of average daily active addresses, where a greater number of blockchain users are interacting with these blockchains than with Ethereum over the time period surveyed.

Notice, however, the degree of centralization. Ethereum has more than 880,000 active validators, Solana has 2,000, while Tron, Cardano, and Avalanche all have more than 1,000 validators, making those blockchains more decentralized. Blockchains with a larger number of validators are more decentralized. As we move from the world of centralized finance into decentralized finance, users would prefer that their transactions would be as secure as possible, with the distributed ledgers being written to as many nodes as possible on the global network. Concerns about concentrated blockchains arise when BNB has 57 validators, Polygon with 105, Cosmos under 500, and Phantom under 100. With a relatively small number of validators running a blockchain, concerns over security issues or computing downtime can arise.

Total value locked (TVL) measures the value of tokens staked or locked into a particular blockchain or DeFi protocol. The greater the TVL, the greater the investment that users have made into a particular protocol. As of January 2024, Ethereum is by far the leader with more than $33 billion staked. Following is Tron at $8 billion, Binance Smart Chain (BSC) at $3.5 billion, Solana at $1.4 billion, Polygon and Avalanche around $900 million, and Cardano at nearly $400 million. The amount of stablecoins, such as Tether (USDT) and USDC, held on each blockchain also denote a level of trust in a protocol. Most stablecoins are held on Ethereum, $70 billion, and Tron, $49 billion, with less than $10 billion held on a variety of other blockchains.

While the previous table tracked daily active addresses, another way to view the number of users of a blockchain is the number of monthly active addresses. Nansen tracks monthly active addresses by chain.[3] As of January 2024, the leaders are Solana, BNB Chain, and Tron with more than 10 million monthly active addresses, Ethereum and Polygon around 5 million, Arbitrum at 2.5 million, and Ronin, Optimism, Linea, Avalanche, Celo, Base, and Phantom between 500,000 and 1.3 million users per month.

Messari tracks the number of validators and their geographic distribution as of May 2023.[4] The economic stakes on POS blockchains are concentrated in the US, Germany, Canada, Korea, and Japan. Between 45% and 65% of all staked tokens on Avalanche, Cardano, Near, Solana, and Aptos are held in those five countries. This study also noted that Avalanche has more than 1,100 validators, with Solana at more than 1,800, Cardano at nearly 2,600, Near at 210, and Aptos at 108. Large validator communities can also be found in the UK, Singapore, Ireland, and Finland depending on the blockchain.

Validators in a proof-of-stake system may source tokens from other investors and share in the staking yield. While validators earn a higher return based on their computing power and technical know-how contributed to the blockchain, the probability that a given validator is chosen for the next block is based on the number of tokens staked. Investors can share in this yield by staking their tokens with a validator, while validators increase their probability of writing blocks by receiving staked tokens from investors. Binance and Coinbase customers are two of the largest sources of tokens staked on proof-of-stake blockchains. Investors are able to stake tokens through these centralized exchanges and earn the staking yields noted in the following table. Notice that staking yields may be higher or lower on one exchange relative to another. Even though each exchange offers trading and custody on dozens of tokens, Coinbase offers staking yields on approximately seven POS tokens, while Binance.US offers staking yields on more than a dozen tokens. There can be risks to staking tokens. Not every centralized exchange offers staking-as-a-service, as the SEC required Kraken to cease offering this service to US investors. Notice that these yields are PIK yields, or paid-in-kind. At the end of one year of staking PolkaDot with Coinbase, users will have 6.92% more DOT tokens, but not necessarily 6.92% more value of DOT tokens in their account.

	Staking Yields	2/19/2024
	Coinbase	Binance.US
PolkaDot	6.92%	12.90%
Cosmos	9.22%	10.90%
Solana	5.01%	6.30%
Tezos	4.62%	3.60%
Ethereum	2.81%	3.40%
Polygon	2.39%	3.10%
Cardano	2.04%	2.30%

Source: Adapted from Coinbase.com, Binance.US.

Each layer 1 blockchain differs in its applications, histories, and staking designs. The later each blockchain was started, the more that could be learned from the experience of the pioneering Bitcoin and Ethereum blockchains.

Cardano started with transfers of value in 2017 and introduced smart contracts in September 2021. Cardano is built by an academic team, with a peer-reviewed process overseeing new developments. While the deliberate academic process at Cardano may lead to slower developments than some would prefer, it shows that Cardano is building for the long run.

A key use case for Cardano is assisting governments worldwide in bringing information storage systems online through NFTs. For example, NFTs built on Cardano are used as a digital identity system to track the school performance of five million students in Ethiopia. NFTs built on a smart contract platform track student grades in a secure, immutable location available across the school system.

Cardano uses a modified proof-of-stake system where validators can run staking pools or token holders can delegate their stake to other validators. The stakes are only monitored at snapshot periods, so validators are not required to continuously hold their stakes.

The Avalanche blockchain was launched in September 2020, six years after the launch of the Ethereum blockchain. Avalanche sold approximately half of its outstanding tokens in private sales raising $42 million. The tokens that were initially sold for less than $0.60 were worth $40 and a total market capitalization of more than $14 billion in February 2024. Of course, not all ICOs were this successful, as the majority of ICOs are worth far less today than when they were sold.

Avalanche is designed so that small stakers and validators can run a node with minimal computing requirements, such as on a laptop, earning an annual staking yield of up to 7.65%. This democratized staking platform is easier to use as staked Avalanche tokens cannot be slashed. Validators with larger stakes may need to contribute a larger computing requirement.

The speed of Avalanche is derived from its ability to process transactions in parallel rather than a strict serial sequence. The Avalanche blockchain can process 4,500 transactions per second with a 2-second block time with smart contract transactions usually costing less than $2. This is much cheaper and faster than the Ethereum blockchain, especially when simply transferring tokens on Avalanche costs less than 10 cents.

DeFi is one of the key use cases for DApps built on the Avalanche blockchain. Trader Joe and Pangolin are key decentralized exchanges running on Avalanche. Aave and Curve are DeFi applications that started on the Ethereum blockchain but are now migrating to other blockchains, including Avalanche.

The success of a layer 1, or a fat protocol, comes with the total value locked – the amount of economic value that's flowing through this ecosystem. The number of decentralized applications and the number of transactions that are going through the system also contribute to its success. If a blockchain like Avalanche can convince Aave and Curve to port their operations over to Avalanche, they have the ability to attract users away from Aave and Curve on Ethereum. This can increase the number of transactions on DeFi platforms such as Aave or Curve, as the lower transaction costs on Avalanche would make smaller transactions more feasible than on the more expensive Ethereum-based DApps.

Ethereum implements all validation, storage, and EVM smart contracts on a single blockchain. The goal of layer 2 blockchains, discussed in the next chapter, is to move the validation and smart contract implementations to a layer 2 or side chain and write the result of the smart contract execution for storage on the Ethereum blockchain.

Somewhat like a layer 2 implementation, Avalanche deploys three separate blockchains to increase the speed and cost-efficiency of its platform. This includes the platform chain (P-Chain), the contract chain (C-Chain), and the exchange chain (X-Chain). Rather than accomplishing all tasks on a single blockchain, such as Ethereum, Avalanche separates these functions. Avalanche runs DApps and EVM-compatible smart contracts on the contract blockchain. The platform blockchain exchanges tokens, while the exchange manages the validation system and staking yields.[5]

Tezos deploys a liquid proof-of-stake protocol that was launched in 2018. Each layer 1 blockchain has different terminology for validators and miners. On the Tezos blockchain, they are called bakers. There are a relatively small number of bakers in the Tezos ecosystem, with 395 active bakers and 86 public bakers as of February 2024.[6] Any Tezos token holders can delegate their tokens to the bakers and share in the block rewards. The bakers run smart contracts and validate transactions. By staking Tezos tokens with a baker, investors are participating in governance and earning a staking yield. Tezos writes information to the blockchain in 1-minute blocks at a rate of 40 transactions per second.

Similar to Avalanche or layer 2 chains, Tezos implements three protocols: the network, the transaction, and the consensus. Tezos offers on-chain governance, where token holders can vote for changes to the Tezos blockchain. New proposals can pass with 80% of the votes cast with the goal of constantly upgrading the blockchain without forking.

The Tezos blockchain mints NFTs through the Teia and Objkt DApps. The Gap uses Tezos-based NFTs to verify the authenticity and rarity of some high-end hoodies.[7] Societe Generale used the Tezos blockchain when participating in the Central Bank Digital Currency (CBDC) trials for the Banque of France.

The Cosmos Hub was launched in 2019 as an Internet of Blockchains. Cosmos' inter-blockchain communication protocol (IBC) exchanges assets and data across 28 blockchains. Similar to ERC-20 compatible tokens being exchanged on the Ethereum blockchain, assets built in the Cosmos ecosystem are compatible across 28 blockchains. Tokens related to the Cosmos ecosystem include Injective, Cronos, THORChain, Akash Network, Kava, Oasis Network, Osmosis, and Fetch.ai.

With only 125 validators, Cosmos is a relatively centralized ecosystem. These validators earn the transaction fees in the proof-of-stake system, but investors can share in the rewards through staking their ATOM tokens. All validators are required to vote using Cosmos' off-chain governance protocol. Cosmos is able to process 4,000 transactions per second with a 7-second block time with fees often less than 1 cent.

Similar to Ethereum, smart contracts on Cosmos can be written in Solidity, a computer language designed specifically for smart contracts. Cosmos also has compatibility with smart contracts written in Rust, a general-purpose programming language that is used outside of the blockchain community. Programmers already familiar with Rust from writing non-blockchain applications may be able to more quickly write smart contract code in Rust rather than taking the time to learn how to program in Solidity.

Binance is one of the world's leading centralized cryptocurrency exchanges. Binance.com is the global website, while Binance.US is the centralized exchange available to US residents, with significant restrictions on what's traded. Binance .com has a significantly greater number of assets available than Binance.US, and non-US users can trade at a much higher degree of leverage than US users. The BNB token can be used to pay discounted trading fees on the Binance platform.

A centralized exchange such as Binance.US chooses which tokens will be available on its platform, with particular consideration paid to avoid listing tokens the US SEC may determine to be securities. Ideally, the due diligence process before listing tokens would determine whether the token has a legitimate business purpose and that it wasn't designed as a scam. While centralized exchanges may offer several dozen tokens to US residents, decentralized exchanges do not typically have the gatekeeper function of deciding which tokens are appropriate for each jurisdiction. Uniswap V2 offers exchanges in more than 1,800 coins, while Uniswap V3 offers access to more than 600 coins.

Binance created the BNB Smart Chain in 2020. The reasoning was that transactions, especially on DeFi DApps and decentralized exchanges, could be accomplished more cheaply than when implemented using Ethereum-based DApps. The Binance Smart Chain (BSC) or BNB chain has the ability to interact with DEXes such as PancakeSwap, 1inch Network, and ApeSwap. Compared to Uniswap V3 on Ethereum, PancakeSwap offers access to 3,600 tokens with cheaper gas fees. With more than 12,700 coins tracked by CoinGecko, even the largest DEXes do not offer access to all cryptocurrencies and digital assets that have been created.

The BNB network is fast and cheap but highly centralized. The 21 validators on the BSC ecosystem earn transaction fees but not block rewards. The BNB protocol is deflationary, as tokens are retired over time, and new tokens are not issued to validators. Smart contracts on BSC are written in Solidity and are compatible with the EVM.

Solana has taken a huge amount of headlines since going live in 2020. The protocol raised $25 million in 2017 and was valued at nearly $50 billion in February 2024. Solana may be the cheapest blockchain, if not the fastest, to transact on. The Solana blockchain can execute as many as 50,000 transactions per second in 2-second blocks. With sub-penny fees and clearing 20 million transactions per month, Solana has been rapidly growing in both market value and popularity

Solana is, perhaps, too fast and too cheap. While processing a multiple of transactions that take place on the Ethereum blockchain, a majority of transactions on Solana may be spam. Because it is so cheap to transact on Solana, bots have created transactions attempting to take advantage of arbitrage opportunities or NFT minting. The volume of messages requesting Solana transactions has been so high that there have been multiple instances in recent years where the network failed to update transactions due to traffic congestion.[8] Solana boasts of its ability to mint 1 million compressed NFTs at a total network cost of $113,[9] perhaps encouraging substantial new network activity. Due to this downtime and trend of network congestion failure, there have been worries about the reliability and security of the Solana blockchain.

Smart contracts are written in the Rust language. After launching in 2020, Solana was accomplishing more than 20 million transactions per month in late 2023. Part of this tremendous growth has been in the NFT market, where the market share of NFTs stored on the Ethereum blockchain has declined from 95% to just 40%; as Magic Eden, Solanart, and Solsea platforms have grown, OpenSea has enabled trading of Solana-based NFTs, and Bitcoin ordinals continue to grow. This trend has been especially prevalent for NFTs priced under $10, where users might pay more in Ethereum gas fees to mint or transfer the NFT than the price of the NFT itself. Reducing gas fees makes it more feasible to perform smaller transaction values in either NFTs or DeFi. Top DeFi apps running on Solana include Raydium, Saber, and Orca.

The Phantom blockchain has been running EVM-compatible smart contracts written in the Solidity language since 2019. Holders of Phantom tokens delegate their tokens to validators to earn a share of the transaction fees and staking rewards. Phantom runs multiple distributed ledgers simultaneously, with sub-penny fees for transactions that are confirmed in seconds. The native DEX of Phantom is SpookySwap, while Curve, Yearn,

Synthetix, and SushiSwap now have DApps that are compatible with the Phantom blockchain.

Tron was launched in 2017 with an investment of $70 million and had grown to a value of $11 billion in early 2024. Smart contracts run on the Tron Virtual Machine are compatible with the EVM. Tron now uses 27 validators who approve transactions using a delegated proof-of-stake protocol.

The stated goal of the Tron DAO is to build a public chain that can support tokens and DApps that will decentralize the internet. The largest DApps built on Tron include the JUST DeFi ecosystem, the APE NFT investment fund that supports galleries and artists, the BitTorrent file-sharing platform, and the WINkLink Oracle.[10]

Proof-of-stake layer-one blockchains continue to grow transaction volumes and corporate partnerships while offering higher speed and lower-cost transactions than Ethereum. While many of these blockchains did not exist in 2017, they are collectively valued at more than $150 billion in early 2024. Many investors believe that these alternative layer 1 blockchains, or altcoins, will continue to take significant transaction activity away from the Ethereum blockchain. Simultaneously, developers of the Ethereum blockchain continue to make improvements to reduce cost and increase capacity. The longer it takes for Ethereum to complete these network upgrades, the longer these alternative layer 1s have to sell their benefits of greater speed and lower cost.

Market statistics show that all of these alternative layer 1 blockchains are growing addresses, total value locked, average daily transactions, as well as the DApp universes they support.

The fat protocol thesis posits that the economics of blockchain networks will accrue more to the layer 1 blockchains, which have been charging users for each transaction. The fat protocol thesis may be somewhat challenged as innovative smart contract layer 1 blockchains continue to scale at low cost. DApps may become more popular and valuable as the layer 1s are more affordable. Cheaper layer 1 transactions may tilt the economics toward the NFTs and DeFi transactions, where platforms may profit due to greater transaction volume and growth in total value locked.

CHAPTER 7

Layer 2 Blockchains and Scaling Solutions

The discussion so far has been focused on the Bitcoin and Ethereum blockchains. These are the base layer blockchains, also known as the settlement layer, layer 1, or even layer 0. The Bitcoin blockchain was originally designed to only store, send, and receive bitcoin. The Ethereum blockchain can store, send, and receive Ether, as well as run smart contracts and save the results of smart contracts to the blockchain. Fungible assets compliant with the ERC-20 standard and non-fungible tokens compliant with the ERC-721 standard can all be stored on the asset layer on top of the Ethereum blockchain. Thousands of validators and miners worldwide work to store information securely and immutably on each blockchain.

Distributed applications are built at the protocol layer, including decentralized exchanges such as Uniswap or DeFi platforms such as Aave and Compound. There is no limit to the types of DApps that can be built at the protocol layer, including exchanges for NFTs, derivatives, and insurance. At higher levels, applications and aggregators can be built on top of the protocols.

The challenge to settlement layer blockchains, such as Bitcoin and Ethereum, is the blockchain trilemma, where it is difficult to be secure, decentralized, and scalable simultaneously. Ethereum and Bitcoin are designed to be highly decentralized and secure but have not yet been able to successfully scale operations.

Bitcoin and Ethereum are relatively slow blockchains, and Ethereum has been expensive to transact on because of the congestion. While Bitcoin's proof-of-work blockchain processes about 7 transactions per second globally, Ethereum's proof-of-stake blockchain currently processes 30 transactions per second globally.

The Mastercard and Visa networks are scalable and secure but not decentralized. Mastercard can process 5,000 transactions per second, while Visa's speed can reach 24,000 transactions per second. If Bitcoin or Ethereum aspires to be used for global consumer transactions, the networks will need to scale to a daily transaction volume like the Mastercard and Visa networks.

Because Ethereum and Bitcoin cannot scale to this level of transactions with the current architecture, the blockchains must be redesigned to meet this level of global demand. Before there is mass adoption of DeFi applications built on the Ethereum network, gas fees will need to decline. Currently, a number of scaling solutions exist that, when used in addition to the Ethereum network, can increase transaction speed and reduce gas fees.

The current design of the Ethereum network tasks validators with running EVM-compatible smart contracts, validating transactions, and securely storing balance information on a single blockchain. Each block of transactions is evaluated and executed by a single validator before another validator evaluates and executes the next block of transactions. The key to scaling the Ethereum blockchain may be to separate the tasks of smart contract execution, transaction validation, and storing balance information. Rather than processing transactions serially or one at a time, transaction volume can increase by moving to parallel processing, where multiple validators simultaneously process different blocks of transactions.

Two of the most significant scaling solutions on the Ethereum network are Arbitrum and Optimism, layer 2 solutions that now process more transactions than the Ethereum network. Transactions that would incur the highest gas fees and create the most congestion on the Ethereum blockchain are outsourced to layer 2 or side chains. Arbitrum and Optimism are not blockchains that securely and immutably store information. They are side chains to which users of the Ethereum network can delegate the costly work of running smart contracts and validating transactions. The results of calculations taking place on the Arbitrum and Optimism networks are recorded on the secure and immutable Ethereum blockchain. Capacity on the Ethereum network is preserved for the secure settlement of transactions. Once the heavy lifting of smart contracts and transaction validation are moved off the Ethereum blockchain, congestion and gas fees are expected to decline. Side chains such as Arbitrum and Optimism are engineered for scalability, while delegating most of the security tasks to the Ethereum settlement layer.

In January 2023, Optimism and Arbitrum combined to process 98% of the month's 28.6 million layer 2 transactions. By August 2023, layer 2 transactions had grown to 116.8 million, with Optimism, Arbitrum, zkSync, and StarkNet combining for a 73% market share, as the Ethereum network was the focus of scaling solutions. In the fourth quarter of 2023, opBNB was introduced to scale transactions on Binance's BNB network. By year end, 65% of more than 400 million layer 2 transactions were executed on the BNB network, showing how quickly protocols evolve in the cryptocurrency market. That is, opBNB processed more than 260 million layer 2 transactions in December 2023, more than nine times the number of layer 2 transactions processed in the first month of the same year.[1]

The scaling dimensions include the choice of fraud proofs vs. validity proofs and on-chain vs. off-chain data. Most of the discussion and transaction volume have used fraud proofs, such as those employed by Arbitrum and Optimism. Validity proofs have mostly occurred through zero-knowledge (ZK) rollups, such as zkSync and StarkNet, using on-chain data.

There are no economies of scale on the Bitcoin and Ethereum blockchains, as each block of transactions is processed serially or one after another. Each transaction is individually validated by verifying the sender's address, balance, and private keys are sufficient to support the proposed transaction.

Rather than evaluating each transaction individually, fraud proofs validate transactions in large batches. In optimistic rollups, fraud proofs assume that every proposed transaction is valid, so every proposed transaction is approved. In order to prevent fraudulent transactions, each transaction is subject to dispute for some period of time. Rather than each transaction being approved and settled during a normal block time on the Ethereum blockchain, each transaction is not finally settled until the dispute period has passed, such as seven days. Transactions not disputed within seven days will be settled as a valid transaction.

Ethereum validators, however, don't want to approve potentially invalid transactions, as that can lead to slashing penalties that reduce the number of Ether they have staked. In an optimistic rollup, transactions are sent to a layer 2 protocol, such as Arbitrum or Optimism. These layer 2 scaling solutions will optimistically assume that all transactions are valid. After the end of the dispute period, those transactions that have not been invalidated will be returned back to the Ethereum mainnet where the results will be securely and immutably recorded.

Validity proofs occur when validators and miners evaluate each transaction but maintain the computational burden of validation off-chain.

Scaling blockchain transactions can be accomplished by either on-chain or off-chain methods. Proposals to increase the block size of the Bitcoin blockchain were rejected and led to the hard fork that created Bitcoin Cash. As a result, Bitcoin has stuck with a block size of 1 MB, which limits the number of transactions that can be processed on the Bitcoin blockchain. After the hard fork, Bitcoin and Bitcoin Cash operated as two separate blockchains, with Bitcoin Cash using 32 MB block sizes. As a hard fork, Bitcoin Cash started with the computer code that manages the Bitcoin blockchain network and modified the code to accept the larger transaction block size.

The higher potential transaction volume of Bitcoin Cash was designed for the token to be used for everyday transactions. After the hard fork, owners of bitcoin tokens were awarded bitcoin cash tokens. While hard forks are relatively rare, soft forks happen frequently, such as all of the planned upgrades to the Ethereum blockchain that Ether token holders have approved. When the Ethereum blockchain upgrades its software, owners of Ether tokens see no change in their holdings as the blockchain continues uninterrupted after the upgrade.

Layer 2 solutions scale blockchain transactions by moving the expensive computing operations away from the crowded layer 1 blockchain. Rather than running the smart contracts on the Ethereum blockchain, smart contracts are executed on another network away from the Ethereum blockchain.

Bitcoin has implemented two software upgrades approved by the community as soft forks. The Taproot and Lightning Network upgrades seek to scale the capacity of the Bitcoin blockchain without increasing the block size or speeding the block time. Both upgrades effectively scale the number of transactions on the Bitcoin network by writing less information to the Bitcoin blockchain.

It is time consuming to verify transactions with multiple sending addresses and multiple private key signatures. The Taproot upgrade allows Bitcoin miners to aggregate private key signatures as a batch, reducing the cost and storage requirements of complex transactions. While increasing the efficiency of the Bitcoin blockchain, Taproot may obscure transaction transparency by publishing aggregate transaction information. Transactions will be posted to the Bitcoin blockchain by noting the aggregate number of bitcoin sent from a basket of addresses rather than from each address individually.

The Lightning Network is another technology used to scale the Bitcoin network. Two trusted parties who frequently exchange bitcoin may agree to open a payment channel. The Lightning Network keeps track of the accumulated exchanges for some period of time until the parties agree to settle the accumulated transactions. Capacity is only used on the Bitcoin blockchain when the accumulated transaction volume is aggregated into a single transaction included in a block and settled to the blockchain. The transactions are only secure and immutable after they have been verified by a miner and written to the blockchain.

Another technology deployed to scale transactions on the Bitcoin blockchain is Segregated Witness or SegWit. A substantial part of the information written on the blockchain is the verification of the digital signature of the owner of each private key. Storage capacity is preserved in each block by removing the witness storage from the block and compressing the data into a new witness structure. The Bitcoin blockchain will record the sending address, the receiving address, the amount of the transaction, and a simple acknowledgment that the private key was present during the transaction.

Again, Bitcoin is relatively straightforward, as the key functionality is to send, receive, and store bitcoin. The network is highly secure and decentralized, but the Bitcoin community has chosen not to pursue significant steps to increase the scalability and transaction volume that can be handled on the blockchain.

The complexity of executing smart contracts, validating transactions, and storing the output of transactions has led to high gas fees and congestion on the Ethereum blockchain. As a result, an entire industry of layer 2 solutions has arisen to reduce the cost and increase the number of transactions that can be settled on the Ethereum blockchain. The key method of reducing cost and scaling transactions has been to execute smart contracts and validate transactions away from the Ethereum blockchain while returning the result of transactions to be securely and immutably stored on the layer 1 blockchain. Users pay gas fees to remove the transaction from the Ethereum blockchain and pay gas fees again to return the transaction to the Ethereum blockchain. However, sending and writing transactions incur much lower gas fees than running smart contracts and validating transactions. Paying lower gas fees for the computing-intense portion of each transaction to the layer 2 protocol results in overall cost savings for the user.

Layer 2 solutions can run Solidity-based smart contracts on their own version of the Ethereum Virtual Machine (EVM). Smart contracts can be executed more quickly and for lower gas fees on a layer 2 scaling solution than on the Ethereum mainnet. Security is assumed to be stronger on the Ethereum blockchain because that is where the ownership data of Ether and ERC-20 tokens is stored. Layer 2 solutions such as Optimism and Arbitrum are non-custodial, so computing resources are directed at executing smart contracts and validating transactions rather than building a robust security system that would be redundant with the strong level of security provided by the Ethereum blockchain.

DApps, such as Uniswap or Aave, are available on layer 2 solutions such as Optimism and Arbitrum. The DApp smart contracts are run on the layer 2 solution at much lower gas fees, with the result of the transaction written back to the Ethereum blockchain. It is cheaper to pay gas fees to move away from the Ethereum blockchain, execute the smart contract on layer 2, and pay gas fees to move back to the Ethereum blockchain, while it is more expensive to simply access the DeFi DApp directly from the Ethereum blockchain.

A variety of layer 2 solutions exist for scaling the Ethereum blockchain. These include Arbitrum, Optimism, zkSync, and StarkNet. While the Ethereum network still processes less than 40 transactions per second, some layer 2 solutions can handle 40,000 or more transactions per second. Layer 2 solutions and alternative layer 1 solutions, such as Solana and Avalanche, will be needed until the Ethereum network has scaled to a speed and a cost that satisfies users' needs.

A key upgrade to the Ethereum blockchain would be sharding, which allows for parallel and distributed processing of transactions by up to 64 validators simultaneously by breaking transaction data into multiple pieces or shards. The current architecture of Ethereum requires a single validator to process all transactions in each 12-second block. Once sharding is implemented, the Ethereum blockchain can scale by the number of shards, as splitting the data into 64 shards can increase the speed of the Ethereum blockchain by 64 times. The speed is accomplished by having each validator working with only a portion of the total transaction data. If each validator works on just a portion of transactions, all combined transactions can be processed more quickly.

Zero-knowledge (zk) rollups use validity proofs in a proof-of-work context. In a zero-knowledge proof, a user can prove a fact is true without revealing that fact. For instance, users can prove they have a password or private key without revealing that information to the verifier of the information.

To speed transactions, succinct non-interactive arguments of knowledge (SNARKs) are used to process multiple transactions as a single transaction. When SNARKs are used to verify transactions, the information regarding the batched transactions is sent back to the layer 1 blockchain. If all transactions in the block are valid, the results will be written to the layer 1 blockchain. If any transactions are invalid, the entire block of transactions will be rejected. Once the layer 1 blockchain accepts the transactions, all transactions in the block are validated.

Loopring uses zk rollups to increase the speed and reduce the costs of managing a DEX and payment protocol built on the Ethereum blockchain.

Polygon is a proof-of-stake internet of side chains to Ethereum with economics driven by the MATIC token. Smart contracts that would have been run on the EVM are delegated to Polygon, which can process 65,000 transactions per second with pennies in fees at 2-second block times. DApps, DEXes, and NFT minting can run cheaply on Polygon, with the transaction results written back to Ethereum for secure storage.

Similar to zk SNARKs, StarkNet deploys zk STARKs, zero-knowledge scalable transparent arguments of knowledge.[2] By deploying zero-knowledge proofs, StarkNet combines thousands of transactions into a single Ethereum transaction, thereby increasing speed and reducing costs.

While Ethereum started the smart contract revolution, the majority of smart contract transactions are now calculated away from the Ethereum blockchain, either on layer 2 solutions built on top of Ethereum or on layer 1 alternatives such as Solana or Avalanche. An increasing number of EVM-compatible DApps and DEXes are now available across blockchains, allowing users to participate in these innovative platforms at a fraction of the cost of applications built directly on the Ethereum blockchain. Lower transaction fees allow for $100 token swaps or the purchase of $10 NFTs and other small value transactions that would be cost prohibitive if executed on DApps built directly on Ethereum. Scaling solutions and low-cost networks are required to build an alternative financial system that brings everyday transactions into the decentralized world of blockchains and fulfills the promise of global peer-to-peer transactions.

While layer 2 scaling solutions can become computationally complex, this book is about investments and not engineering. The goal of this brief chapter is to explain that the Ethereum blockchain has become extraordinarily expensive and congested by combining smart contract execution, transaction validation, and immutable security of ownership data of ERC-20 and ERC-721 assets. Sending the burden of smart contract execution and transaction validation to layer 2 side chains relieves the Ethereum blockchain of these burdensome tasks and allows users to participate in the decentralized economy at a much lower cost than when the Ethereum blockchain is responsible for all required computations. Ethereum is highly secure and decentralized, but it is currently better to leave the scaling tasks to alternative solutions.

CHAPTER **8**

Stablecoins, Crypto Yields, and Central Bank Digital Currencies

Many investors are concerned about the volatility in cryptocurrency and digital asset prices. At times, the prices of bitcoin, Ether, and other cryptocurrencies have exceeded more than 100% annualized volatility or standard deviation of returns. With stock market indices averaging annual volatility of around 20%, many cryptocurrencies and digital assets have price volatility more than five times that of the stock market. Of course, investors like volatility when prices are rising, but volatility is often symmetric. Since September 2014, bitcoin prices have experienced weekly volatility of 9.9%, which annualizes to 71.6% by multiplying by the square root of 52, the number of weeks in a year.

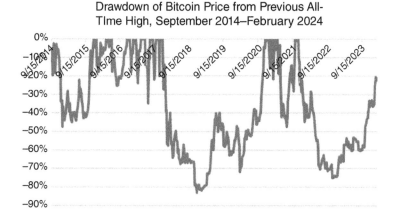

Drawdown of Bitcoin Price from Previous All-TIme High, September 2014–February 2024

493 Weeks	September 2014–February 2024	
Drawdown	Frequency	% Of Weeks
0%	78	100%
–5%	30	84%
–10%	20	78%
–15%	24	74%
–20%	23	69%
–25%	16	65%
–30%	18	61%
–35%	32	58%
–40%	47	51%
–45%	23	42%
–50%	32	37%
–55%	43	30%
–60%	32	22%
–65%	33	15%
–70%	21	9%
–75%	12	4%
–80%	9	2%

Source: Adapted from Yahoo Finance, author calculations.

In fact, from September 2014 to February 2024, bitcoin spent the majority of weeks at prices at least 40% below all-time highs. Bitcoin prices traded below $3,600 in January 2019, 83% below the previous all-time weekly high of $16,400 reached just a year earlier in January 2018. Bitcoin prices hit an all-time high of more than $65,000 in November 2021, only to fall back to under $20,000 by June 2022, another 70% drawdown. The bitcoin price fell by more than 10% in 10% of all weeks since 2014 and rose by more than 10% in almost 30% of all weeks.

While this volatility is exciting for speculators and short-term investors, many investors are not interested in digital assets to make money. Those who live in countries with hyperinflation or weak banking systems are looking for an escape from volatility and a way to invest in a more stable store of value.

Stablecoins are digital assets designed to have nearly zero volatility relative to a specific asset. Stablecoins may be pegged to the value of one US dollar, euro, or ounce of gold. Rather than experiencing the cryptocurrency market's volatility, stablecoins function as a fiat currency asset in a digital asset environment. While many bitcoin evangelists are very negative on fiat currencies and the inflation caused by excessive money supply growth, many consumers in emerging markets see the US dollar and euro as extraordinarily strong currencies when compared to their home market currency, which is being devastated by inflation that can average more than 50% to 100% annually.

One key use case of stablecoins is for consumers in financially distressed countries to be able to hold a store of value. For investors in developed markets with more stable currencies and lower inflation rates, stablecoins may function as a place to park assets in digital asset wallets at times when they are not invested in more volatile cryptocurrencies. This may be familiar to equity investors who sell a stock and hold the proceeds in a money market fund until they are ready to repurchase the stock, ideally at a lower price. Similarly, investors may wish to sell their bitcoin, Ether, or other digital assets during times of high prices and hold the proceeds in stablecoins until the price drops back to a level where they are comfortable reestablishing the position.

With $2 trillion invested in the cryptocurrency universe in February 2024, approximately $1.35 trillion was held in bitcoin and Ether with a combined dominance of more than 67%. The three dominant US dollar stablecoins, Tether ($98 billion), USDC ($28 billion), and DAI ($5 billion), hold a total of $131 billion, or 6.5% of all crypto assets. Bitcoin, Ether, and the three US dollar stablecoins hold 74% of the total market cap of all cryptocurrency assets.

Similar to money market yields, investors can deposit stablecoins to earn a yield, perhaps 4% to 5%. Investors should carefully investigate the source of this yield, including the credit and counterparty risks, as crypto lending was a source of substantial losses in 2022, as will be discussed in Chapter 25 on frauds, thefts, and crypto risks. Both stablecoins and money market funds are designed to trade at a stable value of $1. While few money market funds "break the buck," stablecoins often trade at $0.99 or $1.01. USDC briefly traded at $0.87 in March 2023, as the stablecoin held more than $3 billion in deposits at SVB at the time of the bank's failure.

Investors need to understand the difference between staking yields and lending yields. As previously discussed, staking yields are earned as compensation for providing financial support to validators verifying transactions on proof-of-stake blockchains. The staking yield is a share of the fees paid by the users of a proof-of-stake blockchain or paid by the blockchain operator by issuing new tokens. There is a concern about the value of the tokens earned as staking yields if the yield comes from the issuance of new tokens, as a substantial increase in the token supply can reduce the value of a token. When a staking yield is stated as a 5% annual percentage yield, the investor will have 5% more tokens at the end of the year, but the value of those tokens may be greater or less than the value held by the investor before the staking process.

Lending crypto or depositing stablecoins to earn yield is analogous to bank deposits. The crypto is deposited into a DeFi protocol offering a yield. The DeFi protocol lends those assets at a higher yield, hoping to earn a positive net interest margin. However, a key difference between a bank and a DeFi protocol is that the FDIC insures deposits in US banks. If an insured US bank fails, the insurance fund will compensate depositors up to $250,000 per person per bank. Deposit insurance does not broadly exist in DeFi, and substantial credit losses were experienced in 2022 when some crypto borrowing and lending platforms lost depositor assets in bad loans. Chapter 25 will discuss the losses at Celsius, 3 Arrows Capital, BlockFi, FTX, and Voyager.

DeFi participants can earn yields for participating as a liquidity provider at a decentralized exchange. Similar to a staking yield, earnings for providing liquidity are payments for supporting the operations of a crypto protocol with both capital and technical know-how.

Staking yields earned through a centralized exchange, such as Binance or Coinbase, may be subject to a minimum holding period or an unbonding period. The period may be stated as a 30-day minimum time to be held on the staking platform, or an unbonding period of 7 to 14 days may take place before staked tokens are released back into an investor's trading balances.

Rather than locking up tokens and staking directly with a validator, some investors will participate in liquid staking. In liquid staking, an investor wraps their Ether tokens into RocketPool (RETH), Lido (stETH), or Coinbase-wrapped staked Ether (cbETH). RocketPool, Lido, and Coinbase run Ethereum validation nodes and use the wrapped or liquid staked Ether tokens to increase the stake size used to select Ethereum transactions' validator. The liquid staking group earns the rewards of validating transactions and running smart contracts on the Ethereum blockchain and shares the rewards with the stakers. In early 2024, investors could earn between 2.8% and 4.8% annual yield paid in Ether for participating in these liquid staking programs, with the validators also earning a portion of the total rewards and fees from running the validator nodes.

Information services, such as Coingecko.com, Coinmarketcap.com, Coindesk.com, DefiLlama.com, and Tokenterminal.com, show the number of tokens staked in each POS protocol, the amount held in liquid staking pools, and the current yield on each staking program.

Centralized exchanges and staking platform operators must be cognizant of the regulatory environment, as the SEC has not written custom guidance for the digital assets industry. Instead, the Securities and Exchange Commission continues to use the Howey Test, a precedent set in a 1946 case at the US Supreme Court. Mr. Howey sold his Florida orchards to investors, leased the orchards from the investors, and shared the profits of the citrus crop.

The Supreme Court ruled that Howey had created an investment contract subject to security registration with the SEC, which required disclosures and investor protections according to the Securities Act of 1933. According to the Howey Test, an investment is a security if it meets four criteria: 1) an investment of money, 2) in a common enterprise, 3) with a reasonable expectation of profits, and 4) derived from the efforts of others.

The SEC requires registration of all investments it deems to be securities before they are sold broadly to retail investors. Before the securities can be sold, all material facts and risks must be disclosed. Investments may be subject to less regulation if they are sold exclusively to accredited investors and qualified purchasers. Many hedge fund and private equity investments are sold to these high-net-worth investors using the private placement exemption. An accredited investor is qualified to invest in private placements with 1) $200,000 in personal annual income, or 2) $300,000 in annual income as a married couple, or 3) $1 million in net worth excluding the value of their primary residence, or 4) qualification as a knowledgeable employee of a private fund or as a registered representative who has passed a FINRA regulatory exam. A qualified purchaser simply has a net worth of $5 million or more. Investments sold exclusively to accredited investors and qualified purchasers do not have the limits on leverage, concentration, and derivatives risk that are required for investments sold to the general public.

In 2018, the SEC stated that bitcoin and Ether were not securities due to their degree of decentralization.[1] However, today's Ethereum blockchain has increasingly concentrated validator networks, especially through liquid staking, that may threaten the degree of centralization required to retain its classification as not being a security. Unfortunately, the SEC hasn't published clear guidelines for classifying digital assets as securities beyond the Howey Test. Most other digital assets, especially the initial coin offerings (ICOs) offered in 2017 and 2018, may qualify as securities under the Howey Test, meaning that the SEC may require registration and disclosure. Regulations are less onerous if tokens are only sold to accredited investors or qualified purchasers. However, most tokens are publicly traded with easy access to retail investors who don't possess the net worth or sophistication of accredited investors. A key part of the SEC's regulatory agenda is ensuring unregistered securities are not sold to retail investors.

Similar to initial public offerings (IPOs) in the stock market, ICOs are tokens sold to investors for the first time. In 2017 and 2018, hundreds of ICOs were sold to investors without regard for whether they had the status of accredited investors or qualified purchasers. Because many of the buyers of ICOs were US investors who did not meet these standards of net worth and sophistication, the SEC determined that most ICOs were sold as unregistered securities.

Some ICOs were sold by projects that distributed a detailed business plan or a white paper detailing the future functionality that would be built for the token or blockchain with the funds raised in the ICO. Some of the most successful ICOs were Ethereum and Polygon, projects today worth billions of dollars. Ethereum raised $18.3 million in a 2014 ICO, where investors exchanged bitcoin for newly issued Ether tokens. Polygon raised $5 million in a 2019 ICO. Some ICOs were highly successful, some used the proceeds of the ICO in a genuine effort to build new crypto businesses and failed, while some ICOs were outright scams without a business plan or any attempt to provide investors value for the contributed capital. Obviously, the SEC was highly concerned with those projects that kept investors' money without even pretending to use it to build a business. If tokens in protocols with a strong business plan were sold exclusively to accredited investors and qualified purchasers, an ICO might have many similarities to venture capital investments but with greater liquidity.

While the Howey Test is often applied to equity-like instruments, the Reves Test is considered to determine whether a fixed-income product is a security. The test has four parts to determine whether a note is a security. First, what are the motivations of the buyer and the seller, such as a profit motive? Second, what is the plan of distribution? Is it broadly sold to all types of investors, or is it a limited issue to accredited investors and qualified purchasers? Third, what are the reasonable expectations of the investing public? Fourth, are there risk-reducing considerations, such as insurance? The SEC does not consider bank products as securities due to the presence of FDIC insurance. A note may be a security if it is an uninsured product broadly sold to public investors anticipating profiting from the investment.

The US Congress and/or the SEC may create or revise regulations when new financial products arise. As the equity crowdfunding market grew, Congress passed the Jumpstart Our Business Startups (JOBS) Act in 2012, with the SEC later enacting Regulation Crowdfunding. This regulation allowed small businesses to raise up to $5 million annually without registering the sales as a securities offering.[2] By 2023, US companies had raised more than $2 billion in equity crowdfunding.

The SEC has not yet formed any crypto-specific regulations and continues to rely on crypto firms to interpret their offerings in the context of the Howey Test and/or the Reves Test. Many firms engaged in creating and distributing digital asset products have been meeting with the SEC and Congress in an attempt to define crypto-specific regulations governing this nascent industry. If clear and modernized regulations were enacted, crypto firms would readily comply. Many investors may hesitate to allocate investment capital to digital assets when regulatory clarity is lacking. With so many regulators in the US, it is unclear to some whether crypto is the jurisdiction of the SEC, the Commodity Futures Trading Commission (CFTC), the Office of the Comptroller of the Currency (OCC), the Federal Reserve Bank, the New York State Department of Financial Services (NYDFS), etc.

In contrast, the SEC has been accused of regulation by enforcement, fining companies for selling unregistered securities in primary or secondary markets. The primary market raises funds for new crypto investments, while secondary markets include centralized exchanges facilitating the trading of existing tokens. The SEC requires that any investment deemed to be a security be registered as such with complete risk disclosures made to investors.

One example of regulation by enforcement includes the SEC's mandate that Paxos Trust stop issuing the Binance Stablecoin (BUSD) as an unregistered security. In 2023, the SEC fined Kraken $30 million and suspended staking as a service for US investors, where investors could stake their POS tokens with validators through the Kraken centralized exchange. As a result, the services offered to US investors by centralized exchanges such as Kraken and Binance are significantly limited relative to what investors can access in other countries. One reason why US centralized exchanges list so few tokens is that they want to avoid facilitating trading in securities. When Ripple was accused of selling unregistered securities, XRP was quickly delisted from the Coinbase exchange.[3]

The US has long been a global leader in finance and technology, with the world's largest stock markets and venture capital investment community. Part of the attraction of raising capital and growing companies in the US is the deep investor pool and the generally pro-business stance of the US regulators. The longer it takes for the US to enact clear rules around digital assets, the longer crypto companies may consider forming and growing in foreign markets. If the US eventually puts substantial restrictions on the development or sale of digital assets, the crypto industry will move to Singapore, Hong Kong, London, Dubai, and/or Switzerland, each of which already boasts significant digital assets activity. If blockchain technology eventually becomes Web 3.0 and the backbone of the global financial system, the US risks losing its dominant market share in banking, technology, and payments companies.

The question becomes whether stablecoins will be regulated as securities, especially if they are not paying any yield and are frequently used for making payments. Remember that stablecoins are widely valued as a store of value and payment method, especially in countries with weak banking and currency systems, such as Venezuela, Zimbabwe, and Ukraine.

If there is no profit expectation and the stablecoin continually retains its value of one dollar, it might appear that stablecoins are not securities according to the Howey Test. Because the CFTC and the NYDFS previously stated that Tether and BUSD were virtual currencies,[4] the market was confused when the SEC required Paxos Trust to cease the issuance of BUSD as unregistered securities.

While the US Congress has been discussing stablecoin regulation since at least 2021, no Act has become law as of June 2024. Topics of discussion include requiring stablecoin issuers to obtain banking charters, requirements to hold and report reserve assets, and to work with banking regulators such as the Federal Reserve.

Let's discuss the three largest stablecoins, Tether, USDC, and DAI. These three stablecoins held a total of $131 billion, or 94% of the value of US dollar stablecoins, in February 2024.

As of February 2024, Tether is the world's largest stablecoin, with a market capitalization of $98 billion. Each Tether token is designed to trade at a fixed value of one dollar. When an investor buys Tether, assets are contributed to the protocol, and new tokens are issued. When an investor sells Tether, stablecoin tokens are burned, and the assets are returned to the investor. Questions have arisen as to where Tether invests the assets under its control. The global accounting firm BDO publishes a quarterly attestation of Tether's reserves and asset base. At year-end 2023, nearly 85% of Tether's assets were held in cash or cash equivalents, including more than $70 billion in US Treasury securities.[5] Now that US Treasury interest rates have risen from near zero to more than 5%, Tether's assets exceed the liabilities in token sales by more than $3 billion, as Tether does not distribute interest income to token holders. Tether has the potential to earn more than $4 billion per year in interest income.

Investors are concerned, however, about the 15% of Tether's balance sheet that is not invested in US dollar–denominated cash reserves. This includes 2.91% in bitcoin, 3.62% in precious metals, 4.95% secured loans (none to affiliated entities), and 3.89% in "other investments." With 3% over-collateralization, a 20% loss of value of these non-dollar assets would leave Tether without sufficient liquidity to repay all token holders.

Tether did not voluntarily post these accounting results. Tether was fined by the New York State Department of Financial Services, and required to provide quarterly transparency for two years, starting in 2021.[6] The Attorney General of New York stated:

> Bitfinex and Tether recklessly and unlawfully covered-up massive financial losses to keep their scheme going and protect their bottom lines. Tether's claims that its virtual currency was fully backed by U.S. dollars at all times was a lie. These companies obscured the true risk investors faced and were operated by unlicensed and unregulated individuals and entities dealing in the darkest corners of the financial system.[7]

Tether had previously loaned $550 million of client assets to a related party, Bitfinex, and $1.8 billion to Celsius collateralized by $2.6 billion in crypto, who declared bankruptcy in 2022. During near-zero interest rates, Tether's balance sheet included investments in loans and commercial paper that incurred substantial credit risk. While Tether invested $20 billion in commercial paper in 2022, the year-end 2023 attestation shows about 8% of investments in money market funds without listing commercial paper investments.

The second largest stablecoin is USDC issued by Circle. At the end of December 2023, a monthly attestation by Deloitte shows that USDC had issued 24.64 billion USDC tokens with backing of $24.69 billion in total assets invested in US Treasury securities, US Treasury repurchase agreements, and cash held at regulated financial institutions.[8] This would appear to be a less risky balance sheet than Tether, as USDC is entirely invested in US dollar–denominated assets. However, Tether has an over-collateralization of $3 billion, while USDC has an over-collateralization level of $52 million. Circle also manages the euro-based stablecoin EURC, valued at 48.7 million euros.

The ownership of stablecoins, such as USDC, is tracked on a blockchain using smart contracts. USDC is available on 15 different blockchains, with more than $24 billion outstanding on Ethereum, nearly $1 billion on Arbitrum, $1.4 billion on Solana, and over $200 million each on Base, Polygon, and Avalanche.[9] Buying and selling stablecoins held on the Ethereum blockchain will cost users much higher gas fees than when the stablecoins are held on other layer 1s, such as Solana or Avalanche, or layer 2s, such as Arbitrum or Polygon.

Tether (USDT) and USDC are fiat-backed stablecoins. They seek to maintain a pegged value of one dollar while investing the contributed assets largely in fiat-based government bonds and money market assets. The protocols seek to earn more interest income than the cost of supporting the stablecoin operations.

Not all stablecoins are backed by fiat. Chapter 25 will discuss the substantial losses incurred by the collapse of the algorithmic stablecoin Terra USD.

DAI is a stablecoin backed by crypto assets. Minted by Maker DAO, DAI had $5.3 billion outstanding in February 2024. The value of DAI is fixed at $1. DAI can be borrowed by depositing an over-collateralized amount of crypto into the project. Twenty different currencies can be used as collateral for DAI-denominated loans. For example, the over-collateralization factor for Ether tokens is 170%, with a $17,000 deposit of ETH tokens qualifying an investor to borrow $10,000 in DAI. The investor's DAI can be sold for cash or used in DeFi applications while the investor continues to own the Ether tokens. The Ether tokens are locked up in the DAI protocol until the loan is repaid. Other tokens can also be posted as collateral, such as bitcoin with an over-collateralization factor of 175%, Curve (CRV, 155%), Chainlink (LINK, 165%), and Yearn Finance (YFI, 165%).

Continuing with the example of a $10,000 DAI-denominated loan using Ether as collateral, the collateral backing the loan declines as the price of Ether tokens falls. Once the value of Ether falls below a stated level, the borrower must repay a portion of the loan or deposit more collateral backing the loan. The trade can be liquidated if neither action is taken within the required time period. Liquidation can be a very expensive process, as the lender may charge a substantial fee or send the loan or collateral to auction. Investors may want to deposit more than the minimum crypto required to maintain the loan to ensure that a decline in the value of the crypto collateral will be sufficient to continue with the loan. Investors may choose to add value to their account to maintain the loan's safety, but failing to do so in the right timing and size can risk a liquidation.

The role of central banks in determining interest rates and the money supply was previously discussed. The Federal Reserve Bank determines monetary policy in the US, while the European Central Bank determines monetary policy in the Eurozone. Outside of the Eurozone, most countries have independent currencies that float freely relative to other global currencies. However, some countries have chosen not to manage their own monetary policy. Ecuador and El Salvador are dollarized countries where the US dollar has been officially adopted as legal tender, and the country's local currency has been retired. The US dollar is widely used in countries with substantial inflation, such as Zimbabwe. Other countries may choose to peg their currency relative to the value of the US dollar. While maintaining an independent currency, the currency's value moves with the dollar rather than independently. For example, the Hong Kong dollar has been pegged at a value close to 7.8 HKD per USD since 1983. Other countries with currencies pegged to the value of the US dollar include Panama and the countries of the Gulf Cooperation Council (GCC: Bahrain, Kuwait, Saudi Arabia, Oman, Qatar, and the United Arab Emirates).

In addition to using the US dollar as legal tender, El Salvador adopted bitcoin as an official currency in 2021. In the US, each purchase using bitcoin is a sale of bitcoin that must be tracked for the purposes of capital gains and capital loss taxes. This makes it infeasible to use bitcoin for everyday transactions in the US. In El Salvador, bitcoin is used as a currency where no tax liability is created when buying or selling bitcoin.

Dollarized countries such as El Salvador and Ecuador have delegated their monetary policy to the US Federal Reserve Bank. The Fed sets monetary policy to influence interest rates, inflation, and employment in the US without generally considering the impact on economic conditions in other countries.

The Fed tightens monetary policy to slow the US economy during times of inflation and above-average growth. If the Fed tightens monetary policy during a recession in El Salvador, Hong Kong, or the GCC countries, those economies experiencing slow growth may be pushed deeper into a recession.

To encourage the use of bitcoin in El Salvador, the country gave all citizens who activated a Chivo wallet $30 in bitcoin. Citizens download the Chivo app to their cell phone, enter their national ID, and $30 in bitcoin is deposited into their wallet. While adoption of bitcoin commerce in El Salvador started slowly, Distribuidora Morazán started to accept bitcoin from its network of 40,000 merchants in November 2023.[10]

One goal of adopting bitcoin as legal tender is to reduce the cost of remittances, which make up 25% of El Salvador's GDP. Many Salvadorans live and work in the US and send a portion of their earnings to support family in El Salvador. Bitcoin ATMs in the US can facilitate the transfer of US dollars directly into Chivo wallets reducing the time to process remittances.

El Salvador is considering borrowing money through Volcano Bonds[11] that would be backed by the country's bitcoin holdings. The proceeds of the bonds would be used to build Bitcoin-related infrastructure, including wallets, ATMs, and Bitcoin mining rigs consuming electricity generated by the steam emitted from volcanoes. Remember that Bitcoin miners use a substantial amount of electricity and seek to locate in areas with low electricity costs. While solar, nuclear, wind, and hydro-generated electricity get most of the headlines, low-cost electricity is available near volcanoes in Iceland and El Salvador. El Salvador seeks to attract capital and bitcoin enthusiasts from around the world by building infrastructure for Bitcoin mining and offering a jurisdiction where bitcoin holdings can be liquidated tax-free.

What is the difference between stablecoins and Central Bank Digital Currencies (CBDCs)? Tether, USDC, and DAI are run by private companies offering digital asset services. Some investors own US dollar–denominated stablecoins because they seek a store of value in a fiat currency stronger than their home country. Other investors own digital assets, including bitcoin and stablecoins, as they seek to be global citizens less controlled by banks and the government. Digital assets, especially when held in personal wallets, are attractive to those with libertarian views, who seek to maximize individual freedoms and minimize interactions with any type of governmental entity.

A central bank digital currency is issued by a country's central bank and is an electronic version of the country's fiat currency. Introducing a CBDC seems to go against the decentralized ethos that drives the crypto economy.

Wholesale CBDCs are available only for interbank transactions. Rather than sending funds via Fedwire, which transfers value between banks in US dollars, a wholesale dollar-based CBDC would transfer digital currency between banks using blockchain technology.

Retail CBDCs are broadly distributed and available for consumer transactions. Countries including the Bahamas, India, Nigeria, and China have issued CBDCs, but the technology is not yet implemented in the US.

The Bahamas Sand Dollar was introduced in December 2019, when the country primarily transacted in cash, with 20% of the population unbanked. Sand Dollars are pegged to the Bahamas dollar, which is pegged to the US dollar. The Bahamas has a relatively rural population on thousands of islands that are prone to the significant damage, isolation, and power failures that can result from hurricanes. Sand Dollars are available through a cell phone app with payment functionality even at times when the internet is not accessible. As such, the Sand Dollar can be a readily accessible alternative to cash payments.

While cash can be used anonymously worldwide, there are concerns that the use of CBDCs might not be anonymous. In the Bahamas, users of Sand Dollars can be anonymous when wallet balances are under $500 or when spending less than $1,500 monthly.[12] Above those levels, users will have to complete a Know Your Customer (KYC) process by providing information such as name, address, and national identification number.

India has historically been a country with a large unbanked population where up to 90% of transactions were conducted in cash. More than 90% of workers paid no income tax, as they were paid in cash and spent cash for their everyday needs. In 2016, the Indian economy went through a demonetization process to reduce tax evasion,[13] where the largest denominations of fiat currency were required to be exchanged for newly printed bank notes. When the new notes were acquired, banks were required to track the size of the transactions, with the largest cash holdings being investigated or fined for tax evasion. The result of the demonetization is to move consumers into the formal economy where banks and taxes are a way of everyday life. Transactions taking place through CBDCs and the banking system can be tracked and taxed.

In 2016, India implemented the Unified Payments Interface (UPI) to facilitate electronic payments from consumer's bank accounts to merchants. After completing a KYC process, consumers used cell phones to access payment apps compatible with the UPI system. UPI apps draw funds from consumers' bank accounts, which can be interest-bearing. This is yet another step in reducing India's cash economy and increasing the portion of electronically cleared transactions.

To the extent that electronic money is easy to send worldwide, CBDCs could potentially challenge the global dominance of the US dollar. CBDCs launched by India and China may increase cross-border payments made in those currencies. The Reserve Bank of India launched the Digital Rupee in November 2022.[14] An Indian bank account is required to transact using the Digital Rupee CBDC.

China is already largely cashless, with many merchants no longer accepting fiat currency. As much as 80% of daily consumer transactions in China are processed using electronic payment methods.[15] Small transactions are almost exclusively completed using fintech mobile applications such as Alipay, WeChat Pay, and Union Pay.

The Chinese government has introduced the electronic Chinese Yuan (eCNY) or digital renminbi, a Central Bank Digital Currency (CBDC), encouraging its use for transactions. Merchants are already set up to receive payments via Alipay and WeChat Pay, which could facilitate the adoption of the eCNY. The account will have limited oversight for wallets with balance limits of 10,000 eCNY and daily transaction limits of 5,000 eCNY.[16]

Nigeria, a very large country with a population approximately the size of the US, has an economy with a large informal sector. This cash-based economy reduces the amount of taxes people pay and can also increase crime when it is known that consumers keep their paychecks or life savings in cash. Nigeria's tax-to-GDP ratio was under 11% in 2021, but would be up to 18% if all income was reported and taxes were collected.[17]

The electronic Naira (eNaira) was launched in October of 2021, with the goals of increasing financial inclusion, reducing the size of the informal economy, and facilitating remittances.[18] Similar to other countries, smaller wallets simply require a phone number to activate. Nigeria's bronze wallet is limited to balances of 120,000 eNaira and a daily withdrawal limit of 500 eNaira.[19]

US President Biden published an executive order in March 2022 titled "Ensuring Responsible Development of Digital Assets."[20] The seven key points include:

- Protect U.S. Consumers, Investors, and Businesses
- Protect U.S. and Global Financial Stability and Mitigate Systemic Risk
- Mitigate the Illicit Finance and National Security Risks Posed by the Illicit Use of Digital Assets
- Promote U.S. Leadership in Technology and Economic Competitiveness to Reinforce U.S. Leadership in the Global Financial System
- Promote Equitable Access to Safe and Affordable Financial Services
- Support Technological Advances and Ensure Responsible Development and Use of Digital Assets
- Explore a U.S. Central Bank Digital Currency (CBDC)

The executive order delegates explicit tasks to the Department of the Treasury, the Financial Stability Oversight Council, the Department of Commerce, and the Federal Reserve Bank. Notable exceptions from the order were the regulatory role of the SEC and/or the CFTC and encouraging specific considerations by Congress. While the order understands the key role of the US in global finance and technology, there were concerns regarding climate change, systemic financial risks, financial inclusion, and the illicit use of digital assets.

The US Federal Reserve is studying CBDCs, as are 85% of large countries. The Fed published a neutral discussion paper on CBDCs in January 2022.[21] The paper was designed to solicit comments by asking 22 explicit questions. Biden's executive order encouraged the Fed to continue researching the potential of a US CBDC.

A US CBDC may be required to maintain the dollar's role as the global reserve currency that can enforce US leadership in global technology and financial markets. If the US is too restrictive on digital assets, the global leadership in both technology and finance can be ceded to other jurisdictions with more accommodative policies.

The Fed will only launch a CBDC if instructed to do so by Congress. The Fed will not develop its own phone app or wallet to hold and trade the digital dollar, but will encourage fintech companies to do so. The CBDC may simply be an additional asset in a consumer's account at PayPal, Venmo, JP Morgan, and Citibank. While the Fed will issue and regulate the CBDC, custody will be held within the existing financial markets infrastructure.

The Fed will require holders of the CBDC to undergo a KYC process with wallet providers building sufficient transparency to deter criminal activity. Similar to the current banking and brokerage system, CBDC custody firms may be charged with tracking transactions and submitting transaction information to the taxing authority, the Internal Revenue Service. The CBDC will likely be available to pay taxes, remittances, and global remittances. Another goal of the CBDC will be to foster financial inclusion, where the unbanked may be required to receive government benefits payments through the CBDC or the banking system rather than by paper checks. Paper checks impose substantial costs and risks on the unbanked, including fees for cashing checks and the risk of holding significant amounts of cash. Cash holdings and transactions do not earn interest or even the cash or point rebates available to bank customers using credit and debit cards. The financial life of the unbanked could be significantly improved by bringing them into the formal economy.

The Fed's discussion paper discusses a number of potential risks that CBDCs may pose to consumers and to the banking system. When the paper was published in March 2022, bank interest rates were near zero, and some stablecoins were offering yields of 8% and more. If that interest rate regime continued, the Fed could anticipate substantial assets leaving the banking system to invest in stablecoins. If the CBDC were to offer a higher yield than bank deposits, capital flight from the banking system could take place. By February 2024, those concerns are much less urgent, as FDIC-insured yields of 4% to 5% are widely available, while it has become more difficult to earn yield in digital assets.

As will be discussed in Chapter 25, the high yields paid on crypto assets in 2021 came crashing down in a series of credit events in 2022. While yields on bank deposits are FDIC-insured and free of credit risks, the yields earned on digital assets in 2021 were paid by borrowers who eventually lost the money (BlockFi, Voyager, Celsius, and Terra) or stole the money (FTX). Not only did digital asset investors not earn the high levels of stated annual yields, but the principal value of many of those loans have been impaired or delayed from withdrawals due to a number of high-profile bankruptcies among crypto borrowers and lenders.

Another key concern of the Fed is the potential effectiveness of monetary policy. The Fed's open market operations designed to grow or shrink the money supply are implemented through the banking system. The Federal Reserve's ability to control interest rates and inflation is based on its relationship with commercial banks and the assumption that most economic activity occurs through the commercial banking system. However, introducing a Central Bank Digital Currency (CBDC) deposited at the Fed and not at these commercial banks could change this dynamic. If a smaller portion of consumer assets and economic activity pass through the banking system, monetary policy may be substantially less effective at reducing the volatility of GDP and inflation over the course of the business cycle.

If people take money out of their bank accounts and invest in stablecoins to earn a higher yield, there could be a problem. If the bank is paying 0.8% on deposits and offering a 5% car loan, but everyone is investing in stablecoins with an 8% yield, it could become difficult to maintain that 5% car loan. The concern of the Fed is that if money moves out of the banking system and into stablecoins, the banks might not have enough money to lend, which could slow economic activity. The availability of low-cost credit may also decline, especially if the base interest rate on digital asset–based loans is substantially higher than the base rate on loans from commercial banks.

There's also a concern that if people perceive a CBDC as safer than bank deposits, it could make bank runs move more quickly as investors move to avoid potential bank failures. The key risk to a bank failing is everyone taking out all their money simultaneously. This was the case with the March 2023 failure of SVB, as depositors withdrew $42 billion in 48 hours, with the withdrawal rate sped up through social media communications and electronic bank transfer capabilities.[22] Because the US system is based on fractional reserve banking, there's not enough money in the banking system for everyone to withdraw all their money at once. Pulling their money out of the commercial banks and moving it quickly into the CBDC could exacerbate this risk.

Digital dollars have pros and cons. Electronic payments are convenient for consumers, both for everyday purchasers as well as for monthly bill payments. CBDCs could potentially streamline payments even further. Government benefits and tax refunds could be paid through the CBDC system, increasing efficiency and reducing the number of unbanked in the US. If the US dollar "Fed Coin" is seen as a global asset, the US dollar could maintain its dominant role with investors worldwide.

The downside of the CBDC is that it could reduce assets in the traditional banking system as well as the ability of the Fed to implement monetary policy effectively.

A key worry about CBDCs is centralization and the potential for government surveillance. Many investors are drawn to digital assets with the promise of individual freedom and less control by banks and governments. While spending fiat cash is anonymous, transactions in the banking system and CBDCs are not. Transactions on money transfer services, such as Western Union and MoneyGram, have been monitored by the US government and law enforcement agencies without a warrant.[23] More than 150 million people from 20 countries, including Americans, had transaction data saved to a searchable database.

CHAPTER 9

Oracles and Insurance Tokens

An understanding of oracles is required before explaining decentralized finance in the upcoming chapters. DeFi encompasses borrowing, lending, insurance, and derivatives markets.

An oracle is a source of wisdom or knowledge. Blockchains, by design, do not interact with the external world and only execute the given code. This design ensures security and immutability.

When participating in DeFi activities such as borrowing money, trading derivative securities like options and futures, and executing transactions on decentralized exchanges to swap one token for another, it is crucial to know the true value of each cryptocurrency and digital asset in real time. If the oracle, or the external data price feed, is incorrect, it could lead to the loss of millions or billions of dollars in a decentralized finance protocol hack or exploit. Therefore, it is extraordinarily imperative to have accurate information.

Accurate and timely external information is necessary because oracles and price feeds have been manipulated to steal millions of dollars from DeFi protocols. Oracles are sources of knowledge, providing price feeds or data feeds. They serve as inputs to smart contracts and help blockchains to be interoperable.

An inbound oracle retrieves real-world information and delivers it to the blockchain and a smart contract application. For instance, if the price of a given crypto asset is a certain value, the investor's position is under-collateralized and is subject to liquidation. An insurance payout can be triggered if the weather reaches a certain temperature.

Outbound oracles send data from smart contracts to the external world, such as the volume and prices traded on a decentralized exchange. The decentralized app requests information from the oracle before trading one token for another. The oracle requests information from sources with the best prior reputation and track record. Ideally, multiple price sources are used.

If a single source is used to verify a given price, that source is subject to manipulation or lagged reporting. However, requesting data from 3, 5, or 13 different sources provides more reliable and timely information. When working with multiple price sources, a single price may be calculated, such as by taking the median price, the average of all prices, or the average of all prices after dropping the highest and lowest prices. The greater the number of inputs, the more accurate the information the oracle reports.

Oracles may also report data tracked by Internet of Things (IoT) devices. Some insurance companies provide drivers with electronic devices that track miles driven, average and peak speed, and the time of day when the car is driven. These inputs can be used to reduce the rates of the safest drivers while alerting insurance companies about the riskiest drivers. Of course, the riskiest drivers are unlikely to volunteer to install an IoT device in their vehicle.

Chainlink (LINK), the largest oracle used in the DeFi markets, had a market capitalization of more than $11 billion in February 2024. Chainlink has built a successful business as an oracle, providing information to smart contracts in a trusted way.

When used in DeFi, the oracle imports feeds of market prices and other data, including prices of stocks, NFTs, digital assets, and cryptocurrencies.

Betting and prediction sites in crypto can import the outcomes of elections and sporting events.

On-chain insurance enabled by smart contracts needs inputs such as weather and flight departures, arrivals, and cancellations. The quicker and more accurate this information is, the better the smart contracts will perform.

Trust in the digital assets system is essential, especially since there's no centralized intermediary. Chainlink, for instance, has a verifiable random number generator, which is crucial for activities including games of chance or queuing for an NFT. If the random number generator isn't truly random and a pattern can be discerned, it could give some participants an unfair advantage in trading and investing protocols.

Chainlink has the capability of overseeing the automation of smart contracts. Proof-of-reserve audits can be performed to verify the assets held by a fiat-backed stablecoin. Smart contracts and oracles also facilitate the sharing of information across blockchains, such as from Ethereum to Cosmos to Polygon, as a two-way flow of information regarding the status of each blockchain is essential to communication.

Chainlink has many use cases in DeFi. Price feeds for cryptocurrency prices are essential for borrowing and lending platforms to track loan collateral and force liquidations. These prices are also used to ensure that limit orders on decentralized exchanges are traded at the appropriate time. Derivatives products, such as futures and options, cannot be priced without accurate information regarding the prices of the underlying assets.

Oracles can also be used to verify the value of tokenized assets, whether on-chain or off-chain. On-chain assets may be wrapped versions of cryptocurrencies trading on their non-native blockchain. Off-chain, prices of assets may be tracked on stock and futures exchanges.

Key verticals of the CeFi industry that are being replicated in DeFi DApps include insurance, banking, and exchanges for securities and derivatives.

Off-chain events, such as travel disruptions or weather events, can be insured through on-chain providers. Insurance is also available for on-chain events, such as hacks, rug pulls, and smart contract failures, all of which are discussed in Chapter 25.

Applications exist in smart contracts, peer-to-peer insurance, index-based insurance, industry agreements, reinsurance, and asset management.

Two key blockchain insurance companies are Nexus Mutual and InsureAce. Investors can buy insurance from these companies based on what happens in their crypto accounts, including smart contract failures and exploits, exchange hacks, protocol coverage for hacks on a specific protocol, or custody coverage for centralized exchanges. Insurance payouts were activated in 2022 for losses related to the FTX exchange fraud and the collapse of the Terra UST stablecoin.

Underwriters determine the cost and availability of insurance coverage by evaluating the probability and severity of potential losses. An insurance company may choose only to offer coverage on a specific blockchain after reviewing a smart contract audit or for a centralized exchange after evaluating security measures. Steps taken to get approval for insurance coverage may reduce the risk and severity of the losses, as the smart contract or centralized exchange may improve security measures as a condition of becoming insured.

Consider a smart contract platform like Uniswap, an open-source protocol that has been audited. The insurance price for such a platform might be relatively low compared to a newer decentralized exchange that hasn't disclosed their code or undergone a third-party audit of their smart contract. The riskier the activity, the greater the cost of the insurance. However, risk management exercises can reduce the insurance cost by reducing the probability of loss.

Combining blockchains, oracles, and insurance could lead to innovative solutions.[1] For example, consider purchasing travel insurance from a website that offers blockchain-based travel insurance. The oracle can access the flight or train schedule to determine whether the train or plane left or arrived on time. If a delay or cancellation goes beyond what is specified in the insurance contract, the buyer of the insurance earns an immediate and automatic payout. The smart contract automatically pays an insurance benefit to those who purchased coverage against delay or cancellation.

While most drivers purchase semi-annual or annual automobile insurance coverage, some drivers do not own a car and only drive occasionally. Using blockchain insurance, perhaps aided by IoT devices that monitor driving activity, can allow drivers to purchase insurance only for the days they are driving a car.

The global insurance industry holds $40 trillion in assets worldwide and sells $5 trillion annually in premiums. Three key lines of insurance are health, life, and property/casualty. Property and casualty insurance covers events like auto accidents or home damage from fires, hurricanes, or floods.

The idea of automating insurance through smart contracts is intriguing. For instance, a claim can be made to a blockchain-based insurance carrier after a hurricane damages a home. The smart contract could then query weather data to verify the amount of rainfall, wind speed, and flooding at the home's specific location. It could even order a drone service or query satellite photos to estimate the property damage, potentially resulting in a faster payout than a traditional insurance company.

Insurance companies, many of which are publicly traded, source their capital from the equity and debt markets. Berkshire Hathaway, Warren Buffett's insurance company that includes Geico, is one of the largest and most famous. Insured customers pay premiums to the insurance companies. Generally, between 80% and 100% of all premiums paid are returned to cover insured losses. An insurance company can potentially profit with loss ratios near 100% through profitable investment of the insurance premiums that are held until paid out as claims.

The concept of peer-to-peer insurance is also interesting. In this model, a group of people pool their risk together by paying into an insurance pool. This can be a more predictable system when dealing with large numbers, as it's relatively predictable how many fires, floods, or deaths there will be in any specific period. Premiums are held in escrow during the term of the coverage to ensure that claims can be paid out. Oracles can confirm losses through the use of external data, such as death records, medical records, and weather readings. Oracles may also use the decisions of real people in a governance vote. For example, if four individuals vote that a loss was sustained, the insurance would pay out at the amount determined by the governance vote.

An insurance claim may be paid out even when the insured did not sustain a loss. Index-based insurance pays claims based on market events, not necessarily personal circumstances.[2] For instance, purchasing a put option on a stock index could result in a payout when the stock market declines, even without any personal loss on stocks. Insurance can be purchased against losses on stock or crypto holdings.

Weather insurance is crucial for businesses like amusement parks, ski resorts, beach hotels, or farming. These businesses are significantly affected by weather conditions such as temperature, rainfall, and snowfall. Amusement parks and beach hotels might prefer less rain. Farmers might want a balanced amount of rain, not too much or too little. Ski resorts need snow and might insure against insufficient snow. Insurance could be bought based on inches of rainfall, amount of snow, humidity, temperature, crop yield, etc. Instead of estimating losses for one specific investor, the payout is based on weather statistics.

For example, a payout is received if the rain is less than X inches or more than Y inches. A payout can also be scheduled if a specific location goes 30 days without rain or if the snowfall in January was less than 12 inches. The idea is that the insurance payout will offset the losses from fewer visitors to a beach hotel, ski resort, or fewer bushels of corn harvested.

Insurance is relatively complex. In car insurance, which is mandatory in many jurisdictions, claims must be paid quickly after a crash. Each driver files claims with their own insurance company, regardless of who was at fault. After each driver is paid for the damages to their vehicle and potentially their medical bills, the insurance companies settle up with each other, with the insurance company of the at-fault driver compensating the other insurance company for the damages. The insurance company pays for the loss and then communicates with the other insurance company based on the accident's facts.

In the realm of cryptocurrencies and digital assets, technical insurance covers smart contract failures, attacks, and exploits.[3] The goal is to ensure no money is lost in a hacking incident. Insurance could be bought against such an incident, but this is subject to underwriting. Before deciding on the availability and cost of coverage, underwriters study the smart contract and read or compile a smart contract audit to identify vulnerabilities. New smart contracts that haven't disclosed the code or completed a smart contract audit process may find that insurance is inaccessible or very expensive.

For instance, insurance on Uniswap smart contracts is likely to be more widely available and affordable than a newly launched decentralized exchange. Uniswap has operated for years, been subject to smart contract audits, and is trusted with billions of dollars of TVL.

Economic insurance pays based on market conditions experienced on DeFi platforms. Insurance can be purchased for impermanent losses, liquidations in lending protocols, and de-pegging of stablecoins. Insured investors may receive a settlement if something goes wrong in a liquidity pool in Curve or Balancer. Issues such as impermanent loss and liquidity pools will be discussed in the chapters on decentralized finance platforms.

Some investors hesitate to interact with decentralized finance and may choose not to borrow from a crypto protocol, trade on a decentralized exchange, or trade options and futures on a DeFi platform. They may be concerned about the robustness of the code or if gains from profitable trading activity will actually be paid.

However, more money is likely to be locked into the DeFi universe if insurance is available. More people will trade on decentralized exchanges, trade futures and options, and borrow and lend in DeFi. Investors are familiar with FDIC insurance for bank accounts and SIPC insurance for brokerage accounts and seek the same level of certainty or protection in the DeFi world.

One of the key areas of crypto is custody, which is the safe storage of digital assets. Leading custodians include Fidelity, Coinbase, Anchorage, Copper, and Fireblocks, among others. One of the most effective risk management methods for the custody of digital assets is cold storage, where assets and private keys are not available online. Hackers cannot access assets in cold storage, as keys are securely held in a physical vault and not stored in any internet-accessible computer. For example, Coinbase stores 98% of assets in custody in hardware wallets, keeping just 2% of assets in hot wallets that are used for trading and immediate liquidity.[4] Once a custodian has implemented strong measures of both physical and digital risk management, insurance can be purchased from firms such as Aon, Coincover, and Lloyd's of London.[5]

The intersection of the Internet of Things (IoT), insurance, and blockchain presents interesting possibilities. With more IoT devices today than people in the world, insurance could be priced based on data from sensors installed in cars, homes, and other assets.[6] For instance, auto insurance could be priced based on driving habits monitored by car sensors. Homeowners' insurance could offer discounts for security systems and automatic fire alarms. Health insurance could be more affordable for those whose health and activity are regularly monitored.

Commercial insurance might monitor a warehouse or a fleet of vehicles. Each pallet or vehicle could have security devices or location sensors. The sensors could notify the fleet manager if a vehicle is stolen or deviates from its route.

Peer-to-peer insurance could allow all participants to contribute to a pool from which insurance claims are paid. Traditional insurance companies like State Farm or Geico could also buy reinsurance to back up their insurance claims. This concept of reinsurance allows an insurance company to pay a certain amount of claims, like a deductible, and buy reinsurance for claims that exceed that amount.

For example, an insurance company may determine that they could afford to pay $1 billion for a single hurricane on the US East Coast or Gulf

Coast during a given year. Of course, the insurance company can't control the damage caused by storms, so the insurance company purchases reinsurance to cover all claims in excess of their ability and willingness to pay. If hurricanes caused $3 billion in insured damages in a given year, the insurance company would pay $1 billion, and the reinsurance company would pay $2 billion. Some insurance companies own reinsurance operations called captive reinsurers. Blockchains and smart contracts can facilitate transactions between an insurance company and reinsurers to automate the payment of claims. As climate change is leading to an increasing frequency and severity of fires and floods, purchasing insurance and reinsurance is becoming more expensive and more difficult. Residents of coastal states with repetitive damage from fires and storms may find that insurance is no longer available and that it becomes economically infeasible to rebuild homes in certain disaster-prone locations.

The central idea of blockchain, cryptocurrency, and digital assets is eliminating intermediaries. It is likely cheaper to send remittances using stablecoins than through a money service business such as Western Union. Consumers wish to reduce the costs of accessing banking and insurance services. The construction of banks, insurance companies, and money transfer services based on blockchain technology can eliminate the middleman and enable peer-to-peer transactions and the pooling of risks.

Blockchain technology offers the promise of reduced settlement and compliance costs. Blockchain asset management can be used to expedite remittances and the settlement of stock, bond, and derivative trades. Rather than trading US stocks on a T+1 schedule where trades settle one business day after the transaction, blockchain technology is already being used for same day settlement of credit default swaps by the Depository Trust Clearing Corporation (DTCC).

Centralized systems may have a single point of failure. For instance, Hurricane Sandy, which hit New York and New Jersey, resulted in significant losses of financial records held in paper form or on computer servers located solely in New York. The risk of losing valuable records is reduced when the information is held on distributed ledgers.

Blockchain technology can also be used to improve risk measurement and fraud reduction. Oracles and insurance are a prerequisite for the mass adoption of decentralized finance (DeFi) platforms, which can lead to efficiencies of on-chain borrowing, lending, and trading functions currently concentrated in real-world banks and securities exchanges.

CHAPTER 10

Privacy Tokens

The cryptocurrency universe was designed to be transparent and decentralized. Transactions can be viewed on a block explorer or Etherscan, providing transparency to the sending address, the receiving address, and the size of the transactions.

Fiat cash is anonymous, while most crypto assets are transparent. Fiat cash is used in criminal activity much more frequently than crypto is. Due to the transparency of most crypto assets, including bitcoin and Ether, law enforcement is able to track transactions. In some cases, law enforcement has recovered funds that were stolen in a hack or through ransomware.

Transactions on the Bitcoin and Ethereum networks are pseudonymous. While the transaction activity of each address is transparent, the addresses are infrequently linked to real-world people or companies.

Many investors assume that their real-world identity cannot be linked to their crypto addresses, and that can be true.[1] However, there are a number of ways that addresses can be linked to their owners.

- Investors must complete a KYC process before converting fiat cash to crypto through an on-ramp such as a centralized exchange. The centralized exchange may be required to submit this identification to a governmental entity when a crime occurs or when trading activity causes a tax liability.
- Consumers who have paid for goods or services using crypto and had them delivered to an email or a physical address have given up the anonymity of their address.
- The real-world identity of a social media user can be linked to an address when an NFT image is posted, as the minting activity of each NFT is disclosed. Some will post their address on a social media platform.

The easiest way for investors to keep their transactions private is to use a new address for each transaction. This is burdensome but is able to enhance privacy. Some will practice merge avoidance by sending two trans-actions to two addresses in a way that the two sending addresses aren't linked when combined into a single transaction.

The founders of the cryptocurrency and digital asset revolution are not big fans of banks, governments, and taxes. Some of the greatest software development is happening in the area of privacy coins. Privacy coins, such as Monero, are illegal in Australia, Japan, and South Korea.[2] Centralized exchanges may choose not to custody privacy coins or allow investors to trade them due to their negative publicity. While some investors may desire to use privacy coins simply to maintain the confidentiality of their transac-tions, others explicitly use them for illegal activity. The Office of Foreign Asset Control (OFAC) banned the use of Tornado Cash after approximately 25% of transactions were traced to North Korea.[3] North Korea is among a number of countries included on OFAC's sanction list, alongside Iran, Iraq, Russia, Sudan, and others. Governments frequently shutter or prosecute leaders of crypto protocols that facilitate money laundering, tax evasion, or sending assets to terrorists or sanctioned countries.

Depending on the jurisdiction, privacy coins may be legal if used to obscure wealth or transactions from the broader blockchain community if the user complies with all governmental regulations, including taxation and the avoidance of banned transactions.

If all transactions were private, it would be hard to track blockchain activity. Without transparency, many cryptocurrencies may be less valuable, as knowledge of the number of coins outstanding and the related market capitalization is required to evaluate the investment potential of a specific digital asset.

There are a variety of methods used to obscure their wealth and their transactions in the digital asset space. This includes privacy coins, mixers, and tumblers.

Individuals wishing to obscure the destination of a transaction may send their crypto to a smart contract that functions as a mixer or a tumbler.[4] The smart contract will accept crypto from multiple senders and mix them together until blockchain analysis cannot track the source or destination of the coins. With 50 input and 50 output addresses, each coin's provenance chain is obscured or broken. Wasabi Wallet and JoinMarket are mixing ser-vices using the CoinJoin technique.

If a specific bitcoin was used in the Silk Road dark web marketplace, stolen in the hacking of the Mt Gox exchange, or paid in a ransomware transaction, investors may view it as tainted. While all bitcoins should be fungible, there may be worries that the specific bitcoins used in criminal activity may be subject to future seizure or refusal by a custodian. Coins that have gone through a mixing or tumbling process may lose or obscure the chain of ownership, potentially removing the liability of the specific coin's history.

Centralized exchanges may know which coins have been through a mixer or a tumbler and choose not to accept coins that have previously used a smart contract stored at a mixing or tumbling address. Mixers and tumblers are illegal in the US, with US Deputy Assistant Attorney General Brian Benczkowski declaring in February 2021 that using these services is a crime.[5] The assumption is that the goal of using the service is typically money laundering, tax evasion, hacking, stealing, and dark web activities.

While mixers and tumblers are banned in the US, Bitcoin's Taproot may also obscure transactions.

Tornado Cash and its cryptocurrency, Tumbler, which runs smart contracts on the Ethereum blockchain, met its demise in 2022. Investors send Ether tokens to Tornado Cash, where the protocol mixes up the tokens with those sent by others and returns untraceable outputs.

Zero-knowledge proofs are used to ensure there's no public link between the sending and receiving addresses. In August 2022, the US Treasury Department, in conjunction with the Office of Foreign Assets Control, made it illegal for US residents specifically to use Tornado Cash because they have evidence that more than $7 billion in illicit funds were used in Tornado Cash as a step in the money laundering process.[6] The Dutch Government arrested the developers of the Tornado Cash protocol for facilitating money laundering. This sets a legal precedent that programmers and blockchain designers can have criminal liability for the activity of users accessing their protocol. Those involved in the transfer and custody of crypto assets must ensure that their KYC and AML processes comply with all applicable regulations.

A straightforward cryptocurrency exchange might have liability for money laundering if it doesn't implement proper steps to comply with AML and KYC regulations. Unrelated to mixers and tumblers, Changpeng Zhao (CZ), the founder of the Binance centralized exchange, was personally fined $50 million, while the US Department of Justice fined Binance $4.3 billion for not implementing effective controls against money laundering.[7]

Blocks written to the Bitcoin and Ethereum blockchains typically contain information on each transaction, including the sending address, the receiving address, and the transaction amount. A transaction is only considered to be valid when evidence is presented that the sender's private key authorized the transaction. Transactions using a single input and a single output address can be easily followed with a block explorer or Etherscan.

Ring signatures can be used to make transactions opaque.[8] In a ring signature, a single sender using their private key creates a transaction and several fake private keys for other addresses. When the transaction is presented to the blockchain, a number of sending addresses appear with the information that the private key of one of the addresses was used to authorize the transaction. Transactions become opaque when the value of the transaction and the identity of the sending and receiving wallets are confused by the extra information submitted.

zk-SNARK stands for "Zero-Knowledge Succinct Non-Interactive Argument of Knowledge." zk-SNARKs allow one party to prove to another that something is true without revealing anything specific, making this solution ideal for private crypto transactions. zk-SNARKs can be used with ring signatures, as the originator of the transaction offers proof that the transaction is valid without explicitly disclosing the private key or the transaction size to the broader blockchain. Whatever happens in the black box has been verified, allowing multiple transactions to be processed as a single transaction. The layer one blockchain, such as Ethereum, accepts blocks of transactions that are valid but rejects any block that contains invalid transactions.

Privacy coins include Monero, Zcash, and Dash.

Monero is a hard fork of Bytecoin, which was one of the original privacy coins. Monero transactions are designed to be secure, private, and untraceable. While some coins allow users to choose between public, semi-private, and private transactions, Monero transactions are completely secure and private by default.

The primary feature of Monero is that each private key is used just once. Transactions are anonymous because multiple transactions can't be linked to the same address. Using an address just once ensures that transactions cannot be tracked for a given user over time.

Monero uses a ring size of 10. Monero creates one-time addresses for each user and mixes genuine transaction signatures with decoys. Some of the transactions are true, and some are false. The sending address, the receiving address, and transaction amounts are obscured.

The US taxing authority, the Internal Revenue Service, paid up to $625,000 to two firms in an attempt to trace transactions made using Monero.[9] Cracking the obfuscation of Monero would allow authorities to evaluate transactions for potentially criminal tax evasion, money laundering, and trading with sanctioned countries.

Zcash offers four levels of privacy for transactions: public, shielding, deshielding, and private.[10]

Public transactions disclose the sending and receiving addresses similar to how the Bitcoin blockchain discloses transaction activity. Deshielding discloses the receiving address and obscures the sending address, while shielding discloses the sending address and obscures the receiving address.

Private transactions use zk-SNARKs (zero-knowledge proofs) to allow confidential transactions and financial privacy by shielding both the sending and receiving addresses.

Dash is a coin that offers optional privacy for transactions using the PrivateSend technology, which uses CoinJoin to mix coins from different senders before redistributing the obscured output.[11] Transactions using PrivateSend can be delayed, as the protocol waits until enough private transactions are requested to have sufficient transactions mixed together to meet the privacy goals.

In addition to its privacy features, Dash offers much faster transactions than are experienced on most other blockchains. Payments can be settled within 2 seconds by using InstantSend. In addition, ChainLocks makes transactions on the Dash blockchain instantly immutable. A block of transactions is written to the Bitcoin blockchain each 10 minutes, with many observers requiring 30–60 minutes before declaring that a Bitcoin transaction is immutable due to the approval of multiple subsequent blocks. While the block time of the Bitcoin blockchain is infeasible for point-of-sale consumer transactions, the InstantSend and ChainLocks features of Dash make everyday transactions feasible.

If the Dash technology is viewed more like Bitcoin's Taproot and less like a mixer or a tumbler, it may successfully avoid increased regulatory scrutiny or being delisted by exchanges.

Transactions in most cryptocurrencies are not anonymous, as blockchain data typically discloses the sending address, the receiving address, and the transaction amount. While addresses are typically not publicly linked to their owners, some owners will disclose their addresses by interacting in public forums by posting NFTs to a social media profile. Investors choosing to keep their transactions private need to take steps to ensure that they do not make any public disclosures that could allow blockchain users to link their address to their real-world identity.

Some choose an extraordinarily public link between their address and their identity. The Ethereum Name Service, or ENS, offers domain names that can be used as Ethereum wallets. Blockchain users know that Vitalik.eth is the ENS address of Vitalik Buterin, one of the co-founders of Ethereum. Having a public address allows blockchain users to review the activity in the wallet and send value and messages to Vitalik's wallet.

Users who have completed the KYC process on a centralized exchange may have their identity disclosed to a governmental entity seeking information on tax liabilities or criminal activity. While fiat cash is inherently anonymous, blockchain transactions are generally traceable. Advocates of privacy coins seek the anonymity of fiat cash in a blockchain environment, a goal that is at odds with many governmental regulatory agencies. These agencies make the assumption that the rationale for using privacy coins and mixers is primarily for tax evasion, money laundering, and dealing with terrorists and sanctioned countries.

CHAPTER 11

Decentralized Finance (DeFi): Borrowing, Lending, and Decentralized Exchanges

This chapter discusses borrowing, lending, and decentralized exchanges in the context of decentralized finance (DeFi). The aim of DeFi is to offer services similar to traditional stock and derivatives exchanges and banks but in a more distributed, global, and peer-to-peer fashion.

In centralized finance (CeFi), borrowing and lending are banks' core businesses. Consumers are lenders when they deposit funds into banks and earn an interest rate. Consumers are borrowers when they take out loans and pay an interest rate. Bank profits are determined, in part, by the net interest margin, which is the difference between borrowing and lending rates.

In centralized finance (CeFi), banks offer both secured and unsecured lending. Unsecured lending, such as credit cards, allows consumers to borrow without posting collateral. This lending is risky for banks, so consumers are charged high-interest rates of 12% to 24%. Secured lending, such as car loans or home mortgages, is collateralized by a real asset that can be repossessed or foreclosed on if the loan is not paid. Due to the lower-risk nature of secured lending, consumers with the best credit may be offered rates of 6% to 10%. Banks only offer loans to consumers completing the KYC process with a history of timely loan repayment, resulting in a strong credit rating. Consumers with lower credit ratings will be charged much higher interest rates or denied credit.

Auto loans and home mortgages generally require a down payment, often a minimum of 10% to 20% of the purchase price. A buyer of a $500,000 home with a 10% down payment would deposit $50,000 and borrow $450,000. This is a 90% loan-to-value (LTV) mortgage, calculated as the ratio of the $450,000 loan to the $500,000 purchase price or subtracting the 10% down payment from the 100% purchase price. Banks take less risk by requiring larger down payments or offering borrowers loans with lower LTV ratios.

Only collateralized loans are available in DeFi. Due to the anonymous or pseudonymous nature of the crypto markets, credit scores and unsecured loans are generally unavailable. Consumers desiring loans on DeFi platforms must submit collateral with a value exceeding the desired borrowing amount. What's exciting about the idea of collateralized loans in DeFi is that we're moving toward a world where transactions can't be censored. A key benefit of DeFi is that anyone with collateral has access to loans regardless of their age, credit history, race, or country of origin. This can add substantial value to consumers who live in countries with weak banking systems or discrimination against specific ethnic groups.

DeFi seeks to eliminate the intermediary. Not only is the banker a centralized point of failure, but the net interest margin may require higher borrowing rates and lower deposit rates. In a peer-to-peer world with less need for an intermediary, depositors can potentially earn higher rates and borrowers may be charged lower rates on loans.

Borrowers in the DeFi world may have a number of motivations. In the US, selling digital assets is subject to capital gains taxes, with lower rates on long-term gains for positions held longer than 12 months and higher rates on short-term gains for positions held for less than 12 months. An investor with a substantial gain on a token over a 10-month holding period may wish to borrow against the position to use the cash for everyday expenses or other investments while continuing to hold the asset to qualify for the lower long-term capital gains tax rate.

Other investors may want to borrow against their digital asset holdings to leverage their assets into even larger crypto investments. While continuing to hold a token, such as Ether, that is used as collateral, the loan proceeds can be reinvested in other crypto assets. This strategy can be profitable as long as the leveraged investments increase in value by more than the cost of the loan. The leveraged trade allows the investor to continue earning Ether's price return while adding additional investments in digital assets that may also increase over time. Leveraged trading increases the volatility of returns of both profitable and unprofitable trades. If an investor were to borrow 100% of their collateral's value, the capital invested in digital assets would double. Before the cost of leverage, the profits of rising crypto assets double, but the losses double when prices fall. Investors with holdings leveraged to 200% of the original investment can lose 100% of their original investment with a 50% decline in the price of the assets in the portfolio.

More sophisticated trades include using the borrowing and lending markets to bet against the price of a specific digital asset. An investor would implement a short sale by borrowing and selling a token to express a bearish view. This strategy can earn a profit if the investor is correct and the price of the overvalued token declines. For example, an investor borrows one Ether token and sells it for $2,000. The investor is required to pay back the loan in the amount of one Ether token plus interest. If the Ether token is sold for $2,000 and the price falls to $1,500, the investor can repurchase the Ether token for $1,500 and repay the loan, netting a profit of $500 before interest costs and gas fees. If the Ether token continues to increase in value to $3,000, the investor must still repay the loan in the amount of one Ether token plus interest, subjecting them to a loss as the token continues to rise in value.

In order to incentivize participation in DeFi, many platforms award governance tokens to borrowers and lenders. The popularity of DeFi platforms is measured by TVL and trading volume. As rewards are offered, new users are given incentives to allocate assets to each DeFi platform. New platforms may start off with high levels of rewards to attract users but then decline over time as the protocol becomes more established. Many users participate in yield farming, switching between DeFi platforms in search of higher rewards. Once a platform becomes established and reduces the incentives to participate, investors may move their assets and trading volume to a newer platform with higher rewards. Often those rewards come in the form of governance tokens, which allow holders to propose and vote on changes to the protocol, such as new tokens, collateral factors, and changes to how interest rates are determined.

Investors participating in yield farming must be careful not to simply allocate to the platforms offering the highest annual percentage yield (APY), as those yields can vary over time. Platforms offering the highest yields may quickly attract significant TVL, reducing the need to pay incentives. While the investor may earn that APY for a short period of time, the yields are likely to decline quickly as the protocol gains users and volume, so the investor is unlikely to earn the high APY for a full year.

Investors must also investigate the source of that yield. Consider a protocol offering a 100% annual APY that comes through the issuance of new tokens. Even if that APY was offered for one year and the investor doubled the initial number of tokens, there is no guarantee that the tokens are worth more than when the investor originally contributed to that protocol. If the protocol doubles the number of tokens outstanding over the course of the year, the value of the tokens is likely to be diluted due to the extra supply.

Remember, if an investment seems too good to be true, it probably is. Risk and return are closely linked in finance, with lower-risk investments typically earning lower returns while higher risks are typically required to earn higher returns. As will be explained in Chapter 25, Terra USD promised a risk-free yield of 19.5% on a stablecoin that quickly moved from $1 toward zero. Investors may be able to earn sustainable yields of 2% to 8% without taking significant risks or printing a significant number of new tokens. Protocols offering annual yields of 20%, 200%, or 2,000%

should be approached cautiously, as those yields are not sustainable in the long run and may indicate very risky propositions. Unscrupulous developers wishing to steal investor funds in a rug pull may offer high yields to quickly attract capital before they disappear with the proceeds and abandon the blockchain project.

Two of the leaders in borrowing and lending are Compound and Aave, both of which offer governance tokens (COMP and AAVE). Investors visit the website compound.finance and connect a crypto wallet to enable the borrowing and lending features of the platform. Compound was originally built as an Ethereum-based DApp, with users incurring gas fees to undertake transactions. Compound later added compatibility with Polygon, a layer 2 solution compatible with Ethereum, that allows users to participate in DeFi with much lower gas fees.

Interest rates on Compound are determined algorithmically, with lower borrowing rates during times of reduced loan demand, and higher rates during times when lending activity is robust. In March 2024, Compound had more than $1 billion in loans outstanding collateralized by TVL of more than $3.2 billion, with more than half of the loans in Ethereum and USDC on the Ethereum blockchain.[1] Compound version 2 offers borrowing and lending markets on 18 crypto assets.

Because Compound and Polygon are built on the Ethereum blockchain, all tokens used in the borrowing and lending process must be compatible with the ERC-20 fungible token standard. The bitcoin used as collateral on Compound must be "wrapped bitcoin," (WBTC) which is bitcoin made compatible with the ERC-20 standard. Bitcoin is held in a crypto account, which issues wrapped bitcoin tokens that are ERC-20 compatible. Each wrapped bitcoin token can be retired or burned in exchange for an original bitcoin token.

Each asset on Compound is assigned a collateral factor, or the percentage of collateral value that can be borrowed. Compound's preferred collateral includes Ether, USDC, and DAI, with collateral factors between 80% and 85.5%. Uniswap has a collateral factor of 75%, while wrapped bitcoin is 70%. Tokens with collateral factors between 25% and 50% include Aave, Compound, ChainLink, Basic Attention Token, Sushi, 0x, Maker, and yearn.finance. Notably, a number of stablecoins are not welcomed as collateral at Compound, as the collateral factor is zero for Tether, Fei USD, True USD, and Pax Dollar.

Ether had a collateral factor of 82.5% in March 2024. Investors are eligible for a loan of $1,000.00 in stablecoins for each $1,212.12 in Ether held on the Compound platform ($1,212.12 multiplied by 82.5% is $1,000.00). Investors will pay an annualized interest rate of 2.58% on the Ether-collateralized loan.

The collateral factor of wrapped bitcoin is 70%. Depositing $100,000 of wrapped bitcoin into Compound allows an investor to borrow up to $70,000 in DAI. That DAI can be used to earn a deposit yield or can be used to purchase other crypto assets or be used on other DeFi platforms.

Many of the stablecoin loans in Compound are collateralized by deposits of Ether and wrapped bitcoin tokens. Remember that stablecoins are pegged to one dollar, while bitcoin and Ether tokens have a volatility substantially greater than the stock market. Investors participating in DeFi platforms must watch their positions carefully. As the value of the wrapped bitcoin and Ether tokens declines, the borrowing limit supported by that collateral also declines. As the collateral value declines, investors must add more collateral to the account to support the current value of the loan or repay the loan until the debased value of the collateral is sufficient to support the amount borrowed.

As a collateralized platform, Compound never wants the value of the collateral to be less than the value of the loan. If that were to happen, a portion of the loan value would be unsecured. To protect against the collateralized loans becoming unsecured, investor accounts are subject to liquidation if they do not quickly add collateral or repay a portion of the loan as collateral values decline.

DeFi platforms allow participants or their bots to liquidate investors' accounts whose collateral value is insufficient to fully back the borrowings. The investor's account retains any residual value after the collateral is sold, the loan is repaid, and the liquidator of the collateral earns a liquidation fee, such as 5% of the value of the required liquidation.

A key source of market volatility is the rapid liquidation of undercollateralized positions. As prices fall, loans become undercollateralized and subject to liquidation. Those liquidations lead to lower prices, which can trigger liquidations in other accounts, and so on. These cascading liquidations happen quickly and automatically, and can often lead to a 10% or greater decline in the price of bitcoin or Ether in a matter of minutes or hours.

Aave is more complex than Compound because it supports a greater number of crypto assets and runs on a number of additional blockchains. Compound focuses on Ethereum and Polygon, while Aave is also compatible with the Avalanche, Fantom, Harmony, Optimism, and Arbitrum blockchains and side chains. Running DeFi platforms directly on the Ethereum network incurs substantial gas fees, while processing transactions on a layer 2 or alternate layer 1 blockchain can greatly reduce transaction costs. In March 2024, the TVL of Aave was $11.5 billion, much greater than the $3.5 billion locked into the Compound protocol.

Aave uses the terms supply and borrow, with supply referring to deposits or lending. Suppliers deposit tokens to earn yield, while borrowers supply tokens as collateral for a loan. Aave offers loans with either fixed or variable interest rates. Borrowers with variable-rate loans must watch their positions carefully to ensure that the rate charged on the loan is affordable compared with the expected profits from the use of the loan proceeds.

Interest rates vary with the collateral token, the borrowed token, and the blockchain on which the smart contract is running. Supplying and borrowing ETH has low rates of 1.66% and 2.39%, respectively.[2] Rates for Tether and USDC on the Ethereum network are approximately 12% to supply and 15% to borrow. Stablecoins DAI, True USD, and USDC can be used as collateral with 75% LTV, while Tether, Binance USD, and Synthetix USD cannot be used as collateral.

DeFi platforms vary by collateral factors, borrowing rates, supply rates, and the underlying blockchain platform. Due to the number of varying platforms and rates, opportunities might be presented for arbitrage. A pure arbitrage is a guaranteed, instantaneous, risk-free profit, such as simultaneously buying a token at $100 and selling the same token at $105 net of fees, with the profit booked in seconds or minutes when the trades are written to the blockchain(s).

What appears to be a risk-free profit may result in substantial losses if platforms vary in credit risk, counterparty risk, or smart contract risk. While it may appear profitable to borrow at 4% and lend at 5%, those profits accrue over time, during which a variety of risks may occur at one or more of the platforms where positions are held. Investors should perform due diligence, such as a smart contract audit, before implementing trades on one or more DeFi platforms.

Investors may wish to hold and supply crypto tokens with greater security or upside return potential while borrowing and selling tokens that are likely to decline in value, whether due to a level of overvaluation or the potential to lose substantial value in a fraud or platform failure. In 2022, it was profitable to take a short position in Terra USD, an algorithmic stablecoin that moved from $1 to pennies in a matter of days. This implosion created a domino effect that led to the bankruptcy of a number of leveraged crypto borrowers, lenders, and traders.

There are infinite permutations of DeFi platforms, tokens to supply or borrow, and blockchains and smart contracts to trade across. Algorithmic traders build trading systems and bots to exploit opportunities to profit across markets. Profits may be especially interesting when cryptocurrencies trade in different countries denominated in different fiat currencies. For example, many traders implemented Kimchi arbitrage between 2016 and 2018 when bitcoin prices were much higher when traded on exchanges in South Korea and denominated in Korean Won.[3] This arbitrage required traders to not only trade bitcoin but to have access to their home country's currency, Korean Won, and to have access to Korean exchanges, which were not easily accessible to foreign investors.

So far, Compound and Aave sound somewhat similar to a CeFi bank with the idea of supplying and borrowing capital in collateralized loans. Many DeFi platforms seek to recreate CeFi institutions and methods in ways that reduce the friction to trading in either costs or time. However, some innovative constructs exist in DeFi platforms that were never available in the CeFi system. A concept only available in crypto is Aave's flash loans.

If an investor is willing to pay the required fees and interest, a flash loan can give a borrower access to a loan of millions of dollars without collateral.[4] The "flash" in a flash loan requires the loan to be repaid after one transaction or a series of transactions, typically executed in a single day, if not a single hour. This is especially convenient for arbitrage opportunities or to earn a liquidation fee, trades that become more profitable when more capital is deployed. For example, an investor may find a token trading at a price 2% different across two exchanges and calculate that the trade would be profitable after all gas fees, transaction costs, and flash loan fees. If the investor is confident in the ability to profit from that trade, they can borrow $10 million, buy the tokens on the cheaper exchange, sell the tokens on the more expensive exchange, and immediately repay the loans and close all the trades.

Unfortunately, flash loans are often used in smart contract exploits. If a hacker spots a vulnerability in a smart contract that can benefit from a large amount of capital, that capital can be borrowed in a flash loan and used to drain most or all of the value locked in a vulnerable protocol.

It's important to note the transactions are atomic. Atomic transactions must be completed in full, or they will not be executed at all. If an account runs out of gas fees or can't afford to pay the flash loan, all attempted transactions will be canceled and it will be as if the execution of the smart contract had never been attempted. This is an important safeguard. Consider a decentralized exchange where an investor sends Ether tokens and requests a swap to another specific token. No one would want this trade to fail halfway through the execution, where the investor sent Ether to the Dex and the trade failed without returning either the Ether tokens or the tokens requested in the swap.

If the transaction is successfully completed, the investor receives the requested tokens. If the transaction fails, they retain the tokens they chose to swap. Decentralized exchanges are designed to be non-custodial and without counterparty risk, as they exchange tokens as requested in a matter of seconds.

Flash loans on Aave have an interest cost of nine basis points or 0.09%.[5] This fee is $900 for each $1 million (or $9 for $10,000) borrowed for a loan that typically lasts less than one hour. The transaction will fail if the wallet does not have sufficient funds to pay the cost of the flash loan. The loan automatically liquidates after a series of transactions, so the loan must be repaid after a transaction or a series of transactions.

Another use of flash loans is to shore up loans that are in danger of liquidation. Using a flash loan, the investor can replace collateral, liquidate collateral, and repay the loan before the liquidators close the loan and charge the substantial liquidation fee. A flash loan fee of nine basis points is much more affordable than having positions liquidated.

While Aave and Compound are leaders in banking services such as borrowing and lending of crypto assets, decentralized exchanges seek to replicate or improve on the CeFi concept of stock and futures exchanges.

Most investors start their crypto journey by exchanging fiat currency for bitcoin or Ether on a centralized exchange such as Kraken, Binance, Coinbase, or Gemini. They send dollars or euros from their traditional bank to the centralized exchange, where the fiat currency can be used to purchase any digital assets listed on the centralized exchange. Centralized exchanges act as an on-ramp, allowing investors to purchase their first cryptocurrencies. Once some digital assets are owned, the investor can hold the tokens on the centralized exchange or move them to a personal wallet away from the exchange, where the assets can be used to participate in DeFi activities and pseudonymous crypto transactions.

Centralized exchanges may look and feel like a traditional bank or brokerage account. Investors are likely to be familiar with interface features such as a login screen, the ability to name beneficiaries, change and reset passwords, and review position information and transaction history. It is important to remember, though, "not your keys, not your crypto." Centralized exchanges control your private keys. This can be very positive in the case that your family is allowed to access your crypto when you are no longer able to, but very negative in the case when that exchange is FTX and the leader of the exchange chooses to use your tokens to make political contributions and live a lavish lifestyle.

Investors who hold assets at a centralized exchange are vulnerable to losing their assets if there is a cybersecurity incident or employee theft that reveals the private keys to investor accounts. Investors may choose to withdraw their assets from the centralized exchange and personally hold them in a non-custodial wallet. Holding assets in a non-custodial wallet eliminates the risk of losing tokens in an incident at the centralized exchange but puts the responsibility for the safekeeping of the crypto assets onto the investor. If the investor loses the crypto wallet in a fire or flood, or simply forgets the password, the assets can be lost.

While Coingecko.com tracks more than 13,000 different cryptocurrencies, the top 100 accounts for about 95% of that market cap. Centralized exchanges only list a few dozen or a few hundred tokens, mostly those with larger market capitalizations and those that might pose less risk to the regulators. Centralized exchanges are unlikely to list tokens that are clearly scams or frauds, those that might be deemed to be securities, or tokens that back mixers, tumblers, or privacy-based applications. Newly listed tokens are not likely to be immediately available on centralized exchanges, as the exchanges take some time to decide on which tokens will be made available for trading. Each token will have undergone some level of due diligence before being listed on an exchange available to US investors. Centralized exchanges available to investors outside of the US may offer a much larger selection of tokens as well as derivative products and leverage levels that are not available to US investors. One example is perpetual futures that can trade at or above 10 times leverage.

Centralized exchanges make it easy to buy dozens of different coins, just as if the investor were buying or selling stocks. Investors don't need to understand how custody works or what blockchain a token is compatible with. The investor may buy Ether, bitcoin, Solana, Avalanche, Cardano, and Polygon in their centralized exchange account without understanding that each of the tokens may be custodied on different blockchains. When trading in a non-custodial wallet, also called a self-custodial wallet, investors must know to not send bitcoin to an Ethereum wallet. The technicalities that are vital to maintaining the value of a non-custodial wallet are not nearly as important to investors when custody is maintained at the centralized exchange.

A centralized exchange will feel a lot like an electronic brokerage account with an interface familiar to investors who have previously traded stocks online. Before making trades, investors need to understand market orders, limit orders, and stop limit orders.

A market order is an instruction to immediately buy an asset at whatever the current price may be. This is certainly an easy way to trade and generally works well for small trades in assets with large capitalizations and high trading volumes. Centralized exchanges, especially when used as smartphone apps, will often default to market orders. The slippage, or the difference in actual vs. expected price of a trade, is likely to be small for a $1,000 trade in Ether or bitcoin when markets are not volatile. Market orders can be very expensive, though, when markets are volatile, or when making a large trade in a less liquid asset. Attempting to immediately buy $1 million in a $10 million token that trades $100,000 in an average day will be much more expensive than the price that appears on the screen.

When markets are volatile or the investor desires to make a trade that is large compared to the market capitalization or volume of a token, limit orders are recommended. Momentum investors and those that desire to trade quickly would prefer a market order that guarantees immediate execution at an uncertain price. More patient or value-oriented investors may use a limit order that specifies the maximum price the investor is willing to pay, but it might take time for the investor to be able to buy at the desired price. If Ether is trading at $1,500, a limit order to buy Ether at $1,000 will only be filled if the price drops by one-third in value, which might take weeks or months or that price may never be reached again. However, if the investor wishes to buy Ether tokens at $1,490, the limit order may be reached by the end of the same day. Investors typically place limit orders to buy at or below the currently trading price and place limit orders to sell at or above the currently trading price. If the investor were to buy an Ether token for $1,490 today, they can place a limit order to sell at $1,990, hoping to profit $500 if and when Ether rises in price in the coming months.

A stop-limit order can be used in hopes of protecting a profit. An investor previously purchased Ether tokens for $1,000 each and has a substantial profit at today's $1,500 price. In an attempt to lock in a profit, the investor places an order to sell their token at $1,400 stop, limit $1,300. Once Ether trades at $1,400 or less, a limit order to sell at $1,300 is activated. As the price of Ether falls slowly, the token will be sold between $1,300 and $1,400, locking in a nice profit from the investor's $1,000 cost basis.

It is important to understand the difference between limit, stop, and stop limit. If the price is currently at $1,500, a limit order to sell at $1,400 will be executed immediately, as the investor is seeking to sell at any price of $1,400 or higher. A stop order to sell at $1,400 triggers a market order to sell whenever Ether trades at $1,400 or lower, which could be at $1,399 or at $1,000 during a flash crash with a big gap lower. A $1,400 stop-limit order places a limit order to sell at $1,400 whenever Ether trades at $1,400 or less. If Ether is trading at $1,500 today, it can rise to $1,600, $1,700, $1,800, $1,900, and continue to move higher without triggering the $1,400 stop-limit order. Some investors will use a trailing stop order. Every time the price of Ether rises $100, the investor increases their stop-limit order. When Ether is trading at $1,500, a stop-limit order of $1,400 is entered. After Ether rises to $1,600, the stop-limit order is moved to $1,500, which seeks to protect a growing portion of gains as the market price continues to rise.

Decentralized exchanges (DEXes) include Uniswap, SushiSwap, PancakeSwap, and SpookySwap, among others. A DEX does not hold private keys or take custody of crypto assets. To use a decentralized exchange, an investor connects their non-custodial wallet to the smart contract address of the DEX. Once the investor has connected their wallet to the smart contract, they send the token they desire to swap and request a specific token in return. For example, an investor can send Ether tokens and request Compound tokens in return. Ether tokens would be exchanged for any ERC-20 token that is compatible with the Ethereum blockchain.

Trades on DEXes are atomic and non-custodial. Atomic transactions are either executed completely or not at all. In the example swap, one of two things happens. Either the trade succeeds (Ether is sent and Compound is returned to the investor) or the trade fails (Ether is sent and returned to the investor). In an atomic transaction, the investor would never send Ether, have the trade fail, and not have their Ether returned.

Non-custodial means that the smart contract never takes custody of the investor's tokens. In a single transaction, the DEX receives the Ether tokens, swaps them for the Compound tokens, and returns both tokens to the parties involved in the swap. Before the transaction is initiated, the private keys are confirmed to be present, but the DEX never takes possession of the tokens or the private keys for investors requesting a swap.

Uniswap and Balancer are examples of liquidity pool-based decentralized exchanges. Liquidity providers (LP) deposit their tokens into the DEX to profit from facilitating transactions with investors. Each LP deposits a pair of tokens, in this case Ether and Compound.

Uniswap V2 charges a flat fee of 0.3% for each swap, while Uniswap V3 has the flexibility of liquidity pools charging fees of 0.05%, 0.3%, and 1%.[6] Stablecoins are likely to be swapped in the lowest fee tier, liquid large cap tokens in the middle fee tier, and less liquid small cap tokens in the highest fee tier. LPs supplying tokens to a trading pair earn a share of the fees paid on each transaction. Before requesting a swap, investors should evaluate the trading fees, the gas fees, and the size of their order relative to the available liquidity and average trading volume of the specific token pair.

While CoinGecko lists more than 13,000 coins, centralized exchanges available to US investors only make available a few dozen of the most popular coins. Non-US investors may see a greater choice of tokens available on centralized exchanges, as exchanges in the US do not want to list tokens that the SEC may determine to be securities. US investors seeking to purchase tokens not available on a centralized exchange must trade on a DEX, such as Uniswap V3, which offers approximately 1,200 coins.[7]

Uniswap is an automated market maker (AMM) where all trading is accomplished through smart contracts. Each liquidity pool has two assets, such as Ether and Compound, that LPs supply in equal amounts. If Ether is trading at $1,000 and Compound is trading at $100, each LP would supply 10 COMP tokens for each ETH token.

The LPs set the pricing strategies and range in which they are willing to trade. Every time ETH is swapped for COMP, ETH enters the pool, COMP leaves the pool, and the relative price of COMP rises. Reserves are rebalanced after each trade. Because assets are supplied in pairs, liquidity will always be available for investors wishing to swap their tokens without waiting for another investor to send a matching order.

Oracles are important to decentralized exchanges because tokens' trading prices should closely match those same tokens' prices on other exchanges. As a token, such as COMP, continually leaves the ETH/COMP trading pair, the price of COMP continually rises while the price of ETH declines. This incentivizes arbitrageurs to supply COMP at the higher price and buy ETH at the lower price, restoring the balance between the two prices to match prices at other external exchanges.

Prices are best kept in line when there is a two-way trading flow with a relatively equal volume of buying and selling for each token in the pair. The easiest pairs for an AMM to manage are tokens with low volatility and a high correlation between prices. A stablecoin pair, such as USDC/DAI, will typically see each asset remain within the range of $0.99 and $1.01.[8]

Pairs matching a stablecoin to ETH will be riskier for LPs, as the correlation is low and the difference in price volatility is high. LPs seek to profit from trading volume but can experience losses when the prices diverge between the pair of tokens. LPs prefer that the pair stays in relative balance with significant volume and low relative price volatility. LPs are trying to earn fees for supplying liquidity and supporting investors choosing to swap tokens on the DEX, but must balance the trading fees earned with the potential price volatility of the asset pair.

LPs can experience impermanent loss as tokens move away from the price balance.[9] Impermanent losses occur when LPs hold one token at a price below the market and another with a price above the market. As investors and arbitrageurs buy the undervalued token and sell the overvalued token, LPs may experience a temporary or impermanent loss. That loss is realized when the LP exits the liquidity pool during a time of unbalanced prices. The loss is avoided when the LP remains in the liquidity pool until the prices of the token pair return to the desired balance. Tokens with prices that are highly correlated and mean reverting are best for LPs, as the periods of impermanent loss will be short if the tokens return to the desired price relationship each day or each week.

There are dozens of DEXes where token pairs are trading at different prices. A DEX aggregator evaluates prices across a variety of DEXes to get the best price for an investor wishing to swap tokens. Aggregators are especially valuable for large trades that would move the price of a trading pair far from equilibrium if executed on a single DEX. By splitting the trade across multiple DEXes, the investor may be able to reduce their trade's impact on the price.

1Inch is a DEX aggregator that allows investors to execute their trade on different DEXes simultaneously or trade on a single DEX over a period of hours or days to minimize the market impact. A DEX aggregator also reduces gas fees by batching trades into a single transaction across multiple DEXes.

CHAPTER 12

Composability, Stacking DApps, and Bridges

While each blockchain was developed separately, there is great potential in sending information and value from one blockchain to another. Composability, stacking decentralized applications (DApps), and bridges can get complex quickly.

The first thing to understand is that every blockchain is different. The Ethereum blockchain is separate from the Bitcoin blockchain, the Solana blockchain is separate from the Cardano blockchain, and most blockchains don't natively interact with each other. Getting the bridges or addresses wrong can have serious consequences. An investor will lose their bitcoin by sending it to an Ethereum address; Ether or ERC-20 compatible tokens will be lost by sending them to a Bitcoin address.

Blockchains were designed for users to stay within a specific ecosystem without crossing over to different blockchains. Different assets are held on different blockchains, with even stablecoins like USDC actually becoming different assets when held on the Ethereum blockchain vs. Polygon.

Most blockchains are not natively interoperable. Everything has been designed to communicate within a specific blockchain community. Interoperability allows different blockchains to communicate with each other without the risk of losing value or data in the translation. If investors are able to move data and assets from one blockchain to another or from one DApp to another, more complex and interactive applications can be built.

Bridges can be designed to communicate and transfer assets and data between different blockchains. For example, a bridge can be used to hold a form of bitcoin in the Ethereum ecosystem, such as posting wrapped bitcoin as collateral in a DeFi DApp.

Much of the bridging activity has been designed to interact with the Ethereum blockchain. Given Ethereum's history of high gas fees, an entire ecosystem of layer 2 solutions has been designed to take advantage of its popularity and security while avoiding the expense of interacting with it. Many DeFi DApps are now compatible with Polygon, Arbitrum, Loopring, and Optimism. An investor pays gas fees to send and receive assets to and from the Ethereum blockchain. The investor can reduce gas fees by executing complex smart contract transactions on a layer 2 blockchain with greater scalability. After the DeFi transactions have been completed on a layer 2 compatible DApp, the transaction proceeds are saved back to the immutable and highly secure Ethereum blockchain.

In March 2024, DeFiLlama.com tracked $115 billion of TVL, including $64 billion on the Ethereum blockchain. Other chains with significant TVL include Tron ($10 billion), BSC ($7 billion), Solana ($5 billion), Arbitrum ($4 billion), with Polygon, Avalanche, and Optimism near $1 billion.

DApps such as Uniswap, Aave, SushiSwap, and Curve originated on Ethereum. With smart contracts written in Solidity and compatible with the EVM, these DeFi platforms and DEXes historically operated on the Ethereum blockchain. Due to the expense of running these DApps directly on Ethereum, many DeFi platforms are now available on alternate blockchains and layer 2 chains. For example, Aave is now compatible with 12 chains, with Uniswap (14), Curve (13), PancakeSwap (9), Balancer (7), and Compound (4), all offering multi-chain compatibility.

DeFiLlama.com notes that 990 DeFi protocols are compatible with the Ethereum blockchain. However, cheaper versions of many of those DApps are available on Arbitrum (563 DApps), Polygon (526 DApps), and Optimism (216 DApps). Outside of the Ethereum ecosystem, BSC lists 706 DApps, while Solana offers 131. Coinbase's Base Ethereum layer 2 solution, started in 2023, already has compatibility with 225 DApps.

Many blockchains have substantially greater bridged TVL than native TVL, showing that coins have been bridged or ported from one blockchain to be used or secured on another. Ethereum has native TVL of $64 billion and bridged TVL of $346 billion, with Tron ($10 billion/$64 billion), Solana ($5 billion/$19 billion), BSC ($7 billion/$17 billion), Arbitrum ($4 billion/$15 billion), and Polygon ($1 billion/$9 billion) all holding much larger bridged TVL than native TVL.

DeFi platforms can be used for borrowing or lending or for trading on a DEX. Trading on a DEX is non-custodial, meaning that the token swap is completed in seconds or minutes with the requested tokens returning immediately to the investor's wallet. Borrowing, lending, and yield farming are longer-term investment programs where the total yield earned increases with the time the tokens are locked into a trade.

While the Bitcoin and Ethereum blockchains are highly secure, they weren't originally designed to interact in a multi-chain world. Bridging bitcoin and Ether assets to other blockchains has encountered a number of security issues.

Bridges are an additional layer of software designed to provide bitcoin and Ether-like tokens on non-native blockchains. When bitcoin and Ether are bridged to another blockchain, the actual bitcoin and Ether tokens do not leave the native blockchain. Ether and bitcoin tokens are locked into a smart contract or held by a custodian in the bridge that serves as an escrow account. Sending Ether to the bridge returns newly minted wrapped Ether (wETH) tokens and sending bitcoin to a bridge returns newly minted wrapped bitcoin (wBTC) tokens. Wrapped bitcoin tokens are ERC-20 compatible tokens that can be used in DeFi DApps based on the Ethereum blockchain or any other blockchain compatible with the EVM. Wrapped bitcoin and wrapped Ether tokens can be returned to the bridge anytime in exchange for an equivalent number of native bitcoin or Ether tokens. Once the wrapped tokens have been exchanged for the native tokens, the wrapped tokens are burned or discarded and not reused. Wrapped tokens should be backed one-to-one with native tokens at all times.

Some of the biggest losses in crypto history have occurred when bridges or DeFi platform smart contracts have been exploited. Investors used the Wormhole bridge between Solana and Ethereum to receive wrapped Ether (WeETH) tokens for use on the Solana blockchain. Unfortunately, a programmer was able to exploit the Wormhole smart contract to allow for the minting of WeETH tokens without providing ETH tokens as collateral. This led to more WeETH tokens existing than were backed by ETH collateral. The hacker sold the WeETH tokens to investors and DeFi platforms that believed that they were fully backed by ETH collateral, causing $326 million in losses.

Similarly, $100 million was lost on Harmony's Horizon bridge and $600 million on the Ronin bridge from Ethereum to Axie Infinity. These incidents highlight that bridges can be one of the weaker links in the crypto world. While the Bitcoin and Ethereum blockchains are pretty well locked down and haven't been hacked, multiple incidents across different bridges have resulted in substantial losses.

An alternative approach is to build a blockchain environment that communicates across blockchains without bridges. Polkadot is a nominated proof-of-stake blockchain that operates a relay chain, which acts like a hub-and-spoke network to connect other blockchains. Through the hub of Polkadot, investors can move from one chain to another with data and tokens shared across chains.

Polkadot's Substrate tool assists in building new parachains that rely on Polkadot for speed and security. There is a limited number of chains that can be developed on Polkadot, which are sold through slot auctions. The winning bidder for a new chain slot may be assisted through a crowd loan, where users stake DOT tokens in exchange for tokens on the new chain. Once the auction is completed, the DOT tokens are paid to Polkadot as a fee for the new chain, and native tokens in the new chain are issued to the backers.

The new chain is called a parachain, which is not a stand-alone blockchain because it relies on the security and speed functionality provided by the Polkadot blockchain. The parachains sit on top of Polkadot and run their own smart contracts.

Kusama is an experimental platform that allows developers to build in a Polkadot-like environment with greater speed and lower cost.[1] It's important to be able to test a new blockchain without impacting the mainnet. The Kusama environment allows developers to build in a sandbox or test environment without risking affecting the Polkadot blockchain or any of the parachains.

One of the more successful projects from the Polkadot and Kusama ecosystem is Bittensor (TOR) which had reached a valuation of $4 billion by March 2024 from its launch in 2022 as a platform for the development and interaction of open-source machine learning and artificial intelligence models.[2] Astar connects the Polkadot ecosystem to Ethereum and Cosmos and assists developers in building new blockchains and smart contracts.[3]

Polkadot can also be used to bridge between permissioned (private) and permissionless (public) blockchains. Blockchains secure immutable records in a publicly accessible environment. A university student may have their academic records stored on a private blockchain that interacts with a smart contract on a public blockchain that can verify the degree awarded (year and major) without revealing the private details of the graduate's attendance, such as the grade point average.

A flight insurance application can be built on the Polkadot network.[4] This DApp interfaces with an oracle for flight schedules, IoT functionality to confirm that the insured passenger was at the airport, and an Ethereum smart contract that will pay the insured in DAI if and when the insured flight is delayed or canceled. The blockchains exchange data and value using multiple sources to provide a valuable financial service. The insurance might be purchased from a smart contract on the Polkadot blockchain, but the insurance settlement will be paid to a wallet on the Ethereum blockchain.

Avalanche and Cosmos, which were discussed in Chapter 6, have some of these cross-chain or multi-chain capabilities. Avalanche was designed with decentralized finance in mind. Trader Joe and Pangolin are Avalanche's native DEXes, which are compatible with Aave and Curve. Because Avalanche is compatible with the EVM, it is relatively straightforward to run Aave and Curve DApps on top of Avalanche.

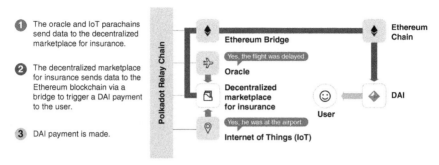

Source: https://polkadot.network/blog/polkadot-bridges-connecting-the-polkadot-ecosystem-with-external-networks

Cosmos, or Atom, is often called the "Internet of Blockchains" because it natively exchanges assets and data across 28 blockchains. The Cosmos protocol is designed as a hub-and-spoke network with the ability to interact with Osmosis or Crypto.com. Cosmos smart contracts written in Solidity are compatible with the EVM, while smart contracts written in Rust are compatible with the Solana blockchain.

One of the key applications built on Cosmos is THORChain, a proof-of-stake Cosmos-based blockchain that allows for cross-chain swaps.[5] Two of the key DeFi building blocks are decentralized exchanges and borrowing and lending platforms. Decentralized exchanges like Uniswap have a liquidity pool of tokens that allow for token swaps using an automated market-making system. DEXes swap one token for another without human intervention, while compensating liquidity providers who make the swaps possible.

THORSwap facilitates non-custodial swaps between Bitcoin, Ethereum, Binance Smart Chain, Avalanche, Cosmos, Litecoin, and Bitcoin Cash without creating wrapped or synthetic tokens. One side of each liquidity pool is THORChain's native token, RUNE. Swapping from bitcoin to Ether requires two swaps, first from bitcoin to RUNE and then from RUNE to Ether.

The settlement layer of the Bitcoin and Ethereum blockchains provides security and settlement of transactions, tracking the balance of bitcoin and ERC-20 tokens on an immutable distributed ledger.

Investors can hold Ether, ERC-20 fungible tokens, and ERC-721 non-fungible tokens (NFTs) on the Ethereum blockchain's asset layer. ERC-20 fungible tokens include Compound, Aave, Curve, and Chainlink, which power DeFi applications.

The protocol layer allows investors to use stacking DApps or money Legos. The DeFi DApps run smart contracts at the protocol layer, and the results of transactions are written to the settlement layer. DeFi DApps include exchanges, such as Balancer, Curve, and Uniswap, and borrowing and lending DApps, such as Compound and Aave. Each of these DApps can work together like Legos, where they are stacked on top of each other. An asset borrowed on Compound or Aave can be swapped using a DEX and settled on the Ethereum blockchain.

Stacking DApps, being interoperable, or using money Legos, allows investors to interchange pieces in any way they choose. Just as a stack of Lego bricks can be built in a large number of combinations, DApps can be built or used in many different ways. DApps can be combined in ways to concentrate liquidity, increase yield, and earn rewards for providing liquidity.

Rather than implementing all DeFi transactions and smart contracts directly on the layer 1 Ethereum blockchain with constrained capacity and high gas fees, investors can execute trades and smart contracts using layer 2 solutions that promise greater scalability and lower fees.

The concept of money Legos is facilitated through the use of open-source smart contracts. When the source code of smart contracts is disclosed, programmers can use application programming interfaces (APIs) and software development kits (SDKs) to easily connect various protocols. Programmers do not need to build new blockchains, as Ethereum, Solana, Avalanche, and others already provide the base layer functionality of settlement. Because functionality exists in a variety of DApps, programmers are freed to build only functionality that does not yet exist while accessing DApps or calling smart contract code that already exists. The ecosystem can grow more quickly and add new applications when programmers build on to the functionality that has already been built, tested, and attracted a significant user base.

Composability combines pieces from different smart contracts to create new services on top of existing applications or completely new applications. Code can be reused from smart contracts that have already been written. Sushiswap used the Uniswap code to build their own decentralized exchange rather than building a new DApp from scratch. While this makes it quick and efficient to build new DApps, it is difficult to protect intellectual property and create sustained competitive advantage in an environment that demands disclosure of the source code.

Because the current layer 1 blockchains are widely tested and trusted, there is little need today to replicate the standard plumbing and build a new blockchain.

The concept of composability allows investors to link DApps such as DEXes, decentralized autonomous organizations (DAOs), and borrowing and lending protocols together to create new financial opportunities. Any protocols within the same blockchain ecosystem, such as ERC-20 tokens and smart contracts compatible with the EVM, can be linked together.

When a number of DApps interoperate seamlessly, various tools can be built in different combinations. An investor can use Maker DAO to mint DAI stablecoins using Ether as collateral and reinvest the DAI on a platform such as Compound. The investor retains their exposure to the return to Ether while being able to simultaneously use a portion of the capital to reinvest in a DeFi platform.

Composability across DeFi platforms can facilitate yield farming or liquidity mining, which invests tokens across DeFi projects to maximize income subject to risk constraints. Investors can access borrowing and lending platforms such as Aave or Compound or contribute to liquidity pools on a DEX such as Uniswap, Curve, or Balancer.

Yearn.finance is a yield aggregator protocol that allows investors to maximize the yields earned on the liquidity provided to DeFi platforms.[6] Yearn deploys trading strategies contributed by users and money robots to automatically move investor assets across different DeFi platforms in search of higher yields.

New DeFi platforms may initially offer substantial incentives and high yields to attract liquidity providers and total value locked. Some yield farmers will move quickly to higher-yield platforms, while others take a more measured approach and remain with well-tested platforms. Investors can choose lower-risk or higher-risk yield farming strategies on the Yearn platform.

Remember that risk and reward in financial markets are closely linked. Lower-risk strategies should earn lower annualized returns, such as 2% to 6%, depending on the level of sovereign debt yields in G7 countries. DeFi protocols offering yields of 19.5% or 195% APY are not risk-free, as investors were painfully reminded by the 2022 collapse of Luna and Terra USD. Platforms may offer high yields denominated in the protocol's native token, which may increase the outstanding supply of the token. If the token supply rises faster than the financial prospects of the protocol, dilution can result, driving down the value of each token through the excess supply. The highest APY offers typically pay the yield for a period much shorter than one year, result in excess dilution, or subject investors to substantial risks.

Money robots, such as Yearn, constantly search the DeFi universe for arbitrage opportunities, such as the ability to borrow at 3% on one platform and lend at 4% on another. Users need to evaluate the risks of each platform, as earning yield differences requires long-term investments on each platform. Before implementing an investment strategy on a yield aggregation platform, investors should seek to quantify the gas fee associated with investing across Ethereum-based platforms and the tax liabilities if tokens are bought and sold in a timing that generates short-term capital gains taxes. Given that a single $1 million transaction may incur similar gas fees as a $1,000 transaction, yield aggregators that combine the capital in each transaction across investors may reduce the gas fee paid relative to those incurred if similar trades were implemented by a single investor. Gas fees are based on the complexity of the smart contract and the number of transactions, not the number of tokens or the value of the transaction. When assets are pooled across the depositors in the yield farming pool, the gas fees are amortized across a much larger number of depositors, reducing gas fees as a percentage of assets.

Gemini provides an example of the yield farming process,[7] where a circular process moves money across DeFi protocols. The idea of yield farming is that money is always moving around and goes where it will be most appreciated.

- ETH is deposited to MakerDAO as collateral
- DAI is borrowed from MakerDAO using the deposited ETH as collateral
- Pay borrow fee on DAI and keep economic exposure to ETH
- The borrowed DAI is deposited to the yDAI vault on Yearn
- The yDAI vault deposits DAI to Curve in order to earn fees
- The liquidity provider token generated from the DAI pool is staked in Curve to earn the CRV token
- The CRV tokens are sold for ETH
- ETH is deposited back to MakerDAO as collateral (back to first step)

Before investing in a DeFi platform, investors are encouraged to investigate the custody risk, the smart contract risk, and the dilution risk of each platform.

Curve is a decentralized exchange where liquidity providers lock tokens to earn a yield.[8] By holding similar assets, such as stablecoins, in a liquidity pool, Curve seeks to avoid the issue of impermanent loss. LPs are paid a portion of the trading fees generated by facilitating trades for platform users desiring token swaps. LPs may stake DAI into the Curve DEX and receive Curve tokens as compensation for providing liquidity. Curve tokens can be sold for DAI, which allows LPs to reinvest their proceeds in an attempt to compound returns.

A yield aggregation protocol such as Yearn simplifies yield farming, which can be complex and error-prone for investors seeking to complete each step independently, not to mention the gas fees paid for each transaction implemented directly on an Ethereum-based DeFi platform.

Curve seeks to concentrate liquidity onto a single platform, reducing trading costs for large trades. The probability of impermanent loss is reduced by concentrating on assets of similar risk in each liquidity pool, swapping stablecoins in one pool and bitcoin and wrapped bitcoin in another pool.

Synthetix is a derivatives protocol that creates synthetic assets tracking the value of stocks and other assets. There is a synthetic Tesla, synthetic gold, a synthetic S&P 500, and synthetic versions of different cryptocurrencies. The investor locks Synthetix (SNX) or Ether tokens as collateral into the Synthetix protocol. Subject to some degree of required over-collateralization, investors can mint any asset of their choosing, as long as an oracle such as Chainlink has reliable access to pricing information. If Chainlink has access to the price of Tesla stock, Synthetix users can mint an ERC-20 compatible token tied to the price of Tesla stock.

Investors can also choose to mint tokens tracked by a basket of assets, perhaps building an index fund of a number of cryptocurrencies. Rather than buying dozens or hundreds of individual cryptocurrencies individually, an investor simply creates a synthetic token that tracks the value of the portfolio. Synthetic tokens are not backed by the underlying asset, so investors owning synthetic Tesla tokens do not own Tesla stock. No Tesla stock is locked into a smart contract guaranteeing the token's value. The value of the token is backed by the SNX or ETH locked into the over-collateralized contract.

1Inch Network offers a DEX aggregator solution that searches prices on more than 500 liquidity sources across 12 different layer 1 and layer 2 chains.[9] Especially useful for large trades, 1Inch can split a trade across multiple DEXes to speed the time or reduce the cost to complete a large trade. By combining prices across multiple liquidity sources, investors may be able to trade more cheaply than when concentrating their trading on a single exchange.

1Inch offers a smart contract that provides security against losses due to unsafe DEXes and runs an AMM that can protect users from front-running. Front-running is when other investors see a large buy order and race to purchase the token in anticipation that the large order will push the price higher. Atomic transactions are the key to providing security against unsafe DEXes, as a transaction will fail rather than sending a token to a DEX and not receiving the appropriate value in return. An atomic transaction either happens in its entirety or not at all. Whenever you're looking across this many Lego pieces to combine, you want to make sure that all of them are hard plastic with the three holes that allow you to build something that's strong together because it's only as weak as its weakest link. The more links are combined, the more attention needs to be paid toward security.

In addition to searching a specific trading pair for the best price, 1Inch can also evaluate whether prices would improve by trading more than one pair to reach the desired ultimate swap. For example, it might not be efficient to trade Ether directly for Trader Joe tokens. Because Trader Joe is a native DEX on the Avalanche blockchain, it might be more efficient to trade Ether for Avalanche and then trade Avalanche for Trader Joe tokens.

1Inch searches multiple paths of arbitrage and trading pairs to minimize the cost of completing the desired swap. This is a complex operation, as prices are compared across 500 DEXes across 12 different blockchains.

Stacking DApps, DEXes, money Legos, composability, and bridges provide many opportunities for investors and programmers. Due to the complexity, investors must be vigilant to diligence and protect against smart contract failures and exploits of brand-new smart contracts. With great power comes great responsibility.

CHAPTER 13

Blockchain Applications Beyond Financial Markets

Blockchain and digital ledger technology applications to financial markets were the key early focus, as evidenced by the title of the Bitcoin white paper "Bitcoin: A Peer-to-Peer Electronic Cash System." This book extensively discusses money transfers, DeFi, borrowing, lending, and securities markets. However, the applications of blockchain technology extend far beyond financial markets.

A distributed ledger's key characteristic is moving data storage from centralized to decentralized counterparties, seeking to eliminate the risk of a single point of failure. To the extent that a peer-to-peer network can be built to eliminate intermediaries, reduced costs and increased efficiencies will likely result.

A key use of blockchain technology is verifying personal identity. Consumers must repeat the KYC process each time they open a new financial account. This time-consuming process requires disclosing a consumer's birth date, address, driver's license, and passport, among other information, which is all stored by the provider of each account. Proving identity is also required every time a consumer accesses a secured account on the internet, which today is largely accomplished through the use of passwords and usernames.

The promise of blockchain is to complete the KYC process once and store the results in a blockchain wallet. The consumer simply unlocks the wallet using their private key whenever credentials need to be verified. Not only does this save time for consumers and businesses, but it also exposes personally identifiable information (PII) to much fewer counterparties. Because a consumer's sensitive information is not stored by multiple unrelated counterparties, there is less risk of exposing this data in a cybersecurity incident.

The identity verification will take place on a permissionless blockchain verified using the consumer's private key. This would allow the consumer to interact anywhere on the internet with a verified identity without using a unique username and password at each site. Credit card details would not be saved at each site, as a consumer's crypto wallet can be used for purchases. The consumer can choose how their data is stored and used.

Companies must comply with Europe's Global Data Protection Regulation (GDPR) and the California Consumer Privacy Act whenever storing the PII of consumers residing in those domiciles. These regulations impose significant penalties for any disclosure or misuse of this personal information. Companies are also required to delete a consumer's information upon request.

Centralized systems storing PII are known as honey pots, which are attractive targets for hackers. Cybercriminals who can successfully attack a bank, insurance company, or healthcare company may get access to information on thousands or millions of consumers in a single breach. If consumers use the same password on multiple websites, the breach allows for access to multiple accounts. It's extraordinarily important to use unique passwords for each individual financial account and ensure that passwords used on financial accounts are not reused on other internet accounts. Security protocols at websites requiring registration, such as a newspaper, might not be nearly as strong as those employed at a bank. Consumers reusing passwords on multiple websites are trusting the information stored at all of those sites to the single site with the weakest security protocols.

Email and cell phone passwords should also be treated with the greatest diligence, as those accounts are used for two-factor authentication that might provide access to reset passwords for financial accounts.

Private keys for identity wallets can be stored locally by each consumer rather than on a centralized server. Local storage of keys requires hacking consumers one at a time, dramatically increasing the effort required to access personal accounts. Rather than having passwords and a username for each website, consumers can deploy a single identity wallet providing access to all of their personal accounts. Identity is proven at each website by connecting the identity wallet.

The identity wallet allows consumers to have a single strong username and password for all of their accounts and online interactions without disclosing the private key. Rather than breaching millions of accounts simultaneously, hackers are forced to breach user accounts one at a time, which is less economically feasible. Users need to be familiar with phishing techniques, which are often attempted by sending emails that wallet credentials and private keys need to be reset or verified, which, of course, is not true.

Identity wallets can also include personal information such as a passport or the verification of a college degree. Credentials that can be globally recognized or verified can be developed, reducing the risk of consumers presenting a fake passport or driver's license that may be unfamiliar to authorities in foreign countries. This technology can reduce identity theft, corruption, double spending, fake credentials, and counterfeiting, making the global economy safer.

NFTs are non-fungible tokens that can be unique and non-interchangeable. Many investors think of NFTs as digital art pictures, such as the series of 10,000 unique Bored Ape Yacht Club drawings. People are non-fungible, with unique birthdays, Social Security or national identification numbers, academic records, and health records. These unique identifiers that will not change over a person's lifetime can be saved as NFTs called soul-bound tokens that cannot be bought, sold, traded, or modified. New information can be added, but all information previously held in the soul-bound token will be immutably stored on a blockchain.

Some information about a consumer's life, such as a home address or phone number, is not immutable. This information will not be saved in the soul-bound token, as the address and phone number will be transferred to others after the consumer has changed their own coordinates.

Every graduate worked hard to be admitted to a university and to earn their degree. Universities with rigorous admissions requirements want to ensure applicants provide accurate information regarding their test scores and secondary school records. It is important that degrees and professional credentials, such as those qualifying attorneys and medical doctors, can be verified as accurate. Academic records can be stored on blockchains in an immutable and publicly verifiable manner that is not subject to manipulation or counterfeiting.

Blockchains are designed to reduce reliance on centralized counterparties. Between 2004 and 2021, 15% of all US colleges closed or merged operations.[1] That trend may accelerate starting in 2025, as fertility rates declined by 7% from 2007 to 2009, as many families delayed childbearing because they were afraid of losing their homes in the GFC.[2] The slowing number of births in 2009 means that there will be fewer 18-year-olds seeking college admissions in 2027, accelerating the financial pressures on universities already struggling financially.

Graduates may be concerned about their ability to verify their degree after a college closes its doors and the registrar's office is no longer in business. A distributed ledger containing college degrees could be used to ensure that everyone who claims to have a degree indeed has one. This ledger would be immutable and secure. A college could contribute its academic records to this distributed database before it closes down, allowing graduates to publicly verify degrees earned from a college or university that no longer exists.

A consumer's digital identity can also contain healthcare records.[3] Currently, those records might be distributed across various pharmacies, doctor's offices, and hospitals concentrated near the consumer's home. These records may not be easily transferrable outside of the patient's current doctor network. The ability to immediately access healthcare records globally could be the difference between life and death when someone experiences a medical emergency far from their home. While traveling globally, a consumer could easily share a digital wallet of healthcare information with a new doctor or hospital in order to quickly facilitate an appropriate treatment plan.

Medical records are very private information that are protected in the US by HIPAA, a regulation that prevents the disclosure of healthcare records to unauthorized parties. Perhaps records will be held on a permissioned blockchain with access limited to authorized healthcare providers. The patient would also have access to their own records and could provide their identity wallet to facilitate emergency treatment. Verifying identity using a blockchain wallet can prevent healthcare fraud by ensuring the identity of the patient being treated.

Blockchains can also facilitate the sharing of information on clinical trials and medical research. By publicly disclosing genomics and cancer research information, global researchers can work together to increase the number of test subjects and move toward improving global healthcare outcomes.

Supply chain management and logistics is a large and complicated global business. Consider the portion of global merchandise trade that crosses national borders. Large vessels with hundreds of shipping containers regularly travel from Asia to the US or Europe and back again. These shipments, worth tens of millions of dollars, involve a complicated chain of custody and require shipment verifications and payments across countries and currencies.

IoT devices can be used in conjunction with blockchain technology to locate the precise location of goods in transit. Businesses ordering goods from global suppliers want to make sure they receive their complete order, while the shipper wants to get paid for the goods as quickly as possible.

Consider the potential of smart contracts to revolutionize the shipping industry. When the goods are shipped, the buyer locks funds sufficient to purchase the items into a smart contract. Each shipping container would contain a unique smart contract–enabled bar code. Once the shipment arrives, the buyer inspects the contents and verifies that the entire shipment has been received without damage. By scanning the bar code and confirming the shipment has been received, the buyer releases the funds held in the smart contract, and the seller receives payment on the same day. Imagine the efficiency gains of smart contract–enabled payments compared to sending cross-border payments using the banker's acceptance market.

Blockchain tracking can assist with logistics, knowing the location of goods in time, perhaps speeding up those shipments. Tracking shipments can also improve quality control and food safety. There are regular issues that threaten the health of people consuming foods that may be tainted, such as lettuce or chicken. Previously, the only solution was to discard a large quantity of the food items, as it was difficult to track specific goods to their origin. Tracking the provenance of goods using blockchain technology can prevent these expensive sweeping recalls while still maintaining public health by being able to target the recall to a specific farm or distributor where the unsafe food has been located and tracked.

Each shipping container or pallet of food has a smart contract–enabled barcode that is scanned each time it reaches a new location or checkpoint. Once people report foodborne illnesses, the location data is used to quickly isolate the specific supply chain where the illness originated. Tracking the illness to specific farms or pallets allows targeted recalls, preventing the expensive disposal of food unrelated to the current health issue.

NFTs can also be used to verify the authenticity of luxury goods, a sector that is subject to frequent counterfeiting.[4] Louis Vuitton and Christian Dior now verify product authenticity using NFTs. Immutable records of the provenance and current ownership of each handbag are stored as an NFT. Luxury goods that are verified to be authentic will be better able to retain their value, while it will be more difficult to sell counterfeited goods at high prices.

Government records must be immutable and transparent. Property rights, such as being able to prove and transfer ownership of a home, are the key to building wealth in a family and in a country. Citizens need to be able to authenticate their birth certificate, passport, driver's license, and title to homes and automobiles. Voting systems need to be auditable and ensure that each voter is eligible and casts only one ballot.

Passports, driver's licenses, and birth certificates can be issued as soul-bound NFTs, which can be immediately verifiable using a code displayed on the user's smartphone. The consumer's identity wallet would contain all of this information, reducing the impact of losing a paper passport or driver's license.

Transferring and securing the title to real estate and automobiles can be streamlined using blockchain technology, reducing fraud and speeding transactions.

The cost of administering government documents and spending can be made more efficient and secure. Government benefits payments can be made to blockchain wallets, reducing costs and increasing security for the previously unbanked population.

The world is uncertain. Many people would like to be able to predict the outcome of an election, the Oscars, financial markets, or sporting events. James Surowiecki's book *The Wisdom of Crowds* notes that the collective opinion of a crowd is typically much more accurate than the opinion of even the smartest person in the crowd. The crowd's wisdom becomes even stronger when the group is diverse and decentralized, a perfect application for blockchain technology.

Blockchain protocols Augur, Gnosis, and Polymarket are prediction markets that provide financial incentives for the crowd to express their opinions. In a prediction market, contracts are listed, encouraging investors to express their opinions on the outcomes of events. Bettors lock value into a smart contract, with payments received after the oracle confirms the outcome of each event.

Contracts covering events that occur may pay $1 after the event, while events that do not take place may pay $0. The price of each contract can be viewed as the crowd's best estimate of the probability of the event's outcome. Investors believing that a specific outcome has a greater probability will buy the contract, while those believing the outcome has a lesser probability will sell the contract. The aggregated predictions of a crowd become more accurate when people bet real money (or real crypto) on the outcome of an event, giving an incentive for the most informed participants to reveal their true opinions. For example, betting markets correctly predicted 17 of the 23 winners at the March 2024 Academy Awards.

Prediction markets can benefit even those who do not trade the contracts by reducing the uncertainty surrounding specific events. Knowing the most likely outcome of an election may allow investors to better position portfolios to increase profits or reduce risks.

Blockchain technology can also facilitate and analyze charitable donations. Charities do good work for causes including healthcare, education, religion, humanitarian services, and improving the inclusion of underrepresented groups. Charities may be able to increase their fundraising efforts by accepting donations of cryptocurrencies and digital assets. Donations of digital assets can be tracked and recorded on the blockchain, increasing transparency and trust.

The most efficient charities spend the vast majority of their income on furthering their stated cause. Charities proving they are good stewards of donations may become more trusted, potentially increasing the amount of donations received. Charitywatch.org rates the efficiency of charities, with those allocating more than 80% of expenses to the charitable cause earning a grade of "A," with those spending more than 50% on fundraising and administrative expenses receiving grades of "D" or "F."[5] Donors care not only about the total allocation of expenses but also the compensation of the charity's leaders. It is not ideal when the CEO of a charity focused on alleviating poverty earns a total annual compensation of more than $1 million, even when other expense ratios are well rated.

Alice.si uses blockchains to track the social impact of charitable projects and to distribute benefits payments to those supported by charities.[6]

Bitcoin miners use a substantial amount of electricity and seek to reduce energy expenses to the greatest possible extent. Energy efficiency is facilitated by smart meters that verify how much electricity is used at a given location at a given period of time. Traditional electric meters report usage over long periods of time, such as a monthly billing cycle, while smart meters can track usage by day and time of day. Bitcoin miners might agree to an interruptible electricity contract that would cut off their access to electricity during times of peak demand in exchange for lower electricity prices. Miners may be willing to shut down their rigs at peak times to earn a substantial discount on their electric bill. Texas is the home to many Bitcoin miners who may be attracted to the incentives to reduce consumption at targeted times.[7] It is important to understand that generated electricity typically cannot be stored and must be used immediately, so Bitcoin miners add value to an electric grid when using excess capacity when solar panels and wind farms are producing more electricity than needed by the network.

Power plants avoid overloads during times of peak demand when the electric company requests the shutdown of Bitcoin mining rigs. Bitcoin miners can use more electricity at times of lower demand and less electricity during times of peak demand, leveling the load on power plants over the course of the day and the year. Peak demand typically comes during times of extreme weather, when electricity usage spikes to provide for cooling or heating needs, especially during the work week when industrial users are at full capacity.

Blockchains can facilitate peer-to-peer electricity trading and automatic trade settlement for traders who must sell electricity before it is wasted.[8]

Renewable energy certificates (RECs) are tradable proof that electricity has been generated from renewable sources. RECs are governmental subsidies awarded to owners of newly constructed renewable energy facilities, such as solar farms or wind farms.

Carbon credits are sold by industrial users who reduce their carbon emissions and purchased by users who emit more than their regulatory limit. Blockchains are very good at avoiding the double spending problem and can be used to ensure that carbon credits and renewable energy certificates are used only once. Buyers want to ensure that they only purchase credits that have not been previously used. Buyers of credits may use them to offset their own pollution or not use them to reduce the total pollution in a country or region.

Ticketing would be much more efficient if artists, teams, and venues were to sell tickets directly to fans. Cutting out Ticketmaster as an intermediary is a desired goal for fans and artists alike, as the ticket seller often charges fees in excess of the cost of the ticket. Event tickets are ripe for disruption by the blockchain, as tickets could be minted as NFTs. When tickets are sold as NFTs, the venue, team, or artist knows who bought the ticket as well as who used the ticket. A person who buys and uses a ticket is a verified fan who might be targeted by the team or artist as a loyal fan. A person who buys and resells a ticket may be identified as a ticket scalper or reseller who might find it more difficult to purchase tickets in the future. Electronic tickets are easier to transfer and easier to reuse than paper tickets in case an event is rescheduled.

A smart contract ticketing algorithm can increase the ability of true fans to purchase tickets while reducing the ability of scalpers to buy tickets. When tickets are resold by the original purchaser, the smart contract could pay a portion of the resale price to the artist or venue, reducing the portion of the total proceeds paid to the reseller.

Advertising is big business. Businesses spend advertising budgets to reach consumers where they spend time. Ad spending previously focused on newspapers and television but has more recently moved to the internet, social media, and even blockchain-based Metaverses. Ideally, the advertiser pays to reach people most likely to purchase their good or service and doesn't pay to reach consumers who are unlikely to purchase.

Blockchains provide transparency and offer benefits of removing intermediaries, avoiding fraud and double spending. Websites earn advertising revenues for each time a consumer views or interacts with an advertisement. Website owners like to earn advertising revenue, while advertisers desire a direct link back to the consumer to maximize the cost-efficiency of their advertising budget.[9]

Unfortunately, some websites participate in click fraud, where bots and click farms generate advertising revenue to websites without providing value to advertisers. Some websites will charge for ads the size of a single pixel that consumers will never be able to see. This fraud provides revenue to websites without directing consumer attention to the advertiser.

Blockchain solutions can eliminate these inefficiencies and reduce intermediaries, reduce fraud, and determine the most efficient advertising locations. Advertisers wish to spend more of their budget on ads that effectively increase consumer attention and spend less on ineffective advertising. Centralized Web 2.0 companies, such as Facebook/Meta and Google/Alphabet, use cookies and other methods to customize advertising to specific consumers. Because consumers don't pay fees to use these services, their data is monetized to create revenue for these large Web 2.0 firms.

Web 3.0 and the blockchain economy believe that data belongs to the individual who can choose to keep it private or monetize it. Users of the Brave web browser experience enhanced privacy that prevents cookies and tracking of consumer behavior. Consumers are given control of the ads they view, and are rewarded with Basic Attention Tokens (BAT) for viewing those ads.

Blockchain technology, which provides decentralized and secure data storage and communications, broadly applies across industries. Blockchains are designed to be more secure, less hackable, solve the double-spending problem, and give consumers more control over their identity and their data. While Web 2.0 companies seek to keep the economics of consumer interaction to themselves, Web 3.0 seeks to enhance consumer choice, independence, and privacy.

CHAPTER 14

NFTs, Metaverse, and Web 3.0

Fungible items are identical and interchangeable. There's no difference between one bitcoin and another or one Ether token and another. Dollar bills, ounces of 24-karat gold, and barrels of light sweet crude oil are all fungible. Fungible items can be mixed together or divided for sale. You can spend a bitcoin or a dollar bill and get change.

Non-fungible items are unique and identifiable, with differences in design, quality, rarity, or condition. For example, real estate is non-fungible, with every house differing in its location and condition. Non-fungible items typically need to be sold in their entirety. Investors don't typically sell half of a house or a non-fungible token (NFT). Non-fungible items are unique, often with personalization or a serial number. Soul-bound tokens can contain data on an individual's identity, including a passport, birth certificate, and educational credentials.

The ownership of both fungible and non-fungible tokens can be tracked and transferred on the Ethereum blockchain. Fungible tokens on the Ethereum blockchain are minted under the ERC-20 standard, while NFTs are minted under the ERC-721 standard. NFTs are minted or created by smart contracts, which also govern secondary trading and proof of ownership. The ownership of each NFT is tracked on the blockchain, similar to how the ownership of fungible tokens is tracked.

To date, the majority of traded NFTs have been related to art, music, and video games. Blockchains maintain and process distributed ledgers with immutable data. The immutable data stored on-chain is the minting date, the ownership history, and the internet location where the sound or image is stored. While the blockchain may store the code used to generate electronic art, computer files containing sound or images can be very large and are typically not stored directly on the blockchain. A key risk of NFT investing is that the sound and image storage at off-chain URLs is not necessarily eternal and immutable. While the blockchain immutably stores a link to the internet location of the sound or image, the website may be maintained by a centralized counterparty that may not be able to guarantee that the link will be eternal and immutable. Simply forgetting to pay to renew the website may cause a loss of the images and sound related to NFTs.

Investors must understand that they are simply buying ownership of a link to an image, a song, or a gaming item. In most cases, owning an NFT does not include the copyright or physical possession of the depicted item. Purchasing a traditional painting or art piece does not necessarily give the buyer the copyright to use that image.

In the traditional art market before 1948, the artist was previously only paid when the image was originally sold. In 1948, the International Berne Convention recognized the right of artists to profit from secondary sales.[1] The UK implemented the Artist's Resale Right provision in 2006, with up to 4% paid on the resale value of fine art during the artist's lifetime and for 70 years thereafter.[2] Royalties are typically not paid to artists in the US, as a 2018 court ruling overturned the California Resale Royalties Act and stated that art is governed by US copyright law.[3] Proceeds of secondary sales at US auctions or galleries are split between the seller and the selling venue without any royalties paid to the original artist.

Some NFT smart contracts pay royalties to the creative team on all future sales. The creative team may draw each NFT by hand or build generative NFTs with artificial intelligence or traditional computer coding. For users willing to pay gas fees, Goblintown and CryptoPunks NFTs were originally given away for free, while the initial price of Bored Ape Yacht Club (BAYC) NFTs was just 0.08 Ether. By March 2024, the trading volume of these three collections of 10,000 pictures was $100 million, $2.8 billion, and $3.1 billion, respectively.[4] Creators earning a 10% royalty on each sale of the most successful collections may be able to earn millions of dollars annually for many years after the project's launch. Owners of these NFTs have also profited, as BAYC and CryptoPunks NFTs are currently priced from $40,000 to $200,000 or more.

An NFT is minted when it is sold for the first time. An NFT project announces a minting date and a limited run, perhaps of 10,000 unique or numbered images. Collectors may find it difficult to secure a newly minted NFT when there is high demand for a limited-edition image. Collectors need to pay gas fees to place an order for an NFT, whether their purchase is successful or not. When the order is placed, the collector sends tokens, such as Ether or Solana, to a smart contract which will determine which orders will be fulfilled. After the minting process is complete, the collector either receives the NFT or a refund of their purchase price less gas fees. Some collectors may pay extra gas fees to incentivize the blockchain validators to immediately process the transaction in the next block, effectively moving to the front of the line.

Collectors who are not able to purchase an NFT in the primary market during the minting period have the option to buy it in the secondary market from a seller who successfully minted it. The original buyer can profit if the NFT has risen in price net of gas fees. Collectors may be able to purchase the NFT in the secondary market at a lower price than during the minting period. Collectors minting NFTs need to be cognizant of gas fees, which tend to spike during times of peak activity.

The Chainalysis NFT Market report states that the most profitable NFT collectors have been whitelisted.[5] Whitelisted buyers are more likely to profit than non-whitelisted buyers, as they are guaranteed a chance to purchase the NFT during a presale period when gas fees are much lower. Collectors are able to be whitelisted on an NFT project by building a relationship with the creator of the NFT. The creator may offer to sell 10,000 NFTs while reserving the first 1,000 for collectors who follow them on Twitter/X or have engaged with them in a Discord or Telegram group. The Chainalysis report details trading volume, whitelist status, and diversification strategies of profitable and unprofitable NFT traders.

The Bitcoin blockchain has historically been used to store and transfer fungible bitcoin tokens. Each bitcoin is divisible into 100 million Satoshis, with each Satoshi identified using an ordinal number assigned at the time of minting.[6] Inscriptions on Satoshis called ordinals were introduced to the Bitcoin blockchain in January 2023 and rose to 42% of all NFT volume by year end.[7] Ordinals inscribe messages on a Satoshi, changing that small value of fungible bitcoin to something unique. The Bitcoin blockchain does not support the use of smart contracts, so Bitcoin ordinals are described as digital artifacts and not NFTs as the data or images stored are attachments to or modifications of bitcoin tokens. Users owning Satoshis as inscriptions may wish to collect them as NFTs, but can still spend them as fungible bitcoin tokens. Many of the Bitcoin ordinals launched in 2023 mimicked popular NFT collections, such as Bitcoin Rocks, Bitcoin Punks, and Pixel Pepes, but Bitcoin-specific images are now being created.[8] Investors may wish to inspect their fungible bitcoin to see if it has been inscribed, as a Bitcoin rock ordinal sold for almost three bitcoin in November 2023,[9] 300 million times the value of the Satoshi it was inscribed on.

Bitcoin ordinals can be controversial, as bitcoin purists may wish the blockchain remained solely for storing and transferring fungible bitcoin tokens.

NFTs are a lucrative and popular portion of the digital asset business. While CryptoPunks were minted in 2017, the 2021 launch of Bored Ape Yacht Club NFTs helped to create explosive growth in NFT prices and volume. Consumers spent more than $24.7 billion on NFTs in 2021 and $25.2 billion in 2022, while falling to $12.5 billion in 2023.

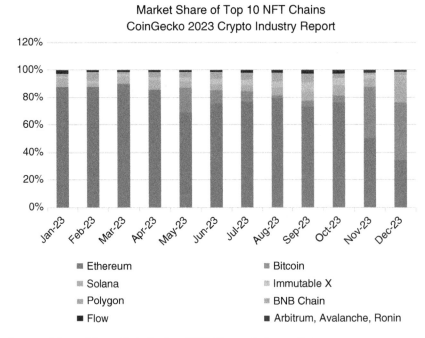

Market Share of Top 10 NFT Chains
CoinGecko 2023 Crypto Industry Report

Ethereum · Bitcoin · Solana · Immutable X · Polygon · BNB Chain · Flow · Arbitrum, Avalanche, Ronin

Source: Adapted from CoinGecko, 2023 Crypto Industry Report.

Before 2023, most NFTs were minted on the Ethereum blockchain, with market share originating at more than 95%. Gas fees for minting and transferring NFTs on Ethereum can be expensive, so market share grew as NFTs started trading on alternate blockchains with lower gas fees, such as Flow, Solana, and Polygon.[10] Ethereum's market share remained above 85% until April 2023, as Bitcoin ordinals exploded to 18.3% of all NFTs minted in May 2023 before rising to more than 42% by December 2023.[11]

DappRadar[12] tracks the largest NFT marketplaces. In February 2024, $646 million of NFTs traded on the Blur marketplace, while Magic Eden, OKX NFT Marketplace, and OpenSea all traded more than $100 million in the same month. A key risk of investing in digital asset businesses is how quickly upstart projects can replace market leaders, as OpenSea previously had dominant market share trading Ethereum-based NFTs. Blur reached its dominant market share quickly, as the marketplace was launched in October 2022. Blur focuses on Ethereum-based NFTs, while OpenSea supports trading of NFTs on Ethereum and Ethereum-related blockchains, such as Polygon, Arbitrum, and Optimism, among others. Magic Eden facilitates NFT trading on Solana, Polygon, Ethereum, and Bitcoin.

To demonstrate how quickly NFTs captured the imagination of both consumers and policymakers, the World Economic Forum published a 2021 report noting the requirements for NFTs to go mainstream.[13] NFTs can gain mass distribution by resolving five challenges:

- Authenticity: Tracking the artist and guaranteeing a limited supply
- Scalability: Processing NFT mints and secondary trading with low fees and congestion
- Interoperability: Allowing NFTs to be used across blockchains
- Storage: NFTs only maintain their value if they can be accessed forever without a loss of the hosting website
- Accessibility: Consumers find it easy to buy, sell, and hold NFTs

That is, the killer app of blockchains likely requires a user interface where consumers do not know they are using a blockchain. If accessing NFTs and other digital assets is as easy as using a smartphone app, consumer adoption can grow substantially. If user interfaces are difficult, mass adoption is unlikely. The easier and cheaper it becomes to access blockchain technology, the broader the consumer usage will be.

The main categories of NFTs today are art, music, and gaming. However, the larger long-run uses for NFTs will likely be for real-world assets (RWAs), such as tickets and real estate.

NFT art can be hand-drawn or computer-generated. Hand-drawn art pieces must be digitized before being sold as NFTs.

Computer programming, artificial intelligence, and smart contracts can be used to build generative art. One of the more famous generative art projects is the Bored Ape Yacht Club. Computer code generated the 10,000 Bored Apes by alternating their characteristics, such as background color, hats, facial expressions, clothing, and whether their eyes are open, closed, or shooting lasers. Each trait is randomly assigned to each ape, with some traits being rarer than others. The apes with the rarest or most desirable characteristics may be the most valuable.

Music is another interesting area of NFTs. Bands can release music with limited distribution and restrictions that the music is not publicly performed or redistributed. Buyers of the NFT may wish to prove that they are among the band's 1,000 most loyal fans and have an experience unavailable to others. The band could also track the wallets holding those NFTs to offer additional exclusive experiences or merchandise, either as NFTs or in real life.

Consider the NFT project called Generative Masks.[14] This collection generated 10,000 NFTs, each varying by the mask's color, shape, the number of circles and triangles, and so on. Visitors to the generativemasks.com website can use an interactive tool to type in the serial number to see the image of the NFT with that specific serial number.

The ownership history of each Generative Mask stored on the Ethereum blockchain can be viewed on Etherscan.io. Masks 3959 and 3960 were purchased in a single transaction on 17 August 2021 for the price of 0.2 Ether each at a time when each Ether token cost $3,011.96 plus transaction fees of $15.11. Transactions for mask 3959 can be tracked through time, showing that it was sold four days after minting for 0.4 Ether. The sending address, the receiving address, and the minting address are all tracked on the Ethereum blockchain.

DappRadar lists the top NFT projects by trading volume in February 2024.[15] BAYC and CryptoPunks continue to be the most valuable and actively traded, many years after their launch. Notice that NFTs often trade in themes or families, with BAYC spawning Mutant Ape Yacht Club, and Pudgy Penguins and Lil Pudgys both in the top 10 for the month. While top collections can trade $23 to $81 million in volume in a month, the majority of NFTs will never be profitable for their owners after accounting for transaction costs. This report also notes that approximately one million wallets interacted with NFT marketplaces on the average day in February 2024 (average daily wallet usage).

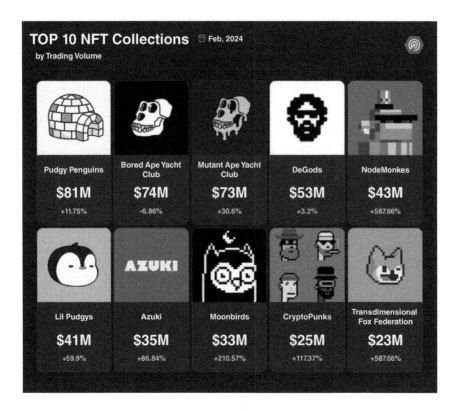

Two of the most expensive NFTs are CryptoPunks and Bored Ape Yacht Club, both generative art NFTs numbered to 10,000. Many owners use these NFTs as profile pictures (PFPs) on social media. Not only does the use of an NFT as a PFP show the owner's social media connections their interest in NFTs, it is also a symbol of wealth. Recent floor prices, the lowest cost to purchase one of the NFTs currently for sale, were $170,000 for CryptoPunks and $46,000 for BAYC in March 2024. Using an NFT as a PFP discloses the owner's public wallet address, as the image can be matched to the NFT number, which can be matched to the wallet where the NFT was most recently transferred. The record price for a Bored Ape was $3.4 million while the highest price achieved by a CryptoPunk was $11.8 million. Remember the original cost of these NFTs was less than $200 each.

The purchase of a Bored Ape NFT comes with much more than ownership of a link to a digital image. The Bored Ape Yacht Club is actually a club with real-life events with other owners including Snoop Dogg, Jimmy Fallon, and other celebrities. Showing the NFT in a crypto wallet is the admission ticket to the real-world event. Those who own these NFTs have proven their wealth, or they were into crypto for some time and were savvy or lucky enough to have purchased or minted the NFT at a much lower price.

Purchases of art and NFTs typically do not include the copyright to the image. However, owners of Bored Apes are granted intellectual property rights to the artwork. Images of Bored Apes are used to sell consumer items such as t-shirts and Adidas shoes.[16] Owners using their NFTs to build a business must be careful to secure their NFT, because if it is sold or stolen, they no longer have the rights to use the image to sell their products.

Believe it or not, the record price for a CryptoPunks pixelated mask NFT is $11.8 million, which does not include the copyright to the image. Proving ownership of a CryptoPunk is a way to flex the owner's wealth.

The NBA is the first sports league to enter the NFT market. Since its launch in October 2020, NBA Top Shot has earned more than $1.2 billion selling NFTs on the Flow blockchain. Investors can purchase a pack of video "moments" analogous to trading cards. A pack might contain three video cards, ranging from common players in a base set to limited-edition highlights of superstars.

Rarity is what drives the price of NFTs. Common versions of NBA Top Shot NFTs may be numbered to 60,000, many of which are from less popular players. For example, a video of a Mike Conley layup was offered at $1, as it was from a base set numbered to 60,000. In contrast, a dunk from Ja Morant numbered to 6,532 from the Hustle and Show set had an average sale of more than $333. The record sale from the NFT Top Shot collection was a one-of-one video highlight of LeBron James that sold for $208,000. NBA Top Shot incentivizes collectors to build sets of teams or players, building a secondary market where the video highlights can be traded.

Video games are the most popular category of DApps, with more than 1.9 million daily active wallets accessing gaming DApps in February 2024.[17] Video game players enter a virtual world, with more successful players minting new objects or stealing objects from other players in the game. Players have an online avatar, which is a digital personality or representation of the player. Players seek to augment their online personality or their game-playing skills by displaying and using clothing (skins), weapons, and accessories.

Interestingly, one reason for the creation of Ethereum was that Vitalik Buterin was disappointed when a spell wielded by his favorite character was lost when a video game upgraded to a newer version.[18] Buterin felt that players should own in-game items, so he helped to create smart contracts to track this ownership. NFTs provide immutable title to in-game objects, ideally with the ability to sell those objects or transfer them for use in another game.

Blockchain gaming has created the category of "play-to-earn," where the most active and successful players may be able to earn a living by winning, building, breeding, and selling in-game items. Gamers can profit in Axie Infinity, Alien Worlds, Galaxy Fight Club, Gods Unchained, and other on-chain games.

The best-selling NFT collection of all time is Axie Infinity with total revenue of $4.2 billion. Participants must purchase three Axie Infinity monsters to start playing the game. Entry-level Axies may cost $20 each, but the rarest Axies with the most attractive traits can trade at much higher prices. In a game somewhat like Pokémon, players breed and fight cute little monsters. The combination of traits from the two parents yields offspring of different colors and rarities.

Play-to-earn games rose in popularity during COVID-19, especially in the Philippines.[19] As workers from hotels, restaurants, and taxi services lost work during the pandemic, they searched for a way to sustain their families online when many in-person jobs were furloughed. Some Axie Infinity players found they could earn more than $400 per month breeding and selling the monster NFTs to new players entering the game, higher than the Philippines' monthly minimum wage of $160.

Thousands of people had full-time jobs minting Axies, but not all Filipinos could afford to buy the three Axies to get started. A venture capital community called guilds arose to fund Axie Infinity players. The guild would purchase the three Axies to get started, perhaps for $100. The Axies would be lent to a scholar who would play the game and split the profits with the sponsoring guild. At least in low-wage countries, play-to-earn games can offer compensation similar to that of an average service industry job.

As the Philippines and the world got back to work full time and fewer new players joined the game, a 2022 crash in NFT prices and the March 2022 hack that drained the Ronin bridge from Ethereum to Axie Infinity of $625 million made it infeasible to continue to earn a living simply breeding cute monster NFTs. Even after the game's creator reimbursed losses from the hack, players who invested more than they sold suffered losses as the game slowed and NFT prices declined.[20]

There is substantial potential for blockchain-based technologies to revolutionize the music industry. Many music fans, including Taylor Swift, dislike services like Ticketmaster that charge significant service fees to ticket buyers while failing to manage a ticket release without crashing computers and selling tickets to bots and scalpers. Many fans believe that tickets should only be sold to those who enjoy the music and plan on attending the concert.

Smart contracts can be deployed to govern sales of concert tickets as NFTs. Wallets connected to consumers who use the purchased tickets to attend the event could have an increased probability of purchasing tickets for future shows, while wallets of consumers who frequently resell their tickets would find it harder to purchase tickets for the next show. Similar to art NFTs, the resale of ticket NFTs could generate royalties paid to the artist, giving the performer a share of the scalper's profits.

Performers could also analyze on-chain ticket sales data to identify the fans attending the most shows. These super fans might be given early access to a ticket sale or the opportunity to purchase exclusive music releases and merchandise. These fans might also be willing to purchase front-row seats at premium prices or even front-row seats for life.

Kings of Leon sold a $50 NFT package for the release of the album "When You See Yourself." Buyers of the package received early access to the album and exclusive alternative cover art. Buyers of the NFTs have bragging rights that they are among the biggest fans or that they heard the album earlier than others.[21]

Music royalties are very complicated, with revenues from a single song potentially being divided among dozens of writers, performers, and producers. Blockchains and smart contracts can collect royalties from radio and streaming services while automatically distributing them to all participants in the creative process.

John Lennon's son, Julian, sold the digital versions of his father's memorabilia as NFTs. The collection included three guitars, John's coat from the

"Magical Mystery Tour," his cape from the movie "Help!," and the notes to "Hey Jude," which Paul McCartney gave Julian as a gift.

Julian Lennon kept physical possession of all six items while selling the digital representations as NFTs for auction proceeds of more than $150,000, part of which was donated to Julian's foundation. Buyers of the NFTs own a digital representation of these Beatles collectibles on a blockchain but do not have access to or ownership of the physical items.[22]

What are Web 1.0, Web 2.0, and Web 3.0? Web 1.0 was the original read-only internet from the early 1990s. Web 1.0 simply replicated existing content in an online format. Rather than receiving a physical newspaper, consumers could access the website of the *New York Times* using slow dial-up modems. Due to the limited bandwidth, content on Web 1.0 was distributed by large media companies, but readers could not interact or comment on the content.

In the late 1990s, Web 2.0 arose as the "social web," where users created their own content. Social media posts, live streams, tags, comments, likes, and even podcasts were posted to centralized platforms, with today's dominant platforms being Facebook, YouTube, TikTok, and Spotify. The criticisms of Web 2.0 are that the economics are skewed toward large centralized companies, including Meta and Alphabet, with 2024 market capitalizations exceeding $1.3 trillion each. While these platforms are free for users, they earn annual revenues of more than $100 billion per year by monetizing data and content provided by users. If an online service is free, the user and their data are products being monetized by the platform. Google allows third parties to read user emails.[23]

While some influencers are paid enough by the platforms to make online content a full-time job, the vast majority of users of these centralized services see none of the revenue. Web 2.0 is very centralized, with a substantial portion of the traffic moving through data centers and cloud computing platforms like Amazon Web Services (AWS). An outage at AWS could impact the ability of major Web 2.0 providers to function.

Another key criticism of Web 2.0 is the "walled gardens," where LinkedIn, Twitter/X, Facebook, YouTube, and TikTok are all different platforms. Once a user has built a following on one of these platforms, there is no way to immediately transfer those followers to another platform. Each community must be built separately, as users cannot copy their LinkedIn followers into TikTok.

The goal of Web 3.0 is decentralization and individual ownership of our persona and our data. That is, to take power away from the Web 2.0 centralized platforms that are among the most highly valued global companies. There's no exact date or definition of Web 3.0, but it may have arrived with the Ethereum smart contract blockchain in 2014. Web 3.0 is built on decentralization, transparency, permissionless participation, and individual ownership.

Each user's wallet is the core of their identity and online persona. Each user owns their own data, avatar, financial information, and social media contacts. The promise of Web 3.0 is the ability to easily transfer any of this information from one blockchain-based platform to another. Once the user's wallet is connected, there is no further need for passwords or identity verification. A user can interact publicly or anonymously through pseudonyms or avatars. Users interact with DeFi platforms using the value in their crypto wallet and with video games using their NFTs, all of which are easily transferrable across Web 3.0. The defining characteristic of Web 3.0 is that users own their content, and assets are portable. Users have the choice to be public or anonymous, to monetize their data or not.

The goal of Web 3.0 is to become more decentralized and less dependent on centralized organizations such as Facebook, Google, and banks. Decentralized Autonomous Organizations (DAOs) promise to build a new form of corporation that will not be traded on centralized stock markets.

What is the metaverse?[24] Blockchain technology allows investors to take control of their investments and their data. While there isn't yet a clear definition of the metaverse and Web 3.0, they could simply be the next iteration of the internet, maximizing decentralization and individual freedom while reducing the power of centralized intermediaries. While the power in Web 2.0 is held by centralized tech giants such as Alphabet and Meta, the power in Web 3.0 shifts to individual participants.

The metaverse is a series of online communities where participants build a digital identity through avatars. While the current internet is a walled garden, separating Twitter/X followers from a user's LinkedIn contacts, Web 3.0 allows the transfer of digital items and relationships across internet or metaverse properties.

Many view the metaverse as an immersive experience using virtual reality (VR) and augmented reality (AR) technologies. VR technologies immerse participants in a virtual world, while AR technologies overlay digital information in the real world. The most famous AR technology is Pokémon Go, where users view the real world through the camera on their smartphone while trying to catch digital Pokémon that appear in the view.

Compared to traditional video games that end when you turn them off, gaming and virtual worlds in the metaverse exhibit persistence, as the game continues even when a user leaves the environment. After users leave the virtual world, it continues without them. Users returning to the digital environment see that the world changed while they were gone.

One of the key players in the metaverse is Decentraland, a 3D universe launched in 2020. Participants can buy one of more than 90,000 plots of virtual land in specific themed neighborhoods. Real-world commerce is planned in this virtual world, where plots of land in the fashion district were sold for $2.4 million to a group planning fashion shows. As fewer consumers watch television and read newspapers, advertisers and brands follow consumers online to both Web 2.0 and Web 3.0 properties.

Consumers build digital avatars, with each identity piece, such as hats, skin color, gloves, and purses purchased as NFTs.

Decentraland is governed through a DAO, a decentralized autonomous organization, the corporate form of blockchain entities. In March 2024, Decentraland's governance token, MANA, was valued at $1.2 billion.

A competing metaverse property is the Sandbox, with SAND governance tokens valued at $1.4 billion. The Sandbox virtual world has more than 160,000 plots of land with a record price of $4.3 million for the sale of multiple lots.

The Sandbox was designed for real-world commerce, with more than 150 corporate sponsorships including Snoop Dogg, The Smurfs, The Walking Dead, Hell's Kitchen, Adidas, and Atari.

Prices of virtual real estate tend to be higher on Ethereum-based metaverse platforms than on Solana-based platforms. The floor price, or cheapest plot of land available in a virtual world, ranges from $1,610 in Axie Infinity, $2,740 in the Sandbox, $3,840 in Decentraland, to more than $4,300 in Otherdeeds. Solana-based platforms Lux and Solace have plots available for less than $200.[25]

Massively multiplayer online role-playing games (MMORPGs) include World of Warcraft, Fortnite, and Final Fantasy. Up to 100 global players meet in each game. Games continue indefinitely in the persistent environment, with players joining from all corners of the globe 24/7. If a player skips a day of World of Warcraft, the game continues without them.

Around the world, 3.6 billion people play video games, which is about half of the global population. Entire industries have arisen around these games, including e-sports teams and paid streaming of games on Twitch. More than 500 million people globally now watch others play video games. E-Sports is becoming a very lucrative league, with more than $180 million in prizes awarded to Fortnite players since 2018.[26]

At $192.7 billion in 2021 revenue, the video game industry easily eclipsed revenues from film ($99.7 billion) and recorded music ($25.9 billion) combined.[27] Gaming could be the basis for the growth of the metaverse and Web 3.0, with players owning, trading, buying, and selling their avatars and their in-game assets through NFTs. Companies such as Unity, CryEngine, and Unreal Engine facilitate these immersive virtual reality and gaming worlds.

Some individuals view cryptocurrencies and digital assets primarily as a means to generate profits, similar to stocks and other tradable assets. Others view them as a way of asserting individual freedoms away from the centralized authorities of banks, governments, and giant internet companies. These users feel trapped by centralized platforms, as there is no easy way to migrate their online audience and contacts to a different platform. This lack of mobility can be frustrating.

Web 3.0 technologies, facilitated by blockchains, give users control over their data and assets, allowing them to move freely across an open internet. Web 3.0 gives users greater autonomy and challenges the dominance of today's internet giants. If Web 3.0 and blockchain technologies thrive, today's largest companies, whether financial or social media giants, will need to adapt their business models toward a more open internet with individual freedoms. Companies that do not adjust to the independence of the Web 3.0 movement may see their revenues and market capitalizations decline over time.

CHAPTER 15

Decentralized Autonomous Organizations (DAOs) and Governance

Many crypto projects are built to parallel and improve upon real-world organizations and institutions. DeFi protocols are built to disintermediate and replicate the functions of traditional banks and securities exchanges. Decentralized autonomous organizations (DAOs) seek to recreate the corporate form of governance in a more decentralized way.

In a corporate form of governance, managers and directors have the delegated authority to make decisions regarding the assets, liabilities, and business plans of a company. The company is owned by shareholders who vote to elect the board of directors and to approve major changes in ownership and company policies. The power in corporations is often concentrated in a hierarchy, led by a CEO and board of directors who delegate the implementation of the business model to others in the organization.

Participants in the world of digital assets often do not prefer a hierarchical structure with centralized authority. While the CEO and board members of traditional corporations can be well known, many leaders of DAOs are anonymous or pseudonymous. DAOs parallel many of the governance roles of the corporate form of ownership but do so in a more collaborative and less hierarchical structure. Few DAOs have a CEO, as participants in these organizations prefer a more collaborative form of governance.

The rules of crypto protocols and DAOs are coded into smart contracts. The collaborative team, many of whom are volunteers, built the initial design of the protocol, which was coded into smart contracts. Updates to the protocol design are subject to governance votes by token holders, such as the Ethereum Improvement Proposals (EIPs) previously discussed.

The governance rules of an organization are important, as many DAOs run DeFi platforms with millions of dollars in TVL and in the DAO's treasury. Updates to the smart contracts have implications for the security and usability of the platform.

DAOs will issue governance tokens that give token holders an economic stake in the enterprise. Investors with the largest economic stake in the protocol will be able to propose changes to the code or governance structure of the protocol. In many cases, DAOs will require that a user own at least 0.1% of the outstanding token supply to suggest a change to the protocol.[1] Chainalysis notes that the governance of DAOs is not as decentralized as many participants believe, as their analysis of 10 leading DAOs notes that 90% of the governance tokens are held by less than 1% of the token holders. This means that many DAOs have less than 100 token holders with an economic stake sufficient to propose changes to the protocol or the governance model. Votes are cast on proposals with one token, one vote, rather than the one person, one vote that occurs in a political democracy.

Maker DAO token holders can vote on proposals to add or delete tokens as collateral acceptable to mint DAI stablecoins or to change the amount of collateral required. DAOs can also vote on revenue sharing, as a March 2024 governance vote approved distributing a portion of the fees paid by users of the Uniswap platform to token holders staking Uniswap tokens. In anticipation of a higher staking yield, the proposal of this "fee switch" upgrade led to a swift increase in the value of Uniswap tokens.

Once proposals have been properly announced, information is disseminated by the protocol's website, with discussion taking place in the protocol's community forum on Discord or Telegram. Once the change to the protocol has been discussed and potentially revised, a time period is set for a vote.

In order to have a highly functional DAO, members must have equal access to the same information for decision-making, face the same costs for transacting their preferred choices, and base their decisions on self-interest and the best interest of the DAO (not on coercion or fear).[2] This may be one of the key values of a DAO, as stakeholders of traditional corporations may find it politically difficult to disagree with a powerful CEO. The promise of a DAO is greater participation in the decision-making process. Ideally, the DAO can reduce the power wielded by any one person, distributing that power across a community of collaborators.

DAOs attempt to solve coordination problems by aligning individual incentives with globally optimal outcomes (for people or corporations).[3] By pooling funds and voting on the use of treasury assets, stakeholders share the costs and incentivize coordination so the entire ecosystem benefits. The goal is to build a long-lasting organization with a respected management team, coders with incentives to build and maintain the protocol, and engaged shareholders who are interested and involved in the governance.

Token holders can benefit economically when a protocol is well run by a respected and collaborative team. While some teams are largely volunteer, it is important to have talented programmers and managers watching the system's progress. In many cases, the team managing the smart contract and blockchain operations will be compensated to do so, often being paid in the project's governance token. Incentives should be aligned, with balanced portions of the economics being allocated to token holders and the developers and managers of the protocol. The development team shouldn't take all of the economics, as there would be no incentive for token holders to participate. Conversely, token holders should not take all of the economics, as there needs to be compensation available for the development team and expenses of the platform.

Chainalysis notes that DAOs have been formed across digital asset sectors, including DeFi protocols, social clubs, grant-makers, play-to-earn gaming guilds, NFT generators, venture funds, charities, and metaverse platforms.[4] The most substantial concentration, with 33% of all DAOs and 83% of DAO treasury value, is found in DeFi platforms. Some of the most well-known DAOs are Maker DAO, Uniswap, and Compound in the DeFi sector, as well as Bitcoin, Ethereum, and Tezos.

Other categories of DAOs include tech-related developer grants, non-tech grants, for-profit investment DAOs, decentralized governance, for-profit DeFi DAOs, DAO software as a service (DSaaS), and protocols/organizations.[5]

An investment fund, analogous to a mutual fund, a fund of funds, or a venture capital fund can be built as a DAO, with assets held in the on-chain treasury.

DAOs can be built as non-profit organizations with the goal of raising funds to provide grants to builders who enhance the crypto ecosystem by building and maintaining software that grows and maintains blockchain protocols. Tokens may be reserved in a DAO to compensate those who develop the software and monitor the protocol. Other non-profit DAOs may fund those who make a positive impact in their local community.

The net worth of a company is the value of its assets in excess of its liabilities. Stock market investors are provided with limited liability, where the amount of their losses is limited to the amount invested in the stock. Token holders of most crypto projects also have their liability limited to the amount invested in the token.

The corporate form of ownership states that when a company goes bankrupt, the worst thing that could happen to investors is a 100% loss of the value of the stock. In the case of a bankruptcy, the assets of the company or protocol may be insufficient to pay the liabilities or the debt that has been issued. Liabilities can explode above the value of the assets when a company has a product liability issue that has resulted in the death or injury of a number of workers or customers.

Crypto investors must be aware that leveraged trading involving positions in futures, perpetuals, and short options can create liabilities that can cause the loss of an investor's entire collateral and potentially an even greater loss if positions are not liquidated before the collateral is exhausted. On decentralized exchanges, those losses may be borne by the protocol or other traders. On a centralized exchange, such as the CME Group, the trader is responsible for those losses.

There are not many legal precedents set for DAOs. If a DAO has distributed operations or an unknown management team, it may be unclear under which country's laws the organization will be accountable. Participants in a business, either managers or investors, may have the status of general partners or limited partners. Limited partners typically have liability limited to the amount of their investment, while general partners may have unlimited potential liabilities. General partners make the decisions, invest the money, design the systems, and employ the coders. Ideally, a DAO could build a structure similar to a corporation or a limited liability company (LLC). Under a corporate or LLC structure, investors and managers can limit their personal liability for the company's debts by delegating the general partner role to the legal structure.

The US SEC filed lawsuits against Sushi DAO in March 2023 and Ooki DAO in September 2022.[6] The leader of Sushi asked DAO token holders to vote to approve a fund of up to $4 million to pay legal costs for members of the programming and management team.

While the US SEC has been accused of regulation by enforcement and not exactly being crypto friendly, other jurisdictions and regulators may be more welcoming of the industry. The US state of Wyoming seeks to attract and support the crypto industry, including the March 2021 revision of corporate law to create the Wyoming DAO LLC structure.[7] DAOs are also legal structures in Switzerland, Liechtenstein, the Cayman Islands and the Marshall Islands as well as the US states of Tennessee and Vermont. The Wyoming DAO structure provides a legal framework for DAOs and provides limited liability to individuals associated with the DAO. As with other US LLCs, the Wyoming DAO LLC structure includes pass-through taxation, where profits are taxed to those receiving distributions and not taxed at the level of the DAO.

DAOs use smart contracts to enable collaborative governance.[8] Smart contracts can be changed through a successful vote on proposed amendments, such as the Ethereum Improvement Proposals previously discussed. Each DAO will have procedures for governance votes, including the size of the holdings of the governance token required to submit a proposal and the portion of voting tokens required to pass a proposal.

After the DAO community has voted in favor of revising the rules governing the protocol, the programmers will implement the new logic in the smart contract. The changes to the code should be rigorously tested and inspected by the community before being updated in the live smart contract. Times when governance updates are applied to the smart contract logic are a vulnerable time for the protocol, as potential bugs or exploits may be inadvertently introduced into the complex programming logic.

Albert Hirschman defines the triangle of tension between the individual, governance, and decentralization.[9] Each participant should have a voice and be able to articulate their discontent regarding governance issues in the community. Individuals have the right to exit a community when they are dissatisfied or perceive better opportunities elsewhere. Individuals may feel a duty of loyalty to the decentralized organization where they are hesitant to speak dissent, whether it is to protect the organization or out of fear of a strong centralized leader. It may be easier for individuals to express loyalty to an organization when leadership is dispersed and there is not a strong leader to be afraid of.

In a typical organization, these are described as principal-agent problems, where the shareholder or token holder is the principal and owner of the organization who has delegated authority to the agent, who is the board of directors and management team of the organization.

The votes of shareholders and token holders are weighted by their economic stake in the organization, with the stakeholders with the largest economic stake having the largest share of the vote. Stakeholders prefer that the organization has a perpetual life, providing economic value to stakeholders and other value to the broader market. If stakeholders are dissatisfied with the direction of the organization, they can choose to vote, sponsor a proposal, volunteer or be hired to solve problems, or simply sell their holdings and walk away.

There are a wide variety of decisions that can be made by a governance community. Shareholders or token holders vote to elect a board of directors as well as issues put to a vote, including mergers, divestitures, closure of the organization, and changes to the design of the corporation or the smart contract protocol. Decisions made at the formation of the organization include profit vs. non-profit status, distribution of voting rights, transferability of ownership shares, and the purpose of the organization.[10] For organizations involved in decentralized finance, governance token holders can vote on fees for using the platform, incentives paid to liquidity providers, and whether revenue is retained in the protocol or partially distributed to token holders.

A key decision is to form a for-profit vs. a not-for-profit entity. While it is relatively easy to merge, sell, or liquidate a for-profit organization, it can be difficult to dissolve a not-for profit organization that has substantial assets.

A governance structure for the team must be identified, including the relationship of the leaders, the board of directors, employees, volunteers, and governance token holders. Are members of the development team compensated with cash or crypto assets, or do they work as volunteers? As seen in the case of Sushi DAO, procedures must be established on how to engage with regulators and whether the DAO will provide for the legal defense of the developers.

There are challenges to governance in DAOs,[11] especially when the development team who built the DAO and coded the smart contracts maintain the majority of the economics. If the development team controls more than 50% of the outstanding tokens, any vote by a token holder wouldn't make much difference as the development team can pass or defeat any proposal they choose.

There is a concern that flash loans can be used to borrow tokens, influencing a vote beyond the token holder's true economic stake. Shadow voting exercises governance rights through borrowed tokens. While there is a cost to the flash loan used to borrow the governance tokens, the cost is much less than a purchase of the tokens required to influence a governance vote. The governance process was designed for those with a large economic stake to have an influence on the vote, with shadow voting beyond the intent of the designed governance process. Shadow voting allows the borrower of the token to influence the outcomes of governance votes without participating in the economics of the token.

A third challenge to DAO governance is that the ownership of crypto wallets is anonymous or pseudonymous. The KYC process is implemented at the point of the fiat on-ramp used to buy the investor's first crypto tokens. Beyond that point, the investor is in the crypto universe and can participate in decentralized exchanges to swap for tokens that can be held in anonymous or unhosted wallets. Developers of smart contract platforms can be known, such as the Ethereum team. Other development teams may choose to be anonymous. Anonymous development teams can be spread around the world while discussing the project on Telegram, Discord, and/or Github. Teams may wish to remain anonymous due to their domicile in a less crypto-friendly jurisdiction or because their participation in a crypto protocol may be a conflict with their full-time employment. Regulators may find it difficult to shut down a protocol run by an anonymous team or prosecute developers for building protocols that do not comply with AML and KYC regulations.

Many DAOs have amassed a significant value of assets in their treasury. This value could come from the proceeds of the ICO or profits earned from user fees on a platform, and can increase if the treasury assets are used to earn staking yields or participate in a DeFi protocol as a liquidity provider. The DAO should have explicit rules on the use of the treasury assets, stating the portion of the assets or revenue that can be used to pay developers during specific time periods.

It is imperative that the treasury assets be held in a safe custody arrangement that is not subject to hack or exploit. Ideally, multiple signatures are required to move the treasury assets. A good governance tool may be that three signatures are required out of five key holders. This rule requires a majority of key holders be present when moving assets, while reducing the liability if a key holder dies or leaves the protocol. There have been significant losses of protocol assets when a single key holder lost the keys or died without disclosing the keys to a business partner.

If the DAO is designed as an investment fund, the tokens held in the treasury must be in compliance with the investment objective disclosed to the investors. Assets disbursed from a fund must be distributed according to the design of the protocol approved by a vote of the token holders.

Many DeFi protocols are designed as DAOs, including DEXes and yield farming protocols. DeFi projects tend to have the largest treasury holdings due to the potential profitability of user fees and net interest margins. Protocols organized as DAOs where token holders have a say in governance decisions include Curve, Uniswap, Aave, Dash, and Compound. Decisions put to a governance vote include the assets that are accepted for collateral, the rules for liquidation, and deposit and lending rates.

MakerDAO (MKR) is one of the first and largest DAOs and DeFi applications built on the Ethereum blockchain. The process by which MakerDAO mints the DAI stablecoin was detailed in Chapter 8. DAI is a community-managed decentralized stablecoin pegged to the US dollar. DAI is minted after the deposit of an over-collateralized amount of Ether or bitcoin tokens. Holders of the MKR governance token can vote on which tokens are accepted for collateral and changes to the required degree of overcollateralization.

While MakerDAO doesn't pay dividends to its token holders, any profits from the minting of DAI will increase the holdings of the MKR treasury, likely increasing the value of the MKR token.

One of the newer DAOs, Arbitrum, is the largest layer 2 scaling solution for Ethereum. In March 2024, Arbitrum held $3.9 billion of total value locked and a market capitalization of $4.4 billion. Arbitrum is a key platform for DeFi DApps, as users move assets away from the Ethereum blockchain in search of lower gas fees for making transactions.

Arbitrum operates as a DAO[12] after distributing 11.6% of its tokens to its users in a March 2023 airdrop.[13] Other holders of ARB tokens include

35.3% allocated to the treasury, 26.9% to the development team, 17.5% to investors, 7.5% to the Arbitrum foundation, and 1.1% to DAOs building DApps on Arbitrum. Airdropped tokens are awarded to early users of a protocol, with the number of tokens awarded often scaled by the number and size of transactions made in a specific wallet over one or more specific time frames. The wallets with the largest number of transactions or transactions in specific categories are awarded the largest share.

A DAO can be organized very quickly. In 2021, one of the 13 surviving physical copies of the US Constitution was put up for sale. In just six days, Constitution DAO was formed, raising more than $40 million in Ethereum from 17,000 investors.[14] Members of the DAO voted to use the money in the treasury to bid on this historical artifact in an auction. The amount the DAO could bid for the document was limited to the value of its treasury holdings, which is transparent to the market. The Constitution was purchased by Ken Griffin, the head of the Citadel hedge fund, who was able to outbid the DAO because he knew the DAO's maximum bid before the auction started.

Because the Constitution DAO was formed for the single purpose of bidding in a specific auction, the DAO was dissolved and the contributions returned to the investors after the auction was lost and the Constitution was no longer for sale.

Crypto has a potential to revolutionize every way we do business. While this book has largely focused on financial markets to this point, DAOs could revolutionize the corporate structure and how distributed collaboration can be designed to meet shared objectives. To date, it's unclear exactly how DAOs fit into the law, especially when it is unclear under which jurisdiction the DAO is regulated. If a DAO is properly registered in a single jurisdiction, such as Switzerland, is the DAO subject to Swiss law even when it is operating in foreign markets? As crypto markets mature and grow, it is expected that these regulatory questions will be answered as jurisdictions clarify regulations in an attempt to become the domicile of choice for a growing business model.

Investing in Cryptocurrencies and Digital Assets

After defining the universe in Part I, Part II introduces information regarding investing in cryptocurrencies and digital assets.

Chapter 16 explains that while crypto investors seek to be global and decentralized, they are still accountable to global taxing authorities and financial regulators.

Chapter 17 discusses how tokenizing real-world assets (RWAs), such as real estate, promises to democratize global markets and provide more than one billion consumers the ability to legally own assets for the first time using distributed ledger technology.

Chapter 18 provides a variety of valuation models for digital assets. The models have been sourced from the commodity, technology, venture capital, and public equity markets.

Chapter 19 builds on the discussion of Chapter 16 regarding the regulations of capital formation in the digital assets industry. Regulations and due diligence processes for evaluating initial coin offerings (ICOs) are discussed.

Chapter 20 discusses the considerations of complementing the fundamental analysis of Chapter 18 with technical analysis. Fundamental valuation methods work better for long holding periods, while technical analysis can be useful for short-term trading and the timing of entering and exiting long-term trades.

Chapter 21 explains how custody arrangements introduce additional risks to digital asset ownership. Investors have the choice of holding digital assets on a centralized exchange or in a self-custody wallet.

Chapter 22 explores derivatives markets, where futures, options, and perpetual swaps regularly trade substantially greater volumes than the underlying spot token markets.

Chapter 23 provides an update on ways to access digital assets through traditional financial market structures, including stocks and spot- and futures-based exchange-traded funds (ETFs). Portfolio construction considerations, including position sizing and rebalancing strategies, are also discussed.

Chapter 24 notes that institutional investors have historically hesitated to invest directly in spot crypto assets but have preferred to invest using the venture capital and hedge fund allocations already approved by their investment committee.

Chapter 25 lists a framework of due diligence and risk management steps investors can use before investing to reduce potential losses. Market risk events of 2022, including Terra Luna and FTX, are used to illustrate the risks of digital asset investments.

CHAPTER 16

Risks, Regulations, and Taxes

Before discussing regulation, taxes, and risks, it must be noted that this book is educational and does not provide legal, tax, or investment advice. The author is not an attorney or an accountant, and the cost of getting these issues wrong is significant. This chapter provides an overview of topics to discuss with appropriate counsel before making tax, investment, or legal decisions. While best efforts were taken to ensure the accuracy of this information while preparing the manuscript, regulations change frequently and tax brackets are revised annually.

US President Joe Biden signed an executive order in March 2022.[1] Biden's tone was constructive for the prospects of the cryptocurrency and digital asset business in the US. The overall positive tone was that the US should reinforce its global leadership in finance and technology. However, he did express concerns regarding the potential of cryptocurrencies to impact risks of global financial stability and national security. While fostering innovation and wealth creation, consumers, investors, and businesses should be protected from fraud. Biden stated that cryptocurrencies have the promise of promoting equitable access to affordable financial services, perhaps by bringing the unbanked into the financial system through smartphone wallet apps. Biden encouraged the Federal Reserve Bank to explore the development of a central bank digital currency (CBDC). The president expressed concern over the illicit use of cryptocurrencies and the environmental impact of proof-of-work cryptocurrency mining.

While Biden's tone was generally encouraging for the industry, the US Congress and SEC have not yet provided clear and updated regulations governing the digital assets industry. The cryptocurrency industry has been asking for clear guidance and updated regulations, while the SEC continues to back the 1946 Howey Test as the key regulation for understanding the regulatory environment for issuing new tokens. As noted in Chapter 8, according to the Howey Test, an investment is a security if it meets four criteria: 1) an investment of money, 2) in a common enterprise, 3) with a reasonable expectation of profits, and 4) derived from the efforts of others.

The industry is generally disappointed by the SEC's stance, which has been "regulation by enforcement" rather than by rule making.[2] In regulation by enforcement, the SEC brings legal action and imposes fines for actions the agency believes to be fraudulent, even if those actions are not specifically addressed or prohibited by current regulations. Even when cryptocurrency companies try to interpret the rules in good faith, the SEC has been accused of introducing new rules during enforcement actions.

Market participants raising new capital, whether in equity or cryptocurrency markets, must understand the process of issuing securities in the US primary market and trading securities in the secondary market. The primary market is for IPOs and ICOs, the single point in time when an investment is first sold to the public. The secondary market is the trading of all securities after their initial issuance. If the SEC believes that a digital asset is a security under the Howey Test, the next questions that will be asked are regarding who the offering was sold to and what disclosures were provided.

By only offering investments to qualified purchasers and accredited investors, venture capital and hedge funds rely on a private placement exemption. Issuers relying on a private placement exemption can offer fewer disclosures and have greater liquidity and concentration risks in their offerings.

When a newly issued investment is sold to any investor that does not have the status of a qualified purchaser or accredited investor, the SEC requires issuers to follow the Securities Act of 1933 and its required disclosures for retail investors. The SEC was specifically concerned that many of the initial coin offerings sold in 2017 and 2018 were unregistered securities that were sold to retail investors without risk disclosures.[3]

Many ICOs published a white paper describing their business plan and the blockchain-enabled technology they hoped to build. To raise money to fund the business plan, enterprises sold tokens to retail and sophisticated investors. In an analogy to venture capital–backed companies, the firms spent the money on programmers and technology resources in an attempt to build the desired platform. When sophisticated investors make a venture capital investment, it is expected that many of the companies will run out of money before reaching business goals and will be worth less than the amount invested. These investors take a portfolio approach and can profit when one winning company in a portfolio returns more than 10 times the amount invested, more than offsetting the losses sustained by the companies that fail to gain traction.

While spending the funds raised in an honest and diligent attempt to build a company is not fraudulent, it is fraudulent when a team publishes a white paper to raise funds and then keeps the funds without attempting to build the proposed platform. Many of the ICOs sold during that time period were fraudulent, with approximately 11% of assets raised going to the 80% of projects defined as scams.[4] In contrast, many successful ICOs of the 2017–2018 vintage reached valuations exceeding $1 billion, including Telegram, Ethereum, Polkadot, Tezos, EOS, and Filecoin, far greater than the $1.3 billion lost to scams in 2017.[5] The large number of ICO scams that were sold to retail investors led to a 2018 crackdown by the SEC that substantially slowed ICO activity.

Security token offerings (STO) are designed to comply with securities laws and are frequently used by venture capital investors allocating to blockchain projects. While traditional venture capital firms often invest in convertible preferred stock, the digital assets industry offers a Simple Agreement for Future Tokens (SAFT), which instead of stock or convertible preferred securities, issues tokens to VC investors at the time of the ICO.

Investors must complete a comprehensive due diligence process before investing, whether in stocks, ICOs, tokens, or tokenized real-world assets. Each investment should have an appropriate balance of risk and potential return and fully comply with Know Your Client (KYC) and anti-money laundering (AML) regulations. Investors need to understand what specific assets or business revenues are being sold in an ICO or a tokenized asset.

The key concerns of regulators have been selling unregistered securities and failing to comply with KYC and AML regulations.

Know Your Client regulations require banks, brokers, lenders, and exchanges to verify the identity of investors and borrowers. This avoids anonymous accounts, which could be used for tax evasion or money laundering. When opening any new account, investors must provide proof of residence, a tax ID, and a passport or driver's license. The investor may also be required to disclose their assets and liabilities, credit history, and the source of funds used to make the deposit into the new account. Investors have an easier time opening accounts when offering full documentation, especially when they have wage income and tax forms supporting the wealth. Self-employed investors, especially in crypto, or those without full documentation may find it more difficult to find a loan, banking, or brokerage relationship.

Investment brokers and advisors need to understand their clients' level of risk tolerance and investment knowledge, which are used to determine the suitability of each investment. Crypto investments are categorized as high-risk and speculative investments, and may not be suitable for conservative or retired investors living on a limited income. Advisors will also recommend portfolio diversification, likely encouraging investors to keep their crypto allocations to less than 10% of investments mixed with investments in stocks, bonds, and real estate.

Centralized exchanges, such as Coinbase, Kraken, and Binance, are on-ramps that allow for the conversion of fiat to cryptocurrencies and digital assets. Centralized exchanges are linked to the traditional financial system, allowing investors to make deposits from bank accounts. Investors must first interface with a centralized exchange to convert fiat into cryptocurrencies before moving to unhosted wallets and decentralized finance. Investors are concerned about having off-ramps that provide the ability to convert crypto assets into fiat currencies that can be reintroduced into the traditional banking system to facilitate everyday spending.

At this point in the development of the distributed ledger business, it is highly unlikely that top protocols such as Bitcoin and Ethereum can be shut down, even due to a government mandate. Even if one or more governments mandate that cryptocurrencies are illegal, investors will continue to own them, especially in unhosted wallets. The concern comes with the off-ramp, as monetizing the gains from cryptocurrencies can be infeasible if the government won't allow banks to accept fiat deposits from crypto exchanges.

Centralized exchanges may be required to report transactions to the taxing authorities. A key goal of anti-money laundering statutes is to ensure that income earned from all sources is declared and that all appropriate taxes are paid. Centralized exchanges can be liable for money laundering if KYC tasks are not performed correctly and clients do not pay taxes on crypto income and realized gains.

Money laundering is attempting to convert illegally obtained assets or income into assets that appear to have been legitimately earned. Illegally obtained assets and income can be sourced through tax evasion, drug trafficking, ransomware, dark web markets, bribes, theft, and scams. Chainalysis[6] notes that the largest source of criminal cryptocurrency transfers is related to sanctioned jurisdictions and entities, as it is illegal to transfer funds related to terrorist organizations or countries such as Iran, Russia, and North Korea.

A number of governmental agencies oversee investigations of money laundering and global criminal networks. These include counter-terrorism financing (CTF), the G7 Financial Action Task Force (FATF), and the US Financial Crimes Enforcement Network (FINCEN). Compliance staff at crypto exchanges and protocols need to understand the regulations and comply with orders from these agencies. Failure to do so can lead to massive fines and the potential closure of the crypto business in some jurisdictions.

Once customers have completed the KYC process, compliance professionals must continue to monitor their deposit and withdrawal activity. Cash transactions more than $10,000 per day require the filing of a suspicious activity report within 30 days of a transaction without notifying the customer. Structured transactions that seek to avoid the $10,000 limit must also be reported. A client would submit a structured transaction by depositing $40,000 in cash in a six-day period without exceeding $10,000 per day. Beyond banks and brokerage firms, sellers of big-ticket items such as automobiles must also file suspicious activity reports. The government wants to ensure that all cash has been appropriately taxed and is not the proceeds of criminal activity. Clients who prefer to transact in cash may trigger investigations due to suspicious activity reports, but will not have any criminal liability if the income was legally earned and fully taxed.

The three steps in money laundering are placement, layering, and integration.

Placement is when illegal funds are introduced into legitimate systems and institutions. Suspicious activity reports are investigated to ensure that money laundering does not occur and that only legal and traceable funds are deposited. Even after clients have passed an initial KYC process, the bank or crypto exchange must continue monitoring all transactions for money laundering compliance. A client with suspicious transactions may be asked to close their account, submit additional documentation, or be subject to criminal investigation and prosecution, even if their background check was approved when the account was opened.

Even when deposits are made by check or wire transfer, transactions are investigated when they are inconsistent with the client's prior transaction activity. Clients who regularly deposit wage and bonus income may be asked questions if a large deposit is made in addition to the traditional source of income. Depositing a large check from a non-taxed consulting project or the sale of a house or a car may be subject to delayed availability of funds and may require documentation on the source of funds.

Layering occurs when a client seeks to obscure the source or destination of funds. Crypto mixers and tumblers are specifically designed to accomplish this step of money laundering. The founders of Tornado Cash were charged with money laundering and sanctions violations for more than $1 billion of crypto that the app mixed and obscured for North Korean and cybercrime organizations.[7] As discussed in Chapter 10, mixers and tumblers obscure the trail of crypto transactions, making it difficult to follow the sending and receiving addresses through on-chain metrics tracked by block explorers and Etherscan.io.

In addition to validating the size and source of deposits, it can be suspicious when assets are moved or withdrawn immediately after a deposit. Most consumers have a normal cadence of their financial life, receiving direct deposits on certain dates and paying recurring bills on a regular schedule. Large deposits that are immediately withdrawn are out of character for this investor and must be investigated as an anomaly. Many significant financial crimes and scams have been uncovered through the quick movement of funds, especially when more than two accounts are involved.

The third step in money laundering is integration. While placement moves illicit money into the legitimate financial system, integration returns previously illicit funds back into the financial system after they appear to have been legitimized.

Fiat cash is entirely anonymous. Terrorists and drug lords are often caught with large stashes of $100 bills or €500 notes, part of $2 trillion in annual global crime facilitated with fiat cash.[8] Up to 2% of global economic activity is involved in using fiat cash for tax evasion, drug dealing, and financing terrorism. Crypto is used much less frequently for crime than cash, because crypto is traceable, leaving a paper trail of criminal activity that is not generated through fiat cash transactions.

Chainalysis tracks crime in crypto transactions.[9] Once an illicit wallet or DApp has been identified, transactions in those accounts are tracked. While the crypto industry previously had substantial transfers used for criminal activity, today's traceable crypto market has much less crime than takes place using untraceable fiat cash.

Bitcoin had an early history of hacks, frauds, ransomware, and dark web markets. The government has been able to seize crypto, reversing transactions of deposits received as the proceeds of theft, scams, and ransomware.

From February 2011 to October 2013, more than $180 million in bitcoin was spent at the Silk Road site on the dark web, where buyers accessed drugs, fake IDs, and stolen credit cards, among other illicit activities. The site has been defunct for more than a decade, with its founder spending life in prison. The more than 80,000 bitcoins seized or stolen from Silk Road had an eventual value of more than $3 billion.[10,11]

Chainalysis notes that 0.34% of all crypto transactions in 2023 were criminal in nature, with the majority related to sanctioned individuals and entities.[12] At 2%, fiat transactions are six times more likely than crypto transactions to be involved in criminal activity. Some crimes, including ransomware and malware, occur outside of the crypto industry with the proceeds being moved through crypto. Some crimes are specifically executed using crypto assets and DeFi platforms. Hacks of bridges, smart contract exploits, and rug pulls are all crypto-specific crimes that investors need to be aware of. Rug pulls occur when the creator sells a crypto token and steals the purchasers' funds without building or supporting the proposed protocol.

The regulatory status of a token may vary based on its classification as a utility token, a payment token, or a security token. Payment tokens and utility tokens are less likely to be classified as securities, as they typically do not have the expectation of a profit that defines a security by the Howey Test.

A utility token is used as payment to access a product or service, such as distributed computing storage or cloud computing capacity. Services like Filecoin and Storj compete with centralized cloud computing services like Amazon Web Services (AWS). A case can be made that Ethereum is a utility token, as it is commonly used to pay gas fees to access DApps. Similar to the way a token can be used in a 1980s video arcade to access various pinball machines and video games, Ethereum tokens can be used to access the various applications running on the Ethereum Virtual Machine.

Payment tokens, such as stablecoins that do not pay a yield, might also be exempt from the definition of a security. The goal of acquiring stablecoins is to transfer or store value and eventually spend it or use it for a payment or a global remittance. The SEC has not defined bitcoin as a security, perhaps due to its use as a store of value and payment mechanism.

The SEC also considers the degree of decentralization of a protocol in its definition of a security. Because Bitcoin was founded by the anonymous Satoshi Nakamoto, the blockchain is inherently decentralized as no centralized authority exists. If staking pools make Ethereum more centralized, there could be a concern that Ether may be considered a security token rather than a utility token.

Tokens that aren't classified as payment tokens or utility tokens are often classified as security tokens. If a token is sold with projections of financial profit or if token holders have governance rights or earn a yield or revenue, the SEC is likely to consider it as a security token. Security tokens sold to retail investors must be registered as a securities offering with sufficient disclosure required regarding the risks of the offering. Security tokens can take the form of either debt or equity securities.

The SEC regulates both new issues in the primary market as well as secondary trading after the fundraising is completed. The SEC deemed many of the ICOs issued in 2017 and 2018 to be securities, a ruling that substantially slowed new issuance at the end of 2018. The SEC has also issued enforcement actions against centralized exchanges offering staking services, such as Kraken, which was required to stop offering its staking-as-a-service to US investors and pay a $30 million fine for the unregistered offering and sale of securities.[13]

In a case that may clarify regulations for the sale of digital assets, the SEC sued Ripple Labs, alleging the sale of $1.3 billion in XRP tokens between 2013 and 2020 were unregistered securities.[14] XRP was highly centralized, with the two founders personally selling more than $600 million in tokens.

The SEC states that "Issuers seeking the benefit of a public offering, including access to retail investors, broad distribution and a secondary trading market, must comply with Federal securities laws that require registration of offerings unless an exemption applies."

"We allege that Ripple, Larsen, and Garlinghouse failed to register their ongoing offer and sale of billions of XRP to retail investors, which deprived potential purchasers of adequate disclosures about XRP and Ripple's business and other important long-standing protections that are fundamental to our robust public market system."[15]

Ripple Labs claimed that the SEC doesn't have clear regulations and that the litigation is a case of regulation by enforcement, while the SEC asserts that the Howey Test is still the standard for defining a securities offering.

Notice the SEC's emphasis on adequate disclosures, which might require issuers of ICOs to provide a prospectus similar to an IPO prospectus for an equity offering. The risk disclosures required by the Securities Act of 1933 would note that all cryptocurrency investments are inherently risky and that any individual cryptocurrency offering could result in a loss of the entire value of the investment. In addition to risk factors, an IPO prospectus includes information on the business plan and financial statements.

Many involved in the cryptocurrency industry look forward to a modernization of the Howey Test with clear rules developed to guide the issuance of digital securities. New regulations could result from legal precedents, such as what may arise in the Ripple case, or could be formed through Congressional legislation or rulemaking from the SEC.

In July 2023, a US court ruled that XRP sold on public exchanges were not unregistered securities offerings, leading the SEC to drop the case in October 2023. However, the case was a split decision, as sales directly to institutional investors were deemed to be illegal.[16]

While the US has been slow to update securities laws to specifically govern digital asset investments, the European Union has passed a comprehensive set of regulations named Markets in Crypto Assets (MiCA).[17] MiCA regulations are implemented in stages from June 2023 to December 2024.

The regulation defines crypto asset service providers (CASPs) to include exchanges, wallets, and custody providers. CASPs are required to complete KYC on their clients and to follow AML regulations, which include not listing or interfacing with any protocol that obscures identity, such as privacy coins, tumblers, and mixers.[18] Crypto asset issuers must publish a white paper and risk disclosures before the assets are listed or traded by any CASP. Crypto asset issuers and CASPs must be properly registered as legal entities in a European country. As with the Undertakings for Collective Investments in Transferrable Securities (UCITS) regulations that govern traditional investment funds, a digital asset company properly registered in a single European jurisdiction can use that registration as a passport to access markets in the 27 EU countries.

Investors must keep track of the purchase price, or basis, of each unit of cryptocurrencies, digital assets, or NFTs purchased. Whenever any digital asset is sold, exchanged, or spent, a taxable event is created, which requires users to track the asset's value at the time of the exchange. Taxable events include:

- Selling: Any sale of assets, such as exchanging bitcoin or Ether for fiat or stablecoins.
- Exchanging: Using a DEX to swap Ether for Uniswap tokens creates a taxable event for the sale of the Ether tokens and sets the tax basis for the Uniswap tokens. Exchanging Ether or Solana tokens for an NFT creates a taxable event for the sale of the tokens and sets the tax basis for the NFT.
- Spending: Any time a cryptocurrency is spent, a taxable event is created, and the sales price of the cryptocurrency must be noted.

Crypto taxes quickly become extraordinarily complicated. A consumer who spends bitcoin to purchase groceries and their daily coffee must track the price of bitcoin at the moment of each transaction, creating hundreds of annual taxable transactions. No taxable event is created when an investor transfers coins between wallets under their personal control.

In the US, prices are listed in dollars, with the value of each dollar being fixed at one dollar. As such, consumers do not need to track their spending, as the dollar's value is fixed, and no capital gains or losses are incurred by spending fiat currency. In El Salvador, bitcoin is legal tender, which allows consumers to spend bitcoin on everyday transactions without incurring any taxable capital gains or losses.

In the US, capital gains tax rates differ by holding period, with short-term rates charged on assets held for less than 12 months and long-term rates charged on assets held longer than 12 months. Taxes for long-term positions are very favorable, with married couples earning less than $94,050 in 2024 owing zero capital gains taxes, 15% capital gains taxes charged up to $583,750 in income, and 20% marginal rates for higher income levels. These tax brackets are updated annually. Short-term capital gains are charged the same tax rate as ordinary income, which is much higher than long-term capital gains tax rates. Below a married income of $383,900, short-term gains are taxed at marginal rates of 10% to 24%, with higher incomes owing taxes with marginal rates of 32% to 37% of the short-term gains.

It's extraordinarily important for investors to keep track of how long they hold each cryptocurrency position, as many prefer to wait beyond a 12-month holding period to realize substantial gains.

While realized capital gains increase tax liabilities, realized losses can reduce them. Losses on assets held short-term offset the tax liability of short-term capital gains, while long-term losses offset long-term gains. If realized losses exceed realized gains in a single tax year, up to $3,000 in losses can offset the tax liabilities owed on ordinary income. Any losses not claimed in a given year create a tax loss carryforward, allowing those losses to be claimed against gains and income in future tax years. In order to reduce tax liabilities, many investors seek to maximize the amount of realized losses in any year where capital gains are claimed.

Tax loss harvesting intentionally sells assets at a loss to generate tax benefits. In the stock and bond markets, wash sales are prohibited, and investors cannot repurchase a substantially similar asset within 30 days of selling an asset to create a tax loss. The tax loss is disallowed if the asset is repurchased within 30 days. As of March 2024, there are no wash sale rules in crypto.[19] This would encourage investors to both sell the dip and buy the dip. When the price of a crypto asset declines substantially below the investor's cost basis, they may wish to realize that loss to reduce their tax liability. However, they may wish to quickly repurchase the asset to maintain exposure to the crypto market.

For example, consider an investor who purchased Ether at $3,000 and saw the price decline to $2,000. By selling Ether at $2,000, a loss of $1,000 per coin is generated that can be used to reduce tax liability in the current year. Short-term losses are more valuable than long-term losses due to the difference in capital gains tax rates. The investor may continue to be bullish on Ether and choose to repurchase tokens for $2,000 on the same day or week. The first trade, buying Ether at $3,000 and selling it at $2,000, creates a capital loss of $1,000 per coin. The second trade, buying Ether at $2,000, establishes a new cost basis, as the profitability of the next sale of Ether is taxed relative to the new entry price of $2,000. This has the effect of reducing tax liability in the current year and increasing tax liability in a future year when the new tokens are sold on a lower tax basis.

Investors are encouraged to watch this area of tax law carefully, as it is anticipated that tax regulations may change to exclude wash sales of crypto assets.[20]

In the US, a 28% tax is charged for any gains from the trading of fine art, coins, sports cards, antiques, and other collectibles, regardless of the holding period. The tax rate on collectibles sales is higher than the long-term capital gains tax rate and even higher than the 2024 tax rate on ordinary income for married couples with incomes below $190,750.

Currently, NFTs and cryptocurrencies have the same tax status, with no wash sale rules and short-term and long-term capital gains tax rates the same as those charged to equity and fixed-income investors. It would not be surprising if the tax rules for cryptocurrencies and NFTs were changed in the future, implementing the wash sale rule and redefining NFT trading to the higher tax rate charged on collectibles.

Most NFTs are purchased using crypto. An investor who purchases an NFT in exchange for Solana or Ether tokens is realizing a taxable sale of those tokens, with the value of those tokens at the time of the exchange setting the basis for the future taxation of profits on the NFT. If the NFT was purchased for one Ether token at a time when it was trading at $2,000, $2,000 is the sales price of the Ether token as well as the purchase price of the NFT.

It is difficult to hold a futures contract long-term because most of the trading liquidity is in contracts with less than 90 days until expiration. The US IRS tax code, Section 1256, notes that 60% of the capital gains taxes on futures contracts will be charged at long-term rates, and 40% will be charged at short-term rates, regardless of the holding period. Bitcoin and Ether futures contracts are traded at the CME Group.

While futures contracts on bitcoin are taxed at 60% long-term and 40% short-term capital gains tax rates, trading bitcoin in the spot market generates capital gains tax liabilities based on the investor's holding period. Traders with short holding periods that regularly generate short-term capital gains tax liability may wish to consider the tax efficiency of futures trading. However, they must be aware of the cash-futures basis that can cause the futures price to move away from the spot price, a topic that is explained in Chapter 21.

Investors can earn crypto tokens as airdrops or as rewards for staking them with validators on proof-of-stake blockchains. Airdrops are given to investors to incentivize early users of a specific crypto or DeFi platform. New protocols may promise airdrops to increase the trading volume or TVL of a DeFi platform. Miners earn block rewards as compensation for the cost of electricity and mining rigs used to validate transactions on the proof-of-work blockchain.

Airdrops, staking yields, and mining rewards are all taxed at the investor's marginal rate as other income, at their value on the date they are received. Miners' taxable income is bitcoin revenue minus deductions for electricity costs and depreciation expense of computer hardware.

Similar to tech stock options awards received by programmers in the late 1990s, investors need to be very cognizant of the tax liability created when receiving highly volatile assets. For example, a small miner received a single block reward for mining bitcoin for a year. The miner received 6.25 bitcoin at a time when bitcoin traded at $30,000 each for a total reward of $187,500. If the miner is in a 24% tax bracket, the tax liability immediately increases by $45,000, with the basis for the price of each bitcoin set at $30,000. To fund that tax liability, the investor may wish to sell 1.5 bitcoin immediately. If they spent the entire proceeds of the block reward or the price of bitcoin declined substantially, the miner may find it difficult to pay the taxes when they are due. Additionally, capital gains taxes are due when the bitcoin is sold above $30,000, while capital loss tax deductions are generated when selling the bitcoin below $30,000.

Crypto rewards paid to users of credit cards issued by centralized exchanges such as Gemini, Coinbase, or Crypto.com are nontaxable rebates or discounts for purchasing goods and services. Selling the coins earned as credit card rewards is a taxable transaction with the basis of the value on the day the rewards were paid. For example, an investor earned $100 of Ether as credit card rewards on a day when it was trading at $3,000. The $100 earned is tax-free, but investors must pay capital gains taxes at the time of sale for any increase in value above the entry price of $3,000 per Ether token.

There are cases when credit card rewards may be taxable, especially when the reward is above $600 when signing up for a new card. A couple earned $300,000 in credit card rewards when spending $6 million in two years on money orders and prepaid cards, which were used to pay the credit card bill. The IRS determined these rewards to be taxable income from a financing business, as it was not a rebate or a discount for purchasing goods and services.[21]

There's a tremendous amount of risk in cryptocurrency, not the least of which is volatility. Bitcoin and Ether tokens have experienced periods of more than 100% annualized price volatility, which is four to five times the volatility of the stock market.

Not only are cryptocurrency and digital asset investments inherently volatile, but investors must also understand that their assets can be lost or stolen in a custody incident. Coins can be stolen in an exploit of a smart contract on a DeFi platform, when an investor gives up their keys or password in an email phishing attack, when a centralized exchange experiences a cyberattack, or even when employees at an exchange such as FTX simply steal the investor's assets. Investors may choose to self-custody in a hardware wallet but can lose their coins if the password is lost or if the hardware device is damaged or stolen.

Another risk of cryptocurrency is inflation. One of the key attractions to Bitcoin is the known monetary policy, which allows a maximum of 21 million bitcoins to be in circulation, less than one bitcoin per US millionaire.[22] Investors are encouraged to investigate the current supply and the maximum supply of tokens, which are tracked at coingecko.com or coinmarketcap.com.

Meme coins are likely worthless in the long run, as they do not have a white paper, a business plan, revenues, or assets. These coins, such as Shiba Inu, Doge, Pepe, and countless others, are simply speculative coins that rely on social media users to hype the potential of instant riches. Unfortunately, the top six meme coins were trading at a combined market capitalization of more than $50 billion in March 2024.

While Shiba Inu, Pepe, FLOKI, and Bonk all trade at a fraction of a penny, speculative investors and influencers claim online that they hope or expect the coins to trade for one dollar, returning more than 10,000 times the current price. Unfortunately, this math is impossible due to the large number of tokens outstanding. There are 420.69 trillion Pepe tokens and 589 trillion Shiba Inu tokens outstanding. There are more than 52,000 Pepe tokens outstanding for each of the world's 8 billion citizens. If either of these tokens were to trade at one dollar, their value would exceed the global stock and bond markets' entire value of $230 trillion.[23] Of course, the global stock market controls massive real estate holdings and produces billions per year in profits, while meme coins produce nothing but amusement and speculative hope.

Another risk of digital assets is the wide variance of tax and compliance regulations required in different countries. El Salvador is likely the most crypto-friendly country, where bitcoin can be used as legal tender and spent without incurring capital gains tax liabilities. China is one of the less crypto-friendly countries, having banned Bitcoin mining in May 2021, despite the fact that China was home to three-quarters of the world's Bitcoin mining rigs at that time.[24] In addition, China banned the purchase and exchange of cryptocurrencies. Investors who own cryptocurrencies may suffer losses if they live in a country that increases the tax rate or prevents the transfer of value to fiat in the traditional banking system.

There are risks that smart contracts can be exploited, which are at their highest when a new protocol is launched, or a software update is installed. Investors can reduce the risk of smart contract exploits by waiting to send value to a protocol until it has become seasoned. After a smart contract has been used for several months, the risk of an exploit declines, especially if a smart contract audit has been published and the code is open source.

The most significant risk in crypto may be the risk of a vampire attack. Many market participants require the source code of a smart contract to be published before investing in a platform, either by buying the tokens or contributing to the TVL of a DeFi platform. While publishing the source code reduces the risk of smart contract exploits, it also makes it impossible for companies to build a competitive advantage through trade secrets. One of the more famous vampire attacks is the one that SushiSwap used on Uniswap.[25] SushiSwap copied the Uniswap source code and started a new protocol. Initially, SushiSwap copied the majority of its code directly from Uniswap's open source as a hard fork, but over time features have been added to distinguish the two platforms. SushiSwap reached a peak valuation of $4 billion in the year after its launch, as it had drained a substantial portion of the liquidity from Uniswap.

In the stock market, companies like Coca-Cola or Kentucky Fried Chicken are able to protect their secret recipe and maintain substantial market share over multiple decades. While trademarks, copyrights, patents, and trade secret protections maintain the value of traditional corporations, crypto protocols find it difficult to maintain a dominant market share in an industry that demands complete transparency. Market share turns quickly in crypto, as Blur had 70% market share in NFT trading just two years after OpenSea had more than 70% market share. This makes it difficult to be a long-term investor in crypto, as it is difficult to say today what the leading platforms will be in five years.

This has been a quick overview of the risks, taxes, and regulations in the cryptocurrency and digital asset business. It has been demonstrated that changing regulations can cause half of the world's Bitcoin mining capacity to move to other countries in just three months or for a platform to lose half its market share in a year or less. For those wishing to start a digital asset business or make substantial investments, it is highly recommended to engage attorneys, accountants, and other professionals with significant experience in this highly specific industry with rapidly evolving regulations.

CHAPTER 17

Tokenization of Off-Chain Assets

The previous discussion of NFTs focused on intangible digital assets, including art, music, and items used in video games. These items are inherently digital, making it easy to see the application of blockchain technology to record ownership and facilitate trading.

Blockchain technology is increasingly being used to provide transparent, permanent, and immutable ownership records of physical and tangible real-world assets (RWAs). Most governments track ownership of some physical assets, such as real estate and automobiles. The ownership of other real-world assets may not have historically been titled, meaning that possession of sports cards or luxury handbags was often deemed to be ownership.

The real-world asset may be in the owner's custody, with the ownership verified by an NFT. Some luxury goods brands, such as Louis Vuitton, now use NFTs to verify the ownership and authenticity of each handbag. Trusted warehouses may hold valuable collectible assets, providing owners with tradable NFTs proving ownership. An owner can take physical delivery of the asset from the warehouse by burning or surrendering the NFT, similar to a claim check. Using NFTs as titles can increase both the liquidity and the security of collectible assets.

Tokenized asset technology has been used for collectibles, fine art, cars, and wine. The use of blockchain technology to tokenize assets may be even more important and valuable than today's leaders of Ether and bitcoin. Once real estate, private equity, hedge funds, infrastructure, and stock and bond mutual funds begin titling assets on blockchains, tens of trillions of dollars of assets may become tracked as tokenized assets. Investors can potentially document the ownership of any real-world asset on a blockchain.

Previously, it was assumed that real-world assets such as real estate, art, and cars were owned in their entirety by a single organization or individual. Tokenization can change this dynamic, making high-priced assets more liquid and available to a broader investment base. Liquidity is the ability to quickly sell an asset at a price close to its assumed value. Stocks and bonds are highly liquid, with small positions being sold instantly and large positions sold within hours or days. Assets such as real estate and shares of private companies are considered to be illiquid, as it takes substantial time to find a buyer, and the price can be highly uncertain.

Consider an office building owned by a single entity with an appraised value of $100 million. Selling this asset can take time, as the number of buyers for large office buildings is relatively limited to a small number of pension funds, real estate investment trusts (REITs), sovereign wealth funds, and publicly traded companies.

Tokenizing the office building may allow 100 investors to each buy a 1% share of the building for $1 million. This fractionalized ownership brings liquidity to the building's owners and provides pricing information whenever a share of the building is sold.[1] By offering fractional ownership of the building, a greater number of investors can participate, increasing the diversification of real estate investment portfolios. Even a large investor seeking to invest $100 million in the office market might prefer to buy 10% of 10 $100 million buildings than to invest $100 million in a single building. By owning portions of 10 buildings, the owner brings diversification to their portfolio, as they are able to invest in different cities or countries and different types of offices and broaden the tenant base. Rather than investing the entire $100 million in the office sector, the investor may prefer to purchase tokenized shares in office and apartment buildings, retail space, and warehouses.

In addition to tracking ownership of RWAs, smart contracts can be used to manage some of its functionality. They can collect rent, distribute income, and manage the voting process for governance decisions.

While tokenized assets increase liquidity, not every tokenized RWA is worth buying. In addition to understanding blockchain technology and the implications of tokenized ownership, investors must perform the same level of due diligence on tokenized assets as on real-world assets. This often includes a physical inspection to understand the condition and location of the real estate or collectible asset.

Investors and issuers of tokenized assets need to understand regulatory and compliance issues, as many of the issues may be deemed to be a security. Some blockchain platforms file registration statements with regulators for tokenized issues, similar to an initial public offering (IPO) in the stock market. Rally, which offers fractional investments in sneakers, cars, comics, historical items, and sports cards, registers each offering with the US SEC and makes the offering available through a FINRA-regulated broker-dealer.[2]

Securities laws consider both the asset being sold and the investor to whom it is sold. Tokenized offerings may be available only to investors in certain domiciles, such as the US or Europe. In the US, some platforms may be available only to accredited investors or qualified purchasers, which allows the issuer to rely on a private placement exemption.

While issuers perform KYC and AML due diligence on investors, investors need to perform due diligence on both the blockchain platform and the assets being offered. Not only is it easy to purchase, but is this real estate or collectible asset offered in excellent condition at an appropriate price?

It's important to understand what legal issues are raised by tokenizing real-world assets, which will likely differ by jurisdiction and type of asset. For instance, if a jurisdiction tracks the title and ownership of real estate and vehicles, will tokenized ownership certificates be acceptable? It might be easier to tokenize collectible assets, as those assets are typically not subject to governmental registration.

Mattereum enables legally binding asset tokenization with legal protection in 170 countries.[3] Assets tokenized on the Mattereum platform have an asset passport and a legal structure that is subject to arbitration under UK law.

Boston Consulting Group and the World Economic Forum anticipate that 5% to 10% of the value of global GDP, or $16 trillion, could be held as tokenized assets by 2030, up from 0.6% in 2023.[4] The majority of the value is expected to be held in listed and unlisted equity, investment funds, bonds, and home equity.

There are five steps to on-chain asset tokenization:[5]

- Assemble the ecosystem: Ensuring coverage for all legal issues, including AML and KYC analysis.
- Register the underlying asset and configure the token: Will the token be publicly available or limited to permissioned investors? Will the token be available globally or only to investors in specific domiciles? Managers appointed to maintain physical real estate holdings. What is the format of the secondary market?
- Set compliance rules: Program the smart contract to include rules on ownership and transferability of the token.
- Store, manage, and distribute the token: Custody arrangements and broker/dealer oversight.
- Execute corporate actions: Set rules for governance, merger, sale, and income distribution.

Traditional asset markets include stocks and bonds, which are often highly liquid investments. Alternative investments can enhance portfolio diversification but at the cost of reduced investment liquidity. Venture capital and private equity investments are designed to enhance portfolio returns, often offering higher returns than publicly traded stocks. Real asset investments, including real estate, commodities, and infrastructure, offer higher returns during times of high and rising inflation when stocks and bonds have below-average returns. Many real asset investments earned positive returns in 2022 when inflation peaked, and the Fed tightened monetary policy. In that same year, bonds suffered their largest losses since the 1970s, and equities entered a bear market, combining for the worst losses to a balanced stock and bond portfolio since the 1930s.

Hedge funds typically underperform stocks during strong bull markets and outperform stocks during strong bear markets, as hedge funds deploy both long and short positions. Private debt strategies can outperform bond market investments through private market loans and can reduce inflation risk through issuing loans at variable interest rates. Smaller areas of alternative investments can provide additional diversification by investing in physical collectibles and royalties from music or pharmaceutical royalties.

A wide variety of assets are already tokenized, including private equity and venture capital funds, real estate, physical collectibles, music royalties, hedge funds, natural resources, private debt, and money market funds. Tokenization can potentially increase liquidity, improve diversification for investors, and reduce the number of middlemen.

Venture capital funds are highly illiquid as are the privately held companies they invest in. A venture capital fund is typically structured as a 10-year closed-end fund where investors delegate investments in startup companies to a venture capital manager. While institutional investors are comfortable with the 10-year life of a venture capital fund, employees of private companies may wish to sell their shares before the company floats an IPO and becomes publicly traded. Tokenized investments in venture capital funds and private company shares have the potential to substantially increase the liquidity of investing in privately held companies.

Security Token Market (STOMarket.com) tracks the trading of more than 500 tokenized debt and equity offerings, with trading volume exceeding $10 million monthly in 2023 and 2024. Offerings are sorted by debt and equity, as well as by the domicile and net worth requirement of investors. The largest tokenized asset tracked by STM is Enegra Group, a $16.9 billion company focused on logistics and risk management for emerging markets commodity miners. 100% of the equity shares of Enegra have been tokenized to trade on the Polygon blockchain.

SPiCE launched the world's first fully tokenized venture capital fund in 2018.[6] Based in Singapore, the SPiCE VC fund has made investments in 13 companies in the blockchain ecosystem, including companies that facilitate asset tokenization. Over its first five years, the NAV of the SPiCE VC fund tokens have risen from $1 to $3.54, with its most successful investments in portfolio companies Securitize and Archaz Custody.

While STM and SPiCE are crypto-native companies, the CeFi giant KKR used the Securitize platform to tokenize its Healthcare Strategic Growth Fund Number 2, which is now traded on the Avalanche blockchain. KKR is an example of a mainstream private equity and venture capital manager embracing the potential of blockchain technology to increase liquidity and access the asset base of the global crypto-native investment community worldwide.

In 2022, the total market capitalization of the global stock market was estimated at $101.2 trillion, while the global bond market had outstanding debt of $129.8 trillion.[7] This is dwarfed in value by the global real estate market, worth an estimated $326.5 trillion in 2021.[8] Savills estimates that the global residential real estate market is worth more than $250 trillion, while agricultural and commercial real estate are valued at nearly $70 trillion. While global stock and bond markets are known for their liquidity, trackable ownership, and well-respected network of exchanges, the real estate market is much less liquid.

The ability to own land, sell it for a profit, and use it as collateral is a key to personal wealth accumulation worldwide. This is even true in the US, a country with well-developed property rights. In 2022, US homeowners had a median net worth of $396,000 and a median income of $94,000, while renters had a net worth of $10,400 and a median income of $42,300.[9]

> Most land in Africa remains unregistered and without formal ownership documents, even when there are legal provisions for the issuance of certificates for all types of land, including customary lands, as in Tanzania, Uganda, and Nigeria. . . The myriad of land tenure systems in Africa complicate the (Western) notion of land ownership and make land ownership statistics difficult to compare across, and even within, countries.[10] In Ethiopia, Nigeria, and Tanzania, land is owned by the state and leased to residents.

Given the importance of real estate to the global economy and the fact that some countries lack the ability to own property or that property ownership is governed by confusing or conflicting claims, tokenized real estate may become by far the most important application of blockchain technology.

In order to immutably record ownership and adjudicate claims of conflicting ownership, property records can note the ownership history of physical real estate as NFTs. Each NFT will be specific to a given property and property owner, with ownership transparent to the market. In the US, property ownership records are tracked within each state or county, with procedures available to record mortgages or other liens against the property's value. A title search is conducted at the time of each transfer to ensure that the stated owner has the right to transfer the property and that all liens have been settled.

In a world of tokenized real estate, NFTs would transparently disclose the history of ownership, and the dates and prices of each transfer.

The key to Bitcoin's success comes from Satoshi Nakamoto's white paper, which contained the algorithm to prevent double spending of digital assets. Tracking real estate ownership through NFTs has the potential to reduce real estate fraud, making it more difficult to pledge the property as collateral to multiple lenders or for someone who is not the true owner to be able to sell the property.

Tokenization of real estate can provide key benefits to individuals who own property in its entirety. Tokenization that allows for fractional ownership of properties can greatly enhance the liquidity of real estate and the ability of investors to own small shares in one or more properties. Tokenized real estate holdings can increase the flexibility of owners to finance properties. Rather than taking out a home equity loan, which requires principal and interest payments, a homeowner could sell 30% of the equity in the home as a tokenized offering. The owner, who still controls a majority interest in the property, has the ability to gain access to a portion of their equity without borrowing. This could revolutionize the ability of seniors to stay in their homes, increasing the cash on their balance sheet without incurring interest expenses or borrowing through home equity lines or reverse mortgages.

Commercial properties may be especially amenable to tokenized ownership, with multiple owners contributing to a building's equity. Smart contracts can be used to collect rent, pay expenses, and distribute net income to property owners.

Blockchain platforms facilitating the tokenized ownership of real estate include Blockchain App Factory, AKRU, Fabrica, HoneyBricks, and Tangible.

Physical collectibles are relatively straightforward to tokenize, as there is no conflict with the ownership registration requirements for real estate and automobiles. The keys to investing in fine art, watches, luxury items, and sports cards are authenticity and custody. The issuers of NFTs representing physical collectibles typically manage or hire a warehouse where the items are secured. With total ownership of a physical collectible, the NFT may resemble a warehouse receipt. When buying partial ownership of a physical collectible, the NFT may resemble shares of stock.

Courtyard and Dibbs offer tokenization of physical collectibles as a service. Brink's and OpenSea are investors in Courtyard.io, a tokenization platform for physical collectibles. Investors can send their physical items to Brink's warehouse, where Courtyard will authenticate and tokenize them.

Investors can hold their assets in the vault or list them for sale on the Courtyard platform. Investors will earn the sales price of their items, less commission, and also receive royalties on all future sales of their collectibles. If the asset is sold, ownership of the NFT is transferred and the asset remains in the vault. Whenever the owner of the NFT wishes to take physical delivery of the asset, the asset is removed from the vault and the NFT is burned. Burning sends a crypto asset or NFT to a wallet without private keys, meaning that the token is inaccessible and removed from circulation.

Many consumer brands participate in NFT markets, including RTKFT, Nike, Azuki, Adidas, Tiffany, and Louis Vuitton.

Music is a significant business with complicated formulas to calculate payments to singers, songwriters, producers, and record labels. In many cases, the songwriter receives royalties greater than or equal to performers. In 1997, long before tokenization, David Bowie borrowed $55 million in a bond offering that was securitized by the royalties from his catalog. The bonds were repaid through the annual income from the performance and streaming of Bowie's songs.[11] A portion of the proceeds from the "Bowie bonds" was used to repurchase the rights to Bowie's songs owned by his former manager. This innovation in securitizing music royalties opened the door for other artists as a new means of financing.

Artists earn income from live performances, the sale of recorded music, and for streaming on Spotify, YouTube, and SiriusXM/Pandora. It is estimated that 7 million streams of an artist's song on Spotify generates a royalty of $27,000.[12] Smart contracts can be deployed to collect the revenues from streaming platforms and automatically distribute the revenue to the creative team at their contracted shares.

Blockchain technology can potentially increase revenue to singers and songwriters while reducing the share paid to intermediaries. If artists can own and publicize their own music through social and blockchain platforms, the cost of distributing their art can significantly decrease. As discussed in Chapter 14, artists can receive royalties from the sale and resale of NFT tickets for live concert performances. NFT ticketing can be used to target fans who will actually attend the concert while reducing the probability that scalpers can purchase tickets. With royalties in place, the share of the revenue paid to the artists increases while the revenue share of the scalpers declines.

Music tokenization platforms, such as Royal, SongVest, and Royalty Exchange, allow for the trading and purchasing of music royalties. Investors can purchase a portion of the royalties that may be sold by the performer, the songwriter, or one of the producers.

Investors in private equity funds must be an accredited investor or a qualified purchaser who agrees that the private equity fund is locking them into an investment for a lock-up period of 7 to 10 years. No liquidity or withdrawal is available until the private equity or venture capital manager sells one or more of the portfolio companies. After the company is sold in an IPO or a merger, the proceeds are distributed to the investors with some portion of the proceeds distributed to the fund manager as fees.

Many hedge funds also require a lock-up period, typically one to three years. New investors in hedge funds must hold their investment for at least the lock-up period before seeking to liquidate their investment. Hedge funds with liquid underlying investments, such as managed futures or long-short equity, may have lock-up periods of one year or even no lock-up period. Hedge funds with less liquid underlying investments, especially distressed debt, will likely have the longest lock-up periods. The lock-up period is used to prevent investor redemptions from causing the hedge fund manager to have to sell illiquid portfolio investments at inopportune times.

It is very disruptive when investor redemptions require a private equity manager to sell a portfolio company, a real estate fund to sell a building, or a hedge fund to sell a defaulted bond in the middle of the bankruptcy process. Forcing liquidity at inopportune times can reduce the sales price of the asset, impacting the value of the fund for both selling investors and the investors sticking with the fund for the long run.

Managers of illiquid alternative funds may not be bothered by investor-to-investor sales of fund interests, as those sales involve only investors and do not require any assets to be sold or withdrawn from the fund. Secondary sales have the promise of improving investor liquidity while not impacting the portfolio value of shareholders remaining invested in the fund.

Tokenization can potentially improve liquidity of private fund investments. In 2019, the hedge fund Protos issued a security token through Securitize.[13] Protos tokens trade on OpenFinance Network, an SEC-registered alternative trading system. OpenFinance also trades other offerings, including SPiCE VC and Blockchain Capital.

Infrastructure investing brings diversification and inflation protection to a portfolio by investing in toll roads, airports, seaports, the electric grid, renewable energy, and solar and wind projects. Physical commodity investments include oil wells, gold mines, and copper mines. While investors desire liquidity in their portfolio, some assets are highly illiquid. Airports and the electric grid are designed to be long-term assets that are not bought and sold frequently. The lives of these assets are likely much longer than the time frame of an individual investor. If infrastructure and natural resource investments can be tokenized, more capital can be committed to the sector while investors will not be required to make the long-term commitment currently required with private funds.

Private debt is a growing market, as the banking industry is shrinking and making it more difficult for corporate borrowers to access the markets. Private debt funds, which initiate corporate loans outside of the banking system, now have assets exceeding $1.5 trillion. Private debt funds offer loans to borrowers for terms of three to five years. Borrowers will pay interest during the life of the loan, and repay the principal at maturity either through their cash flow or by refinancing the loan. Because of the illiquid nature of a private debt loan portfolio, investors in private debt funds typically cannot request a return of their capital before the maturity of the fund or the full repayment of some of the loans. While interest is paid to investors in private debt funds on a quarterly or semi-annual basis, the principal of the loans is only available for redemption after the loans have been repaid.

When private debt investments are tokenized, investors are able to create liquidity without requesting redemptions from the fund managers, which would disrupt the underlying asset portfolio. In addition to facilitating secondary trading, smart contracts can automate loan covenants, collect interest and principal payments, and distribute income to token holders. If private debt investments become more liquid through tokenization, more capital may be attracted to the space.

In 2023, DEFYCA released a platform trading private debt on the Avalanche blockchain.[14] DEFYCA is registered in Luxembourg under the MiCA regulations. Its first offerings include a private credit fund with direct lending to small and medium European businesses and a fund investing in infrastructure debt.

Other private debt platforms include Frigg, DexStar, Clearpool, Jia, Credix, Sapling, and Polytrade Finance.[15]

Finally, some of the world's largest CeFi asset managers are introducing tokenized money market funds. In April 2023, Franklin Templeton launched the first US mutual fund with ownership recorded on the Polygon blockchain. Shares of the Franklin OnChain US Government Money Fund can be purchased as BENJI tokens from a smartphone app. Franklin Templeton notes that the on-chain fund will be more secure and more efficient, with lower costs and faster processing times. Fund assets were more than $320 million in February 2024.[16]

The Blackrock USD Institutional Digital Liquidity Fund launched as a government money market fund on the Ethereum blockchain in March 2024, quickly raising $250 million. Investors are especially excited about Blackrock's entry into the tokenized asset space, as the asset manager is the world's largest, reaching more than $10 trillion in assets before the markets started to decline in early 2022.

CHAPTER 18

Fundamental Valuation Models

Blockchains and distributed ledgers are revolutionary technologies that allow data and assets to be stored, secured, and sent in a global and trustless manner. The goal of distributed ledgers is to disrupt the centralized financial system, seeking to build a decentralized world that gives power to consumers and breaks the power of national regulators and financial institutions. Some investors believe that selected blockchain protocols may soon put banks and securities exchanges out of business.

More than 20 years ago, another revolutionary technology captured the imagination of investors worldwide. At the time, it was termed the internet, populated by dot-com stocks. In the crypto world, this is now called Web 2.0. From 1995 to 1999, there was massive speculation in internet stocks; simply mentioning a company building a website would cause its stock to rocket higher. Some investors believed that the internet would soon put brick-and-mortar retailers out of business. Outside of some notable exceptions such as books, music, and travel, dot-coms 25 years later account for just 15% of retail sales, and brick-and-mortar stores continue to do business.[1]

More than 2,000 private companies issued initial public offerings (IPOs) during the five years from 1995 to 1999. These IPOs had prices that were as lofty as the expectations, at more than 40 times trailing revenues, with operating losses and cash burn rates that needed to be contained.[2] The speculation was that these internet stocks would soon take over the real world of retail. The problem was that many of these companies didn't have enough cash to last until the end of the year.

During that time, the Nasdaq Composite Index rose by more than 570% to its 10 March 2000 peak. The euphoria surrounding tech stocks drove the Nasdaq to trade above 90 times earnings because the growth expectations were as spectacular as the stock prices. The Nasdaq fell by more than 75% between March 2000 and October 2002. More than $1.7 trillion of the value of tech stocks was lost between March and November 2000. The Nasdaq wouldn't regain its high of March 2000 until April 2015.

Is it different this time? Although history might not repeat itself, it often rhymes. Are cryptocurrencies and digital assets a repeat of the dot-com speculations of the late 1990s, where investors bet on a new technology to revolutionize an old industry? Rather than being captivated by the technology, it may be more instructive to model cryptocurrencies and digital assets as publicly traded venture capital or even a new stock market.

How did the venture capital market play out in the dot-com era? Although venture capital investors posted record profits, they did so by selling their companies into public markets, where broadly distributed investors suffered massive losses. In 2000, investors lost more than $1.7 trillion as most of the nascent internet stocks succumbed to their negative cash flows and high burn rates.

Venture capital is an exciting business, but investors must realize that many venture capital investments lose most or all of their value, because it takes time and money to prove that some business models work and others don't. Venture capital works as a business model even if most of the portfolio company investments are losers. If 80% of portfolio companies lose half of their value and 20% earn returns of 1,000%, investors have a total return of 140% before fees on the entire portfolio of companies. The goal of venture capital investing is to find those big winners, the $1 billion unicorns or even the $10 billion decacorns.

The reason some companies are winners, and the majority are losers is that many industries end up as oligopolies, where a small number of firms control the majority of the revenues and profits. Looking at the dot-com stocks more than 20 years later, there are some enormous winners, many of which are household names. Amazon, Priceline, eBay, and Broadcom all went public between 1997 and 1999. The combined market cap of these four firms today is larger than the entire $1.7 trillion drawdown that occurred as the Nasdaq market crashed in 2000. That is, just these four companies together were worth more than all the losses from a notorious era of speculation, volatility, and technological innovation.

Company	IPO Date	2024 Valuation
Amazon	May 1997	$1.9 Trillion
Broadcom	April 1998	$631 Billion
Ebay	September 1998	$27 Billion
Priceline	March 1999	$124 Billion
Netflix	May 2002	$272 Billion
Google	August 2004	$1.9 Trillion

Source: Adapted from Institutional Real Estate, / https://irei.com/publications/article/cryptocurrencies-new-dot-com-bubble/ Last accessed on 15 May 2024.

Notice that each of these companies is very different. Each picked a business model and disrupted traditional industries, such as buying retail goods, booking travel, or selling collectibles and used goods. Each of these companies dominates an industry with relatively few competitors. Many tried to compete with them, but most failed. That is, the winner takes all. Massive industries are dominated by just one to five companies. Oligopolies reign.

Although there are more than 13,600 cryptocurrencies in April 2024, the venture capital and oligopoly models tell us that fewer than 1,000 of these will have any value in the long run. The actual number might be fewer than 100. That is, more than 95% of the cryptocurrencies trading today likely have no long-run value. Today's cryptocurrency market already has a cap-weighted structure similar to stock market indexes. Bitcoin accounts for 50% of the $2.6 trillion cryptocurrency market, Ethereum makes up 15%, and the next 10 coins add another 12% of market capitalization. The top 50 coins comprise approximately 90% of the market cap, while stablecoins are valued at 5%. The remaining 13,500 plus coins are valued at less than 5% of the entire crypto universe.

Notice that the cryptocurrency market's $2.6 trillion value is similar to the market capitalization of a single large technology company, with Microsoft, Apple, Nvidia, Alphabet, and Amazon each valued between $1.9 trillion and $3.1 trillion.

Total Cap ($ Billion)	**$2,616**		coingecko.com
Number of coins	**13,669**		3 April 2024
Coin	Cap ($Billion)	Dominance	Cumulative Weight
Bitcoin	$1,303	49.8%	49.8%
Ethereum	$400	15.3%	65.1%
Binance	$84	3.2%	68.3%
Solana	$82	3.1%	71.4%
XRP	$31	1.2%	72.6%
Dogecoin	$25	1.0%	73.6%
Cardano	$20	0.8%	74.4%
Toncoin	$17	0.6%	75.0%
Avalanche	$17	0.6%	75.6%
Shiba Inu	$15	0.6%	76.2%
Bitcoin cash	$12	0.4%	76.7%
Polkadot	$11	0.4%	77.1%

Microsoft	$3.1 Trillion
Apple	$2.6 Trillion
Nvidia	$2.2 Trillion
Alphabet	$1.9 Trillion
Amazon	$1.9 Trillion

Source: Coingecko.com, Yahoo Finance

In the long run, the value of the digital assets market may be far beyond the $2.6 trillion market capitalization experienced in April 2024. In the long run, thousands of digital assets will trade at prices far below today's levels. How can investors today analyze the cryptocurrency market? Focus on the oligopolies and the sectors in traditional industries most likely to experience substantial disruption from the burgeoning digital asset community. Although thousands of coins and tokens will be worth far less in the future than they are today, some of the biggest companies in the world 20 years from now already may have been started in the crypto sector.

A framework can be built to evaluate the value and potential of each specific crypto asset. This starts with understanding how a venture capitalist evaluates startup firms, including a complete due diligence process and an idea of the long-term value of each firm. Ideally, investors would only buy assets that they understand and focus on those that have a chance to prosper in the long run. The first step of valuation is to investigate the probability of long-run survival. Of course, there is little interest for a long-term investor to spend the time to value a crypto project that is not expected to succeed in the long run.

The first step is understanding the various use cases for cryptocurrencies and digital assets. In terms of a stock market or venture capital model, in which industry does the crypto asset operate? This book has already discussed crypto assets seeking to disrupt traditional businesses in various industries, including payments and stablecoins, bank deposits and loans, securities trading, global money transfers, and insurance. Others are creating completely new business models, such as smart contracts, non-fungible tokens, and the metaverse. Some crypto assets are used as utility tokens to access services competing with real-world technology companies. Examples include Filecoin (FIL), used to access distributed cloud storage similar to AWS and Azure, Basic Attention Token (BAT), which powers the Brave web browser, a privacy-first web browser competing with Google Chrome, and The Graph (GRT), which is a query system that indexes and searches blockchain protocols, such as a Google search for data stored on blockchains.

If cryptocurrencies and digital assets are considered as publicly traded venture capital investments, a valuation model can be built. The valuation process only begins once the investor is convinced the crypto asset represents a project with true potential value. There is no point in going through the valuation process for any asset that is deemed to be a scam, a fraud, or a joke. Unfortunately, meme coins are trading at market capitalizations in

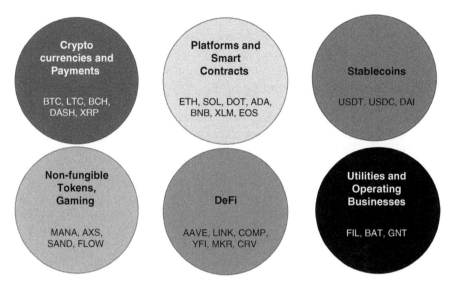

Source: Cryptocurrencies and Digital Assets / Keith Black.

the billions, despite the founders' admission that they are built as a joke and have no use case. These coins will likely have a much lower value in the long run than today's level of market capitalization.

An article by Appinventiv outlines the factors that help decide the success of an ICO[3] :

What industry is the protocol seeking to create or disrupt? What is the size of that addressable market? Does the market have need for the utility that the crypto asset provides?

Has the project published a well-drafted business plan or white paper? Is the project currently being built or is it already functioning?

What are the skills, experience, and success of the programming team as well as the management team? Is this the right team to lead this project?

What is the popularity of the project? This can be measured by the number of users or wallets, the number of software developers contributing to the GitHub, or the number of followers on Twitter, Discord, Telegram, or Reddit.

Does the project exhibit well-designed technology? Is the code efficient and error-free or can it be exploited? Has the project passed an audit from a consulting firm familiar with blockchain design and smart contract code? Is the custody and security design of the project sufficient to protect investor assets?

Is the project well-designed from a financial point of view? Are there scenarios in which the coin can be attacked financially, such as a stablecoin being backed by another crypto asset that it launched? Are the tokenomics appropriately shared between investors and owners of the project, leaving income and assets to pay the software development team for building, upgrading, and managing the project?

Does the market have a real need for this project? Does it run on a standardized blockchain, such as by offering an ERC-20 token that can use the Ethereum blockchain, or is it trying to create a new blockchain? With more than 10 layer 1 protocols already functioning, new projects would be well advised to use an existing protocol unless a new blockchain is required to implement their use case.

At least seven models can be used for valuing crypto assets. Hougan and Lawant discuss the total addressable market, valuing crypto assets as a network, and the cost-of-production valuation.[4] Burniske and Tatar discuss the equation of exchange,[5] and Plan B details the stock-to-flow model.[6] This chapter adds the ideas of using price-to-sales multiples and discounted cash-flow models based on the yield paid as rewards for mining, staking, and providing liquidity.[7]

These valuation models are sourced from various disciplines, including public and private equity, commodity markets, macroeconomics, and the valuation of technology stocks. Some of the models come from traditional valuation methods for public equity and private equity, such as discounted cash flow on staking yields, price/revenue and revenue growth based on income to miners, stakers, and liquidity providers, and the value of existing businesses in the total addressable market. The stock-to-flow and cost-of-production models are sourced from the commodities market. The equation of exchange is related to the macroeconomic modeling of inflation and money supply. Technology stocks have been modeled using Metcalfe's law regarding the value of the network.

Traditional fixed-income securities can be valued using the discounted cash flow of the interest payments, and stocks can be valued using a dividend-discount model. The size, timing, and duration of future cash flows are estimated, and the discounted present value of those future cash flows is calculated. The discount rate uses a risk-adjusted required return, which is likely to be higher for cryptocurrencies and lower for investment-grade fixed-income securities.

Owners of cryptocurrencies can earn yield by staking their assets with validators on proof-of-stake blockchains, with many centralized exchanges offering staking services. Yields are stated on an annual basis and typically are paid in the coin being staked. For example, if the yield on Curve (CRV) is 8% per year, depositing 100 CRV tokens will yield 108 CRV tokens after one year, but the dollar yield is unclear because many of the underlying crypto assets have substantial volatility and the price of the token may increase or decrease substantially during the course of the year.

Staking yields vary substantially based on the risk of the protocol, the issuance rate of tokens, and the urgency with which the protocol seeks to attract wallets and total value locked (TVL). Trust Wallet is Binance's unhosted wallet enabling the custody of tokens across 64 blockchains. There are 18 assets that can access native staking in Trust Wallet, ranging from Ether at 3.52% APY to Stargaze at 22.75% APY.

Token	Staking Yield
Ether	3.52%
Tezos	5.75%
Kava	6.88%
Akash Network	15.66%
Cosmos	13.67%
Stargate	22.75%

Source: Adapted from Trustwallet.

Internet stocks created new and ill-fated valuation methods to justify price levels of companies with zero to minimal revenues; however, many of today's crypto protocols earn substantial revenues. A key difference between internet stocks and crypto assets is noted in the fat protocol thesis.[8] The creators of the internet did not successfully monetize the plumbing of the internet; they didn't, for example, charge a small fee for each email sent or each webpage viewed. This thin protocol value allowed for the fat application layer, where the value of the internet was earned largely by applications such as Amazon, Priceline, and Google. In the blockchain world, there are fat protocols and thin applications. Today's crypto asset market capitalization is dominated by layer 1 protocols, with Bitcoin, Ethereum, Solana, and Cardano alone accounting for more than two-thirds of the total market value of all crypto assets. Because the market currently charges fees for each transaction, much of today's crypto market value has been concentrated in the companies building the base-layer plumbing that facilitates the blockchain revolution.

Those substantial revenues earned by blockchain protocols and applications may be paid to stakers or to miners and liquidity providers. For example, bitcoin is mined using a proof-of-work process, in which substantial computing power is applied to solve an encryption problem while publishing the next block of transactions. By minting 6.25 new bitcoins every 10 minutes, bitcoin miners earned more than $600 million in revenues during the year ending March 2024. Those processing transactions on the Ethereum blockchain earned more than $3 billion for publishing transaction blocks and processing smart contracts. Fees earned by the Uniswap platform were $700 million. Crypto assets, including Uniswap, Lido DAO, and Tron, trade at price-to-sales multiples similar to those of top tech stocks. In order to compare price-to-sales multiples, investors need to evaluate profit margins, dividend policies, and revenue growth rates.

	Market Cap ($ Billion)	Revenue ($ Billion)	Price/Sales
Microsoft	$ 3,124	$ 228	13.7
Apple	$ 2,619	$ 386	6.8
Nvidia	$ 2,224	$ 61	36.5
Alphabet	$ 1,933	$ 307	6.3
Amazon	$ 1,894	$ 575	3.3
Ethereum	$ 400.0	$ 3.1	129.0
Uniswap	$ 6.5	$ 0.7	8.9
Bitcoin	$ 1,303.0	$ 1.0	1,303.0
Lido DAO	$ 2.3	$ 0.8	3.0
Tron	$ 10.3	$ 0.5	22.8

Source: Yahoo Finance, DeFiLlama.com

Venture capitalists are fond of understanding a product's total addressable market. They seek to estimate the revenue potential of a product or service by estimating the market share a new product can achieve and multiplying that market share by the annual revenue of that product's entire industry. That is, the potential value of a protocol offering a new product or service can be estimated by comparing the project to the current market capitalization of existing companies in the same business.

To apply this to cryptocurrencies, investors need to find comparable real-world companies with which the new crypto protocols seek to compete. With its total token supply limited to 21 million, some investors believe that bitcoin will serve as a long-term store of value, similar to the role played by gold today. If bitcoin is believed to compete with gold as a store of value, its $1.3 trillion valuation can increase by nine times to match the current $11.7 trillion market value of gold.

Cryptos with business models in the decentralized finance (DeFi) areas of decentralized exchanges, borrowing, and lending are seeking to disintermediate banks such as JP Morgan ($570 billion) and exchanges such as CME Group ($76 billion). With a combined market capitalization of approximately $100 billion, led by Aave, Chainlink, Uniswap, and Maker, DeFi assets may have substantial upside if they succeed in taking market share from the titans of the centralized finance world.

Asset	April 2024 Price	April 2024 Market Capitalization
Gold	$2,300	$11.7 Trillion
Bitcoin	$66,000	$1.3 Trillion
Ethereum	$3,320	$400 Billion
DeFi Sector		$100 Billion
JP Morgan	$198	$570 Billion
CME Group	$213	$76 Billion

Source: Yahoo Finance, coingecko.com

In the commodities market, prices can be estimated using a stock-to-flow model. In this model, the current inventory level, or stock, is divided by the current-year production or flow. This ratio points out the scarcity of a commodity and has been used to explain the role of gold as a store of value. This scarcity can be noted by a nearly 100-year period in which the supply of gold increased by 1.52% per year, and the US monetary base increased by 7.17% per year during the same time period.[9] At the current production rate, it would take almost 60 years to double the current stock of gold. The constrained supply may explain how gold was able to beat inflation by more than 3% per year during the past 30 years.

Plan B expects the price of bitcoin to continue rising as the growth of its supply continues to slow.[10] In 2019, Plan B's stock-to-flow model estimated the bitcoin price would reach $100,000 before the April 2024 halving.[11] With 19.6 million bitcoins outstanding in April 2024, supply growth is strictly limited, with an explicit schedule to reach a maximum supply of 21 million bitcoins in the year 2140.

When Bitcoin started in 2009, 50 bitcoins were awarded each 10 minutes to the miners securing the network and posting all recorded transactions to the Bitcoin blockchain. Every four years, the size of the block rewards is halved, falling to 25 in November 2012, 12.5 in July 2016, 6.25 in May 2020, and 3.125 in April 2024, etc. These block rewards continue to be halved each four years until all 21 million bitcoins have been released by the year 2140. This halving schedule and known monetary policy is a key element to the value proposition of bitcoin, especially in a world where central banks have been printing fiat currency for many years without regard for the inflation rate that degrades the currency's value.

As an example of stock-to-flow, consider the supply-demand imbalance created by the launch of spot bitcoin ETFs in the US. From their launch on 11 January 2024, until 3 April 2024, the largest four ETFs reached total assets under management of more than $20 billion in just 11 weeks. These ETFs shattered the largest ETF launch when the gold ETF (GLD) raised $1 billion in its first three days in 2004.[12] The Blackrock iShares Bitcoin Trust (IBIT) reached $9.76 billion in AUM in its first 11 weeks, aided by inflows of $3.1 billion in just six trading days between 27 February and 5 March 2024.[13]

At a bitcoin price of $68,350, these four ETFs purchased nearly 300,000 bitcoins in just 11 weeks. The demand of 300,000 bitcoins from just four ETFs in 11 weeks exceeded the supply of 83,700 newly minted bitcoins paid to miners as block rewards over the same time period. With block rewards at 6.25 each 10 minutes, 900 bitcoins are minted daily (6.25 block reward x 6 blocks/hour x 24 hours per day). The reason the April 2024 bitcoin halving is expected to be bullish is that the supply will be cut in half from 900 to 450 bitcoins mined each day. If demand stays strong while supply is cut in half, supply-demand analysis predicts rising bitcoin prices.

Bitcoin Spot ETFs	AUM	Bitcoins Purchased
iShares Bitcoin Trust (IBIT)	$9.76 billion	142,794
Wise Origin Bitcoin Trust by Fidelity (FBTC)	$6.68 billion	97,732
Ark/21 Shares Bitcoin Trust (ARKB)	$2.18 billion	31,895
Bitwise Bitcoin ETP (BITB)	$1.56 billion	22,824
Total	$20.18 billion	295,245
1/11/2024 to 4/3/2024	Bitcoin mined in 93 days	83,700

Source: Adapted from BLOCKWORKS INC.

Closely related to this halving schedule is the cost-of-production model.[14] In a proof-of-work mining process, producers of bitcoin compete to solve a cryptographic puzzle. The first to solve this puzzle in each 10-minute period can publish the next block of transactions and earn the block reward. A block reward of 3.125 bitcoins is worth $200,000 when bitcoin trades at $64,000. The difficulty of bitcoin mining adjusts automatically given the amount of computing, or hashing, power currently deployed on the network. As more miners come online, the difficulty of mining increases to make sure that the block time on the bitcoin blockchain averages 10 minutes. After each halving occurs, it is assumed that the variable cost of production would double, because the same amount of electricity is expended to earn block rewards that have been reduced by half.

Bitcoin miners make substantial investments in computer hardware, focusing on custom-designed bitcoin mining rigs built using application-specific integrated circuits. Each rig may cost $5,000 to $10,000 and successful miners deploy thousands of mining rigs. These rigs also are substantial users of electricity; they are said to consume between 0.2% and 0.9% of the world's electricity.[15] Given that electricity costs are a key driver of miner profitability, miners seek to locate in areas of low electricity costs, especially those that are driven by natural sources such as steam-driven turbines from volcanoes or hydroelectric dams. Due to the continued addition of mining rigs by publicly traded bitcoin mining firms, the cost of mining a single bitcoin reached an all-time high of more than $51,000 in March 2024.[16] This includes both the fixed cost of mining rigs and data centers and the variable cost of electricity.[17] Miners with the lowest average production costs are likely to be the longest-lasting and most profitable, and those with the highest production costs are likely to stop mining when the price of bitcoin falls below the variable cost of the electricity used to generate the new supply of bitcoin. As the highest-cost miners shut off their rigs during times of low crypto prices, this acts as a support for the price of bitcoin and serves to increase the profitability of the remaining miners who have a higher probability of publishing the next block given the smaller number of miners remaining. Another reason for the bullish sentiment surrounding the April 2024 halving in block rewards is that double the electricity is required to mine each new bitcoin, raising production costs far above the recent $51,000 record. If higher-cost miners shut down their rigs after the halving, the production cost of the remaining miners can decline due to declining competition. According to the cost of production model, as the cost of mining each bitcoin rises, the price of bitcoin is likely to rise, and the number of active mining rigs is expected to decline. In commodity markets, the price is expected to match the marginal cost of production, meaning that the price of bitcoin is likely to rise after each halving increases the marginal cost of production.

Proof-of-stake networks are more difficult to value using the cost-of-production method because the minting of the next block is awarded based on the size of each miner's stake in the network. That is, a miner who owns or controls 1% of the staked tokens on the network has a 1% probability of publishing the next block of transactions. Proof-of-stake mining uses 99% less electricity than proof-of-work mining because proof-of-stake mining requires only the selected miner to perform the complicated cryptography required to secure the network rather than the redundant efforts of thousands of mining rigs in the proof-of-work system. Given the lower variable costs of proof-of-stake mining, miners will be less likely to reduce supply during times of low token prices.

Burniske and Tatar adapt Fisher's equation of exchange to value bitcoin.[18,19] The famous equation, MV=PQ, notes that money supply times velocity equals the price of goods and services times the quantity of goods and services. The high level of consumer price index inflation experienced in 2021 and 2022 can be explained using this equation, because the quantity of goods and services has been constrained by COVID-19 and supply-chain related shortages, while the money supply simultaneously increased through both monetary and fiscal policy stimulus. The velocity of the US dollar, or the speed of spending money, has ranged from 0.9 to 3.5 during the past 30 years. Bitcoin may have a higher velocity than US dollars, with the average bitcoin holding period of just more than two months, resulting in a velocity of about 5.

With an estimated $10 trillion annual trading volume and a velocity of 5, the value of bitcoin is estimated at $2 trillion. When fully diluted by the eventual bitcoin supply of 21 million, this implies a long-run value of $95,238 per bitcoin.[20]

The last method of valuing crypto assets comes from network theory. Metcalfe's law states that the value of a network is proportional to the square of the number of participants. This model is easily applied to crypto assets, given the transparency of blockchains that report the number of total wallets on each blockchain and the frequency of their use. This model has been used successfully for relative valuations of social networking companies whose values have increased with the size of their user bases. Crypto assets also tend to follow Metcalfe's law because the protocols with the most users have earned higher valuation levels.[21] Peterson empirically validated that the medium- to long-term price of bitcoin has followed Metcalfe's law.

There were 17 million wallets at the end of 2017, when bitcoin was priced near $14,000,[22] which rose to 48 million wallets in August 2023[23] when bitcoin was valued at around $26,000. Metcalfe's law predicts that this increase in the number of wallets would increase bitcoin's price by nearly 800% to $111,612, by squaring the ratio of 48 million wallets to 17 million wallets.

Although more than 13,000 cryptocurrencies exist today, fewer than 100 of today's cryptocurrencies likely will have substantial value in 10 years. Today's market capitalization is already highly concentrated, with more than 75% of value in the top 10 crypto assets and 95% of value in the top 100. However, those crypto assets that survive and thrive and succeed at disintermediating substantial current businesses or those that create brand new industries may individually have valuations on the order of those enjoyed today by Amazon.com, Google, or Apple.

The challenge for today's investors is to pick the relatively small number of today's crypto assets that will be among the largest winners during the next decade. By following the due diligence and valuation processes of today's public equity and private equity investors, analysts may increase the odds of finding the large, long-run winners in the crypto assets space. By having the discipline of following a time-tested process, investors will at least be able to avoid speculation by focusing on crypto assets that have business plans, operating protocols, growing numbers of users, and the potential to create or disrupt a large industry. Buying crypto assets without a business plan or white paper and a growing user base is more speculation than investing and will likely be unsuccessful in the long run. That is, Shiba Inu and Dogecoin may be the equivalent of the dot-com era pets.com.

CHAPTER 19

Initial Coin Offerings (ICOs), Security Token Offerings (STOs), and Tokenomics

Capital formation is the process of funding a company as it grows. In TradFi markets, companies are often funded by angel investors or venture capital funds.[1] The less developed a company is, the lower its valuation, the higher the risk, and the more difficult it is to receive funding. A company is in its pre-seed stage when it is just an idea and a prototype has not yet been developed. The pre-seed stage is the riskiest time to invest, as there is no guarantee that the company will ever earn revenues or profits. Companies raising funds before earning revenue do so at relatively low valuations, as investors are taking a risk on a company with a high probability of failure.

Startups reach the seed stage or seed round of funding by receiving investments from external sources, typically after the company has a product and at least some revenue. Angel investors are individuals who make investments in startup firms, with 60% of angel investments made during the seed round.[2] Angel funding is rare, as angels may fund 60,000 US startups in a typical year, a small portion of the 6 million US companies with employees.[3] For seed-stage companies that are able to raise capital, the typical equity raise is between $500,000 and $2 million, valuing companies at $5 million to $15 million.

Venture capitalists often start investing in startups with the A round of funding, which follows the seed stage and precedes the B, C, and later-stage funding rounds. While venture capital funds invested $2.5 trillion globally in 2023,[4] little of this funding was provided to companies with valuations below $15 million.

As the startup passes each milestone, the company's valuation rises, and the risk declines. With each milestone achieved, the probability of failure declines. Milestones include developing a viable product, earning patent protections, securing initial customers, reaching $1 million in revenue, and so on. Venture capitalists (VC) don't provide startups with all of the required capital at once but portion out the investments according to milestones.

The VC and the entrepreneur negotiate the time and cost of meeting the next milestone. If the entrepreneur is able to meet the next milestone as agreed and on budget, the VC will provide the next round of funding. VCs continue to invest in companies that grow revenue and meet milestones while reducing or eliminating future funding rounds for companies that fail to meet milestones. VCs are prepared to invest in companies that fail but prefer to invest less in companies that fail and more in companies that succeed.

Capital provided to entrepreneurs by VCs and angel investors is meant to be spent on growing the business and meeting milestones. The funding can be used to build prototypes, secure patents, hire programmers, and build inventories. As the company grows its revenue, its need for capital can increase, with investors often anxious to invest in enterprises with strong revenue growth. Once a company becomes profitable, its need for external capital may decrease.

What is the process by which angels and VCs decide which companies to invest in? The goal is to find companies that can reach a specific level of revenue by a specific date. In order to do so, the entrepreneur needs great ideas and an experienced and motivated team that can deliver on those ideas.

Angels and VCs need to understand the technology they are investing in and be able to trust that the entrepreneur has the right combination of ideas, technical skills, and passion to bring the product or service to market. While the long-term financials of startup companies are notoriously difficult to project accurately, the key is understanding the total addressable market (TAM). The potential revenue of startup companies is typically projected as a market share goal based on a TAM, such as 5% of a $10 billion market. To estimate the TAM, the investor needs to understand the business model of the startup and the industry in which the company competes. It is easier to estimate the TAM in an established industry, such as banking or securities exchanges than in an emerging industry, such as NFTs and the metaverse. By definition, emerging industries have a less certain growth rate and revenue trajectory.

Investors need to understand the startup, its products, its team, and the competitive environment. In many markets, there is a first-mover advantage, where the first team to launch a product or service often maintains a significant market share, even after superior offerings are subsequently released. Development teams may be encouraged to launch products as quickly as possible while resisting the temptation to delay the launch for months or years to develop a perfect product. That is, once a viable product has been developed, it may be advantageous to launch quickly to gain market share and release improved versions of the product as they become available.

Angels and VCs dilute or reduce the equity stake of the founding team when investing in startup firms. If a VC takes a 20% stake in a startup that has never before accessed external capital, the founding team's holdings are reduced to a maximum of 80% of the firm's value. It is important to note that angels and investors in VC funds located in the US must be accredited investors or qualified purchasers. In addition, equity investments made by angels and VC funds are illiquid, as it can take years to sell the holdings in an IPO or a merger/acquisition.

In 2017 and 2018, many crypto projects sold tokens through initial coin offerings (ICOs). During an ICO, investors purchase tokens in a startup crypto project for the first time, often using Ether tokens as the payment method. Rather than raising funds from angels and VCs, ICOs seek funding directly from crypto investors globally.

Typically, these projects were in the pre-seed stage when raising capital through the ICO. The most reputable ICOs raised money for projects that had released a white paper or a business plan detailing the team's roadmap to the launch of a successful new crypto protocol. Because most ICOs raised capital during the pre-seed stage before the crypto protocol was built, the investments were highly speculative. Due to the extreme uncertainty of when and if these crypto protocols would be launched, investors purchased tokens at relatively low valuations. Had the crypto projects been more developed at the time of the ICO, the protocols may have been able to raise capital at higher valuations, leaving greater economic value to the development team.

ICOs may have more in common with crowdfunding platforms than angel or VC investments. Angel and VC investments are highly illiquid investments made by accredited investors and qualified purchasers. Retail investors can make investments in crowdfunding campaigns. The US Congress passed the Jumpstart Our Business Startups (JOBS Act). Title III of the JOBS Act, titled Regulation Crowdfunding, allowed companies to raise up to $5 million in any 12-month period. Regulation Crowdfunding allowed retail investors, or those investors who do not qualify as accredited investors or qualified purchasers, to invest limited amounts into the equity funding of small businesses. Even greater amounts can be raised under Tier 1 and Tier 2 of Regulation A offerings, with annual limits of $20 million and $50 million, respectively. Crowdfunding campaigns take place on FINRA-registered funding portals such as Kickstarter or IndieGogo. Investors must hold securities purchased through crowdfunding campaigns for at least 12 months. Portals are required to perform due diligence on issuers of crowdfunded securities, and transparency must be provided to investors.

ICOs may resemble crowdfunding, where the internet facilitates capital formation from retail investors. Unfortunately, the US Congress passed the JOBS Act to facilitate fundraising from small companies, but has not yet passed legislation clarifying regulations regarding fundraising by new crypto protocols and DApps. ICOs may have greater liquidity than crowdfunded equity investments if the tokens start trading on a centralized or decentralized exchange. Tokens can be difficult to sell or exchange if not listed on a centralized or decentralized exchange.

Tokens are not native to a blockchain but are created on top of a smart contract platform, such as the ERC-20 compatible tokens that are built on the Ethereum blockchain. Similar to venture capital, investors in ICOs are investing in a young and speculative startup business. There is a potential, however, for the tokens purchased in an ICO to be much more liquid than venture capital investments, as tokens represent fractional ownership. The stakes held by VCs are typically sold in their entirety at the time of an exit.

What distinguishes ICOs that receive funding from those rejected by investors? Before investing, professional investors complete a due diligence process.[5] Due diligence includes an evaluation of the team, the business plan or white paper, the market's need for the product or service, as well as the economics of the investment. When investing in crypto assets, the economics of the investment are termed tokenomics.

Each project funded by a VC or an angel investor has prepared a business plan. This plan provides bios on the project team, a project definition, and technical specifications. It also includes financial projections for both the time and the costs to develop the project and the revenues that could be earned if the project is successful. Investors evaluate the prospects of an ICO by reviewing the white paper, which is similar to a business plan.

While VCs and angels typically wait to invest until the company has a product and some revenue, ICOs raise funds much earlier in the project's life. In many cases, ICOs seek funding based on the ideas and team outlined in the white paper rather than on products that have already been developed. Investors should choose to not invest in any ICO that has not provided a white paper or a working prototype, as the potential valuation of an undisclosed project is too uncertain for anyone but the most speculative investors to participate in.

Investors need to judge the potential success of the project by evaluating the need for the project, its technology plan, the use of the token, and what competing platforms have built or plan to build. With available smart contract platforms, including Ethereum, Polkadot, Cosmos, Solana, Avalanche, Cardano, and others, it is often faster and easier to build a DApp on an existing blockchain rather than a new one. At this point, development teams should present a very clear reason why they might choose to build a completely new blockchain. Developers that offer their code as open source will make it easier for experienced coders to evaluate the skill of the developers and the uniqueness of the DApp.

The fundraising goal of the ICO should be stated with the amount of funds raised ideally sufficient to fund the majority of the development costs of the project. Clear tokenomics should be presented, offering reasonable portions of the tokens for public investors while reserving tokens for the founders and for ongoing distribution to developers participating in the project.

In addition to understanding the utility of the DApp, the project should offer appropriate levels of security and custody.[6] Given that a key to token valuation is the size of the user community, the popularity of the project's website and social media communities, such as Twitter/X, Discord, Telegram, Reddit, and GitHub, are extraordinarily important. What code has been contributed to GitHub and how many developers are involved with the project?

Angels and VCs have relatively standard ways of investing in startup businesses, such as by investing in convertible preferred stock. Investors in convertible preferred stock will convert to common equity when the startup has reached substantial success, while retaining the option to participate in a liquidation of a less successful company as debt investors. Angels and VCs typically require their investments to include governance rights and potential cash flows as terms of the investment. The valuation placed on the company by angels and VCs is proportionate to the potential revenue and future market capitalization of the startup.

In contrast, the tokenomics of crypto projects are much more varied. This means that investors must study the tokenomics carefully before investing. While entrepreneurs seek to maximize their stake in the company, investors want incentives to be balanced.[7] If the company is successful, the founders, the hired developers, and the investors should all share in the success in a balanced way. The white paper should disclose the maximum number of tokens planned to be issued, as well as the split of the tokens reserved for investors, developers, founders, miners, and stakers, and those reserved for future airdrops to early adopters or sale at some future date. The viability of the project should be evaluated, including the ability of the project team to adapt the product's design for changes in the market over time. Is the token designed as a governance token or equity in the project, or are they designed as utility tokens that will be used to access a valuable service?

Investors prefer tokens that provide cash flows, but providing cash flows and governance votes to investors can put the token in regulatory crosshairs. When Uniswap disclosed a February 2024 plan to distribute trading fees to tokenholders, the price of the token doubled within two weeks. Unfortunately, Uniswap received a Wells Notice from the SEC in April 2024, which is a precursor for an enforcement action. The SEC asserts that Uniswap runs an unregistered securities broker and exchange.[8] The Wells Notice was sent to Uniswap when the fee-sharing idea was a proposal that had not yet been implemented. The legal status of a token is a key consideration for investors.

Additionally, investors will investigate whether the token is designed using a proof-of-work or proof-of-stake validation system. For a proof-of-stake protocol, it is important to know what the staking yield is likely to be and how those tokens will be provided to stakers and validators.[9]

One of the most important considerations is the number of tokens that can potentially be issued and whether the protocol is inflationary or deflationary over time, with tokens continually being issued or burned, respectively. Investors prefer relatively rare tokens, not Shiba Inu with more than 589 trillion tokens outstanding. Despite a token price of less than one-hundredth of one cent, Shiba Inu had a market capitalization of $13.4 billion in April 2024 that would rank in the top 700 US stocks. Even though Shiba Inu is just a joke and has no revenue or business plan, its market capitalization is similar to real world companies such as Fox, News Corp, United Airlines, Stanley Black & Decker, Molson Coors, MGM Resorts, Key Bank, Franklin Resources, and Campbell Soup. These companies have revenues between $6 billion and $53 billion with annual profits of as much as $2.6 billion. In the long run, the value of all assets is related to its revenues, assets, and cash flows, making inflationary tokens such as Shiba Inu highly speculative and likely to decline substantially in value.

The tokenomics should be designed to support the community, providing incentives for developers to build the project and for liquidity providers to lock value into the DApp. As Metcalfe's Law suggests exponentially increasing levels of valuation based on the growth of the community, tokens should take steps to increase the number of developers and users involved with the project.

Teams should only consider raising funds through an ICO if they are building a product that is needed by the market and is likely to earn customer attention and revenues.[10] The team should have the skill to build the project and be passionate and focused on its development. Teams that keep full-time jobs while developing a crypto protocol in their spare time may not have the passion or the focus to quickly build a strong new company. The key to success is the ability to quickly design a strong technology platform that will be in demand by consumers.

Unfortunately, crypto entrepreneurs often sell too much of their equity quickly and cheaply. Retail investors can get in on the ground floor in crowdfunded projects, whether sold on Kickstarter or an ICO. By interacting with the development team on a social media platform, investors may be whitelisted or able to purchase the offering early or at a discount.

As previously discussed, the valuation of a company is at its lowest before the product is developed and the revenue begins. This makes ICOs one of the most expensive ways to fund a business, as many of the development teams sell up to 80% of the planned tokens to fund the project. This provides substantial upside to investors for successful projects but subjects investors to the risk that most of their investments will lead to losses. Developers are encouraged to delay fundraising as long as they can, as the valuation of the token is likely to rise with each milestone reached. Rather than selling all of the tokens in a single ICO, entrepreneurs may increase the proceeds of token sales by spacing out the fundraising over time, perhaps selling 10% of the tokens every six months or after each milestone is reached.

In contrast, angels or VCs often purchase 20% of the equity in a startup firm, but only after the product and revenue have been at least initially established. When ICOs are sold globally without regard for the net worth of investors, there is a substantial chance that the token sale will not comply with securities laws. An offering of a utility token or one that complies with crowdfunding regulations may potentially be able to be sold without registration or regulatory intervention. Of course, teams are encouraged to seek legal advice while structuring their fundraising activities.

A key concern of investors is whether they will be able to sell their tokens. Many ICOs are sold without the guarantee that the token will be available for trading on a centralized or decentralized exchange. Without such liquidity, it will be difficult for investors to sell their tokens at any significant level of valuation.

Milestones that increase a token's valuation and reduce the probability of the project's failure include patents, prototypes, significant code contributions, a growing social media following, a listing commitment from a centralized exchange, and the establishment of a liquidity pool on a decentralized exchange. The further the project progresses in building the tech and the user community, the greater the valuation and the lower the risk.

Half of the ICOs sold in 2017 and 2018 quickly failed.[11] Many of the failed projects did not offer a strong team, a rational business model, or a professional white paper. Investors skilled in due diligence or venture capital valuation techniques may have been able to distinguish between projects with very high and much lower probabilities of failure. If a white paper can't discuss a rational business model or present a high-quality development team, it likely isn't worth investing in. Some projects actually attempted to raise money through an ICO without even offering a white paper. Investors who purchase tokens without a business model or a white paper are highly likely to lose their money, as professional investors only allocate assets to projects with a reasonable probability of success. That is, don't invest unless there is a strong white paper that presents a rational and compelling business plan.

Another mistake entrepreneurial teams make is hiring talented engineers and programmers intent on building strong technology without balancing the team with others skilled in finance, marketing, and sales. If the project can't get the attention of users or investors, a strong tech offering may not attract the capital the team needs and desires.

As many as a quarter of the ICOs were scams that raised money and quickly failed. What distinguishes a scam from a legitimate investment opportunity? Remember that capital is raised to build a business. Investors who have read the white paper invest money with the goal of spending that money on engineering and marketing talent that can grow a great business. Teams can be charged with fraud if they raise money and do not invest that money in a good-faith effort to build a new business. It is fraud when money is raised, and no promised efforts to build a business are made. In contrast, a business can fail even when making a strong effort to build the business. Early investors take the risk that a company can run out of funding before reaching milestones or that another project with similar or better tech is released while the team is still building their project. Early investors take these risks because they know that a relatively small number of successful projects can earn substantial financial returns. It is not a crime or a fraud to spend capital raised on an honest attempt to build a business. There is a clear distinction between stealing money without even trying to build a business versus spending money to build a business that did not reach the desired level of success.

Another key risk of investing is that the token lacks utility or a user community. The team may build a project with strong tech, but if there is no demand for the functionality of the blockchain or the DApp, investors can lose money even when the promised project was built on spec and on time.

In all types of companies, VCs and angel investors know that a substantial portion of their portfolio companies will not meet their milestones or build a product that lacks demand, which leads to financial losses. The reason these investors continue to engage with startup companies is that they seek to lose a small amount of money on a large number of companies while making a large amount of money on a small number of companies. Investors are profitable when the size of profits on winning investments exceeds the size of losses on the losing investments.

Pre-seed and seed stage investments have the highest probability of failure, while investing in the A or B round after many milestones have been met can reduce the risk of investing in startup companies. Each milestone achieved reduces the risk and increases the company's valuation.

When investing in ICOs or VC funds, it is OK for companies or projects to fail. The companies wisely spent the capital raised and could not build a product that met consumer demand within the time and budget allowed. It is important to understand the burn rate of a project. For example, a pre-revenue company spending $1 million per month will burn through $10 million in ten months. If the startup has not started earning revenue by the tenth month, it will fail if it can't raise a new round of funding.

Even if a project is making progress, building great smart contracts, attracting a strong community of developers and users, and executing all the milestones in the business plan, there is no guarantee that investing in that project will be profitable. Beyond building the business, the key for investors to profit is the liquidity of the token. It is unlikely that investors can sell at a substantial profit if the token is not listed on a centralized exchange or included in a liquidity pool on a decentralized exchange.

While 1,785 ICOs successfully raised capital from 2016 to 2019, 3,685 projects tried to raise capital and didn't receive funding.[12] ICOs that succeeded in fundraising attracted $26.5 billion, with $21.5 billion raised by Ethereum-compatible projects. Over two-thirds of the capital raised was for projects domiciled in the United States, Singapore, Switzerland, the United Kingdom, the British Virgin Islands, and the Cayman Islands.

The majority of the ICOs by number failed. However, consistent with the winner-take-all track record of venture capital, a small number of ICOs grew rapidly in market capitalization. Just seven ICOs that raised $2.5 billion were valued at nearly $65 billion in April 2024. These included Telegram, Filecoin, Tezos, Polkadot, Hedera, Tron, and Cardano. By far, the biggest winner was Ethereum, which raised $19 million and reached a valuation of $372 billion. It is not possible to directly calculate the return from the ICO funds raised to today's valuation, as the number of tokens outstanding may have increased from airdrops, staking or mining rewards, and subsequent token sales after the ICO date. ICO investors who did not purchase tokens in one of the 20 most successful projects likely lost money on their investment.

Project	ICO Proceeds	April 2024 Market Capitalization
Telegram	$1,700 million	$22 billion
Filecoin	$257 million	$3.2 billion
Tezos	$236 million	$1 billion
Polkadot	$121 million	$9.7 billion
Hedera	$100 million	$2.8 billion
Tron	$70 million	$9.8 billion
Cardano	$63 million	$16.3 billion
Ethereum	$19 million	$372 billion

Source: Adapted from ICOBench.com.

Selling a stock through an initial public offering, an IPO, often takes three to six months or even longer. There are required filings with the securities regulator in each country where the offering is listed, the time it takes to build the prospectus, the roadshow to meet prospective investors, and the required disclosures for retail investors.

In contrast, ICOs can be accomplished very quickly, with more than 77% of 2017 ICOs completed within 10 to 50 days and less than 10% taking more than 70 days. While ICOs took longer to complete in 2018, the process is still much quicker than that of IPOs.

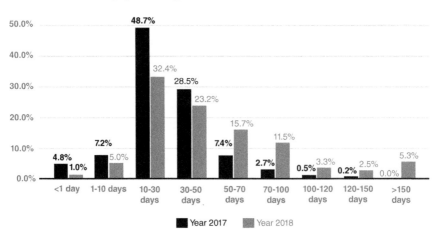

Source: Why do ICOs Fail? Are They Still Worth Investing in 2019–2020?, Appinventiv.com

More than 80% of the ICO activity in 2017 and 2018 was used to fund Ethereum-based projects. As many of the tokens offered as ICOs were purchased with Ether tokens, the ICO activity substantially increased the demand and use case for Ether tokens.

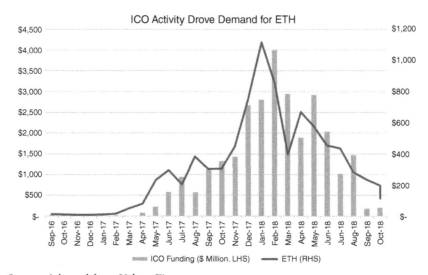

Source: Adapted from Yahoo Finance.

Ether tokens were priced at $200 in April 2017 and rose to more than $1,000 in January 2018, near the peak of ICO fundraising in February 2018 when ICOs raised $4 billion in a single month. Many ICOs required investors to pay with Ether, which increased demand for those tokens. By the third quarter of 2018, the SEC's ruling that many ICOs were unregistered securities offerings led to a dramatic collapse in ICO activity. ICOs were sold to investors globally without regard for their status as retail or high–net worth investors.

As the ICO fundraising activity declined, so did the demand for Ether tokens, which declined to below $200 by October 2018, entering crypto winter, a time of low prices and low demand for tokens. Crypto assets, such as Ether and bitcoin, experience tremendous volatility. Ether tokens rose to more than $4,000 in 2021 with the rise of Ethereum-based DeFi DApps.

A key risk of ICO investing is that there is no guarantee that the investor will ever be able to sell their tokens. Selling illiquid tokens that are not available for trading on a centralized or decentralized exchange can be difficult. Liquidity, or the ability to sell a token at a price close to what is expected, increases substantially when a centralized or decentralized exchange lists the token for trading.

Many ICOs were launched without an exchange listing, and token holders needed to wait until the project was successful enough to attract the attention of a centralized exchange. In 2024, centralized exchanges in the US typically offered less than 100 tokens for trading, with offshore platforms offering a much wider selection due to fewer regulatory concerns.

Liquidity risk is substantially reduced when the tokens are first sold as an Initial Exchange Offering (IEO) or an Initial DEX Offering (IDO or IDEO). When an IEO fundraising is completed, the project has an agreement for the tokens to be immediately listed on a centralized exchange, such as Binance, Coinbase, Kraken, or Gemini. Before listing any token, the centralized exchange will perform a limited due diligence process to ensure that the offering has some potential for success and is not clearly a scam.

In exchange for providing immediate liquidity for the tokens sold in an IEO, the centralized exchange may require a listing fee and a percentage of tokens sold. Simply by listing this new blockchain protocol, the centralized exchange is adding significant value to it. Polygon, Band, Sandbox, Harmony, Elrond, and MultiversX now have significant valuations after being sold as Initial Exchange Offerings.

Investors may prefer an IEO to an IDO, as the centralized exchange has completed at least some level of due diligence. Less due diligence may be performed in an IDO, as the listing on the DEX may be as simple as a liquidity provider contributing the new tokens in a trading pair on the DEX. The liquidity pair would require a contribution of equal amounts of the new token and a corresponding paired token, which could be Ether, a stablecoin, or another token of similar value and liquidity.

A key difference between an ICO and an IDO is the number of tokens sold.[13] ICOs often raised very expensive capital by selling up to 80% of the tokens in the pre-seed stage of the protocol. Many IDOs will list 10% to 20% of the supply of the newly issued token, reserving the majority of token sales for a later time after milestones have been reached and the tokens have reached higher valuation levels. This provides more economics to the development team because they're not selling everything at the initial speculative valuation. They're waiting to sell more tokens until after the project has made more progress and has a higher valuation.

Users can be whitelisted by interacting with the project's smart contract or by building relationships on the team's social media platforms. Because the project sells relatively few tokens, whitelisted users can initially buy less than $1,000 worth of an IDO. By investing early in the life of a project, investors may experience a total loss of value or potentially earn multiples of 10 times or greater on their initial investment.

Investors may be required to own launch pad tokens to participate in IDOs offered by Polkastarter or the Binance Smart Chain pad.

Crypto Potato compares ICOs, IEOs, and IDOs. An ICO places all of the responsibility on the company. The company has to market, build, and sell its project. The offering will be highly speculative, as no third party has completed a due diligence process. ICOs are a lot of work for the protocol that is trying to complete a fundraising offering.

Protocols selling an IEO have a centralized exchange as a partner in their fundraising that will complete some initial due diligence while providing marketing assistance and the exchange platform. These contributions of the centralized exchange may make tokens sold in an IEO less speculative than those sold in an ICO.

An IDO has characteristics of both an ICO, where the developer has substantial responsibility for the fundraising process, and an IEO, where tokens are initially more liquid than those sold in an ICO.

The ICOs offered in 2017 and 2018 were not designed to comply with regulations regarding securities offerings and were largely shut down in late 2018 due to this lack of compliance. After the decline in ICO activity, security token offerings (STOs) gained prominence, raising $1 billion in 2021. STOs are tokens that go through the process of registering as a securities offering. Many STOs hold off-chain assets, such as ownership in real estate or equities.[14]

STOs are carefully designed to comply with all laws, disclosures, and regulatory registrations regarding the sale of securities. Organizers of STOs understand that the Howey Test defines securities offerings that must be registered with US regulators when there is a pooling of money, with the expectation of profits, through the efforts of others.

	ICO	IEO	IDO
FUNDRAISING IS CONDUCTED AT	The token issuer's website	The platform of the exchange	Launchpad platform / DEX
CROWDSALE COUNTERPARTY	The project's developers	A cryptocurrency exchange	The project's developers
SMART CONTRACT MANAGED BY	The company conducting the token sale	The cryptocurrency exchange	The company conducting the token sale
AML/KYC NEEDED BY THE TOKEN ISSUER	Yes, it can vary between the different projects	Not necessarily - the exchange conducts AML/KYC on its users	Yes, it can vary between the different projects
MARKETING BUDGET NEEDED FOR FUNDRAISING COMPANIES	Significantly high, the project will have to invest many resources in order to get the attention of the public	Relatively low - the exchange actively markets the tokens of the startups	Medium - Marketing efforts are done by both the Launchpad and the project's team
SCREENING REQUIRED BEFORE A STARTUP CAN LAUNCH A CROWDSALE	No - anyone can launch an ICO (in a country where it is legal)	Yes - the exchange screens the company before it allows it to raise funds on its platform	Screening is done by the launchpad platform
AUTOMATIC TOKEN LISTING AFTER CROWDSALE	No - the startup has to reach out to exchange to list its tokens	Yes - the exchange where the IEO is conducted list	Token listing happens almost immediately after the sale on a DEX

Source: What is an IDO – Initial DEX Offering?, Crypto Potato.

While ICOs were broadly distributed to retail investors, often without substantial disclosure, STOs may be restricted for sale to accredited investors. The US SEC offers private placement exemptions, which require less regulatory burden when securities are sold exclusively to high–net worth investors such as accredited investors and qualified purchasers. STOs may be available in a limited geography, as the organizers of the fundraising efforts have only registered the offering with regulators in a single domicile, such as the US, Europe, or Hong Kong.

Many STOs are backed by real assets, such as real estate or equity in an off-chain corporation. While ICOs are seeking funding for blockchain-based businesses, STOs can use blockchain-based fundraising efforts to raise capital for real-world projects.

There are a number of benefits to security token offerings (STOs).[15] STOs create tokenized and fractionalized ownership of businesses, increasing liquidity and price discovery. Transparency is created when token ownership is immutably tracked on a blockchain. Real estate properties were traditionally owned by a single investor, which may require a capital investment of $100 million or more. With tokenized ownership facilitated by an STO, the business increases the potential number and diversity of investors, offering ownership to investors with a much smaller capital contribution. Fractionalized ownership increases liquidity, as the owner of a $100 million property may choose to sell $10 or $20 million in an STO, raising some capital while continuing to own a controlling stake in the venture.

Deloitte lists five phases of an STO offering.[16] Because the offering is designed to comply with securities regulations, the process is more time consuming than an ICO and may share many characteristics of the IPO process for publicly traded equity securities. The first phase involves preparing all required documents, including business plans and all risk disclosures required by securities regulators. Second comes the design phase of tokenomics including the governance rights of token holders, the cost of each token, the value that will be offered for sale, and the potential income distributed to token holders.

Once the offering has been designed, service providers should be evaluated and selected. Service providers include custodians, exchanges, distributors, and wallets. The fourth step is capital raising, where investors must be made aware of the size, timing, and merits of the offering.

Finally, the token will be listed as a security on a regulated exchange venue. The tokens may be sold to a special purpose vehicle (SPV), which is going to issue the tokens on the exchange.

There are challenges to the growth of STOs.[17] Because there is no common global framework of global securities regulations, an STO is typically designed to comply with a single regulatory regime, whether it is in the US, the UK, Europe, Hong Kong, or elsewhere. Once the security token has been built and listed, only investors who are domiciled in countries compatible with the laws of the listing domicile will be allowed to participate. Investors will be required to complete KYC and AML processes and verify their net worth status before investing in the tokens.

Issuers will have ongoing responsibilities for communicating with investors by offering transparency, such as a quarterly net asset value (NAV) and an annual appraisal or audit.

The greater the number of investors, the greater the liquidity on an exchange, the greater we have a global regulatory framework for digital assets, the more successful STOs can be. The growth of an STO market can support the ability of well-seasoned, off-chain businesses to access capital investments from a new, natively digital type of investor.

Because STOs issue regulated securities, the tokens must be traded on regulated exchanges. Many centralized exchanges have become regulated in specific domiciles, including Archax and Gemini in the UK, and OSL Hong Kong.[18] A digital payment token services license is available for companies doing business in Singapore.

CHAPTER 20

Trading and Technical Analysis

Traders need to understand the implications of market volatility and trading methods when investing in any liquid asset, including stocks, futures, options, and crypto.

Most crypto investors will solely trade long positions, a bullish view in which digital assets are purchased in hopes of higher prices. Short positions can be established through the options and futures markets or by borrowing and selling a crypto asset. Short positions are bearish positions that profit when the asset's price declines.

Some investors will simultaneously take long and short positions, focusing on the difference between the returns in two assets rather than on the market direction. For example, options and futures will be discussed in Chapter 21. The price of a bitcoin futures contract does not always match the price of bitcoin tokens in the spot market. When the futures market is in backwardation, the futures price is below the spot price. Conversely, a futures market is in contango when the futures price is above the spot price. A trader may seek to capture the cash-futures basis by placing offsetting trades in the futures market and the spot or cash market. In a contango market, traders would purchase bitcoin tokens and sell bitcoin futures. In a backwardated market, traders would sell short bitcoin tokens and purchase bitcoin futures.

A long-short hedge fund may have skill in selecting tokens that might outperform but wants to reduce the risk factor of investing in the crypto market. This trader may purchase a basket of altcoins and sell short Ether or bitcoin tokens or futures against the basket. This trader would profit if the return to the coins in the basket was higher than the return to bitcoin or Ether, even if the cryptocurrency market declined. For example, if the basket of altcoins declined by 10% while the price of Ether or bitcoin declined by 20%, the hedge fund would profit 10% by selecting tokens that outperformed the market. The 20% profit from the short position in bitcoin or

Ether would net against the 10% loss on the tokens in the basket, to earn a total profit of 10%.

While liquidity can be defined as the ability to quickly sell an asset at a price close to its assumed value, it can also be defined by the volume of trading and the bid-asked spread.

Investors need to evaluate the cost of trading, where slippage is defined as the difference between the actual price traded and the price at which the investor assumed the trade would take place. The three key factors determining slippage are the bid-ask spread, the urgency of the trade, and the size of the trade relative to the size of the market.

Crypto trading is highly fragmented with different prices trading on each centralized exchange and in each different fiat currency. For example, even at Binance.US, the price of bitcoin differs relative to whether it is being traded for Tether or USDC.

	Bid	Ask	Size	Size * Ask	Bid-Ask Spread
Bitcoin	$ 63,430.00	$ 63,470.00	10	$ 634,700.00	0.06%
Ether	$ 3,070.00	$ 3,073.00	100	$ 307,300.00	0.10%
Filecoin	$ 5.95	$ 6.05	500	$ 3,025.00	1.65%
Flow	$ 0.86	$ 0.88	500	$ 440.00	2.27%

Source: Adapted from Binance.US.

Professional traders, liquidity providers, or market makers seek to buy at the lower bid price and sell at the higher ask or offered price. Every time they can buy on the bid and sell on the offer, they will earn the bid-ask spread, which is the dollar difference between the bid price and the ask price divided by the average of the bid and asked prices. Occasional traders, users of liquidity, or market takers, typically pay the bid-ask spread as compensation to the market makers for providing liquidity.

Notice that the spot bitcoin and Ether markets on Binance.US are highly liquid. Market takers will only pay a bid-ask spread of 6 to 10 basis points while being able to trade more than $300,000 immediately without any market impact. Market impact is the change in the price caused by a specific trade. Market impact is likely to be small when the size of the investor's trade is smaller than the market size. When these quotes were obtained, 10 bitcoin or 100 Ether tokens could be traded at the bid or asked price with minimal market impact. Stocks or tokens with large market capitalizations and significant trading volume tend to have smaller bid-ask spreads and lower market impact.

Investors desiring to trade less than $10,000 of bitcoin or Ether tokens may choose a market order, which is designed to immediately trade at the bid or ask price. The slippage will be minimal because the investor's trade is small relative to the market volume. An investor wishing to purchase three Ether tokens with a market order is likely to have the trade completed close to the ask price of $3,073 per token. A market order to buy guarantees immediate execution or completion of the trade at whatever the ask price is when the order reaches the market, while a market order to sell guarantees execution at the bid price. When markets are moving quickly, bid-ask spreads may widen and the volume listed at the bid and ask prices may decline, driving up the cost of trading.

Smaller capitalization stocks and tokens may have significantly wider bid-ask spreads and less market depth. For example, only 500 Filecoin or FLOW tokens could be traded at the bid or ask price when these quotes were obtained. Notice that the bid-ask spread has widened to approximately 2%, a significantly greater trading cost than bitcoin or Ether. The market impact can be significant for an investor attempting to immediately purchase 5,000 flow tokens, a trade valued at approximately $4,400. If the quantity offered at the ask price is not sufficient to complete the investor's order, a market order will purchase all tokens at the current ask price, and all tokens at higher ask prices until the order is completed.

Because a market order to buy 5,000 FLOW tokens demands immediate liquidity, the investor may purchase 500 at the lowest ask price of $0.88, another 1,000 at $0.90, 1,500 at $0.92, 1,000 at $0.95, and the final 1,000 at $1.00. This slippage is significant, as the investor assumed the price was $0.88 per token, while one-fifth of the order was filled at $1.00, a price 13% higher than assumed.

An investor who desires to trade a much larger quantity than is listed at the bid or ask price may choose to break the order into smaller trades or use limit orders. For example, the investor may purchase 1,000 FLOW tokens with a market order, splitting the price between $0.88 and $0.90. As soon as new liquidity comes to the market at a price of $0.88 or $0.90, the investor buys another 1,000 tokens, and so on.

Alternatively, an investor can place a limit order, guaranteeing price but not execution. The investor may place a limit order to buy 1,000 or 5,000 FLOW tokens at a maximum price of $0.90. This order will purchase all tokens offered at $0.90 or less. The limit order to buy 5,000 may immediately purchase 500 at $0.88 and 1,000 at $0.90. After the order is partially filled for 1,500 tokens, the remaining 3,500 tokens will be shown as the best bid price of $0.90 until the order is filled or the price rises with new bidders above $0.90. There is a chance that the trader will only purchase the 1,500 FLOW tokens offered at $0.88 and $0.90, and the size of the trade drives the price higher, making it difficult for the investor to buy any more tokens at $0.90 that day or that week. Of course, the bid at $0.90 may attract new sellers, with the trader's order being filled within the hour or the end of the day.

Once a position has been established, the investor may wish to protect profits or limit losses by placing a stop order or a stop limit order. For example, an investor purchased bitcoin at $50,000 and saw its price rise to $60,000 after several weeks. The investor may choose to place a stop order at $55,000 or a stop limit order at $55,000 limit $55,000. Under normal market conditions, this protects most of the trader's profit from the entry price of $50,000 to the stop price of $55,000.

A stop order at $55,000 places a market order to sell bitcoin that becomes effective whenever bitcoin trades at $55,000 or less. The market order is not activated as the price of bitcoin continues to rise. Some investors will implement a trailing stop order, moving the stop price $5,000 higher every time bitcoin rises another $5,000. That is, the $55,000 stop is moved to a $60,000 stop after bitcoin rises to $65,000, seeking to protect an ever-growing profit when the price of bitcoin reverses. Investors need to be careful with stop orders, because they turn to market orders. In this example, the market order is activated when bitcoin trades below $55,000, which could be $54,998 or $35,000 in a market crisis or a flash crash when bitcoin falls $20,000 in just one trade.

To avoid this scenario, the trader could place an order to sell bitcoin at $55,000 stop limit $55,000. This order places a limit order to sell at $55,000 whenever bitcoin trades at $55,000 or less. If bitcoin trades at $54,998, the limit order to sell is likely to be quickly filled. In the flash crash scenario when bitcoin trades from $56,000 to $36,000 with no trades in between, the trader automatically places a limit order at $55,000, avoiding the sale of bitcoin at the flash crash prices.

The efficient markets hypothesis (EMH)[1] assumes that asset prices immediately and fully respond to all available information. When a crypto mining firm announces earnings or the number of bitcoins mined in a given month or quarter, the stock's price should quickly move to a new valuation consistent with the information released and perform in line with the sector or the market until new news is released. If the EMH is true, investors will find it difficult to consistently outperform the market through the active management of buying and selling specific stocks or crypto assets.

Evidence shows that assets with the largest market capitalization and the largest trading volume are close to efficiently priced. S&P Dow Jones Indices completes an annual study titled SPIVA (S&P Index vs. Active).[2] At year-end 2023, the SPIVA report calculated that 60% of actively managed US large-cap domestic equity funds underperformed the S&P 500. The percentage of actively managed funds underperforming the S&P 500 ranged from 87% in 2014 to 45% in 2007. Since 2001, active managers beat the index in only three years, when 45%, 48%, and 49% of active managers underperformed the index. Over 15 years, S&P notes that there was no category of equity or fixed-income funds where the majority of active managers could outperform the benchmark index. Underperformance in small-cap stocks is less prevalent, where active managers typically have a better chance of outperforming small-cap indices than large-cap indices.

If the EMH is correct, it is difficult for investors to use available information, either fundamental analysis or technical analysis, to outperform the market. Investors can use fundamental information to value assets, such as price-to-sales ratios, revenues, revenue growth, and the total addressable market. Alternatively, investors can use technical analysis to value assets, such as momentum, trend lines, reversals, price, and volume. The logical conclusion of the EMH is that if it is difficult to beat the market, investors should minimize trading costs and asset management fees and choose to buy and hold broad exposure to the market, such as in a low-cost index fund.

Assets with larger market capitalization and trading volume often have more information available and more investors studying that information. Assets with a smaller market capitalization and lower trading volume may have fewer investors studying the asset, which may make it more lucrative to spend time evaluating the prospects of lesser-known investments.

If there is a greater probability of underperformance in large-cap stocks and a lower probability of underperformance in small-cap stocks, perhaps bitcoin and Ether are close to efficiently priced. Bitcoin, Ether, and three US dollar stablecoins hold 74% of the total market cap of all cryptocurrency assets. With 26% of crypto market cap held in over 13,000 coins, the altcoin market may potentially be less efficiently priced.

Alternative theories to the EMH include behavioral economics and the adaptive markets hypothesis (AMH). For the EMH to hold true, economists make a key assumption that all market participants are informed and act rationally. Those assumptions are not true, especially when it comes to crypto, where investors buy meme coins and trade based on what they read on Twitter/X or Reddit, whether it is true or not. Rather than being informed, many investors buy coins because social media influencers are buying them or because the price is increasing. In a madness of crowds, everyone buys at the same time, driving prices higher, and sells at the same time, driving prices lower. Many investors do not act rationally but swing between fear and greed. Rather than buying low and selling high, many investors end up panic selling in a crash after buying in a rally due to the fear of missing out (FOMO).

Behavioral finance notes that investors don't always act rationally and are subject to a number of biases. Rational and professional traders seek to buy low and sell high, letting gains accumulate, while realizing losses quickly. Many investors trade with loss aversion, finding it difficult to sell assets at a loss, even when the sale may realize tax benefits and reduce exposure to an overvalued asset. Investors tend to overreact and succumb to their fear and greed, selling at the lows and buying at the highs. Investors also tend to suffer from overconfidence, where the estimated probability of profit or outperformance is much higher than the actual probability.

Andrew Lo from MIT has proposed the Adaptive Market Hypothesis,[3] which seeks to reconcile the EMH with behavioral finance. When studying the physical world, the laws of physics are easy to predict and not subject to change. Lo suggests that markets are comprised of investors who make mistakes. If investors adapt or evolve their behavior by learning from their mistakes, it will be extraordinarily difficult to model financial markets. Those who build a model that is able to explain market behavior during the 2021 low interest rate bull market find that the model explains little about the 2022 bear market characterized by higher interest rates. As market factors and investor behavior change over time, models to predict and explain that behavior must also evolve.

The Adaptive Market Hypothesis suggests that markets will often be close to efficiently priced when volatility is low, and investors are likely to act more rationally and not move to the extremes of fear and greed. However, when market volatility increases, investors become less rational and more likely to make investment decisions due to fear and greed.

Behavioral finance tells us that individual investors, unfortunately, sell low in a crisis, and then reenter the market at much higher prices after the factors driving the crisis have been resolved.

Traders and investors can vary by their trading behavior, risk and return expectations, and holding periods. Value investors and speculators may have different views, as may those using fundamental or technical analysis.

Fundamental analysis, which studies business metrics such as profitability, market size, and revenue growth, tends to focus on the long-term value of an investment. In contrast, technical analysis, which studies how price and trading volume influence future prices, tends to have a much shorter-term orientation. Warren Buffett paraphrases his mentor, Benjamin Graham, when he said "In the short-run, the market is a voting machine – reflecting a voter-registration test that requires only money, not intelligence or emotional stability – but in the long-run, the market is a weighing machine."[4]

In the short term, price matters, sentiment matters, volume matters, and speculation matters. In the short run, a mob of Reddit-fueled speculators can move Game Stop's stock price from under $10 to more than $120 on a split-adjusted basis in just a few weeks. In the long run, it matters that Game Stop has minimal profitability, with the stock price returning to $10 more than three years later. What matters in the long run are assets, profits, and revenues, all of which are valued by Mr. Market's weighing machine.

Crypto prices are subject to extreme volatility and speculation, which can drive the price of a meme coin up 1,000% in just a few days. The key to trading meme coins is to buy before they pump or rise quickly and sell them before they crash. Notice that meme coins are trades and not investments, as they require near-perfect timing to both buy and sell at the right time to realize the profits.

In the long run, what matters are the number of wallets, the business use of the protocol, the number of transactions, and the total value locked. The tokens that are valuable in the long run are those with real users and a legitimate business model.

Different investors have different holding periods. Investors with longer holding periods may prefer to employ fundamental analysis, when the market is a weighing machine. Investors who analyze a crypto protocol and believe that the number of wallets, developers, and transactions will continue to grow may find the value of their holdings increase in the long run after those fundamental milestones have been reached. While the price might seem random for days, weeks, or months, the protocols that continue to increase price, volume, and users, are likely to increase in value over the years. In the US, lower capital tax rates are available to long-term investors who buy and hold (or HODL, a misspelling of hold that has been reinterpreted as hold on for dear life) for periods longer than one year. US investors who die can leave their assets to their heirs with a step-up in basis, where capital gains taxes are charged based on the price on the date of their death, rather than on the date of their purchase. As such, some value-based fundamental investors believe that the optimal holding period is forever, as their family will be able to sell the inherited shares after having been forgiven of a substantial capital gains tax burden.

Technical analysis is more important for shorter holding periods. Even fundamental investors who will hold a token for years may use technical analysis to find the right time in a day or week to purchase the token. Swing traders hold positions for days or weeks, seeking the optimal timing to enter and exit a trade. Swing traders want to make a 10% to 50% trade from market volatility or short-term factors, not hold for years to make a multiple of their capital on a single position. Day traders hold positions for minutes or hours, often exiting positions before the close of a trading day.

Some people choose to be liquidity providers, scalpers, or market makers, making a large volume of short-term trades by hand. They seek to earn small profits by frequently capturing the spread between the bid and ask prices. This is a full-time job, where the trader is present on a trading floor or in front of an electronic trading screen for the majority of the time the market is open.

High-frequency traders (HFT) deploy algorithms that may hold positions for a matter of seconds or minutes, capitalizing on providing liquidity to investors using market orders. HFT algorithms are liquidity providers seeking to buy at the bid price and sell at the ask price. The key to high-frequency trading algorithms is analyzing the bid price, the ask price, and the size offered or bid at each price. When the size on the bid is growing and the size on the ask is declining, the HFT predicts that the price will increase over the next seconds or minutes.

Whether their goal is a short-term or a long-term holding period, investors need to manage risks carefully. A key risk in crypto is market risk, especially when the annualized volatility of bitcoin and Ether can be between 50% and 150%, or two to six times the volatility of a stock market index.

Liquidity risk is the risk that assets may be locked up or difficult to sell. Crypto investors may face liquidity risk when buying a token before it opens for trading on a centralized or decentralized exchange or when agreeing to a 30-day withdrawal period when staking a token.

Operational risk and counterparty risks are significant concerns in crypto. Investors must carefully evaluate their custody arrangements and audit code to minimize the probability that smart contracts can be exploited. Users of DeFi platforms may experience credit risk when loans go unpaid and liquidation risks when the value of collateral falls short of the requirement.

Each market has a variety of investor types. Value investors and fundamental investors are seeking to make long-term investments in projects that will grow substantial market share in a large total addressable market. These investors tend to be patient, often taking time to build a position using limit orders during times of market weakness.

Speculators tend to be attracted to short-term holdings of highly risky positions. They may be influenced by social media personalities and buy meme coins after a time when they have risen rapidly. While a key consideration of risk management is diversification and small position sizes, many speculators say, "You only live once" (YOLO) and concentrate most or all of their net worth on a small number of trades. If they can buy before the coin rises and sell before it falls, speculators can and do make millions of dollars on a single trade. However, many other speculators can lose half or all of their total net worth in a matter of days or weeks by betting too heavily on a speculative position that crashes in price before they can exit.

Liquidity traders and market makers may lock tokens into a liquidity pool on a decentralized exchange to earn trading fees and bid-ask spreads.

On some DeFi platforms, liquidity providers who are early to support a new protocol are rewarded with airdrops of governance tokens.

There are also news traders. While news traders may have never traded bitcoin or Ether tokens before, they may buy them immediately before a halving or a merge event, seeking to profit from increased attention on a specific protocol. If the event takes place without any negative issues arising, the token value may increase after the risk of the event has passed.

Some traders focus on technical analysis indicators, such as trend following, seeking to buy tokens that have been rising in value and sell short tokens that have been declining in value. Technical analysis may be especially useful in crypto due to the extreme volatility and presence of speculative trading. Most of the value and fundamental investors are likely invested in the top 10 to top 50 crypto assets by market cap, leaving the thousands of other coins to the other types of traders who may be less concerned with the long-term prospects of the protocol.

Ultimately, investors need to understand the balance of supply and demand. Prices rise when the demand is stronger than the supply, and prices fall when the supply is larger than the demand.

In crypto, three main factors affect the price of individual coins: macroeconomic factors, crypto industry factors, and token-specific factors. Macroeconomic conditions that may affect the prospects of cryptocurrencies include price inflation, interest rates, the value of fiat currencies, and the return to technology stocks. For example, from the beginning of 2018 to March 2024, 15% of the variance in the price of bitcoin is directly explained by the returns to the Nasdaq-100 stock market index. If investors are currently rewarded for investing in risky technology stocks, they are likely willing to also invest in crypto assets. When the stock market turns lower and investors are experiencing losses on technology stocks, they may also choose to sell their digital assets as an extension of the risk-off trade.

Crypto industry factors are concerns that apply to the entire cryptocurrency industry. Notably, bitcoin and Ether declined substantially in 2022 due to the fears surrounding the losses at FTX and Terra Luna. If investors are worried about fraud, custody risk, tokenomics failures, or whether the regulators will outlaw digital assets, they may choose to leave the crypto universe entirely rather than seek to find the specific assets that will survive after the current scandals subside. As an example of a cryptocurrency industry factor, 60% of the variance in the price of Ether tokens since 2018 is directly explained by the return to bitcoin.

The fundamentals specific to a single coin are the third factor driving the prices of digital assets. When evaluating the price outlook for Ether tokens, it is important to understand the roadmap for building the Ethereum blockchain, including the merge, the surge, the purge, and so on. The ecosystem built around the Ethereum blockchain is also very important, including the number of DApps, the total value locked, and the success of layer 2 chains such as Optimism and Polygon.

Investors will likely earn the most profit from investing in Ether at a time when the Ether-specific fundamentals are favorable, but only when investor attitudes toward both tech stocks and the crypto universe are also favorable.

In some months, the price of bitcoin and Ether may change little, while the price of Solana and ICP may rise 20% while Flow and Tezos decline 20%. These are the times when the market is focused more on the individual developments at each project while not expressing concerns over the broader stock or crypto market.

Both fundamental and technical analysis in crypto make substantial use of on-chain data.[5] Because crypto transactions are transparent, significant data regarding the prospects for individual tokens can be gleaned from querying Etherscan or a block explorer. While publicly traded stocks disclose revenue and earnings quarterly, information regarding the fundamentals of crypto protocols is available in real-time.

With bitcoin prices hitting an all-time high in March 2024, an analysis of holders making money at the current price would show that every prior bitcoin purchase was profitable. When bitcoin is below all-time highs, analysts may note that one-third of coins in wallets were purchased at prices higher than today's price, leaving those traders at a loss. If investors suffer from the behavioral bias of loss aversion, fewer will sell at lower prices, and more will sell at a time when they have finally earned a profit after holding through a long time period of losses. The market can resume its upward move after the weak hands sell after finally reaching a profit.

Significant attention is paid to the wallets with the largest holdings of specific tokens, noted as whales. Whales with a large amount invested in a specific token may be founders of a protocol or a prescient trader who purchased the tokens at lower prices with a fundamental view that the protocol would be successful. Many wallets owned by whales trade infrequently, as the position benefitted from prices rising over a long time period. When trades are made in a whale's wallet, the market often follows with similar trades in hopes of replicating the success of the whale. In the spirit of the whales, many investors follow transactions valued at more than $100,000. The assumption is that large trades are made by successful and sophisticated investors who may be worth following.

Another technical indicator is the dominance of bitcoin relative to Ether. When bitcoin dominance is rising, bitcoin prices are outperforming Ether prices. When Ether dominance is rising, bitcoin prices are underperforming

Ether prices. Some traders believe that bitcoin prices outperform in a defensive market when crypto prices overall are flat to weak. At the same time, Ether's outperformance is during a time when the crypto market is rallying. Altcoin season is a time when coins beyond bitcoin and Ether outperform. This is often during a time of a strong bull market and after a time of first bitcoin and second Ether outperformance.

Coins held in wallets for less than one month are more likely to be traded soon. Coins held for one to 12 months may be traded or held, while coins held in a wallet for more than one year are much less likely to be traded. It is a bullish sign when the greater portion of the supply of a specific token has remained in wallets for longer than one year because the token is relatively scarce, with less supply available to be sold to other investors.

Similarly, a key technical indicator is the flow of tokens from centralized exchanges to unhosted wallets and back. The assumption is that tokens that move from unhosted wallets to a centralized exchange are likely to be sold soon, while tokens moving from centralized exchanges to unhosted wallets are likely to be held as longer-term investments. As a result, it is assumed to be bearish when tokens move from unhosted wallets to a centralized exchange, especially if those tokens were in the personal wallet for a long holding period. Conversely, it is a bullish sign when tokens move away from centralized exchanges, as fewer tokens can be sold to new investors.

Patterns of geographical and time zone trading are also an area of analysis. If the trades have different characteristics when taking place in Asian, European, or American time zones, investors may be able to profit from those patterns. Does price action during weekends and holidays differ from that taking place during the work week in a discernable way?

With Metcalfe's Law predicting that the value of a crypto protocol increases exponentially with the number of users, long-term fundamental investors closely track the number of wallets and the amount of TVL of each protocol.

Momentum or trend following is one of the most popular technical indicators. It's a very simple idea that when prices are rising or trending higher, they will likely continue to rise. Investors take long positions when prices are trending higher and take short positions when prices are trending lower.

Trend following is more profitable with long holding periods when prices have time to move substantially. Momentum trading is most profitable when trends are well-defined. However, losses can occur in a choppy market, where what seems to be an uptrend quickly moves lower or what seems to be trending lower suddenly increases. Some traders will mix shorter-term countertrend strategies with longer-term trend-following strategies. While holding a core long-term position, shorter-term trades are placed in the opposite direction to potentially gain from choppy markets.

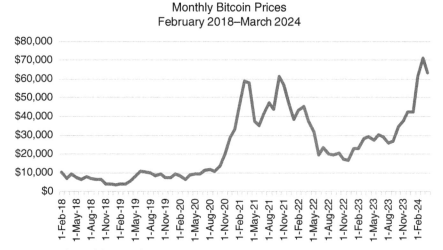

Source: Adapted from Yahoo Finance.

When looking at a long-term bitcoin chart, investors may wish they made just five trades from 2020 to 2024. In order to maximize the benefits of trend following, investors may wish to hold trades until the market reverses. Investors may have bought into an uptrend when bitcoin increased from $9,000 to more than $13,000 from June to October of 2020. This long position could have been held until the peak price of more than $59,000 in March 2021 with a signal to exit the trade and/or take a short position in May 2021 when prices crashed to $37,000. The short position is short-lived as a new long position is created when prices rallied from $35,000 in June to $47,000 in August. The long position is held until the peak of $61,000 in October, reversing to a short position as prices fell to $57,000 in November and $46,000 in December. This short position was likely held until the market bottomed near $16,000 in December 2022 or when it started to rally to $23,000 in January 2023 or $28,000 in March 2023. A long position at that point is held until the peak of more than $71,000 in March 2024, likely closing or reversing the trade as bitcoin fell to below $60,000 in April 2024.

In summary, trend followers need to stay with trades for long time periods to catch the moves from 1) $13,000 to $59,000, 2) $35,000 to $61,000, 3) $46,000 to $23,000, and 4) $23,000 to $71,000. While a buy-and-hold investor may have purchased bitcoin at $13,000 and held to $71,000 four years later, a successful long-term trend follower may have been able to profit more than $143,000 per bitcoin on four long-term trades, three long positions, and one short position with some losses from choppy countertrend trades in between. Notice that the trend follower had short positions in 2022, a time when the buy-and-hold investor experienced a 69% drawdown.

One of the key leaders of the early technical analysis was Dow Theory, created by Charles Dow, familiar to us as one of the partners in Dow Jones. Dow Theory states that markets are typically efficiently priced, but a trend in one asset price isn't confirmed unless observable in another asset price.[6] When one stock or one crypto price rises quickly, it is hard to believe the rally will stick if the rest of the market is not moving higher at the same time. The rise in the price of a single asset is more bullish when accompanied by positive price action in other areas of the market. Price trends are also more sustainable when confirmed by high volume. If a price is moving higher on thin volume, the market has less conviction in the trend and the price is more likely to reverse. Dow Theory places more confidence in price trends that are confirmed with heavy volume. Once a trend is confirmed, it is assumed to continue until there's a definite reversal. Once the market is confirmed to be moving higher, investors are encouraged to hold long positions until it is confirmed that the market has entered a negative trend.

The Wyckoff method is a five-step method:[7]

1. Determine the trend. Is it an uptrend? Is it a downtrend?
2. Are strong assets moving with or against the trend? For instance, what does it mean when Ether is moving up and bitcoin is moving down? Does that mean that there's something fundamentally different about Ether, is the market confused, or is there not a lot of conviction on either of them?
3. Find assets with sufficient cause. This could be a technical indicator or a fundamental indicator.
4. Is the reward worth the risk? Before entering into a trade, the investor should determine the profit target for that trade. For example, is the investor purchasing bitcoin just to make a quick $1,000, or will they set a loss target of $5,000 with a profit target of $10,000 or more on the upside? Ideally, the upside potential of the trade is larger than the downside of the trade.
5. Assess the likelihood of the movement. Do the price and the volume suggest the asset is ready to move? What happens if the price isn't moving but the volume is growing? A big price move may be imminent if key investors are increasing positions. Once it is determined that a move is likely, technical analysis can be used for the timing of the trade.

Technical analysis, called charting, predominantly looks at price changes and trading volume. One of the most popular charts used by crypto traders is a candlestick chart.[8] Each bar or candle represents one trading day in a one-day candlestick chart. The market moved lower when the bars were red or empty and higher when the bars were full or green. Each candle notes the open, high, low, and closing price for each trading day. When trading from a long-biased position, traders enjoy green candles and are frustrated by red candles.

Some traders will draw trend lines on a chart. If a market continues to move higher with prices remaining above a trend line, perhaps bouncing off the trend line at least twice, it is assumed that the trend line offers support, and prices will continue to increase. Investors will continue to hold a long position until the price has clearly broken below the trend line.

Trend lines can be used as support or resistance, where support is a price floor in an uptrend and resistance is a price ceiling in a downtrend.[9] Support, once broken, becomes resistance. That is, if a trend line fails to support the price, investors assume that it will be difficult for the price to rise above that resistance line in the short term. A resistance line, once broken, becomes support. Once a price breaks out of its downtrend, it is less likely to return to that downtrend.

Support and resistance lines may become self-fulfilling. If the price is unlikely to fall through a support line or a price floor, many traders may buy near the support line, as they believe there is a low probability that the price will decline through the support. This provides a trade with a high probability of profit and a smaller probability of a loss, a skewed risk-reward tradeoff in the trader's favor. However, the price can fall quickly once breaking through the support line, as the initial thesis of the traders has been invalidated, and many traders placed stop-loss orders to sell below the support line. Once the support line is broken, it becomes resistance or the top of a trading range where traders place sell orders believing that the resistance line is a short-term top for the price.

Technical analysis might believe that trading volume is the most important statistic, with large volume preceding both large positive and negative price moves. When volume increases, the market draws attention from traders expecting a big move. With trends assumed to be stronger during times of strong volume, an increasing number of traders may buy into a large volume uptrend, further accelerating the move. Again, technical analysis can be a self-fulfilling prophecy, accelerating a trend by attracting an increasing number of market participants.

Some large trades may be broken up into pieces and executed over the course of hours or days. There is a tradeoff between reducing market impact and taking too long to complete the trade that the price moves beyond the initial estimate of the market impact. When working to complete a large order over hours or days, a trader may be benchmarked to a volume weighted average price (VWAP) or time weighted average price (TWAP).[10] The TWAP is simply the average of the prices over a certain period, say 30 days. Many traders believe that the VWAP is more relevant than TWAP, especially when volume varies over the time the order is in the market. Price levels that trade in lower volumes have less weight in the VWAP while prices that trade in higher volumes have greater weight in the VWAP. The goal of a trader when buying a large order is to achieve an average price for the trade equal to or lower than the VWAP. Algorithms can be used to trade in greater size during times of greater volume and lesser size during times of lesser volume in an attempt to complete the order at a price more favorable than the VWAP.

Price oscillators, such as the Relative Strength Indicator (RSI), can be used by countertrend traders. Countertrend traders look to buy in markets where prices have fallen too far and to sell in markets that have risen too quickly. That is, they buy when the market is oversold and sell when the market is overbought. RSI is calculated on a scale of 0 to 100. Different traders may use the RSI in different ways, with some buying at 20 and selling at 80, while others might buy at 30 and sell at 70. Some may buy below 20, but only after the price has started to move higher.

The idea of oversold markets is that the price has fallen so quickly that buyers are likely to emerge to drive the price higher. Conversely, when a market has risen quickly, traders are likely to sell to take profits, which can lead to lower prices.

It can be difficult to determine a price trend simply by looking at a chart. Many traders augment charts with linear trend lines or non-linear moving averages. Looking at each individual price point, or even each candle, represents significant volatility. By using one or more moving averages, traders can view a smoother price chart. The idea is to buy when the price moves above the moving average or sell when the price moves below the moving average.

To smooth price signals even further, some traders use two moving averages, perhaps a fast moving average of 30 or 60 days (or hours) and a slow moving average of 100 or 200 days (or hours). Traders will buy when the fast moving average moves above the slow moving average and sell when the fast moving average breaks below the slow moving average.

Moving averages might not adjust for volatility, but Bollinger Bands do.[11] The distance between the top and the bottom band increases with volatility. The middle band in Bollinger Bands is a slow moving average. Bollinger Bands are used as a counter-trend indicator, triggering sales of overbought positions near the top band and purchases of oversold positions near the bottom band.

Because so much information is available either online or on-chain, talented programmers can perform complicated data analysis to support their trading. The data analysis can be focused on long-term fundamental valuation or shorter-term technical trading. On-chain metrics can be sourced from a variety of sites including DeFi Llama, The Defiant, The Block, Dune Analytics, Messari, Coinglass, Ultra Sound Money, Glassnode, and others.

Crypto prices, especially at very short time frames, are highly influenced by sentiment expressed on YouTube, Twitter/X, and Reddit. Some programmers will use application programming interfaces (APIs) to download all of the content moving through a social media platform. Once all of the tweets have been downloaded, they must be sorted to find those expressing an opinion on a specific cryptocurrency. Tweets using cash tags such as $BTC or $ETH will be relatively easy to sort. Once the tweets discussing crypto are identified, machine learning and natural language processing techniques are used to determine the sentiment. For the tweets expressing an opinion about bitcoin, the sentiment is calculated as highly positive, slightly positive, neutral, slightly negative, and highly negative. The more positive the sentiment expressed on a social media platform regarding a specific token, the more likely the token will increase in price over the coming hours or days, at least until sentiment reverses.

While some analysts will analyze every tweet regardless of the sender, more sophisticated models will focus only on the tweets sent by one person (Elon Musk) or the 50 people determined to be the most significant influencers on crypto Twitter, those with the most followers, or those whose prior tweets were most correlated to the subsequent price action.

Short-term speculative traders may place a significant weight on sentiment, such as buying Dogecoin when Elon Musk expresses a positive opinion on his social media platform. These speculative traders are focused on the short-term price action and may choose to ignore the weak long-term fundamentals of meme coins. It is likely easier to build a trading system that reacts only to Elon Musk's tweets than to sort through all of the content on Twitter/X, searching for relative content on crypto market sentiment.

Beyond price and volume, volatility can also be a technical indicator. Realized volatility is the standard deviation of prices over some period of time, while implied volatility is derived from options prices. Implied volatility, or the volatility predicted by traders between the trade date and the option's expiration, determines the price of call and put options.

Option prices and implied volatility tend to increase when markets are volatile or when significant news is expected. For instance, if earnings reports are due for a stock or if a significant event like the Ethereum merge is upcoming, option prices and implied volatility might rise. Increasing levels of implied volatility signal expectations of increased future volatility in the asset price.

Why would people pay more for options this week than last week? It suggests that volatility expectations in the market have risen, and traders believe that a significant price movement is likely to occur. For example, if the Federal Reserve is expected to increase interest rates in the following week, we might see that stock market volatility or bond market volatility expectations might be very high leading up to that Fed meeting.

After the Fed makes its announcement or Ethereum has successfully completed the merge, implied volatility and options prices are likely to decline, as much of the market uncertainty has been resolved.

Another observation from the options market is that prices might be skewed if traders are paying more for put options than they are for call options at an equivalent strike price. When the demand for bearish put options is strong relative to the demand for bullish call options, asset prices may be predicted to move lower, as market participants are expressing fear and paying a high price to ensure against losses in a falling market.

CHAPTER 21

Investing Directly in Crypto: Wallets, Custody, and Security

The most important saying in this business is, "Not your keys, not your crypto." Even if an investor is highly discerning and carefully buys the tokens that increase the most in value, their investment analysis skills can be wasted if something goes wrong in the custody arrangement. Custody is the safekeeping of an asset in physical and/or digital form.

While it may be tempting to opine that the most risky aspect of the crypto markets is price volatility, others may argue that custody arrangements are the most risky part of the cryptocurrency experience. Billions of dollars of crypto assets have been lost when held on centralized exchanges and in non-custodial wallets where users have taken control of their own tokens.

Crypto users lost more than $6 billion to hacks, scams, and exploits in 2022 and 2023.[1] Chainalysis estimates that up to 3.7 million bitcoins have been lost when users forget their password, lose their wallet, or suffer a hard drive crash.[2] This estimate of 3.7 million lost bitcoins makes the scarcity argument for the value of bitcoin even stronger, as the maximum supply may be 17.3 million rather than 21 million.

In TradFi, deposits at US banks and credit unions are insured. The Federal Deposit Insurance Corporation (FDIC) and the National Credit Union Administration (NCUA) insure deposits at banks and credit unions, respectively, for up to $250,000 per depositor per institution. If the bank or credit union fails, the insurance fund will reimburse depositors for their losses. Banks and credit unions pay insurance premiums to build the value of the insurance funds.

Depositors with $1 million may be encouraged to split their assets across four or more banks to maximize the insurance coverage and diversify the risks of bank failures. Two large US banks, SVB and Signature Bank, failed in 2023. While assets were protected above the FDIC insurance limit of $250,000 per depositor at each bank, US Treasury Secretary Janet Yellen stated there is no guarantee that deposits above the limit will be reimbursed in future bank failures.[3] If the insurance fund has insufficient assets to cover losses, some losses will be uninsured, or the American taxpayer will insure deposits at failed banks.

Similarly, assets in brokerage accounts are insured by the Securities Investor Protection Corporation (SIPC). Assets of individual investors are insured for up to $500,000 in securities and $250,000 in cash at each brokerage firm. high–net worth investors may wish to diversify their holdings across a number of brokerage firms to maximize insurance coverage. Notice that the insurance covers losses due to the failure of the brokerage firm, not a decline in the value of investments due to falling asset prices or a stock market crash.

It's important to know that digital assets are typically not insured. There's no insurance fund backing deposits at centralized exchanges. That is, the SIPC, FDIC, or NCUA will not insure digital assets lost due to the failure of a centralized crypto exchange.

There are various custody arrangements for digital assets. Assets can be held on a centralized exchange, the investor could self-custody their assets in an unhosted or non-custodial wallet, or they can be held by a third-party independent custodian. To date, the independent custody option seems to have been the safest, but professional custodians will charge fees for their security services.

In the libertarian spirit of crypto assets, investors may choose self-custody. Remember that each crypto wallet has a public key address and a private key passphrase. Both the wallet address and the private key are needed to move crypto assets. In self-custody, the investor is solely responsible for securing their digital assets and maintaining their private keys. When an investor stores their private keys offline, and those keys have never been disclosed to a centralized exchange or another counterparty, there is zero probability a hacker or a data breach will steal their crypto. However, with great power comes great responsibility. From the one who has been entrusted with much, much more will be asked.[4]

While taking control of crypto assets through self-custody reduces the probability of theft, it increases the risk of loss. The investor needs to ensure the physical safety of the keys, whether they are stored in a phone, a computer hard drive, a USB-like hardware wallet, or on paper. If the investor loses their phone, suffers a hard drive failure, or a fire or flood destroys their home, the private keys can be lost. If the private keys are lost, the crypto is inaccessible, and there is no help desk to recover private keys. Investors also need to consider what will happen to their crypto if they die, disappear, or become incapacitated. If the investor's family or business partner does not know how to access the crypto assets, those assets will be lost at the time of the investor's death.

There are stories in the crypto business of people who have either died or disappeared, when they were the only person with access to the private keys. When that person died or disappeared, the private key went with them, and the entire business was gone. A key part of enterprise risk management is to ensure business continuity even when a facility or a key person is no longer available. Crypto exchanges and custodians need to have checks and balances in place so that the loss or corruption of a single person will not compromise the integrity and continuity of the business. In order to avoid the risk that a single person can steal the entire value of a custody business, large transactions often require approvals from three or more people before being completed. A business may have five individuals capable of approving transactions and no transaction is approved without verification of at least three of their private keys.

Investors with substantial investments in digital assets should consider a split custody situation. A crypto wallet can be designed to only be unlocked using two or more private keys. Two business partners or a husband and wife may design a security system where two of three keys must be used to send value from a wallet. In most cases, the signatures will come from the husband and wife or from the two business partners. However, if one of these parties is no longer able to sign, the spouse or business partner may have previously arranged for a financial advisor or crypto-security service to be able to provide the second signature. Notice that the financial advisor or crypto-security service cannot unlock the wallet without one of the owners also signing off on the transaction.

Institutional investors, such as mutual funds and exchange-traded funds (ETFs), typically use professional independent custodians to secure crypto assets. Crypto custodians include specialists such as Fireblocks, Copper, or Anchorage, diversified financial firms such as Fidelity, and diversified crypto firms, such as Gemini and Coinbase.[5] Independent custodians who take numerous physical and digital security measures may qualify to purchase insurance against the loss or theft of digital assets entrusted to their safety. Professional custodians take multiple security measures to insure against the loss or theft of assets. The custodian may secure private keys in one bank vault and public keys in a second bank vault that are only accessible to certain trusted parties who provide biometric information to gain access. Ideally, at least three people would be required to move the assets: one to access the private key, one to access the public key, and a third to make the transaction.

There are four ways to store private keys: the combination of hot wallets or cold storage and investors or a third party.[6] Hot wallets are connected to the internet and allow for immediate trading of crypto assets. Of course, wallets that are connected to the internet are subject to hacking or the loss of private keys through phishing attempts. Private keys held in cold storage are physically disconnected from any externally accessible electronic system and may take time to retrieve before trading. Some investors choose to keep long-term holdings in cold storage and a smaller amount to trade in a hot wallet.

Hot Wallet	Hot Wallet
Investor Controls Private Key	Third Party Controls Private Key
Cold Storage	Cold Storage
Investor Controls Private Key	Third Party Controls Private Key

Source: Burniske and Tatar, *Cryptoassets*, 2018.

While hot wallets are convenient for placing trades, they also place the investor's private keys at risk. A key risk is phishing, where a hacker tricks the investor into revealing their private keys or accepting a mal-intended transaction. Investors need to be extraordinarily careful to only transact on safe platforms when they intend to make transactions. In a phishing attack, a hacker sends an investor an email, an infected file, an NFT, or a link to a smart contract. Once an investor's public key has been disclosed, they may receive phishing links directly in their wallet, such as NFTs designed as vouchers. When the investor connects their wallet to "redeem" the voucher for crypto assets, stablecoins, or more NFTs, they are likely to interact with a smart contract that will steal assets from the wallet.

The goal of the phishing attack is to gain the investor's password or private key, either by the investor interacting with a fraudulent site or by the investor accepting malware downloaded to their computer that seeks to access financial information. To avoid phishing attacks, investors should never click on links in emails, as emails that require the verification of private keys or the unlocking of a wallet are almost always fraudulent. If the investor receives an email from "Binance" requiring action on their account, they should never click on the link in the email. Instead, the investor should directly access their account as they always do on the official website Binance.com or Binance.us. In most cases, accessing the official Binance account will show the user that their account is in good standing and that no actions to verify their keys are required.

Using a hot wallet or storing crypto assets on a centralized exchange is very convenient, as crypto assets can be traded or moved with ease. Storing coins in a hot wallet may be like carrying cash in a wallet or a purse. While carrying cash is convenient, it also presents the risk of loss of theft. Just as consumers typically choose not to carry their life savings in their wallet, it is recommended that long-term crypto holdings be stored offline, while smaller trading balances are held in hot wallets that are immediately accessible.[7]

Assets held in cold storage are not available to be immediately traded because the private keys are stored in a location not connected to the internet. To reduce the risk of theft, investors are encouraged to HODL their long-term assets in cold storage.

Even though they are held offline, cold storage wallets can receive coins. Each wallet has a public key address that can receive any value that is sent. Similar to an email address that continues to receive email when the computer is turned off, a public key address can accept any value whenever it is sent, whether the address is in a hot wallet or cold storage status.

To avoid any probability of compromised private keys, some custodians deploy cold storage with computers that have never been online. If the computer has never been online, there is no way for it to be exposed to viruses or have any software installed that could expose the private keys.

While cold storage is safe, it takes time to process withdrawals. In many cases, moving assets held in cold storage can take up to 48 hours. During the KYC process, the custodian collects information from the investor, including their email, phone number, photo, and list of approved crypto wallet addresses. Withdrawal requests must originate from the approved email or phone number and be sent to a previously approved wallet address. Two-factor authentication methods will be used to verify the investor, with significant withdrawals perhaps requiring a video conference where the investor must appear on camera to verify they match the photo previously provided.

Investors have many options for cold storage, including paper wallets and hardware wallets. A paper wallet is literally a piece of paper printed with the wallet address, or the public key, and the seed phrase, or the private key. Of course, investors need to take great care of paper wallets, with many choosing to store it in a safe deposit box. In order to offset the worries about ink that fades or paper that crumbles over time, some investors choose to carve their private keys into wood, plastic, or metal. Some investors store their wallet address in a separate physical location from the private keys, perhaps using two different safes or safe deposit boxes. If either the wallet address or the private keys are found, the crypto assets are still safe, as both are needed to access the value.

Some investors will go to great lengths to protect their private keys. In a story made famous in the film "The Social Network," Cameron and Tyler Winklevoss developed a social networking website while students at Harvard. After the site was substantially developed, Mark Zuckerberg was added as a partner on the project team. Rather than work with the team, Zuckerberg published Facebook on his own as a copy of the company started by the Winklevoss twins. After a series of lawsuits, Zuckerberg paid the brothers a settlement of $65 million in Facebook stock.[8] In 2013, using $11 million of the lawsuit proceeds, the twins bought 110,000 bitcoins at prices averaging

$10 each. It is rumored that they continue to hold 70,000 bitcoins as of March 2024, with their suspected holdings valued at more than $4.4 billion.[9] The Winklevoss brothers also founded the Gemini cryptocurrency exchange in 2014. Mark Zuckerberg now has a net worth of more than $160 billion, as he continues to own 13% of Facebook/Meta stock.[10]

In order to protect their bitcoin fortune, the brothers sharded their keys and rented safe deposit boxes in a dozen banks in small towns across the Midwest. There are four sets of private keys, each broken into three pieces.[11] Even if their phone or computer breaks or someone breaks into their home or office, they would not lose access to the coins held in the paper wallet. They simply sent bitcoins to wallet addresses and locked the keys in geographically diversified safes.

Hardware wallets can also be used as cold storage devices. Trezor and Ledger wallets store private keys on a computer hardware device that is usually not connected to a computer or the internet. Hardware wallets can be as small as an external USB thumb drive and can be easily stored in a safe or a safe deposit box. When investors desire to move or trade their crypto assets, the hardware wallet is connected to a computer to provide the private keys for each transaction. Once the transactions have been signed, the hardware wallet is detached from the computer and returned to cold storage. If the hardware fails, or if it's lost, you can recreate the private keys from the seed phrase. Some investors will have both a hardware wallet as well as a backup paper wallet.

While paper and hardware wallets are not vulnerable to hacking or phishing, care must be taken to protect them from fires, floods, and physical theft.

Hot wallets can be custodial or non-custodial. Wallets can be used in web browsers such as MetaMask, or smartphones, such as Coinbase or Trust Wallet. Centralized exchange accounts are classified as custodial hot wallets, as the centralized exchange has access to the investor's private keys, and the assets are available for immediate movement. Coinbase offers both custodial and non-custodial smartphone wallets. In a non-custodial or a self-custody wallet, such as MetaMask or Trust Wallet, the private keys are held by the investor and not any third party. While non-custodial wallets store the private keys in an internet-accessible location, investors are encouraged to back up the seed phrase using a paper or metal wallet to avoid losing value when a phone or computer breaks or is lost or stolen.

There is a risk of loss of crypto assets whenever the private keys have been disclosed to any third party, including a centralized exchange. In 2022, the FTX centralized exchange used private keys to move investors' crypto assets for the use of the FTX exchange and its sister company, Alameda Research. Investors are encouraged to investigate centralized exchange practices to determine whether they are comfortable with a custodial wallet or if they would rather take self-custody of the assets.

To avoid hacking incidents, it is recommended that investors use multi-factor authentication (MFA) on all bank, brokerage, and crypto accounts. After enabling MFA, investors are required to enter a username and a password to access a financial account. Once the username and password are correctly entered, an extra step is added to further authenticate the user. The user will only be able to access the account after verifying a code sent to a previously provided email account or cell phone number. The use of MFA prevents hackers with stolen passwords and usernames from accessing financial accounts unless the investor's email or cell phone accounts have also been compromised. Microsoft states that users who enable multi-factor account authentication can block 99.9% of automated attacks.[12]

In order to further secure assets, investors are encouraged to use separate passwords for all accounts. Each financial account should have a unique password. The passwords used to access email and cell phone accounts should also be unique. Passwords should be carefully chosen and closely guarded because the investor's phone and email accounts are used for MFA and to reset passwords on financial accounts.

While some MFA systems will send a verification code to the user's phone or email address, other MFA systems require a smartphone application. An authenticator app will generate a new MFA verification code every 15 seconds.

MFA does not stop phishing attacks. If the user is tricked into providing access to their computer, email account, or their phone, hackers may be able to access many of the user's accounts. Phishing attacks may include emails directed to fake websites requesting passwords and private key phrases, spam NFTs pointing to smart contracts designed to drain user wallets, or malware installed on a user's computer to capture keystrokes or information stored in password manager files. A smartphone that is stolen when it is unlocked or when the thief has viewed the passcode can also provide access to an investor's financial accounts.

This book has discussed smart contracts in a positive way, where they can be used to trade NFTs, invest in DeFi DApps, or store critical ownership and identity information. Unfortunately, smart contracts can also be used for nefarious purposes. Hackers finding bugs in smart contracts have stolen billions of dollars by exploiting vulnerabilities in DeFi platforms.

The user experience and interfaces in crypto can be very difficult to understand. Investors may be anxious to interact with smart contracts, but might not know if the smart contract is designed to help or hurt the investor. Investors may be prompted to approve a smart contract whenever their wallet is connected to a smart contract site. Ideally, investors would be initiating the transaction by choosing to swap tokens on a decentralized exchange or buying NFTs from a brokerage site.

Investors are encouraged not to interact with any email saying your Coinbase account, your Trust Wallet, or MetaMask needs to be authenticated, or your private keys have expired and need verification. It's a trick. It's a lie. It's a scam.

In order to protect themselves, investors should understand the implications of executing a smart contract before approving the transaction. A browser extension, such as joinfire.xyz, can provide an overview of which assets will move into and out of a wallet based on the actions of a smart contract. This is critical, as the Meta Mask interface will not list the implications of providing the private keys to approve a smart contract transaction. joinfire.xyz will stand between the MetaMask wallet and the smart contract and simulate the implications of approving the smart contract execution.

Smart contracts may have very different implications, some of which are desired and some of which are not. For example, an investor interacting with a DeFi platform may willingly exchange 0.033 Ether tokens for 100 DAI when Ether is valued at $3,000 per token. The simulated smart contract execution shows 0.033 Ether tokens plus gas fees leaving the investor's wallet in exchange for 100 DAI being sent to the investor's wallet. If that is the intended transaction, the user signs the smart contract and the trade is executed.

Unfortunately, some smart contracts have malicious intent, especially if received as a link in a spam email or a spam NFT. Verifying a malicious smart contract with joinfire.xyz before approving the transaction may show that a $300,000 CryptoPunk NFT will be leaving the wallet, and what is received by the wallet isn't worth nearly 100 Ether tokens. The investor should be careful not to sign that smart contract and immediately exit the potential transaction, and the spam email or NFT should be immediately deleted.

Some investors use multiple wallets, holding valuable crypto assets and NFTs in cold storage and using a nearly empty wallet for transactions or a new wallet for each transaction. By estimating the value of each transaction and holding only the amount needed for that specific transaction in the wallet, the investor can limit their losses when interacting with a malicious smart contract.

Most people will start their crypto journey by sending fiat currency to a centralized exchange. Perhaps they will send $10, $1,000, or €500 to Binance, Kraken, Coinbase, Gemini, or Crypto.com. Opening the account will require a KYC process in which investors confirm their identity by providing a driver's license or passport and a social security number. The investor cannot complete any transactions until the KYC process has been completed.

Interacting with a centralized exchange may seem very familiar to investors who have previously used an online brokerage account to trade stocks and bonds. The centralized exchange will allow investors to name beneficiaries for their accounts and change their passwords using MFA.

A centralized exchange may offer investors a single account with access to tokens housed on multiple blockchains, allowing for a single account to hold tokens including bitcoin, Solana, Polygon, and Ethereum. In non-custodial wallets, investors must be careful to hold tokens in separate wallets compatible with each specific blockchain.

Some investors will choose to hold their tokens in the custody of the centralized exchange, which is easy and convenient. However, investors must remember that a centralized exchange account is a hot wallet where the private keys have been provided to the exchange. Some investors will use the centralized exchange as a fiat on-ramp or off-ramp, where dollars or euros are moved to and from TradFi bank accounts and centralized exchanges. Once the investor has converted their fiat currency into crypto assets, they may choose to immediately move the crypto assets into a non-custodial wallet in cold storage.

Even though centralized exchanges appear to be hot wallets, the best crypto exchanges store the vast majority of their crypto assets in cold storage. For the sake of security, a large exchange will not leave 500,000 bitcoins in a public hot wallet. The exchange will estimate what portion of the bitcoin holdings will leave the exchange in a given day or week and hold only that amount in a hot wallet. Assets can be held in cold storage for investors who will be long-term holders or for traders who move bitcoin from one investor to another on the same centralized exchange. For example, thousands of investors hold bitcoin balances on the Binance centralized exchange. Not every bitcoin traded on a specific centralized exchange will be recorded to the Bitcoin blockchain. The exchange may have a wallet with large bitcoin balances held in cold storage and simply debit and credit investor accounts as a portion of the bitcoin held in the exchange's large wallet. Trades will be written to the bitcoin blockchain only when assets are moved out of a specific centralized exchange to a non-custodial wallet or to another centralized exchange. That is, investor accounts at centralized exchanges may own a portion of the crypto assets held in the exchange's wallet rather than holding assets that have been segregated on-chain into their personal address. This exchange design minimizes the risk of theft of the majority of the assets that are held in cold storage while also reducing the gas fees incurred when transactions are written to congested blockchains.

Trades on decentralized exchanges, such as PancakeSwap or Uniswap are atomic and non-custodial. When an investor requests a trade on a decentralized exchange, they send tokens to the DEX's smart contract with a request for the token they are choosing to swap for. Atomic trades will be either executed in full or not at all. As a safety mechanism, DEXes are designed to return the investor's tokens if the trade cannot be completed as requested. It would be very dangerous to send Ether tokens to a smart contract and to not have those tokens returned if the wallet couldn't pay gas fees or if the smart contract couldn't return the appropriate quantity of the tokens requested. That is, when Ether tokens are sent to a DEX's smart contract, the investor will either receive the tokens requested in the swap or a return of their Ether tokens (minus gas fees). A well-designed DEX will have no scenario where the Ether tokens are sent and nothing is received in return.

A DEX is non-custodial because the decentralized exchange never takes custody of the user's tokens. The user sends tokens to the DEX's smart contract, which immediately returns the tokens requested in the swap. Because the DEX does not store the user's private keys, users can safely interact with a DEX in a non-custodial wallet.

Investors need to remember that each blockchain is different when using non-custodial wallets. Value can be lost when sending bitcoin to an Ether wallet or sending Ether to a bitcoin wallet without first wrapping the token on a bridge. Only bitcoin tokens can be held in a bitcoin wallet and only ERC-20 compatible tokens can be held in an Ethereum wallet.

Remember that custody arrangements are the most important consideration in digital asset investments. When holding assets in self-custody, investors are taking responsibility for their own digital assets. While they are less likely to be stolen in a hacking incident, crypto assets are often lost in fires, floods, and hard drive crashes, or when someone dies without providing the keys to their spouse or their business partner. In self-custody, there are no help desks or password resets. It is almost certain that the value held in a crypto wallet is lost when the private keys are lost.

Similarly, there are risks of holding crypto assets on a centralized exchange. Any time keys are exposed to the internet or provided to a third party, there is some chance that the assets can be lost through theft or a cybersecurity incident. While many centralized exchanges take great care of investor assets, examples from Mt Gox in 2014 to FTX in 2022 show that risks remain to this day for assets held on centralized exchanges.

Whether assets are held in custodial or non-custodial wallets, investors must guard their passwords and private keys. To keep assets as safe as possible, they must use MFA, use strong passwords, create unique passwords for each site, and avoid interacting with phishing emails.

Investors with a significant amount of crypto assets should investigate professional custodians and multi-signature wallets and backup arrangements to minimize the probability of loss and to provide continuity of the value of the assets for their family or business partners for when the investor is no longer able to access the assets on their own.

CHAPTER 22

Derivative Markets: Futures, Options, and Perpetual Swaps

In finance, derivative products include options, swaps, and futures contracts, where the price is derived from the price of an underlying asset. Derivative products are zero-sum games, as every long position requires a short seller. The losses of one side are the gains of the other side.

Derivatives markets differ from the underlying markets, such as stocks or crypto, where buying positions in the spot market gives long-term ownership in the shares or tokens. The spot market is not a zero-sum game, as millions of shares or tokens are all owned by investors or the issuer. Investors all have long positions, and can profit together as the market rises, and lose together when markets decline in value.

Ownership of stocks, crypto, futures, and swaps all provide linear payoff profiles, where a $1 change in the price leads to a commensurate gain in the value of the investor's position. Long positions are limited to a loss of 100% of the invested value while gains are potentially unlimited if the price continues to rise.

Options, however, have non-linear payoff profiles. Purchasing call and put options exposes an investor to a loss of 100% of the price paid for the option and potential gains that could be large multiples of the price paid for the option. Options can be seductive, as investors have the potential to leverage small investments to earn large gains.

Option buyers and sellers have very different risk profiles. While option sellers' potential gain is limited to the price the option was sold for, they can potentially lose large multiples of the option premium. On average, option sellers tend to profit and option buyers tend to lose. That is, option buyers are willing to pay to access the leverage embedded in call options or the insurance embedded in put options.

Buyers of call options have the right, but not the obligation, to buy the underlying at a strike price before expiration, while buyers of put options have the right, but not the obligation, to sell the underlying at a strike price before expiration.

Investors purchase call options, taking a long position when they expect the price of the underlying market to rise quickly in a short period of time. This bullish position profits when the underlying market's price rises above the option's strike price by more than the option's price before expiration.

Selling put options, taking a short position is another way for investors to express a bullish view on the price of the underlying market. Because the put seller has sold insurance against a decline in the price of bitcoin, they profit when the put option reaches expiration before bitcoin has fallen below the put's strike price.

That leaves short calls and long puts as the ways to express bearish positions and profit when the price of the underlying market declines below the strike price. In a short call position, the seller gets to keep the entire price of the call option they sold when the price of the underlying market is below the strike price at expiration. In a long put position, the buyer purchases insurance against the decline in the value of the underlying market. If the bitcoin price is below the strike price at expiration, the option seller pays the buyer based on how far the price moved below the strike price.

If the underlying market is expected to make a small move or settle close to the strike price, sellers of options can profit by keeping the premium of all options that expire worthless, or out-of-the-money.

Investors who are expecting large moves to the upside can earn the most profit by buying call options, while those expecting large moves to the downside can earn the most profit by buying put options. While selling options that expire out-of-the-money allows sellers to keep the entire premium, buyers of options that finish deep in-the-money can earn gains of many multiples of the price paid for the option. In a simple example, an investor that sells an option for $1 keeps the $1 when the option expires worthless at expiration. Conversely, a buyer may purchase a $1 option that is worth $5 or more after the underlying market made a sharp move beyond the strike price.

In-the-money options are call options where the underlying price is above the strike price, while put options are in-the-money when the underlying price is below the strike price. Options are out-of-the-money when the underlying price is below the strike price of the call option or above the strike price of the put option.

Over the long run, it pays to be a seller of options. In most commodity, equity, interest rate, and currency markets, options are slightly overvalued in the long run.[1] The main factors in the profitability of professional options traders are implied volatility and realized volatility. Options sellers profit when implied volatility exceeds realized volatility, while options buyers profit when realized volatility exceeds implied volatility.

Realized volatility is the actual standard deviation of the price in the underlying market over the option's life. Of course, when the option is traded, neither the buyer nor seller knows what the realized volatility will be between the date the option is traded and when it expires. Implied volatility is the volatility assumed or included when the option is priced. The nonlinearity of option payoff profiles benefits buyers of options and can be costly for sellers of options. Because buyers of call options value the leveraged upside returns, while buyers of put options value the insurance coverage provided, option sellers price options at an implied volatility that exceeds the expected realized volatility. That is, if the market expects bitcoin to trade at a realized volatility of 75% over the next month, one-month options may be priced with an implied volatility of 80%. If estimates of realized volatility are accurate or overstated, sellers of options will be able to profit by difference in the option price generated by a 5% difference in volatility assumptions. A careful, systematic option seller who understands hedging can profit by selling options over long periods of time. While option sellers can be consistently profitable, there are times when option buyers do make large gains. Options sellers tend to profit during most market conditions while experiencing substantial losses during large market events. While seeking to earn an annualized profit of 5 volatility points, a 20% to 50% market move in a single day, week, or month may subject the seller to losses of 20 volatility points or more. In extreme market scenarios, option sellers may forfeit one year of gains during a single week of volatile market action.

There are many different ways to combine call and put options trades. While many traders will simply buy or sell call or put options as a single trade, others will create combinations that may include multiple options and a position in the underlying market.

Covered calls and put writes are ways to monetize the volatility of the crypto assets already owned by the investor.

A very popular trade, especially in a highly volatile asset like crypto, is a covered call option. An investor who owns bitcoin or Ether tokens would sell call options. With bitcoin at $60,000, the investor may sell a one-month call option with a $62,000 strike price for a $5,000 option premium. If the price of bitcoin is below $62,000 at the end of the one-month life of the option, the option expires worthless, and the option seller keeps the entire $5,000 option premium. While the covered call gives the seller the right to profit from a flat to declining bitcoin price, it also allows the call buyer to profit from an increase in the price of bitcoin. That is, the gains to the option seller on the combination of the bitcoin holdings and the option is limited. Profitability is determined by the breakeven price, which is the strike price plus the premium for call options and the strike price minus the premium for put options. If bitcoin were to rise above $67,000 ($62,000 strike plus the $5,000 premium) at the date of the options expiration in one month, the call seller faces a loss on the trade. That is, all of the profits above a bitcoin price of $67,000 in one month accrue to the buyer of the call option, limiting the gains of the covered call seller.

Investors can also sell put options, which offer insurance against the decline of bitcoin prices over the option's life. For example, with bitcoin at $60,000, an investor can sell a one-month put option with a strike price of $58,000 for a price of $4,000. The breakeven price on this trade is $54,000 ($58,000 price less the $4,000 premium). If the price of bitcoin is above $58,000 at the option's expiration, the seller keeps the entire premium. If the price of bitcoin declines below $54,000 by expiration, the buyer of the put option experiences a profit on the trade. Investors may view the sale of put options as a way to potentially buy the underlying at a lower price. The investor who sells the put option is happy if bitcoin prices are stable or slightly rising, as they get to keep the $4,000 put premium, which can be viewed as reducing the cost of buying bitcoin at higher prices. If the price of bitcoin declines below $58,000, the investor participates in the downside price of bitcoin, similar to purchasing bitcoin in the spot market.

Buying options is expensive, but having insurance is desirable. To purchase insurance at a reduced cash cost, a collar strategy can be employed. When Ether is priced at $3,000, the investor might sell a one-month call option with a $3,100 strike price for $220, and purchase a one-month put option with a $2,900 strike price for $220. That is, the value of the investor's Ether tokens combined with the pair of options is guaranteed to be between $2,900 and $3,100 in one month, placing a collar around the potential returns. When the premium on the call sale matches the premium on the put purchase, the strategy is called a costless collar, as the price of the call options exactly offsets the cost of the put options. Collar strategies are customizable, as some investors may wish to sell call options at higher strike prices, such as $3,200 or $3,300, to forfeit less of Ether's upside return potential. Of course, call options with higher strike prices have lower prices, causing the investor to pay part of the put premium to complete the collar.

Options prices increase with the volatility of the underlying, with more volatile assets having more expensive options premiums. This is because more volatile assets have a wider range of potential price outcomes. Investors are willing to pay higher prices for options that can potentially expire a greater distance beyond the strike price.

Ether and bitcoin prices exhibit substantially greater volatility than a stock market index such as the S&P 500. Over a five-year period, bitcoin's annualized volatility reached as low as 41%, calculated as the standard deviation of daily returns over 30-day rolling time periods, while Ether's price volatility briefly exceeded 200%. The more frequently prices are observed, the greater the calculated volatility. That is, bitcoin prices measured hourly will have greater measured volatility than prices measured daily.

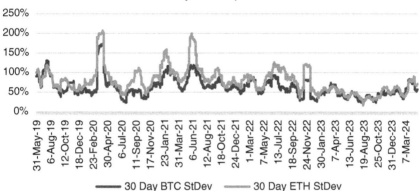

30–Day Rolling Standard Deviation
Bitcoin and Ether Returns
May 2019–April 2024

━━━ 30 Day BTC StDev ━━━ 30 Day ETH StDev

Source: Adapted from Yahoo Finance.

Over this 5-year period, bitcoin volatility in some years was as low as 42% in 2023, and more than 78% in 2021. Notice the spikes in volatility, where bitcoin reached more than 171% for at least one 30-day period in 2020. On average, Ether experienced greater price volatility than bitcoin in this time period. While the volatility of Ether averaged an annualized daily volatility of 45% in 2023, its volatility spikes were higher than those of bitcoin, exceeding 207% volatility for at least 30 days in 2020.

	30 Day BTC StDev	30 Day BTC StDev	30 Day ETH StDev	30 Day ETH StDev
	Average	Maximum	Average	Maximum
2020	63.2%	171.7%	86.0%	207.2%
2021	78.2%	117.5%	102.3%	197.8%
2022	62.4%	92.0%	84.1%	123.5%
2023	41.8%	73.4%	45.3%	64.9%
Jan-Apr 2024	56.3%	83.4%	60.5%	89.0%

Source: Yahoo Finance, author calculations.

To calculate the price of an option, the investor needs to know the strike price, the expiration date, interest rates, dividends, the price of the underlying market, and the assumption of implied volatility. Options on bitcoin and Ether futures traded at the CME are European style, meaning they can't be exercised before maturity. American-style options, which can be exercised before expiration, have higher prices than European options on underlying assets that pay dividends.

	1 Month	2 Months	3 Months
Call Price, 80% Volatility	$62,000 Call $4,787	$62,000 Call $7,131	$62,000 Call $8,994
Call Price, 100% Volatility	$6,184	$9,074	$11,357
	1 Month	2 Months	3 Months
Put Price, 80% Volatility	$58,000 Put $4,424	$58,000 Put $6,508	$58,000 Put $8,118
Put Price, 100% Volatility	$5,771	$8,381	$10,396

Source: Author calculations using the Cboe options calculator.[2]

Once the inputs are known, the investor can estimate prices using an options calculator, such as the one provided by Cboe. This example calculated call and put prices for bitcoin options with one, two, and three-month expirations with implied volatility assumptions at 80% and 100% at a time when bitcoin was priced at $60,000. Interest rates are assumed at 4%. The dividend yield on bitcoin is assumed to be zero, while investors pricing Ether options may wish to include the estimated annualized returns to staking as a dividend yield.

The buyer of each option will lose their premium if the underlying price does not move beyond the strike price at expiration. If the underlying price moves beyond the strike price at expiration, the buyer will receive payment from the seller determined by how far the option is in-the-money.

Options prices increase with the implied volatility assumption and the square root of the time until maturity. If a one-year option is priced at 100%, a six-month option is priced at 75% (square root of 50% of one year), while a three-month option is priced at 50% (square root of 25%), and a one-month option is priced at 28.9% (square root of 1/12). Due to this accelerated time decay, option sellers may focus on shorter-term options with a higher dollar price per day of option maturity. Conversely, option buyers may wish to focus on longer-term options with a lower price per day of option maturity. Collars can be constructed by buying longer-term put options and selling a series of shorter-term call options. For example, the investor buys a three-month put option and sells a one-month call option today, and sells another one-month call option at the maturity of the first option. The $62,000 bitcoin call options priced at 80% implied volatility cost $4,787 for a one-month option, $7,131 for a two-month option, and $8,994 for a three-month option. If implied volatility remained stable for one month, an option seller could receive a greater premium for selling two consecutive one-month options ($4,787 × 2 = $9,574) than for selling a single three-month option ($8,994).

To illustrate the benefits of buying options, consider purchasing a three-month $62,000 call option on bitcoin priced at $9,000. Compared to buying a full bitcoin for the current price of $60,000, the buyer of the call option potentially has greater upside and lower upside over the three-month life of the option. The breakeven price for the call buyer is $71,000, the $62,000 strike price plus the $9,000 premium. If bitcoin rises to $71,000 the investor breaks even and earns a zero return on the trade. If bitcoin moves an additional $9,000 higher to $80,000, the investor doubles their investment on the $9,000 call option premium. At $89,000, the investor earns a return of 300%, 400% at $98,000, and so on. As bitcoin moves from $60,000 to $80,000, the call buyer earns 100% return, while holders of bitcoin tokens earn 33% (($80,000–$60,000)/$60,000). That is, the leverage purchased by call buyers allows them to earn higher returns than bitcoin HODLers for sharp moves higher in bitcoin prices over a short period of time. Buying options also provides benefits in down markets. The call option buyer loses their entire $9,000 premium when bitcoin is at any price below $62,000 at the three-month expiration. Compared to buying bitcoin at $60,000, the call option buyer is better off at any bitcoin price below $51,000. That is, if bitcoin was priced at $40,000 in three months, the owner of bitcoin tokens would lose $20,000 per token, while the buyer of the call option would only lose $9,000. This demonstrates how option buyers have a non-linear payoff profile with potentially unlimited gains and losses limited to the price of the option purchased.

As implied volatility increases, option prices also increase. The two-month $62,000 call option is priced at $7,131 using an implied volatility assumption of 80% and at $9,074 using an implied volatility assumption of 100%. Put options are slightly less expensive than call options, as the maximum gain on a put option is the strike price minus the option premium, while the gains to long call options are potentially unlimited.

With bitcoin at $60,000, the $62,000 strike call options are $2,000 out-of-the-money, meaning that bitcoin prices have to move $2,000 higher before the call option buyer sees any return of their investment. Similarly, the $58,000 strike put options are $2,000 out-of-the-money, as bitcoin prices must move $2,000 lower before the put options become in-the-money.

These options are very expensive because the high trailing realized volatility leads investors to believe that bitcoin prices can trade in a wide range before the expiration of the option. Some investors may buy these options to make a leveraged bet on bitcoin prices reaching $100,000 by the end of the year, while others may buy put options to profit when bitcoin reaches their price target of $20,000 by year-end.

	1 Month	2 Months	3 Months
	$62,000 Call	$62,000 Call	$62,000 Call
Call Price, 80% Volatility	$4,787	$7,131	$8,994
	$70,000 Call	$70,000 Call	$70,000 Call
Call Price, 80% Volatility	$2,335	$4,476	$6,261
	1 Month	2 Months	3 Months
	$58,000 Put	$58,000 Put	$58,000 Put
Put Price, 80% Volatility	$4,424	$6,508	$8,118
	$50,000 Put	$50,000 Put	$50,000 Put
Put Price, 80% Volatility	$1,515	$3,091	$4,427

Source: Author calculations using the Cboe options calculator.

Call options become cheaper as the strike prices increase, as further out-of-the-money options have a lower probability of reaching the strike price before expiration. Bitcoin prices only have to move $2,000 before the $62,000 call is in-the-money, while a $10,000 price move is necessary before the $70,000 strike calls have any value at expiration. That is, a $70,000 call will always be less expensive than a $62,000 call for the same underlying and the same expiration date. Similarly, a $50,000 strike put will always be less expensive than a $58,000 put for the same underlying and expiration date.

While regular sellers of options tend to profit in the long run, they can also suffer substantial losses when the underlying market makes large moves in a short period of time. An investor may choose to sell a three-month $62,000 strike call option for $9,000. This seller is happy if bitcoin is below the break-even price of $71,000 in three months. However, they may regret selling these options if bitcoin reaches $91,000 in three months, as they experienced a $20,000 loss by selling that option. To minimize this regret, some traders may choose to sell call spreads rather than selling call options at a single strike.

Call Spread	1 Month	2 Months	3 Months
$62,000–$70,000	$2,452	$2,655	$2,733
Put Spread	1 Month	2 Months	3 Months
$58,000–$50,000	$2,909	$3,417	$3,691

Source: Author calculations from previous tables.

An investor who owns bitcoin wants to sell covered calls to earn options premium but is worried about the April 2024 halving of block rewards to bitcoin miners, as many market analysts predict that the halving could drive bitcoin prices sharply higher. Rather than selling the three-month $62,000 call for a premium of $8,994 and miss out on all bitcoin returns above $71,000, the investor chooses to also purchase the three-month $70,000 call for a premium of $6,261. This $62,000 – $70,000 call spread earns the investor a net premium of $2,733 ($8,994 – $6,261) while only exposing the investor to a potential loss of $8,000 ($70,000 – $62,000, the difference between the strike prices). Given the investor's underlying bitcoin position, they retain all upside returns above the $70,000 strike price.

Similarly, a three-month $50,000-$58,000 put spread could be sold for a net premium of $3,691 ($8,118 – $4,427), exposing the investor to only a potential payout of $8,000, the difference between the strike prices. Selling this put spread allows the investor to profit from selling insurance but limits the losses experienced if bitcoin prices were to move sharply below $50,000 within three months.

The Chicago Mercantile Exchange (CME Group) trades listed futures and options on Bitcoin and Ethereum. Because the CME Group operates the world's largest futures exchange, many institutional investors already have accounts to trade futures contracts on assets such as gold, oil, interest rates, and stock market indices. This makes it easy for institutional investors to access the returns to crypto assets without worrying about the custody arrangements of holding spot bitcoin or Ether tokens.

Each CME bitcoin futures contract is denominated at 5 bitcoins per contract.[3] When investors take a position, either long or short, in one futures contract worth 5 bitcoins (approximately $333,500 as of April 2024), a maintenance margin of $79,932 per contract is required. The maintenance margin on bitcoin futures is scheduled to rise regularly until reaching $90,666 in December 2025. This allows an investor to control bitcoin using leverage of 4.17 times, the reciprocal of the 24% margin to contract value ($333,500 divided by $79,932).

Similarly, Each CME Ether futures contract is denominated at 50 Ether tokens per contract.[4] When investors take a position, either long or short, in one futures contract worth 50 Ether (approximately $161,750 as of April 2024), a maintenance margin of $43,065 per contract is required. The maintenance margin on Ether futures is scheduled to rise on a regular basis, until reaching $47,412 in December 2025. This allows an investor to control Ether tokens using leverage of 3.76 times, the reciprocal of the 26% margin to contract value ($161,750 divided by $43,065).

Investors can access bitcoin futures directly on the CME or through exchange-traded funds (ETFs). In December 2021, the US SEC allowed the trading of ETFs based on bitcoin futures while it took until January 2024 to approve ETFs based on spot bitcoin. While a specialized account is required to trade futures, ETFs can be traded in any account where stock market trades are allowed.

Bitcoin futures do not always match the bitcoin spot price, but can differ by the degree of contango or backwardation. Spot and futures prices must converge at the expiration date of the futures contract.

4/23/2024	CME Bitcoin Futures	Spot Bitcoin Price	$ 66,469	
Contract Month	Expiration	Days to Expiration	Futures Price	Annual Contango
April	26 April 2024	3	$ 66,435	
May	31 May 2024	38	$ 67,155	9.9%
June	28 June 2024	66	$ 67,880	11.7%
July	26 July 2024	94	$ 68,510	11.9%
August	30 August 2024	129	$ 69,085	11.1%
September	30 September 2024	160	$ 69,590	10.7%

Source: Adapted from CME Group / https://www.cmegroup.com/markets/cryptocurrencies/bitcoin/bitcoin.quotes.html#venue=globex / Last accessed at 15 May 2024.

When futures prices are in contango, the futures prices are higher than spot prices, creating a negative roll yield. For example, consider the futures markets listed in this table, with the spot bitcoin price at $66,469, and the May contract expiring on the last Friday of the month (31 May) priced at $67,155. If the spot price did not change between 23 April and 31 May, the investor would lose $686 on the futures contract ($66,469 – $67,155). The negative change in the cash-futures basis of $686 is about 1% for the five-week futures contract, which annualizes to 9.9%. Investors holding the September contract to expiration would experience a negative roll yield at an annualized rate of 10.7%.

It can be expensive to buy and hold bitcoin futures during times when the futures curve is in contango. However, hedge funds often capitalize on this by monetizing the futures curve. For example, an investor could buy spot bitcoin at $66,469 and sell September futures for $69,590, profiting $3,121 per contract before trading and financing costs. By holding the long bitcoin, short futures position for 160 days, the investor earns an annualized profit of 10.7%. This strategy is relatively low risk as long as the spot bitcoin is held in a secure custody arrangement and the investor has the required cash to maintain the margin required by the futures exchange at all times. Regulatory filings show that hedge funds are among the largest owners of spot bitcoin ETFs, which are likely paired with short futures positions.

Conversely, backwardation occurs when futures prices are below spot prices. Suppose bitcoin is $66,000 today, and September futures are trading at $65,000. Buying September futures at $65,000 allows the investor to outperform the spot price of bitcoin by $1,000 over the holding period.

There are a number of key differences between futures listed on CeFi exchanges, such as the CME, and futures traded on centralized crypto exchanges.

The CME was founded in 1898, with an initial focus on agricultural commodities such as oats and corn. Options and futures on US Treasuries were added in 1976, while S&P 500 products started trading in 1982.[5]

CME bitcoin futures contracts trade 23 hours a day from Sunday to Friday and are closed for trading on Saturday. CME futures contracts expire monthly, so investors desiring long-term exposure must roll positions into new contracts at or before the expiration of the current contract. As of April 2024, maintenance margin requirements on CME futures contracts allowed maximum leverage levels of 3.7 for Ether futures and 4.1 for bitcoin futures. CME futures contracts are marked to market daily. Investors with positions in CME futures contracts receive cash in their account twice each day when the position moves in their favor, while cash exits their account twice each day the position declines in value. Investors deposit the initial margin requirement before initiating new trades and must hold cash, gold, or a variety of US and foreign debt issues in their account in at least the amount of the maintenance margin requirement.[6] Some asset types are accepted for margin deposits with a haircut, such as 30% of the value of stocks and ETFs. Whenever the account falls below the required maintenance margin level, investors must add assets to the account or reduce the size of the futures positions. Investors unable to quickly return their account to compliance are subject to liquidation of their positions within 24 hours. Should an investor lose more than the value of their account through leveraged futures trading, the investor's broker or clearing member is initially responsible for the losses. Losses that cannot be paid by clearing members are insured by the CME clearing guarantee fund, holding more than $8 billion. Notice that neither the CME nor its clearing brokers will liquidate any positions of investors who remain compliant with position limits and maintenance margin requirements.

Contrast the CME futures with the world of crypto derivatives trading at global centralized exchanges. US customers are typically not allowed to trade on offshore exchanges, due to the high levels of leverage available and the unregulated status of exchanges. Much of the crypto derivatives trading takes place in perpetual swaps, which have similarities to futures contracts but without expiration dates. Crypto derivatives markets never close and are available for trading 24 hours a day, 7 days a week.

CME bitcoin futures often trade in contango, where the futures price exceeds the spot price, which carries a cost for investors holding long futures positions. The parallel in the perpetual swaps markets (pcrps) is the funding rate. Similar to contango, when funding rates are positive, the price of the perpetual swap is above the spot price, and investors with long positions in perpetual swap markets pay the funding rate to the sellers of perpetual swaps. When funding rates are negative, similar to backwardation, the price of the perpetual swap is below the spot price, and the sellers of perpetual swaps pay those with long positions in the perps. Funding rates are paid or received every eight hours.

Positive funding rates can be used as a positive signal in technical analysis, which assumes that spot prices can move higher when holders of long positions in perpetual swaps are willing to pay the funding rate to maintain the long positions.

Funding rates, which are often between 0.01% and –0.01% daily, vary over time and across exchanges. When there is a large spread of funding rates across global crypto exchanges, some investors may build arbitrage positions taking long exposure to perpetual swaps on exchanges with the lowest funding rates and short positions in perpetual swaps on exchanges with the highest funding rates. The combination of long and short positions cancels out the price movements of bitcoin, leaving investors to earn the difference in the daily funding rates. While this may be a relatively low-risk trade, investors need to understand the custody risks on each exchange and ensure that sufficient capital is available at both exchanges to prevent the liquidation of one side of the trade.

Most investors are very familiar with spot markets, such as the stock market, or buying bitcoin tokens on a centralized exchange such as Coinbase. Once a trade is completed without margin in the spot market, the investor can hold that share of stock or crypto token as long as they choose.

Many investors will be surprised to learn that the volume of the bitcoin perpetual swaps market ranges between 5 and 10 times that of the spot bitcoin market.[7]

Similarly, open interest in bitcoin and Ether options tends to be lower than open interest in the perpetual swaps market. Volume counts the number of options or swaps contracts traded over a given time period. Open interest counts the number of options or swaps contracts outstanding at a particular point in time. Volume is a shorter-term measure of trader's interest in an underlying market, while open interest is a longer-term measure of interest. If volume is high and open interest is low, traders are holding positions for very short periods of time, typically minutes or hours, and exiting those positions before open interest is counted at the end of the trading day. If volume is low and open interest is high, investors are holding the swaps or futures contracts for longer periods of time.

In April 2024, bitcoin futures contracts at the CME had the largest open interest with open positions of $8.35 billion. Binance was second at $6.93 billion, while Bybit was third at $4.51 billion. Other exchanges with more than $1 billion in open interest include Bitget, OKX, Deribit, and BingX.[8] The CME ranks first in open interest and sixth in global trading volume, at $2.48 billion. Binance leads in the volume of bitcoin perpetual swaps at $32.4 billion, while OKX, Bybit, and Bitget all have volumes exceeding $10 billion. The ratio of volume to open interest at CME is 0.29, while the ratios at Binance, Bybit, Bitget, and OKX were 4.7, 5.2, 3.0, and 5.2 respectively. This means that positions are held at the CME for longer periods of time, while the offshore swaps markets are more popular with day traders who close positions before open interest is counted.

The volume and open interest in Ether perpetual swaps are much lower.[9] Open interest on Binance, Bybit, and OKX are $3.6 billion, $1.9 billion, and $1.6 billion respectively. CME ranks sixth in open interest and is not ranked in the top six in volume. Binance and OKX dominate trading in Ether perps with $16.3 billion and $11.2 billion in volume, respectively, while Bitget, Bybit, and BingX have volume between $1.8 billion and $5.6 billion.

One explanation for the higher ratio of volume to open interest at offshore exchanges relative to the CME is the higher level of leverage available. Bitcoin and Ether futures on the CME Group trade at a maximum allowed leverage of around four times, which varies with the price of the underlying token. At four times leverage, a 25% move in the underlying asset causes a 100% loss in the investor's equity contribution to the trade.

Exchange	Maximum Leverage
Coinbase	10
Kraken	50
KuCoin	100
Bybit	100
OKX	125
Binance	125
MEXC	200

Source: Adapted from BeInNews Academy / https://beincrypto.com/learn/crypto-leverage-trading / Last accessed at 15 May 2024.

Notice the leverage levels available to traders outside the US. Traders on KuCoin or Bybit can access 100 times leverage, while Binance and OKX offer 125 times leverage, and MEXC offers 200 times leveraged trading.

May 2019–April 2024	1828 days	
Daily Range	Number of Days	% of Days
0%	1	0%
2%	287	16%
3%	509	28%
5%	411	22%
6%	270	15%
8%	120	7%
9%	82	4%
11%	56	3%
12%	23	1%
14%	26	1%
More than 15%	43	2%
Average	4.5%	
Median	3.7%	
Maximum	61.7%	
Minimum	0.4%	

Source: Adapted from Yahoo Finance.

The daily price range of bitcoin can be calculated as (high price – low price)/close price. Over the five-year period from May 2019 to April 2024, the daily range of bitcoin prices averaged 4.5% with a median of 3.7%.

Leverage and volatility don't mix. With a median daily price range of 3.7%, a trader using 27 times leverage (1/3.7%), could lose 100% of their equity in half of all trading days. The volatility of bitcoin combined with high leverage explains why the trading volume is high and the open interest is low in bitcoin perpetual swaps. Traders should not leave their trading screen for lunch or to sleep when holding positions at maximum leverage. When trading at 100 times leverage, a 1% move in the underlying market causes a loss of 100% of the trader's equity contribution to the trade. That is, highly leveraged traders should close positions when they leave for lunch, as it is likely their position could be liquidated in an hour. Leveraged traders are encouraged to close all positions when they are done trading for the day, as crypto markets are open 24/7 and the trade is likely to be liquidated as the trader sleeps.

If a trader loses all of their equity at a 1% market decline, they may wish to have relatively small profit targets. They may enter the trade willing to risk a 0.5% to 1% market decline, so they may wish to take profits when the market rises by 1% to 3%. Liquidations of leveraged traders are a key cause of volatility in the price of bitcoin and Ether, as cascading liquidations can move the price of a token by 5% to 10% or more in minutes or hours. Leveraged traders with long positions that are liquidated during a 1% move will see their positions immediately sold, which moves the price lower, triggering liquidations for traders based on a 2% move, and so on.

CME is a centralized exchange for commodity and financial futures, while Binance, OKEx, and Bybit are centralized exchanges for crypto futures or perpetual swaps. Decentralized exchanges that trade derivatives include Uniswap, dYdX, Kine Protocol, and Jupiter. Investors must understand the implication for gas fees is based on what blockchain the DEX is built on. Gas fees will cost almost nothing for investors trading derivatives on Jupiter, because it is built on top of Solana. Gas fees will be substantial for investors trading on the Ethereum-based version of Uniswap, but can be greatly reduced by trading on Uniswap based on a layer 2 platform such as Optimism.

It's extraordinarily important to understand the difference in liquidation and margin procedures on CME relative to an offshore centralized crypto derivatives exchange, such as Binance. CME marks gains and losses to the market twice daily. Futures traders are known to their broker, who has accepted the trader's account based on the trader's income and assets. The futures broker may offer lines of credit, allowing traders time to repay losses on liquidated trades. Subject to the discretion of the investor's broker, a small shortfall in maintenance margin might not lead to immediate liquidation, but the investor may have a few hours to meet the margin call under normal market conditions. When an investor fails to meet a margin call in a timely manner, the trade can be liquidated. The liquidation of the trade will typically be charged regular fees and commissions and not a large liquidation fee. With a lower maximum leverage of just four times investor equity, positions at the CME are much less likely to be liquidated.

Things move much more quickly on offshore crypto exchanges, where investors often trade at 50 times leverage or more. It is important to note that crypto markets allow for anonymous trading, especially at decentralized exchanges. This means that all trades must be collateralized, as the exchange may not be able to recoup losses from anonymous traders in excess of the collateral posted before the trade. Due to the greater leverage and more anonymous nature of trading, liquidations of undercapitalized traders happen quickly and are algorithmically enforced. Traders of offshore perpetual futures not only have a smaller dollar cushion on leveraged trades but also a smaller time cushion, leaving little room for errors or negotiations.

When a trader's positions are liquidated at the CME, losses are assessed first to the trader, next to the trader's clearing firm broker, and then to the CME clearing corporation, which is an insurance fund that is highly capitalized from trading fees paid by clearing members. Losing traders experience losses while winning traders can stay in their trades as long as they comply with the margin requirements.

There are three models of how losses are funded on global crypto exchanges: the insurance fund, a socialized loss system, and auto-deleverage liquidations. Similar to a traditional futures exchange with a clearing corporation, an insurance fund allows the exchange to use excess funds to cover losses. This insurance is funded by contributions from liquidation fees or the remaining equity from liquidated positions. Notice that when trades are liquidated, there may be a substantial liquidation fee (5% to 15%) or the investor's entire remaining equity is forfeited to the insurance fund.

The last two methods used to fund losses of losing traders assess a direct cost on the winning traders on the exchange. In a socialized loss system, the losses of bankrupt traders are paid by the winning traders. Even worse is a system of auto-deleverage liquidations (ADLs). In an ADL system, trades of winning traders are automatically liquidated to cover the losses of losing traders starting with the most highly leveraged positions. That is, a winning trader can be forced out of their position even when the trade is well funded and in compliance with leverage limits. Notice that well-funded traders on the CME who are in compliance with all rules and position limits will never have trades liquidated by their broker or the exchange.

CHAPTER 23

Building Portfolios of Stocks, Bonds, Crypto Stocks, and ETFs

The discussion so far has focused on the risks and returns of directly investing in digital assets. The default way to access crypto assets is through centralized exchanges, with some investors choosing to move the assets to a non-custodial wallet. Chapter 21 discussed the custody risks of holding tokens on centralized exchanges and non-custodial wallets.

Assets held on centralized exchanges and in non-custodial wallets are typically not eligible to be held in tax-deferred accounts, such as individual retirement accounts (IRAs) in the US. ETFs, OTC funds, and crypto stocks can be held in tax-deferred accounts. All annual transactions in taxable accounts must be reported to the US Internal Revenue Service (IRS), including short-term and long-term gains and losses and mining and staking income.

At the end of 2023, Americans held $24.2 trillion in tax-deferred retirement accounts, including $13.6 trillion in IRAs and an additional $10.6 trillion in defined contribution plans, such as 401(k) plans, that may be eventually rolled into IRAs.[1] Considering the significant role of IRA assets in the financial planning of the average American, the option to invest in crypto through retirement accounts is gaining traction. In these accounts, all transactions are tax-deferred, which means investors don't have to worry about holding periods, such as those required to qualify for long-term gains tax treatment. This allows investors to trade as frequently as they wish in tax-deferred accounts, with all tax implications incurred at the investor's marginal tax rate on each withdrawal made during retirement.

In addition, institutional investors may be hesitant to invest directly in crypto assets but may choose to invest indirectly in the space. Foundations in the US controlled $1.25 trillion in assets in August 2023,[2] while US and Canadian college and university endowments held $839.1 billion as of June 2023.[3] At the end of 2023, US corporate and government defined-benefit retirement plans held $11.9 trillion[4] while global sovereign wealth funds totaled $11.3 trillion in assets at the end of 2022.[5] With these large pools of capital totaling nearly $50 trillion in assets, the crypto industry could double its $2.5 trillion market cap by attracting a 5% allocation from the average individual and institutional investor.

A variety of investment vehicles have been designed to offer access to crypto assets in the form of futures contracts, closed-end funds, stocks, spot ETFs, and futures ETFs. Chapter 24 will discuss accessing crypto assets through hedge funds and private equity funds, which are available to institutional and high–net worth investors.

Bitcoin futures ETFs started trading in the US in December 2021, more than two years before spot bitcoin ETFs commenced trading. During the time period, returns to the largest bitcoin futures ETF experienced a 0.99 correlation to spot bitcoin prices with a beta of 0.96. Because the futures market was generally in contango over this time period, the bitcoin futures ETF underperformed spot bitcoin by approximately 11% from December 2021 to March 2024, about 4.8% annualized after fees.

However, this fund proved popular, as it allowed investors to access bitcoin in tax-deferred and stock trading accounts without worrying about holding custody of bitcoin on centralized exchanges or non-custodial wallets. Because ETFs create new shares when investors are adding assets and retire shares when investors are withdrawing assets, they trade very close to the net asset value of the underlying assets. That is, during trading hours, the price of the ETF closely matches the value of the futures contracts held by the fund.

In contrast to ETFs, closed-end funds can trade at a substantial premium or discount to the net asset value (NAV) of the fund's holdings. Closed-end funds issue a specific number of shares in initial or ongoing offerings. Because there is a fixed number of shares of each closed-end fund, the fund can trade at a premium above net asset value when investor demand for the fund is strong, and trade at a discount to net asset value when investor demand for the fund is weak. Because shares of closed-end funds are not retired when investors are selling, the price typically declines below NAV when there is a strong supply of shares for sale.

Grayscale launched the Grayscale Bitcoin Trust (GBTC) in 2013, as the first fund vehicle available for US investors desiring exposure to spot bitcoin. GBTC started as a private placement in September 2013,[6] where investors bought shares of the bitcoin trust knowing that there was no immediate way to sell their holdings. GBTC started trading in the over-the-counter (OTC) US market in May 2015. Due to the fund's uniqueness and popularity in the early days of bitcoin trading, GBTC predominately traded at a premium until February 2021 of up to 39% of the NAV.[7] At a 40% premium, a $1,000 purchase of GBTC shares held $714 of spot bitcoin. As new options for bitcoin investing became popular and several bankrupt entities discussed in Chapter 25 held large positions in GBTC, the fund traded at a 49% discount at the end of 2022. Investors in GBTC substantially underperformed spot bitcoin returns when holding from its peak premium of nearly 39% in December 2020 when bitcoin was priced near $30,000, to its peak discount of nearly 49% in December 2022, when bitcoin was priced near $17,000. Conversely, investors nearly doubled the return to bitcoin while holding GBTC from its peak discount of 49% in December 2022 until GBTC converted to a spot bitcoin ETF at a zero discount in January 2024, a time when bitcoin prices surged from $17,000 to $63,000.

At the end of 2023, GBTC reached assets under management (AUM) of more than $60 billion and controlled more than 620,000 bitcoins or nearly 3% of the maximum bitcoin supply.[8] Once spot bitcoin ETFs started trading in the US in January 2024, GBTC converted to a spot bitcoin ETF, and lost assets to newer funds offered by Fidelity, Blackrock, and Bitwise.

In April 2024, the largest remaining US closed-end fund is the Bitwise 10 Crypto Index Fund (BITW), with AUM of approximately $1 billion.[9] The index fund holds approximately 90% of its assets in bitcoin and Ether, and 10% in other key crypto assets, including Solana, XRP, Cardano, Avalanche, Chainlink, Polygon, and Uniswap. As a closed-end fund, BITW has a fixed number of shares that may trade at a substantial premium or discount to the NAV of the tokens held in the fund.

Spot bitcoin ETFs were approved by the US SEC and started trading in January 2024. Spot bitcoin and Ether ETFs are scheduled to start trading in Hong Kong in April 2024, while spot ETFs were traded in Canada, Germany, and Switzerland long before they were approved in the US. In December 2022, before the US spot bitcoin ETFs were launched, global spot and futures-based ETFs held more than 170,000 bitcoins plus the 622,000 held in GBTC.[10]

	US Bitcoin Spot ETFs with AUM more than $100 Million	AUM ($ Million)	# Bitcoin Owned at $65,000
GBTC	Grayscale	$ 23,750	365,385
IBIT	Blackrock	$ 17,740	272,923
FBTC	Fidelity	$ 10,170	156,462
ARKB	ARK 21 Shares	$ 3,130	48,154
BITB	Bitwise	$ 2,170	33,385
HODL	VanEck	$ 596	9,169
BRRR	Valkyrie	$ 537	8,262
BTCO	Invesco Galaxy	$ 418	6,431
EZBC	Franklin	$ 342	5,262
	Total	$ 58,853	905,431

Source: Adapted from Yahoo Finance.

After the US launch of spot bitcoin ETFs in January 2024, eight new spot bitcoin ETFs raised more than $35 billion through mid-April 2024, with some of the fastest-growing ETFs ever launched. Blackrock's IBIT and Fidelity's FBTC quickly reached AUM of $17 billion and $10 billion, respectively. While GBTC quickly lost more than 40% of its AUM to funds offered by CeFi giants at lower fees, the nine largest US spot bitcoin ETFs controlled more than 900,000 bitcoins, or 4.6% of all bitcoins outstanding as of mid-April 2024. CoinGecko reports that the US held 83% of total global spot bitcoin ETF assets, with over USD 3.6 billion held in European ETFs and over USD 3 billion in Canadian ETFs. The largest ETFs are Canada's Purpose Bitcoin ETF at over CAD 2 billion and Germany's ETC Group Physical Bitcoin at over USD 1.2 billion.

Spot bitcoin ETFs have a number of advantages relative to futures ETFs and closed-end funds. Spot bitcoin ETFs tend to have much lower fees than the earlier fund vehicles, and do not suffer from the drag of contango on the futures-based funds or the potential premium or discount of the closed-end funds. That is, spot bitcoin ETFs are designed to offer returns exactly matching the return to holding spot bitcoin before custody and management fees. Investors are encouraged to understand the custody and fee arrangements before investing in spot bitcoin ETFs.

Some investors may hesitate to invest directly in tokens, as they may be unsure of which tokens will increase in value over the next decade. Additionally, bitcoin mining is highly competitive. Top bitcoin miners continuously add mining rigs, yet their market share remains relatively constant. Despite significant investments in mining capacity, the probability of earning block rewards doesn't change if all miners add a similar number of mining rigs.

At each halving, the bitcoin block reward is cut in half. With bitcoin prices stable at $65,000, the 6.25 bitcoin block reward was valued at $406,250 in March 2024, while the 3.125 bitcoin block reward was valued at half of that, $203,125, after the April 2024 halving. The thesis for owning stock in mining companies is that increasing scarcity will continually drive the price of bitcoin higher.

As mining becomes more competitive, selling services to miners rather than mining yourself is often more profitable. This concept, known as the picks and shovels theory, is reminiscent of the California Gold Rush in the 1840s, where selling picks, shovels, and jeans to gold miners was more lucrative than mining gold directly. Businesses serving the crypto industry, such as publicly traded mining stocks, hardware suppliers (GPUs and ASICs), and financial institutions like banks, brokers, and asset managers, might offer interesting investment opportunities.

As of 15 April 2024, there were seven US-listed ETFs focused on crypto-related stocks holding at least $100 million each. The AUM of the funds combined reached nearly $1.5 billion.

	Equity ETFs with AUM more than $100 Million	AUM ($ Million)
BLOK	Amplify	$ 750
BKCH	Global X	$ 164
BITQ	Bitwise	$ 124
WGMI	Valkyrie	$ 112
DAPP	VanEck	$ 111
LEGR	First Trust	$ 105
FDIG	Fidelity	$ 102
	Total	$ 1,468

Source: Adapted from Yahoo Finance, 2024.

	Common Holdings of Crypto Equity ETFs
MSTR	Microstrategy
COIN	Coinbase
SQ	Block
NVDA	Nvidia
PYPL	Paypal Holdings
RIOT	Riot Platforms
HUT	Hut 8 Corp
BITF.TO	Bitfarms
CLSK	CleanSpark
MARA	Marathon Digital
CIFR	Cipher Mining
WULF	TeraWulf

Source: Adapted from Yahoo Finance, 2024.

While each of these funds has unique holdings, they share a number of stocks or themes. Microstrategy is a publicly traded software company that held nearly 175,000 bitcoins on its balance sheet at the end of 2023, prompting investors to value it for its bitcoin holdings rather than its software business.[11] Fintech companies, such as Paypal, Coinbase, and Block, earn trading fees from customers trading crypto assets on their platforms. Nvidia is a key provider of computer chips and graphics processing units that support the crypto and artificial intelligence industries. Crypto miners, such as Riot Platforms, Hut 8 Corp, Bitfarms, CleanSpark, Marathon Digital, Cipher Mining, and TeraWulf are core holdings of crypto ETFs. Many of these miners had a cost of mining each bitcoin of under $15,000 in August 2022,[12] when global bitcoin mining rigs produced approximately 220 exahashes per second (EH/s).[13] With continuous additions to global mining rigs, EH/s reached 700 immediately before the April 2024 halving. Between the increase in mining rigs and the April 2024 halving, the cost of mining each bitcoin may have increased from $15,000 to more than $90,000 over the last two years. The increase in hash rate has made it 3.2 times more difficult to mine each block (700/220), while halving the block reward immediately doubles the cost of mining each coin.

The question is raised whether crypto stock prices are more sensitive to changes in stock prices or changes in bitcoin prices. Because equity ETFs were launched years before spot and futures-based ETFs, returns can be analyzed since March 2018. For the six years ending March 2024, the total returns were calculated for however many of the seven ETFs referenced earlier were outstanding in each month. Regression analyses were performed to estimate the portion of returns explained by tech stocks as represented by the Nasdaq-100 Index (QQQ) and spot bitcoin (BTC). While the returns to crypto ETFs are explained by both tech stocks and bitcoin, the crypto ETFs have more in common with stocks than crypto. In single regressions, the crypto ETF basket had a beta of 1.666 to QQQ with an r-squared of 0.50, and a beta of 0.39 to BTC with an r-squared of 0.33. That is, on a standalone basis, tech stock returns explained half of the return of the crypto stock ETFs, while bitcoin explained approximately one-third. When combining both tech stocks and bitcoin in a single regression, the portion of return variance explained by the two factors rises to 0.60, with a tech stock beta of 1.34 and a bitcoin beta of 0.24. Interestingly, the return to tech stocks explains 15% of the variance in bitcoin returns, with bitcoin offering a beta of 1.36 to QQQ, showing its greater volatility.

Ether tokens rallied in late 2023 and early 2024 when spot bitcoin ETFs were approved and earned record inflows. Investors may buy Ether tokens in anticipation of the launch of spot Ether ETFs, hoping for a portion of the asset flows that led the spot ETFs to become the faster-ever ETFs to reach $10 billion in AUM. It is unclear if or when the SEC will approve spot Ether ETFs. However, spot Ether ETFs already trade in Canada, Switzerland, and Germany, with $1.8 billion in AUM as of February 2024.[14]

Risk management, diversification, and rebalancing are all key elements of meeting investors' long-term goals. While many investors will brag on social media about the millions they earned holding meme coins, those gains typically came from holding concentrated positions of between 50% and

100% of the investor's net worth. As will be explained in Chapter 25, many investors lost their entire life savings during the bankruptcies experienced in 2022, such as Terra Luna, Celsius, BlockFi, Voyager, and FTX. Concentrating all of one's assets in a single YOLO trade ("You only live once") can lead to riches or ruin. The crypto market is unpredictable and substantial losses are possible. Coins that increase in value by 100 times in a month may decline by 99% in the next month, especially if there are no fundamental developments in the protocol warranting a long-term valuation.

The volatility of an investment portfolio depends on three factors: 1) the volatility of the individual assets in the portfolio, 2) the weights of each asset in the portfolio, and 3) the correlation between the returns to assets in a portfolio. From January 2018 to March 2024, bitcoin experienced an average annualized volatility of 73.9%, more than four times the volatility of the S&P 500 stock market index at 17.8%. Over the same time period, bitcoin experienced a maximum drawdown or decline in value of 75.6%, more than three times the maximum losses experienced by the S&P 500 at 23.9%. Fortunately for investors, the correlation of bitcoin returns to stock and bond returns was relatively low over this time period, at 0.37 and 0.20, respectively. If correlations and weights are small enough, portfolio theory calculates that it is possible to add extraordinarily volatile assets to a portfolio without substantially increasing the risk of the portfolio.

A long-term investment strategy involves combining different asset classes and holding a mix of stocks, bonds, private equity, hedge funds, and cryptocurrencies within a single portfolio. Investors should hold a diversified portfolio and rebalance the portfolio often.

Consider the impact of adding a small allocation of bitcoin to a portfolio holding stocks and bonds. The analysis starts in January 2018, a time when bitcoin had reached $10,000 per coin. Studies starting at earlier dates when bitcoin could be purchased for $100 or even $1 will show substantially greater returns and risk. From January 2018 to March 2024, a portfolio invested 60% in stocks represented by the S&P 500 and 40% invested in investment-grade bonds as measured by the Bloomberg Aggregate Bond Index, rebalanced monthly, earned an average annual return of 7.3% with a standard deviation of returns of 11.8% and a maximum drawdown of 20.1%. In contrast, bitcoin earned a much higher return of 33.4% per year, with an annualized standard deviation of returns of 73.9% and a maximum drawdown of 75.6%. It can be hard for investors to HODL bitcoin long term due to the extreme losses experienced during each market crisis or downturn.

Jan 2018–Mar 2024	Bitcoin	S&P 500	Bloomberg Agg	60/40	1% Bitcoin	2% Bitcoin	3% Bitcoin	5% Bitcoin	10% Bitcoin
Return	33.4%	11.4%	0.6%	7.3%	7.7%	8.1%	8.6%	9.4%	11.4%
Std Dev	73.9%	17.8%	5.7%	11.8%	11.9%	12.1%	12.3%	12.8%	14.6%
Drawdown	–75.6%	–23.9%	–17.2%	–20.1%	–20.5%	–20.8%	–21.2%	–22.0%	–24.3%

Source: Adapted from Yahoo Finance.

Next, consider the impact of replacing a small portion of the stock market allocation with holdings in spot bitcoin. A portfolio that invests 3% in bitcoin holds 57% in stocks and 40% in bonds and is rebalanced monthly. Notice that investing 3% in bitcoin slightly increases portfolio risk (from a standard deviation of 11.8% to 12.3% and from 20.1% to 21.2% drawdown). While there are marginal increases in risk, the portfolio return is much greater, at 8.6% vs. 7.3% annually. Portfolio risk starts to increase substantially once the weight on digital assets reaches 5%, 10%, or more.

Many advisors recommend that investors control risks by allocating a small portion of their net worth to digital assets. In many cases, the recommended allocation is between 1% and 3%. At this allocation, investments in crypto can potentially increase portfolio return but not subject the investor to catastrophic losses. That is, if the 3% crypto allocation were to lose 100%, the investor would still be able to pay their rent or mortgage payment, buy groceries, and potentially retire.

Rebalancing is the process of returning the weights of assets in a portfolio to the desired long-term weights. When rebalancing, investors will sell a portion of the assets that have outperformed the portfolio and use the proceeds to reinvest in assets that have underperformed the portfolio. Rebalancing forces investors to buy low and sell high and ensures that no one asset grows to a substantially overweight position. When risk and return are modeled, specific weights are assumed. Given that crypto and equity assets typically outperform fixed-income holdings, a failure to rebalance will lead to ever-growing allocations to the outperforming assets, which increases their weights and the risk of the portfolio.

Rebalancing is especially valuable when asset returns are mean reverting. Mean reverting assets have a negative autocorrelation, where periods of strong returns are followed by periods of weak returns. There have been many periods where bitcoin investors who regularly rebalanced substantially outperformed buy-and-hold investors. Bitcoin prices were approximately $10,000 in January and February 2018, declined to below $4,000 from December 2018 to February 2019, before returning to $10,000 in June and July 2019 and falling again below $7,000 in March 2020. Investors who bought in January 2018 and held to September 2020 earned a zero

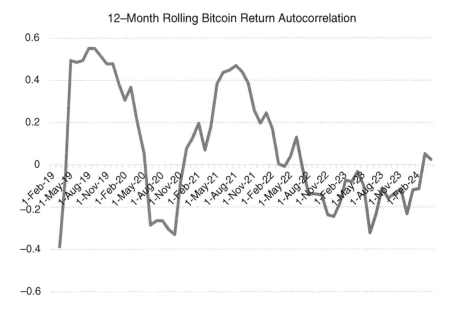

Source: Adapted from Yahoo Finance.

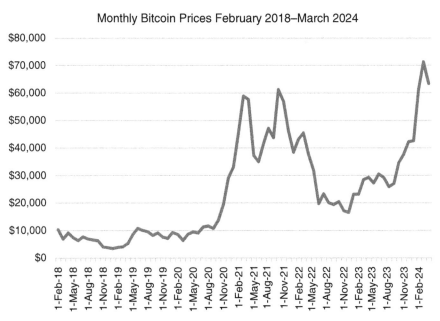

Source: Adapted from Yahoo Finance.

return on bitcoin, as the price started and ended near $10,000. Investors who rebalanced may have earned $10,000 in trading profits while still holding a similar amount of bitcoin at the end of the nearly two-year period.

When the autocorrelation is positive, prices are trending and investors benefit from longer holding periods and less frequent rebalancing. Clearly, investors would desire to hold bitcoin while it rallied from $11,000 in July 2020 to more than $61,000 in October 2021. Of course, it is important to understand the volatility of bitcoin, as prices declined below $17,000 by December 2022, before hitting new highs above $71,000 in March 2023.

Diversification return is the additional return earned through rebalancing when assets experience high volatility and low correlation to the return of other assets in the portfolio. Crypto assets and commodities have earned the highest level of diversification returns in recent years.

An August 2023 study by Bitwise discusses the impact of rebalancing strategies when bitcoin is added at a 2.5% weight to a portfolio originally invested 60% in stocks and 40% in bonds.[15] Using data from January 2014 to June 2023, the annualized standard deviation of the 60/40 portfolio was 11.37%, while a portfolio with 2.5% allocated to bitcoin rebalanced monthly, quarterly, or annually, had standard deviations of returns between 10.86% and 11.38%. While the 60/40 portfolio experienced drawdowns of 23.9%, the portfolios that rebalanced back to 2.5% bitcoin allocations experienced drawdowns between 24.17% and 24.72%. Neglecting to rebalance, however, led to a substantial overweight of bitcoin that resulted in portfolio standard deviation of 20.71% and a maximum drawdown of 51.35%. That is, starting with just a 2.5% allocation to bitcoin and not rebalancing more than doubled the maximum portfolio drawdown from 24% to more than 51%.

The Sharpe ratio is a reward-to-risk measure calculated as the return on the portfolio in excess of the risk-free interest rate divided by the standard deviation of the portfolio. Investors prefer higher Sharpe ratios, as each unit of risk is rewarded with a higher return. Bitwise notes that the Sharpe ratio of the 60/40 portfolio is substantially enhanced by adding 2.5% bitcoin to the portfolio and rebalancing, as the 60/40 portfolio offered a Sharpe ratio of 0.275 while the rebalanced bitcoin portfolios earned Sharpe ratios of between 0.42 and 0.603. When the 2.5% bitcoin allocation is not rebalanced and portfolio standard deviation soars to more than 20%, the Sharpe ratio declines to under 0.40. That is, the additional risk of holding large allocations to bitcoin has not adequately rewarded investors with a ratio of return, as the reward per unit of risk actually decreases as the allocation to crypto becomes larger and larger.

In conclusion, adding crypto assets to a well-diversified portfolio in weights of 1% to 3% with a disciplined rebalancing strategy has historically enhanced returns without a substantial increase in risk. However, investing more than 3% of assets in crypto or failing to rebalance before large drawdowns can substantially increase portfolio volatility and drawdown risk. Investing in crypto can be highly profitable over long periods of time. Still, investors are encouraged to rebalance regularly and to keep crypto holdings to a maximum of 3% to 5% of total assets. To maximize returns and minimize risks in the long term, investors are encouraged to avoid trendy and speculative coins and focus on assets backed by solid fundamentals. The top 10 layer 1 and layer 2 blockchains and several US dollar stablecoins comprise approximately 80% of the market capitalization of today's digital asset universe. While more than 13,000 coins are tracked today by coingecko.com, the vast majority of those coins will be worth much less in the coming years. The challenge for investors is to understand the business models, use cases, and user communities to identify the crypto protocols that may one day rule the oligopoly and reach market capitalization levels similar to today's leaders, such as Google, Amazon, and Microsoft.

Investing Through Private Equity and Hedge Funds

Chapter 23 discussed that the institutional investors that globally control more than $50 trillion in assets have so far been hesitant to invest directly in cryptocurrencies and digital assets. This may be due to concerns about custody issues or difficulty in where crypto fits into an asset allocation model. Is crypto its own asset class? Does it fit in the equity portfolio? Should it be allocated into the alternative investments category? Another reason might be that the investment team at each pension fund must explain all new investments to an investment committee or board of trustees before being allowed to invest. This does not mean, however, that institutional investors do not have the demand or interest to invest in crypto. In fact, an increasing number of institutional investors are investing in crypto assets through their previously approved hedge fund, private equity, and venture capital allocations. By investing in crypto through existing VC and hedge fund allocations, crypto can potentially enter the portfolio at a small allocation without returning to the investment committee to receive approval. As previously discussed, crypto investments have much in common with venture capital investments.

As of the fourth quarter of 2023, Crypto Fund Research counts 417 VC and 421 hedge funds that invest predominately in crypto assets.[1]

This same report notes that these funds have more than $70 billion AUM, up from less than $20 billion at the end of 2019. This is a small portion of the global assets invested in alternatives, as McKinsey counts VC assets of $2.57 trillion, other private equity and private credit assets at $6.37 trillion, and $2.73 trillion in real estate, infrastructure, and natural resources.[2] That totals $11.7 trillion and does not count the $4.3 trillion in global hedge fund investments.[3]

VC and hedge funds dedicated to crypto assets are relatively small, with a median AUM of $45 million, and just 9% of funds managing more than $100 million.[4] The majority of non-crypto focused hedge funds have AUM exceeding $100 million.

While the median funds are relatively small, more than 25% of all AUM is concentrated in five large funds. VC funds have a median number of 38 portfolio company investments.

Alternative investments, like hedge funds and venture capital, charge significantly higher fees than traditional stock and bond funds. An actively managed fund might charge an annual management fee of 50 to 100 basis points, 0.5% to 1% of assets, while index funds often charge 0.25% or less. In the US, funds available to retail investors cannot charge asymmetric performance fees.

US funds sold exclusively to accredited investors and qualified purchasers qualify for a private placement exemption. In addition to an exemption from regulations governing transparency, portfolio leverage, and concentration, funds with private placement exemptions can also charge incentive fees. Also called carried interest or performance fees, VC and hedge funds often earn 15% to 25% of investor profits without the requirement that the fund manager share in investor losses.

Fees on VC funds average 1.43% and 22.86%, which is an annual management fee of 1.43% of assets and an incentive fee of 22.86% of the profits on all exited investments.[5] VC investments are exited when the underlying company floats an IPO or is sold in a merger or acquisition transaction. At between 1.5% and 2%, management fees on hedge funds tend to be higher than VC funds, while performance fees at 15% to 20% tend to be lower. Note the incentive fees on hedge funds are typically paid on both realized gains from exited transactions and unrealized gains from assets still held in the portfolio.

To make a fair comparison to investing in publicly traded assets, such as crypto tokens, the return to investing in private funds should be calculated on a net-of-fee basis, subtracting all fees before making performance comparisons.

Investing in crypto tokens, stocks, and ETFs is highly liquid, as investors can choose to sell their holdings at any time. Investing in VC and hedge funds incurs substantial liquidity risk, as the fund's structure and documentation enforce long holding periods.

A specific VC fund will raise capital for a period of time and then be closed to new investors. After gathering commitments from investors for 6 to 18 months, the fund will stop gathering assets from new investors. The VC is not likely to raise a new fund until the current fund is fully invested, which might take two to four years. While VC funds do not accept withdrawal requests, they typically provide a quarterly NAV to investors, which is useful for evaluating fund performance and asset allocation.

VC funds typically have a drawdown structure, where investors only contribute capital when it is needed by the VC to complete an investment in a portfolio company. It may take two years or longer for a VC to call an investor's entire capital commitment. The total life of a VC fund can be 10 years or longer, with capital only returned to investors when an investment is exited. Crypto VC funds may have greater liquidity than traditional VC funds, as investments may turn into liquid tokens earlier than a traditional VC fund would seek an exit for a portfolio company.

Hedge funds typically accept commitments from investors on a monthly basis and allow withdrawals each month for investors who have provided a 30-day notice of their request for liquidity. Many hedge funds are subject to an initial lock-up period, which requires a minimum holding period before the investment can be submitted for redemption. Discretionary long/short crypto, market neutral, and quantitative long/short crypto funds have an average lock-up period of 6 to 12 months. Discretionary long-only crypto funds may have lock-up periods of three years or longer.[6]

Hedge funds may require a hard or a soft lock-up period. Hedge funds that require a one-year hard lock-up period do not allow withdrawals during the first year of an investment. Some strategies may be less liquid, such as investing in pre-launch tokens or staking tokens with waiting periods required for unstaking. Hedge funds may charge investors a withdrawal fee for withdrawing assets during a soft lock-up period. A soft lock-up fee, or an early redemption fee, may vary between 1% and 5% of the amount of the investor's withdrawal request. The fee is paid into the fund to compensate other investors for the trading costs incurred in fulfilling the withdrawal request of the exiting investor.

Hedge funds implement a variety of trading techniques, many of which have already been discussed.

- Cash/futures arbitrage – When futures are in contango, investors can profit from a long crypto, short futures position. When futures are in backwardation, investors may short crypto, and take offsetting long positions in the futures market. Funding rates can be arbitraged across exchanges.
- Geographic/triangular arbitrage – bitcoin and Ether trade globally with exchanges often segmented by fiat currency and country. The kimchi arbitrage trade is implemented when bitcoin trades at a higher price when denominated in Korean Won (KRW).[7] While the South Korean government restricts capital controls in fiat currency, those with connections in Korea or the ability to carefully move crypto assets can buy bitcoin in the global market at lower prices and sell it in the Korean market at higher prices. Triangular arbitrage profits from variations in the prices of three assets, such as USD, KRW, and BTC.

- Fundamental analysis – Purchase crypto assets that are believed to be undervalued. The fund will have higher volatility when investing only in long positions, while volatility can be reduced in a long-short strategy that purchases undervalued crypto assets and sells bitcoin or Ether as a hedge
- Quantitative analysis – High-frequency trading strategies can profit by providing liquidity, while trend-following strategies profit from sustained moves in crypto assets
- Mining and staking – Some hedge funds manage their own mining rigs or validation platforms or lend crypto to validators to earn staking yields
- Yield farming – Moving assets across DeFi platforms in search of the highest rewards to liquidity providers
- Airdrops – Early users of new DeFi protocols are often rewarded with tokens based on their trading volume

The percentage of hedge funds participating in yield farming is estimated at 14%, while 8% of crypto hedge funds earn staking yield by running their own validator node, and 21% earn staking yield by delegating tokens to a third party.[8]

Investors must evaluate the fees paid to managers of private funds relative to the value added. If the private fund earned returns similar to or less than that of simply holding bitcoin, investors would be better off buying a bitcoin ETF or spot bitcoin and not paying the additional fees to the VC or hedge fund manager. The CFR Crypto Fund Index earned higher returns than bitcoin from its 2017 inception until the end of 2023. Note that much of the outperformance was earned by avoiding losses from the crypto bear market of 2021 and 2022. That is, investors may earn higher long-term returns if they are able to earn 80% of the upside of the crypto market while participating in only half of the drawdowns. Hedge funds with hedged strategies, or those that hold both long and short positions, are often able to earn returns that are much less volatile than a long-only position in bitcoin.

Hedge funds have been largely successful in reducing volatility compared to a long-only, buy-and-HODL investment in bitcoin. When measuring risk using the beta to bitcoin, multi-strategy funds have been the least risky hedge fund strategy with a beta of 0.61, with algo/quant strategies, long-only funds, and index funds, posting beta risks of 0.68, 0.88, and 0.91, respectively. An investment with a beta of 1.0 is expected to have the same risk as the underlying market, as beta is a linear measure of risk relative to the returns of a specific asset. That is, an asset with a beta of 1.0 to bitcoin is expected to have both upside and downside returns of approximately 100% of that of the underlying bitcoin price.

CFR Crypto Fund Index vs. Bitcoin

December 31, 2016 - December 31, 2023

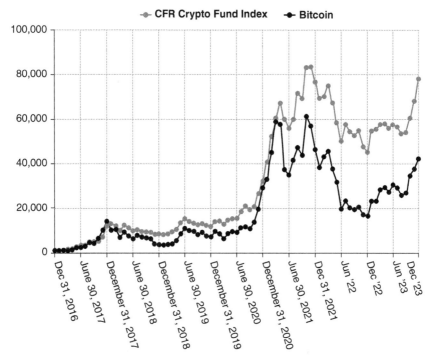

Source: Crypto Fund Research Quarterly Report Q4 2023, https://cryptofundresearch.com/q4-2023-crypto-fund-report/

Beta / Relationship to Bitcoin

Q1 '17 - Q4 '24 by Fund Strategy

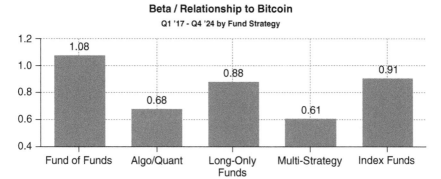

Source: Crypto Fund Research Quarterly Report Q4 2023, https://cryptofundresearch.com/q4-2023-crypto-fund-report/

Investors consider many facets of investment performance, including returns, fees, and net-of-fee returns, as well as standard deviation and drawdown risk. Some investors may prefer to allocate to investments with lower returns if the investment also experiences low risk. One way to measure the risk-return tradeoff is by the Sharpe ratio, which is calculated as the (return on the asset – the risk-free rate) / the standard deviation of the return on the asset. For example, an asset has a Sharpe ratio of 0.5 when its return is 13%, the risk-free rate is 3%, and the volatility is 20% ((13%–3%)/20%). For assets with returns that are approximately normally distributed, investors prefer assets with higher Sharpe ratios, as they are earning a higher return for each unit of standard deviation risk incurred.

Median Sharpe Ratio Across Fund Style

Q1 '17 - Q4 '23 by Fund Strategy

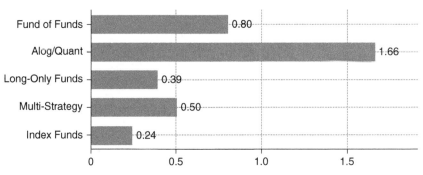

Source: Crypto Fund Research Quarterly Report Q4 2023, https:// cryptofundresearch.com/q4-2023-crypto-fund-report/

Notice the index funds and long-only funds have the lowest Sharpe ratios across hedge fund strategies, at 0.24 and 0.39, respectively. These funds are likely to be the most volatile, as no short sales or hedges have been implemented to mute the volatility of returns. The hedge fund strategy with the highest Sharpe ratio is algorithmic or quantitative funds which often have very short holding periods. These funds may take positions that are held for seconds or minutes, allowing the funds to earn profits from arbitrage or providing liquidity without being in the trades long enough to experience substantial market volatility.

Hedge funds make substantial use of derivatives, with 61% of hedge funds trading options, futures, or other derivatives.[9] The largest portion of funds trade futures, 57%, while 28% of funds trade options. Futures and options can be used to increase or decrease the risk of a hedge fund. The risk of a hedge fund can be reduced when it holds a portfolio of tokens by selling short CeFi futures contracts or DeFi perpetual swaps. Selling covered calls or options spreads can monetize volatility and provide income to the hedge fund without substantially increasing the volatility of the fund. Futures and options can be used to increase the risk of the fund when positions are used to increase the fund's leverage or when options are sold without having a position in the underlying or other options positions.

An exciting development that has the potential to substantially increase crypto adoption is that 29% of hedge funds that are not crypto-focused hold a median allocation of 7% of assets in crypto.[10] This can include systematic trend-following funds that have added CME bitcoin or Ether futures to their holdings of gold and Treasury bond futures or long-short equity funds that hold crypto stocks or bitcoin ETFs.

Many of the assets and trading venues used by hedge funds will be familiar to readers of this book. More than one-third of hedge funds had long positions in Solana, Polygon/Matic, Uniswap, Avalanche, Polkadot, and/or Cosmos, while more than 10% held Chainlink, Binance, Cardano, XRP, Litecoin, Doge, and/or Tron.[11] As a group, hedge funds tend to focus on the largest capitalization tokens backing the key layer 1 and layer 2 protocols.

More than one-quarter of hedge funds traded on SushiSwap, Curve, and/or dYdX decentralized exchanges with an overwhelming preference for swapping tokens at Uniswap, at 75%.[12]

In an AIMA survey, 56% of hedge fund managers stated that their top concerns were either the globally fragmented regulatory environment or regulation by enforcement.[13] In a global environment, it can be unclear whether investors must follow the requirements of the US, British, European, Chinese, or other regulators.

A key differentiating factor in hedge fund performance is whether its investments included exposure to Terra/Luna, FTX, or both. In 2022, 53% of crypto hedge funds were able to avoid both of these problems, while 13% were exposed to both, and 34% were exposed to one of the two.[14]

In reaction to these issues, hedge funds are now focused on custody arrangements. In 2023, no hedge funds held tokens in commingled accounts at a centralized exchange, which is often the default arrangement for individual investors. In contrast, 80% of hedge funds now employ a third-party custodian, while 35% hold segregated accounts at centralized exchanges.[15] Hedge funds may split custody of assets, as 39% self-custody in cold wallets while 16% self-custody in hot wallets. Custody arrangements may vary with staking needs, the frequency of trading, and for holding tokens that may lack liquidity or are based on blockchains not supported by exchanges or custodians.

To further focus on security, the majority of hedge funds now require client asset segregation, mandatory financial audits, and independent statements of reserve assets. Approximately one-third of hedge funds now complete background checks on key personnel, require insurance coverage, and minimum capital requirements.

While crypto hedge funds are relatively small, there are some very large crypto VCs, including Andreessen Horowitz (A16Z) and Katie Haun, who raised a combined $4 billion to invest in nascent crypto projects. Notably, A16Z was a key investor in Web 1.0, posting big profits on exits from internet companies in 1998 and 1999.

Crypto projects can be funded in a variety of ways. Chapter 19 discussed the angel, ICO, crowdfunding, and VC models. ICO activity has slowed substantially since 2018, when the US SEC warned that most ICOs were offerings of unregistered securities. The SEC was concerned that the ICOs were broadly offered to retail investors without providing the disclosures routinely offered in the IPO market.

While VCs and angel investors do invest in liquid tokens, several other investment types include equity in the token-issuing entity, convertible notes, non-equity tokens, and simple agreements for future tokens (SAFTs). VC firms or sovereign entities may host incubators or accelerators. An incubator provides shared resources for startup firms, such as office space, legal, and accounting services. In addition to providing the services of an incubator, an accelerator also offers funding for startups. Crypto protocols that sell a minority stake to an angel or a VC in the seed or later rounds may maximize the long-term ability to raise capital, as ICOs previously sold a majority stake in the pre-seed round at much lower valuation levels. Angels and VCs are used to being patient investors and may be willing to buy tokens or ownership stakes that are not liquid for several months or years.

Many corporations have a venture capital unit that invests in startup companies. The goal may be purely profit, to keep in touch with the emerging tech space, or to identify early acquisitions that may be a good fit for the corporation's core business. Top corporate venture capital (CVC) investors include Google, Intel, Qualcomm, Salesforce, Novartis, Samsung, Comcast, and GE.[16]

Many crypto firms, including Coinbase and Binance, also have a CVC arm. CoinGecko reports that the largest crypto VCs ranked by the number of deals include Coinbase Ventures, NGC Ventures, AU21 Capital, Shima Capital, LD Capital, Animoca Brands, Hashkey Capital, Pantera Capital, Binance Labs, and BigBrain Holdings. Each of these VCs invested in at least 170 deals between January 2017 and September 2023.[17] Binance Labs was spun out of Binance in March 2024.[18]

Traditional VCs operating in the equity markets typically invest in convertible preferred stock. If the investment goes well and the VC can exit through an IPO or acquisition, the preferred stock is converted into common stock. If the investment goes poorly, the convertible stock remains a debt issue, participating in the entity's liquidation at a higher place in the capital stack than common equity. While convertible preferred stock may receive some recovery value, common equity is typically worthless after a bankruptcy or liquidation process.

After the SEC cracked down on ICOs in 2018, VCs created simple agreements for future tokens (SAFTs) to invest in nascent crypto projects while remaining compliant with US securities laws.[19] Even though SAFTs are still securities, they comply with US laws because they are sold exclusively to accredited investors and qualified purchasers. Similar to convertible preferred stock, SAFTs convert to tokens when issued but remain an investment in the enterprise even if tokens are not issued.

SAFTs can be codified as a smart contract. Terms of the agreement include events that will trigger conversion into tokens, the ownership stake granted to the investor, the price of the tokens at a discount to the price at issuance, and the ability of the investor to participate in future funding rounds.

SAFTs may provide value to both VCs and development teams. VCs can invest at a discount before a protocol issues tokens. The development team can raise needed cash from the VC at the pre-seed stage but may only be required to sell a small minority stake. Because the cash from the VC investment sustains the development team while they reach milestones, the protocol can eventually raise a greater amount of capital by delaying a greater quantity of token sales until a time when the protocol is well-developed and trades at a much higher valuation.

While founders of a new crypto protocol may raise funds through the sale of ICOs or SAFTs, not all tokens are issued or sold. Most protocols will reserve a portion of tokens for future issuance, often in exchange for services rather than fiat cash or crypto assets. Tokens can be issued to founders, developers, miners, validators, and airdropped as incentives to early users of the platform. In addition to providing funding through SAFTs, VCs and other investors may participate in the growth of the protocol by operating a validator node to earn staking yields or providing liquidity to earn airdrops and token rewards.

Fundraising provided by crypto VCs was relatively quiet, raising less than $10 billion for crypto startups in 2017 to 2020 combined. Fundraising soared to $20 billion in 2021 and $35 billion in 2022, before falling back to less than $10 billion in 2023.[20] VC investments in traditional technology companies also declined substantially in 2023 after the decline in equity markets and the aggressive increase of interest rates by the US Federal Reserve in 2022. In most quarters since 2017, the majority of assets invested were sourced from crypto-native VCs, either corporate VCs sponsored by centralized exchanges or VCs focused exclusively on Web 3.0 technologies.

Because the crypto economy is still relatively young, approximately half of the deals since 2017 have been made in the pre-seed or seed stage.[21] In the pre-seed stage, the protocol is not yet operating, and investors allocate capital solely on the strength of the white paper and conversations with the developers and the management team. In the seed stage, the protocol has some operations and may be starting to attract attention from users. Investors in pre-seed and seed-stage companies make relatively small investments, often under $5 million, in search of returns 10 or more times the initial investment. Because these investments are made before the company has met substantial milestones, pre-seed and seed-stage investments are highly risky, with a substantial portion of the ventures losing money for their investors by failing to develop a timely and cost-efficient protocol that attracts users' attention.

While approximately half of the deal count since 2017 was invested in pre-seed and seed-stage investments, the vast majority of the capital invested was in early- and later-stage deals.[22] Protocols attracting capital for early- and later-stage deals have become less risky and more valuable by meeting a number of developmental milestones. Having progressed far beyond a white paper, the protocols are operational and attracting interest from developers and users. Due to their more advanced stage of operation and the building of a consumer following, protocols in the early and later stages can attract larger amounts of capital at higher valuations. As each milestone is met, the probability of failure of the protocol declines, and the valuation increases. As the valuation increases, the future profit potential declines. VCs investing in later-stage rounds are less likely to experience a 100% loss of their investment but are also less likely to earn a profit of 100 times their initial investment. Of course, VC investors at each stage complete a comprehensive due diligence process to minimize the probability of losses, especially by determining the skill and honesty of the team.

ICOs may be characterized as liquid venture capital investments with some key differences. First, ICO investors may be more likely to invest in a losing project, as many retail investors have not been trained in due diligence processes. While ICO investors in 2017 and 2018 were very likely to invest in a scam or a rug pull, VC investors are generally able to quickly eliminate the riskiest projects and those most likely to fail. Another important distinction is that ICO investors may have invested substantial amounts in one or a few tokens, while VC funds invest in dozens of protocols. VCs ideally invest in stages, offering all management teams small investments to start and adding more funds to the protocols that are most successful in meeting their milestones. When an ICO investor invests in just one or two tokens, there is a high probability their entire investment will be lost. When a VC general partner invests in two dozen projects, odds are that the profits from the winning projects will exceed the losses from the losing projects. That is, the VC tries to lose a small amount of money on many investments while making a large profit on a few investments. Most ICO investors likely missed the due diligence and diversification aspects of investing and may not have understood to increase investments as given protocols increased their success over time.

Different VC investors may focus on different sectors within the crypto community. Most investments at several large VCs, including Polychain, Coinbase Ventures, Pantera Capital, and NGC Ventures, were made to support infrastructure and DeFi projects.[23] In contrast, Animoca Brands focused investments on gaming and NFT projects.

While capital dedicated to various sectors changes over time, the sectors generally attracting the largest capital investments include infrastructure, trading/exchanges/investment/lending, and Web 3.0/NFT/metaverse/gaming.[24]

These three sectors attracted 51% of the investments made by VCs in the first quarter of 2024.[25] Another 27% of the number of investments were made into the DeFi, payments/rewards, layer 2/interoperability, and data sectors. Sectors attracting fewer funding deals included privacy/security, AI, tokenization, wallets, compliance, custody, and others. As the industry matures, investors may anticipate funding fewer projects in infrastructure and exchanges and more projects in AI and tokenization.

Sectors also vary in the stage of investment. In the first quarter of 2024, the majority of investment capital contributed to the AI, banking, DeFi, enterprise blockchain, and privacy/security sectors was made at the early and later stages of protocol development. Sectors focused on pre-seed and seed-stage investments included custody, mining, tokenization, and compliance.[26]

Finally, the number of project investments varies by blockchain. Across blockchains, DeFi projects have been the most popular target of investors. More than 2,000 projects operating in the Ethereum ecosystem have been made, focusing on infrastructure, DeFi, and NFTs. More than 1,000 projects using Polygon and BNB Chain have been funded, while more than 500 projects built on Arbitrum, Avalanche, and Solana have been funded.[27]

CHAPTER 25

Due Diligence and Technology Risks: FTX, Terra Luna, Hacks, and Scams

This chapter discusses the algorithmic failures, scams, fraud, and bankruptcies that rocked the crypto industry in 2022, including Terra Luna, Three Arrows Capital, FTX, Voyager, BlockFi, Celsius, and rug pulls.

The returns to individual crypto assets are driven by four factors: the return to the broader crypto market, the return to the equity market, price inflation, and developments regarding the fundamentals of individual crypto assets, such as an increase in transactions and total value locked.[1] Over a five-year period, the correlation between monthly returns on US stocks and bitcoin averaged 0.24, while the correlation to fixed income returns averaged a statistically insignificant 0.01. Notice that these correlations are highly volatile. The highest correlation between bitcoin and stock prices was experienced during the tumultuous year of 2022.

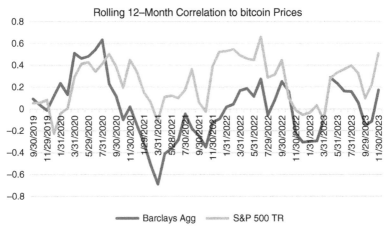

Source: Adapted from Yahoo Finance.

Many investors would prefer not to relive the year 2022, as stock, bond, and crypto markets experienced sharp simultaneous losses. The S&P 500 declined 18.3%, while the Barclays Aggregate Bond Index crashed more than 13%, marking the worst year ever for the US bond market. These market developments were spurred by US CPI inflation rising to more than 9%, triggering the US Federal Reserve Bank to increase short-term interest rates by more than 4%. After reaching nearly $65,000 in November 2021, bitcoin fell below $17,000 by the end of 2022, moving the market capitalization of the crypto industry from $3 trillion to $800 billion.

At a time when sentiment regarding the crypto industry is negative, it can be difficult for any tokens to increase in value, even when the fundamentals of a specific token may be overwhelmingly positive. That is, when faith in the concept of crypto assets is shaken, the vast majority of crypto assets will experience losses. Scams, hacks, and frauds, especially when causing large domino effects of losses, can quickly turn sentiment regarding the industry in a very negative direction.

The key to understanding the losses in the crypto market in 2022 starts with the first domino falling, which triggered a cascading wave of bankruptcies and liquidations. The first domino to fall was the collapse of the Terra UST algorithmic stablecoin system (along with Anchor and Luna), which triggered Three Arrows Capital's bankruptcy, leading to credit losses at Celsius, Voyager, BlockFi, and FTX.

Terra UST was an algorithmic stablecoin launched in South Korea in December 2020. By June 2022, the stablecoin and related Luna and Anchor tokens had failed, leading to losses of $18 billion on UST and $35 billion on Luna in a single month.[2] Note that the liabilities of Lehman Brothers, whose failure sparked the global financial and real estate crisis in 2008, exceeded its assets by only $26 billion.

There was an immediate contagion effect, with the crypto industry losing more than $600 billion in value in a single month, including substantial losses in the value of bitcoin, Ether, and other assets that were not directly related to the collapse of the Terra ecosystem.

Terra UST was an algorithmic stablecoin pegged to $1, backed by an arbitrage mechanism to its related token, Luna.[3] When UST rose above $1, Luna tokenholders could exchange their tokens to mint new UST. The new issuance of UST drove the price back toward $1, while the burning or retiring of Luna tokens supported the price of that governance token. When UST fell below $1, UST could be exchanged for Luna tokens, driving the stablecoin's price back toward $1. This circular arbitrage attracted substantial TVL and trading activity.

It is important to note that the stablecoin was backed by Luna, a token created internally by the Terra ecosystem. The stablecoin was not backed by fiat, such as US dollars or Korean Won, nor was it backed by over-collateralized holdings of externally created tokens, such as Ether or bitcoin, as is the case with the DAI stablecoin. Algorithmic stablecoins may be inherently fragile, as it can be difficult to incentivize independent investors to always act to support the stabilization of the system.[4] That is, the stablecoin may be vulnerable to sentiment leading to quick withdrawals and may be attacked by investors noticing any degradation or withdrawal in the assets supporting the system.

Luna's staking yield of 8% to 10% attracted capital to the protocol and the Anchor DeFi protocol, which paid 19.5% yields on UST deposits, including Luna's staking yield. In 2021, the price of Luna tokens rose from $0.66 to $89, further attracting assets to the ecosystem. The system was marketed as a cash equivalent, even offering debit cards accepted for consumer purchases in South Korea through the Chai Network.[5]

What lessons can be learned from the collapse of the Terra UST stablecoin and the related Luna and Anchor tokens?

First, investors should realize that risk and return are closely linked. Investors seeking risk-free returns may earn a yield commensurate with money market assets or investment-grade bonds, around 5% in April 2024. Investors looking to earn much higher yields, such as 19.5%, should expect to take a much greater level of risk. As a result, investors should be skeptical of a risk-free 19.5% yield, as if something looks too good to be true, it usually is. DeFi investors should always consider the annual percentage yield (APY). Yields that are sustainable in the long run are less than 10% APY. There can be substantial risks to crypto protocols offering APYs substantially above 10%. In the best-case scenario, the protocol will offer high yields for some time, attract a significant amount of capital, and reduce the yield to sustainable levels once the protocol has attracted the desired level of TVL. In a middle scenario, the high APY will be paid by issuing new tokens, which dilutes the value of the existing tokens. When the APY is paid in the tokens of the protocol, investors are not guaranteed to increase the value of their tokens in dollar terms. For example, an investor depositing tokens in a protocol with 100% APY will end the year with twice as many tokens as they started. On average, tokens in an inflationary protocol where new tokens are continuously minted will decline with the degree of dilution. That is, unless the protocol is earning substantial profits, the investor should expect the value of the tokens to decline by 50% per year to offset the dilution or the doubling in the number of tokens. The worst-case scenario is when the protocol is fraudulent, and the creators steal the funds invested after attracting the desired amount of capital.

Second, investors need to understand where the yield comes from. Is the yield paid from borrowers to lenders, from market takers to market makers, or from an unsustainable source of capital that may eventually run dry?

In the case of Anchor, depositors or lenders were earning 19.5% on $14 billion in deposits, while borrowers were paying 15% on $3 billion in outstanding loans. This is a negative cash flow situation, temporarily supported by venture capital investors who funded the losses to earn equity in the Terra-Luna-Anchor ecosystem. Reserves declined each month, as payments to depositors/lenders were substantially larger than the income to the ecosystem. When the venture capitalists run out of money or patience, the protocol is forced to break the stablecoin's peg to $1. Because crypto protocols disclose information on-chain, it may be clear when the system runs low on reserves. This information can start a bank run, as savvy investors may bet against the assets in the system in anticipation of its demise. In a classic bank run scenario, as withdrawals from the system increase, assets may be insufficient to support the withdrawals and cause the failure of the system.

Third, don't ignore risk events. US Dollar Stablecoins are designed to be pegged to $1, while other stablecoins may be pegged to the value of one euro or one ounce of gold. Investors should carefully evaluate the volatility of the stablecoin, as the value should not diverge from a range close to $1, such as $0.995 to $1.005. When UST was just six months old, the price of the Luna token fell from $15 to $4, which led the stablecoin to "break the buck" and trade below $1. After only six months, the algorithmic stablecoin has already started to fail.

Fourth, and a key to many of the incidents in 2022, is that a protocol can't print its own collateral. Following the example of Venezuela and Zimbabwe, whose money printing led to inflation rates of 1,000% or more, crypto protocols such as Celsius, FTX, and Terra Luna could not maintain their value and prevent bankruptcies. The value of the currency continues to decline as more is printed, minted, or issued. Investors prefer hard currencies minted elsewhere, such as dollars and euros in the case of fiat currency, and bitcoin and Ether in the case of digital assets.

The final lesson is that once investors lose confidence in a system, bank runs happen very quickly, leading to losses of up to $50 billion in a matter of hours or days. With advancements in technology, including online bank transfers, social media, and crypto protocols, bank runs now occur at an accelerated rate, as trading is now available 24/7. In March 2023, SVB experienced the largest US bank failure since 2009, after a "Twitter-fueled bank run" led to $42 billion in withdrawals in 24 hours.[6]

Given the size of the Terra-Luna-Anchor ecosystem, these substantial losses reverberated quickly across the crypto landscape. These losses led to the bankruptcy of Three Arrows Capital, a Singapore-based hedge fund with $10 billion in assets. The losses at Three Arrows Capital (3AC) triggered bankruptcies at Voyager, Genesis, BlockFi, and Celsius, creditors of highly leveraged crypto hedge funds such as 3AC. Losses at these crypto lending firms led to withdrawals and an examination of the balance sheet at FTX, which exposed fraud and led to the bankruptcy of the centralized exchange.

3AC borrowed more than $3.5 billion in partially collateralized loans from 27 lenders, including $2.3 billion from Genesis and more than $600 million from Voyager.[7] 3AC used borrowed funds to invest in the Terra Luna–Anchor ecosystem in search of the offered 20% returns. Leveraged trading can be highly profitable when the return on investment exceeds the cost of borrowing, such as when borrowing at 10% and lending at 20%. Investors may become overconfident and trade at high levels of leverage. Of course, losses multiply when the investments lose value while the borrower pays interest. Investors trading at 10 times leverage suffer a loss of 100% of their equity when the underlying assets experience a 10% loss.

In addition to investments in Terra Luna–Anchor, 3AC invested in dozens of other crypto assets and held more than 6% of the Grayscale Bitcoin Trust (GBTC) shares.[8] Before its conversion to a spot bitcoin ETF in January 2024, GBTC was an over-the-counter trust holding spot bitcoin. Investors would purchase restricted shares from GBTC at NAV, which would convert to tradable shares after a six-month minimum holding period. After declining from more than a 70% premium in 2018, GBTC traded at a 10% to 40% premium to the value of its bitcoin holdings in 2019 and 2020.[9] Intended as an arbitrage trade, investors would purchase GBTC at NAV and hedge against the movements of bitcoin in the trust by selling bitcoin in the spot or futures market. Investors profited by selling GBTC at a premium at the end of the six-month lockup period. If the premium remained at 20% for one year, investors could profit 40% through two six-month trades, each earning 20% returns.

GBTC traded at a premium for years when there were few other options to invest in bitcoin outside the spot and futures markets. Investors were attracted to GBTC as a way to invest in bitcoin in a retirement account while not having to worry about custody arrangements.

GBTC became an extraordinarily large fund, holding nearly 620,000 bitcoins before converting to a spot bitcoin ETF in 2024.[10] Because there was no withdrawal mechanism, investors continuously added assets to GBTC as long as the shares traded at a premium to NAV. The reason that GBTC traded at a premium or a discount was that there was no mechanism to withdraw assets from GBTC, so investors needed to trade shares in the market.

Unfortunately for arbitrageurs, GBTC traded at a constant premium to NAV from 2018 until it traded at a constant discount to NAV from February 2021 to December 2023. By the time of the Terra Luna collapse in spring

2022, GBTC was trading at a 30% discount to NAV. Traders holding who purchased GBTC shares at NAV using more than three times leverage lost their entire capital invested in this trade.

What are the lessons learned from 3AC?

First, a lesson that should have been learned long ago during the 1998 collapse of the Long-Term Capital Management hedge fund is that highly leveraged trades are extraordinarily risky. Leveraged trades frequently lead to spectacular bankruptcies when combined with high volatility or low liquidity. Trading GBTC at three to five times leverage entirely wiped out investor capital as the fund moved from a premium to a discount. Similarly, trading bitcoin or Ether at just two times leverage leads to a complete loss during a 50% drawdown. Losses from Terra Luna decimated even unleveraged investor capital.

The second lesson is to fully evaluate counterparty risk and credit risk. Before extending credit, lenders must understand the borrower's entire balance sheet, including the assets the loan will support and information on all outstanding loans. Consider the 2022 collapse of Archegos Capital Management.[11] The TradFi fund used equity swaps at up to nine banks to take positions at up to 10 times leverage in a concentrated portfolio of stocks. Because regulators did not require the firm to report aggregate exposures, each bank only had access to the positions held at its firm. This lack of transparency allowed Archegos to provide incomplete and misleading information regarding the size of the debt and the concentration of its portfolio. While each bank set credit limits based on only the positions held at the bank, the aggregate credit limits across banks were much higher than would have been allowed by any bank with a careful risk management process.

Third, lenders need to understand which collateral is pledged against which loan. While loans in the crypto universe are typically fully or over-collateralized, many of 3AC's loans were undercapitalized. As the value of their crypto asset holdings declined, the collateral value guaranteeing the loans also declined. While the largest losses at 3AC were likely related to Terra Luna, holdings in GBTC and other crypto assets also declined in value due to the contagion risk of the Terra Luna collapse. Both lenders and investors must realize that not all "arbitrage opportunities" are risk-free and last forever. Many forget that arbitrage is defined as a risk-free, instantaneous profit. Lots of risky things can happen in the six-month holding period required before being able to liquidate new positions in GBTC.

Finally, lenders and investors must perform due diligence on the principals in the firms where they are building relationships. Before moving into the highly volatile crypto space, the principals at 3AC were unable to profit trading emerging markets currencies, even though currency trading is much less volatile than crypto.

The first domino to fall was Terra Luna–Anchor, which led to the bankruptcy at 3AC. The losses at 3AC toppled a number of firms that lent to the highly leveraged crypto hedge fund. Voyager Digital lost half of its assets after lending $650 million to 3AC. Genesis Global Trading lent 3AC $2.3 billion, while blockchain.com provided an additional $270 million in capital.[12]

Voyager, BlockFi, Celsius, Gemini, and Genesis were crypto lending platforms where investors could earn a yield by depositing crypto. Rather than using the crypto assets to earn staking yield, the tokens were lent to hedge funds and other traders seeking to leverage their investments in cryptocurrency trading. While some investors may have viewed these deposit products as similar to earning interest on bank accounts, it must be emphasized that crypto lending platforms are not accounts at banks or brokerage firms that are eligible for FDIC, NCUA, and SIPC insurance coverage.

While the losses at 3AC started the decline of BlockFi, it was later revealed that the firm had lent more than $1.2 billion of its $2.7 billion in client assets to FTX and its sister firm Alameda Research.

A lesson to be learned here is that lenders of any type need to manage counterparty risk and diversify their balance sheets across borrowers. Voyager's lending of half of its assets to 3AC is a clear failure of risk management and diversification, while BlockFi's exposure to FTX was more than 40% of assets. Investors also need to diversify deposits, as losses would be mitigated if assets were held at other centralized exchanges such as Binance or Coinbase rather than holding all of their assets on the FTX centralized exchange.

If Voyager lends half of its deposits to Three Arrows Capital, it can fail simply due to the credit losses to 3AC. Voyager may have survived if it had diversified its balance sheet across borrowers, perhaps lending just 5% or 10% of assets to 3AC or other single counterparties. BlockFi had significant deposits at FTX, which led to its bankruptcy. Custody risk would have declined if assets were held outside of FTX.

Celsius attracted $25 billion in customer deposits by promising yields of up to 18.5%. While Celsius looked to lend those assets at a higher yield, the yield earned on Celsius' $8 billion in loans was insufficient to pay the yield promised to depositors.[13] Depositors on the Celsius platform could earn discounts on loans and trading fees by holding the Celsius token, which paid higher yields than other token deposits. In the fine print of the yield agreement, Celsius noted that customer funds were unsecured loans to Celsius and that customer funds might not be recovered in the case of bankruptcy.

Investors must always understand the source of the yield. At Celsius, yields paid to customers were substantially greater than the income earned on loans. The loans and investments Celsius made were to creditors and platforms such as Anchor and FTX. If Anchor paid sustainable yields of

19.5%, Celsius may have been able to pay depositors 14% to 18% for some period of time. Of course, the crash of Terra Luna–Anchor not only ended the source of 19.5% yields, but also caused a loss of nearly all capital invested in the system.

Celsius was accused of running a Ponzi scheme, where the funds of new customers were used to pay the yields of existing and exiting customers.[14] In addition, Celsius was accused of using up to $558 million in customer funds to inflate the value of the Celsius tokens, even when the Celsius team was personally selling tokens. Celsius tokens comprised a growing portion of the firm's balance sheet, which made it important for the CEL tokens to remain at high values.

What are the lessons to be learned from Celsius? It can be difficult to support a high yield to depositors, as Celsius paid $1.3 billion more to customers than it earned on its loans and investments. To be sustainable, banks and leveraged investment firms must earn a positive net interest margin, earning more interest and income on loans and investments than is paid in deposits. When it is difficult to find lucrative loans and investments, banks and investment firms should reduce the yield paid on deposits to ensure that the interest paid is less than the interest earned.

The second is to avoid an asset-liability mismatch. Many crypto firms allowed investors to withdraw their assets daily, but invested customer funds in long-term and illiquid investments. Celsius was one of the largest investors in the staked Ether tokens offered by Lido.[15] While staking Ether tokens with Lido earned a staking yield of 6% to 8%, the tokens that Lido staked with Ether were locked until the Ethereum Shanghai upgrade was completed in April 2023. Ether tokens staked in 2021 could not be withdrawn until the merge was completed, which was at an unknown future date. While it was assumed that Lido's staked Ether tokens would trade at the same price as liquid, unstaked Ether tokens, that peg was broken in the summer of 2022 during this string of bankruptcies, as staked Ether tokens traded to at least a 6% discount to the value of liquid Ether tokens.

While DeFi platforms can offer great transparency, crypto lending firms and centralized exchanges do not offer the same transparency. This makes it difficult to understand the size of deposits and loans as well as the concentration of assets and liabilities on the balance sheets of these privately held firms.

No discussion of crypto losses in 2022 would be complete without telling the story of FTX, Alameda Research, and Sam Bankman-Fried. Sam Bankman-Fried eventually chose to domicile the FTX centralized exchange in Bermuda.

While centralized exchanges operating in the US offer investors low leverage levels and dozens of token choices, exchanges operating offshore have much lower regulatory requirements. While Binance.US and FTX.US had limited products available for US investors, non-US investors could access Binance.com and FTX.com which had a much wider array of investment choices, most of which were not compliant with US regulations. While some might say that US investors are not seeing the full opportunity of crypto, others would say that US regulations are protecting US investors from participating in highly leveraged trading, fraudulent tokens, and unregistered securities.

Offshore exchanges may offer hundreds or thousands of tokens and leverage on crypto trades of 10 to 100 times equity capital. In finance, an offshore domicile denotes that an entity may be searching for a headquarters location that would be subject to a much lower regulatory burden than a traditional jurisdiction with a strong regulatory environment, such as Hong Kong, the US, and the UK.

Sam Bankman-Fried (SBF) might have thought that if FTX was operating in Bermuda, the firm was not accountable to US law, even though it had a US subsidiary. Because $1.1 billion of the $1.7 billion FTX received in venture capital investments came from US investors, US regulators have jurisdiction over some of the actions of SBF and FTX.

In March 2024, SBF was sentenced to 25 years in a US prison after being convicted of the fraudulent use of customer funds.[16] When investors held assets in custody at the FTX centralized exchange, the terms of service they received promised that customer funds would be segregated and only used for the benefit of customers. As discussed in Chapter 21 on wallets and custody, investors do not fully own their crypto assets if the private keys have been shared with anyone, including a centralized exchange. At the collapse of FTX, customers faced losses of $8 billion, investors lost $1.7 billion, and lenders lost $1.3 billion.

SBF and other FTX directors took personal loans from FTX totaling more than $2.1 billion. Client assets were used to purchase luxury homes in the Bahamas, Super Bowl advertisements, planes, naming rights to the Miami Heat arena, and political contributions to US senators and representatives designed to influence crypto industry regulation. SBF also made numerous investments in public and private equity investments, including a stake in Robinhood. Creditors and customers recovered their losses when these assets and the crypto held in FTX wallets were liquidated after a substantial increase in their value. Investors may even try to recover some of the funds spent on Super Bowl advertisements by recouping payments to celebrities such as Tom Brady, Larry David, and Kevin O'Leary, Mr. Wonderful from Shark Tank.

Global users of FTX.com were allowed to participate in highly leveraged crypto trades. Investors deposited a small amount of capital but were held accountable to software that liquidated their trades the moment the collateral became insufficient to support the trade.

FTX had a sister company, a hedge fund–like vehicle called Alameda Research. Alameda accumulated billions of dollars in losses by participating in many of the trades previously discussed that sank firms such as 3AC. Not only was Alameda Research using client funds to make these highly leveraged and money-losing trades, but the software governing Alameda's leveraged trades was coded to not liquidate trades no longer supported by collateral. In addition, the software allowed Alameda to borrow up to $65 billion in client assets without their permission.[17] Alameda was losing money before the FTX exchange was founded, with an influx of client funds allowing Alameda to continue money losing trades for a longer period of time.[18]

There was no incentive for Alameda's traders and algorithms to manage risk because the losses were supported by customer assets, a substantial credit limit, and safety from liquidation when trading on FTX. Due to the lack of immediate financial consequences, SBF and Alameda may have been unaware of the extent of the losses and the amount of risk the operations incurred. The market eventually learned that Alameda had borrowed $10 billion in funds from clients of FTX, despite the assertion that client assets were segregated from the assets of FTX and Alameda.

Of course, customer assets can only be fraudulently used to prop up trading losses as long as customers continue to custody crypto assets at FTX. A liquidity mismatch is created when clients can withdraw assets at any time, while investments in houses, staked crypto, and private equity deals take time to liquidate.

As bankruptcies and liquidations cascaded through the crypto industry in the spring and summer of 2022, investors began to examine counterparty and credit risk more closely. Many investors sought to reduce risk by consolidating assets into their self-custody wallets and recalling all loans and staked tokens. While FTX made overtures to save bankrupt crypto lenders in the summer, the lack of liquidity at FTX was publicized in a now-famous CoinDesk article published 2 November 2022.[19] The article noted that Alameda Research's balance sheet as of 30 June 2022, held $14.6 billion, including nearly $6 billion in self-issued FTT tokens and more than $1 billion in Solana tokens, much of which had restricted liquidity. This article led to an immediate liquidity crisis, as the price of FTT tokens crashed when Binance planned to sell its holdings due to the disclosure of the composition of Alameda's balance sheet.

What lessons can be learned from FTX and Alameda Research?

Interestingly, this fraud wasn't directly related to crypto but was a simple misuse of client funds and understating losses and debt, which had previously occurred at both banks and large corporations. Ironically, the new

CEO of FTX was previously involved in the liquidation of Enron. Enron was a publicly traded Texas-based natural gas and electric utility that declared bankruptcy in December 2001. While Enron was posting strong revenue growth and increasing in value as a stock, the company's executives were losing money and covering the losses with debt held in off–balance sheet special purpose vehicles (SPVs) that were not disclosed to investors.[20] The debt in the SPV was collateralized by the company's stock, but as the stock price declined, the collateral value became insufficient to support the loans. Enron falsified company financials, partially by placing overly optimistic valuations on long-term energy derivatives contracts.

When performing due diligence on any type of investment, investors must investigate commingled assets and conflicts of interest. If a centralized exchange is running a hedge fund or if a hedge fund is running a brokerage firm, it is imperative to investigate whether there is a strict segregation of client funds. No matter how strong the returns or how charismatic the founder is, investors must be willing to walk away from any investment where there is even a hint of operational risks. When assets are commingled, losses of the firm become losses of their clients.

A lesson commonly experienced in 2022, is that issuing your own token does not strengthen a balance sheet. It is important that externally issued assets are held on balance sheets, whether dollars or euros, bitcoin, or Ether. Printing money, whether tokens or fiat currencies, is inflationary and subject to a dramatic loss in value when the market loses faith in the currency.

Due diligence processes also involve an evaluation of the principals of a business. Some investors were so concerned about the behavior of SBF that they asked Michael Lewis to spend time with him. Michael Lewis is one of the world's most famous financial biographers and historians, having written books including *The Big Short, Flash Boys, Moneyball*, and *Liar's Poker*. Lewis's biography of SBF, *Going Infinite*, was published in 2023. In hindsight, many wonder how and why SBF became entrusted with more than $10 billion in client assets before age 30. FTX and Alameda Research were populated with traders and programmers and lacked the traditional experienced compliance, accounting, and risk management teams commonplace in the financial industry. Investors should have been concerned that FTX did not employ senior managers who had CEO or CFO experience at well-respected financial firms. While SBF may have been deemed quirky by some, playing League of Legends while being interviewed by CNBC or when speaking to investors should be seen as a red flag.[21] Multi-tasking often leads to underperformance at both tasks and should not be tolerated during important meetings.

At this point, the reader is referred back to the discussion in Chapter 21 regarding the risks of holding coins on centralized exchanges relative to holding tokens in self-custody. Investors must be cautious to avoid phishing attempts, whether they arrive as emails, web pages, or spam NFTs in a crypto wallet. Investors should verify every transaction in a wallet or a smart contract using a tool such as joinfire.xyz, which shows the assets that will enter and exit a wallet when a transaction is approved.

Investors must also be concerned about vulnerabilities in DeFi protocols. As of May 2023, 148 smart contract exploits had caused $4.28 billion in losses.[22] Investors are encouraged to wait before interacting with a new smart contract or decentralized exchange. If the smart contract governing the protocol has an obvious flaw, it is likely to be exploited within weeks of its publication. The risk of smart contract exploits declines with the age and TVL of a platform. A decentralized exchange, such as Uniswap, presents less risk than many other smart contract platforms because smart contract audits have been performed, the open-source code has been available for years, and investors trust the DEX with substantial TVL. Of course, even a seasoned platform can be vulnerable for some time after a new code update has been released. Developers are encouraged to carefully evaluate the updated code in a test environment before publicly releasing the update.

Blaize has identified Nine Common Smart Contract Vulnerabilities:[23]

Vulnerable price feed – oracles can be exploited when the price feed is stale or inaccurate

Reentrancy – exploits can take place when one smart contract calls functions of other smart contracts

Incorrect deploy settings – incorrect settings can be manipulated or exploited to cause losses

Inflation attack – smart contracts can be manipulated to mint or burn tokens in large amounts

Compromised private keys – developers of crypto protocols need to zealously guard their private keys, as the source code can be changed by unauthorized entrants

Attack with fake contract – smart contracts executing smart contracts can lead to outcomes unexpected by the original protocol developers

Calculation and accuracy issues – calculations can be difficult, especially division, as smart contracts only work with integers

Race conditions and order dependency – the order in which transactions are included in a block may affect the outcome of unrelated transactions

Incorrect work with ERC-20 tokens – Tokens incorrectly configured to comply with ERC-20 standards can cause compatibility issues

With constant vigilance by investors and developers, ideally losses due to crime and fraud will decline over time. The value of crypto lost in scams, hacks, and rug pulls declined from $1.9 billion in the first half of 2022, to $1.69 billion in the second half of 2022, to $656 million in the first half of 2023.[24] In addition, the portion of lost assets recovered increased from 8% in 2022 to 45% in 2023. More than 70% of losses are due to smart contract exploits, nearly 20% are due to phishing, and more than 10% come from rug pulls.[25]

In a rug pull, developers raise money by selling a new coin. Investors buy the coin in anticipation of profits and expect the developers to support the coin, perhaps by building a new DApp and ecosystem. The developers manipulate the price of the coin by pumping it to higher and higher prices, seeking to attract new investors to the coin. Once the price has peaked, the developers implement an exit scam or a rug pull, draining the coin of its assets and abandoning the project undeveloped and without value.

Coin Telegraph provides seven signs of how to spot and avoid rug pulls.[26]

1. Unknown or anonymous developers: Anonymous developers may be a red flag
2. No liquidity lock: Ideally, at least 80% of the money that comes into the project should be locked into the project one year or longer. If there is no liquidity lock in the code, the assets can be immediately withdrawn.
3. Exclusive selling rights: Some unscrupulous developers of a token and smart contract will limit the ability of wallets outside the developer community to be able to sell the token. The development team buys the token, drives it to higher prices, and attracts buyers to the project. When buyers want to take profits, they are not able to sell and know they have been scammed.
4. Test before you invest: Before investing in a new coin, investors may wish to buy a small number of tokens and immediately sell them. If the investor can easily buy and sell the tokens, the development team did not code exclusive selling rights into the token. If the investor is unable to sell the tokens, a rug pull may potentially be coming.
5. Watch for a large price increase without a large number of buyers: When a token is rising quickly in price, or pumping, investors are encouraged to use block explorers to find how many wallets own the tokens. If the price is increasing while it is being purchased by just a few wallets, the price rally is less believable.
6. If it looks too good to be true, it probably is: The fact is that investors are not likely to earn a 2,000% APY in dollars from any crypto project. Stablecoins are not likely to pay 20% risk-free yields. In the best-case

scenario, the protocol attracts substantial TVL and reduces the APY to a sustainable level. In the worst-case scenario, the project is a scam.
7. No external audit: Investors are encouraged to wait for a smart contract audit before investing in any new project.

It's important to summarize the risk management lessons learned from the catastrophic year of 2022, as those who don't learn history are doomed to repeat it.

You can't print your own collateral in unlimited amounts, whether fiat currency or cryptocurrencies.

Leverage and volatility don't mix. If you're trading at 10 times leverage, a 10% loss in the value of that asset wipes out your entire investment.

Leverage and liquidity risk don't mix. Investors who are unable to quickly liquidate assets may not be able to service the debt or add the capital required to maintain a leveraged position. It is important to match the liquidity of the asset to the liquidity of the liabilities. If investors agree to be locked into staked Ether from 2021 until the unknown date of the merge, they need to have other assets available.

Beware of commingled assets and related party transactions. Perform due diligence. Ask a lot of questions. Understand the value of the collateral, the risk management process, and the team's experience.

14%, 18%, and 20% are not risk-free yields. Investors must understand the risk of earning these yields and investigate who is paying them. Sustainable investments earn a positive net interest margin by paying lower yields on deposits and higher yields on loans.

While the FDIC, NCUA, and/or SIPC insure bank and brokerage accounts for US investors, no insurance is currently widely available for crypto held on centralized exchanges. When insurance does exist, assets are covered for the failure of the bank or brokerage firm, not a loss of value.

2022 was a painful year. I hope that you have learned something in this book that will keep your investments safe and you have learned some skills in evaluating the true risk and potential reward of digital asset investments.

Notes

CHAPTER 1   Money, Banking, and Inflation

1. "The Gold Standard Throughout US History." APMEX.com
2. https://fortune.com/2021/11/01/used-car-prices-high-carmax-2021/
3. https://fred.stlouisfed.org/
4. https://caia.org/blog/2020/07/16/socially-distant-inflation
5. https://fred.stlouisfed.org/
6. cnbc.com

CHAPTER 2   Centralized Finance (CeFi) and Traditional Finance (TradFi) Markets

1. https://www.sec.gov/Archives/edgar/data/719739/000119312523064680/d430920dex992.htm
2. https://www.dtcc.com/blockchain
3. Mackintosh, Phil. "Short Interest in Decline." Nasdaq.com. March 3, 2022.
4. finance.yahoo.com
5. https://data.worldbank.org/indicator/BX.TRF.PWKR.DT.GD.ZS?locations=SV
6. Social Security mortality tables. https://www.ssa.gov/oact/STATS/table4c6.html
7. https://www.worldbank.org/content/dam/Worldbank/Research/GlobalFindex/PDF/N2Unbanked.pdf

CHAPTER 4   Bitcoin Mining and Proof-of-Work Protocols

1. Diffie, Whitfield, and Hellman, Martin E. "New Directions in Cryptography." *IEEE Transactions on Information Theory*, Vol. IT-22, No. 6, November 1976.
2. Chaum, David. "Computer Systems Established, Maintained, and Trusted by Mutually Suspicious Groups." Dissertation, Computer Science, UC Berkeley, June 1982.
3. https://worldcoin.org/articles/history-of-cryptocurrency
4. https://crypto.com/university/what-is-cryptography
5. https://bitcoin.org/bitcoin.pdf
6. https://worldpopulationreview.com/country-rankings/millionaires-by-country
7. https://bitcoin.org/bitcoin.pdf
8. https://cointelegraph.com/news/bitcoin-lightning-network-vs-visa-and-mastercard-how-do-they-stack-up

9. https://coincodex.com/article/36709/bitcoin-vs-bitcoin-cash/

10. https://hash.online-convert.com/sha256-generator

11. https://www.pcmag.com/news/inside-the-gpu-shortage-why-you-still-cant-buy-a-graphics-card

12. https://www.blockchain.com/charts/pools

13. https://news.climate.columbia.edu/2022/05/04/cryptocurrency-energy/

14. https://www.nytimes.com/2022/03/22/technology/bitcoin-miners-environment-crypto.html

15. https://bitcoinminingcouncil.com/bitcoin-mining-council-survey-confirms-year-on-year-improvements-in-sustainable-power-and-technological-efficiency-in-h1-2023/

16. https://www.nrel.gov/news/program/2023/how-renewable-energy-is-transforming-the-global-electricity-supply.html

CHAPTER 5   Ethereum Blockchain and Smart Contracts

1. https://decrypt.co/resources/what-is-ethereums-shanghai-upgrade

2. https://www.coingecko.com/research/publications/2023-annual-crypto-report

3. https://www.sec.gov/news/press-release/2023-25

4. Szabo, Nick. (1996). Smart Contracts: Building Blocks for Digital Markets. http://www.fon.hum.uva.nl/rob/Courses/InformationInSpeech/CDROM/Literature/LOTwinterschool2006/szabo.best.vwh.net/smart_contracts_2.html.

5. https://d3h0qzni6h08fz.cloudfront.net/Smart-Contracts-12-Use-Cases-for-Business-and-Beyond_Chamber-of-Digital-Commerce.pdf

6. Ibid.

7. https://www.ccn.com/education/crypto-hacks-2023-full-list-of-scams-and-exploits-as-millions-go-missing/

8. https://ethereum.github.io/yellowpaper/paper.pdf

9. https://ethereum.org/en/roadmap

10. https://www.coindesk.com/learn/what-is-mev-aka-maximal-extractable-value/

CHAPTER 6   Proof-of-Stake Protocols and Other Layer 1 Blockchains

1. https://www.usv.com/writing/2016/08/fat-protocols/

2. https://coinmarketcap.com/academy/article/coinmarketcap-december-2023-market-overview

3. https://dailycoin.com/solana-tops-active-wallets-with-99-month-over-month-surge

4. https://messari.io/report/evaluating-validator-decentralization-geographic-and-infrastructure-distribution-in-proof-of-stake-networks

5. https://coinmetrics.substack.com/p/state-of-the-network-issue-246?utm_source=post-email-title&publication_id=6269&post_id=141084244&utm_campaign=email-post-title&isFreemail=true&r=lsse&utm_medium=email

6. https://tezos-nodes.com/

7. https://www.techtimes.com/articles/270511/20220113/gap-launches-nft-tezos-blockchain%E2%80%94physical-wearable-hoodie-cost-much-500.htm
8. https://beincrypto.com/latest-solana-network-outage-arbitrage-bot-spam/
9. https://solana.com/news/state-compression-compressed-nfts-solana
10. https://coinmarketcap.com/academy/article/what-is-tron

CHAPTER 7   Layer 2 Blockchains and Scaling Solutions

1. 2023 Annual Crypto Industry Report. CoinGecko.
2. https://www.theblock.co/learn/251463/what-is-starknet-and-how-does-it-work

CHAPTER 8   Stablecoins, Crypto Yields, and Central Bank Digital Currencies

1. https://www.cnbc.com/video/2018/06/14/sec-bitcoin-ethereum-not-securities.html
2. Black, Keith. "Capital Formation and Crowdfunding." In *The Emerald Handbook of Fintech: Reshaping Finance*, edited by H. Kent Baker, Greg Filbeck, and Keith Black, Emerald Publishing Limited, 2024.
3. https://beincrypto.com/is-xrp-a-security-coinbase-wallet-delists-ripple/
4. https://www.foxbusiness.com/money/stablecoins-attract-scrutiny-secs-drive-control-crypto
5. https://tether.to/en/transparency/#reports
6. https://ag.ny.gov/press-release/2021/attorney-general-james-ends-virtual-currency-trading-platform-bitfinexs-illegal
7. Ibid.
8. https://www.circle.com/hubfs/USDCAttestationReports/2023/2023%20USDC_Examination%20Report%20December%202023.pdf
9. https://www.circle.com/en/multi-chain-usdc
10. https://bitcoinmagazine.com/business/supplier-of-over-40000-merchants-in-el-salvador-now-accepts-bitcoin
11. https://finance.yahoo.com/news/el-salvador-bitcoin-volcano-bonds-050823244.html
12. https://equitybankbahamas.com/en/central_bank_sand_dollar_updates_lionpressspring2020
13. https://www.bbc.com/news/world-asia-india-37974423
14. https://www.ey.com/en_in/financial-services/what-will-it-take-for-the-digital-rupee-to-be-widely-acceptable-in-india
15. https://ctmfile.com/story/chinas-global-digital-payments-dominance-catalysts-and-future-prospects#:~:text=China%20is%20almost%20a%20cashless%20society%2C%20with%20US%24434, a%20report%20from%20Chinese%20card%20payment%20company%20UnionPay.
16. https://www.atlanticcouncil.org/blogs/econographics/a-report-card-on-chinas-central-bank-digital-currency-the-e-cny/

17. https://www.mondaq.com/nigeria/tax-authorities/1410508/unaccounted-taxes-in-nigeria-the-hidden-drain-on-the-economy#:~:text=Nigeria%3A%20Unaccounted%20Taxes%20In%20Nigeria%3A%20The%20Hidden%20Drain, Consequences%20of%20Unaccounted%20Taxes%20...%204%20Footnotes%20

18. https://www.imf.org/en/News/Articles/2021/11/15/na111621-five-observations-on-nigerias-central-bank-digital-currency

19. https://enaira.gov.ng/

20. https://www.whitehouse.gov/briefing-room/statements-releases/2022/03/09/fact-sheet-president-biden-to-sign-executive-order-on-ensuring-responsible-innovation-in-digital-assets/

21. https://www.federalreserve.gov/publications/money-and-payments-discussion-paper.htm

22. https://www.cnbc.com/2023/03/10/silicon-valley-bank-collapse-how-it-happened.html#:~:text=All%20told%2C%20customers%20withdrew%20a%20staggering%20%2442%20billion,enough%20collateral%20from%20other%20sources%2C%20the%20regulator%20said.

23. https://news.yahoo.com/know-u-governments-surveillance-money-202500939.html

CHAPTER 9   Oracles and Insurance Tokens

1. Blockchain: A Catalyst for New Approaches in Insurance. PWC.
2. Ibid.
3. Why DeFi Insurance Needs a New Design. CoinDesk. Sep 7, 2022.
4. https://www.benzinga.com/money/best-crypto-and-defi-insurance
5. Crypto Custody Firm Copper Inks $500M Insurance Deal With UK Giant Aon. CoinDesk. Nov 9, 2022.
6. https://www.mckinsey.com/industries/financial-services/our-insights/digital-ecosystems-for-insurers-opportunities-through-the-internet-of-things

CHAPTER 10   Privacy Tokens

1. Privacy in the era of cryptocurrencies, Bitcoin Suisse Themes – Technology
2. https://elementalcrypto.com/tips-and-tricks/is-monero-legal-in-us/
3. Ibid.
4. https://www.coindesk.com/learn/bitcoin-mixers-how-do-they-work-and-why-are-they-used/
5. https://www.lexology.com/library/detail.aspx?g=b46073d7-0731-42d2-b319-270bd0c17c6e
6. https://www.cnn.com/2023/08/23/business/tornado-cash-crypto-roman-storm/index.html#:~:text=The%20US%20Department%20of%20the%20Treasury%20sanctioned%20Tornado, those%20under%20US%20jurisdiction%20from%20using%20the%20mixer.

7. https://www.investopedia.com/crypto-exchange-binance-charged-with-money-laundering-fined-usd4-3-billion-8405545#:~:text=The%20world%27s%20largest%20cryptocurrency%20exchange%2C%20Binance%2C%20has%20pleaded,and%20agreed%20to%20step%20down%20from%20his%20position.
8. https://medium.com/asecuritysite-when-bob-met-alice/ring-signatures-and-anonymisation-c9640f08a193
9. https://decrypt.co/43451/irs-1-million-contracts-data-firms-crack-monero
10. https://www.publish0x.com/cryptocurrency/what-is-zcash-a-comprehensive-guide-to-understanding-zcash-xxzkjd
11. https://coinmarketcap.com/currencies/dash/

CHAPTER 11   Decentralized Finance (DeFi): Borrowing, Lending, and Decentralized Exchanges

1. https://compound.finance/
2. https://app.aave.com/markets/?marketName=proto_mainnet_v3
3. https://www.imnepal.com/premium-crypto-phenomenon/
4. How to DeFi. Coin Gecko.
5. https://www.okx.com/learn/aave-flash-loan-tutorial
6. https://docs.uniswap.org/concepts/protocol/fees
7. https://www.coingecko.com/en/exchanges/uniswap-v3-ethereum
8. https://blog.uniswap.org/uniswap-v3
9. Harvey, Campbell R., Ramachandran, Ashwin, and Santoro, Joey. *DeFi and the Future of Finance*. John Wiley & Sons, 2021.

CHAPTER 12   Composability, Stacking DApps, and Bridges

1. https://coinmarketcap.com/currencies/kusama/
2. https://coinmarketcap.com/currencies/bittensor/
3. https://coinmarketcap.com/currencies/astar/
4. https://polkadot.network/blog/polkadot-bridges-connecting-the-polkadot-ecosystem-with-external-networks
5. https://decrypt.co/resources/what-is-thorchain-defi-bitcoin-ethereum https://www.coindesk.com/tech/2021/04/13/thorchain-is-ready-to-grease-the-wheels-of-crypto-to-crypto-trading/
6. https://www.gemini.com/cryptopedia/yearn-finance-defi-lending-protocol#section-what-is-yearn-finance
7. https://www.gemini.com/cryptopedia/yearn-finance-defi-lending-protocol#section-what-is-yearn-finance
8. https://www.gemini.com/cryptopedia/compound-finance-defi-crypto#section-c-tokens-as-legos
9. https://1inch.io/

CHAPTER 13   Blockchain Applications Beyond Financial Markets

1. https://hechingerreport.org/proof-points-861-colleges-and-9499-campuses-have-closed-down-since-2004/
2. https://www.cdc.gov/nchs/data/hestat/births_fertility_2010/births_fertility_2010.htm
3. https://www.dock.io/post/blockchain-identity-management
4. https://www.coindesk.com/markets/2019/03/26/louis-vuitton-owner-lvmh-is-launching-a-blockchain-to-track-luxury-goods/
5. https://www.charitywatch.org/our-charity-rating-process
6. https://blockchainforsocialimpact.com/members/alicesi/
7. https://www.energy.gov/femp/demand-response-and-time-variable-pricing-programs-southeastern-and-midwestern-states
8. https://www.protokol.com/insights/top-5-blockchain-use-cases-in-energy-and-utilities/
9. https://www.kearney.com/digital/article/-/insights/how-blockchain-will-disrupt-digital-advertising

CHAPTER 14   NFTs, Metaverse, and Web 3.0

1. https://news.artnet.com/art-world/us-appeals-court-strikes-royalties-law-1314857
2. https://artistscollectingsociety.org/artists-resale-right/
3. https://news.artnet.com/art-world/us-appeals-court-strikes-royalties-law-1314857
4. https://www.cryptoslam.io/
5. The Chainalysis 2021 NFT Market Report. Chainalysis.
6. https://www.bitstamp.net/learn/blockchain/what-are-bitcoin-ordinals/
7. https://www.coingecko.com/research/publications/market-share-nft-blockchains
8. https://www.bitstamp.net/learn/blockchain/what-are-bitcoin-ordinals/
9. https://decrypt.co/205540/pet-rock-jpegs-bitcoin-ethereum-sell-over-100k
10. https://www.cryptoglobe.com/latest/2022/01/ethereum-eth-is-losing-nft-market-share-to-solana-sol-jpmorgan-analysts-say/
11. https://www.coingecko.com/research/publications/market-share-nft-blockchains
12. https://dappradar.com/blog/crypto-hype-pushes-dapp-industry-adoption-to-new-all-time-high-with-67-million-daily-wallets
13. https://www.weforum.org/agenda/2021/08/nft-boom-cryptocurrency-digital-collectible-artwork
14. https://generativemasks.on.fleek.co/#/
15. https://dappradar.com/blog/crypto-hype-pushes-dapp-industry-adoption-to-new-all-time-high-with-67-million-daily-wallets
16. https://public.com/learn/bored-ape-yacht-club-bayc-guide
17. https://dappradar.com/blog/crypto-hype-pushes-dapp-industry-adoption-to-new-all-time-high-with-67-million-daily-wallets
18. https://www.polygon.com/22709126/ethereum-creator-world-of-warcraft-nerf-nft-vitalik-buterin

19. https://manilastandard.net/pop-life/368517/axie-infinity-philippines-changing-lives-for-the-better.html
20. https://time.com/6199385/axie-infinity-crypto-game-philippines-debt/
21. https://www.rollingstone.com/pro/features/music-crypto-blockchain-nfts-guide-1116327/
22. https://www.julienslive.com/auctions/catalog/id/417
23. https://tech.hindustantimes.com/tech/news/google-s-gmail-allows-third-party-developers-to-read-your-emails-report-story-W9IObo6sjRWCWSAeeZneDN.html
24. https://www.wired.com/story/what-is-the-metaverse/
25. The Chainalysis State of Web3 Report. Chainalysis.
26. https://www.esportsearnings.com/games/534-fortnite
27. https://www.statista.com/chart/22392/global-revenue-of-selected-entertainment-industry-sectors/

CHAPTER 15 Decentralized Autonomous Organizations (DAOs) and Governance

1. The Chainalysis State of Web 3 Report. Chainalysis.
2. Samman, George, and Freuden, David. "DAO: A Decentralized Governance Layer for the Internet of Value." SSRN Electronic Journal, May 2020.
3. Ibid.
4. The Chainalysis State of Web 3 Report.
5. DAO: A Decentralized Governance Layer for the Internet of Value.
6. https://www.zeroplusfinance.com/sec-summons-sushiswap-as-dex-submits-legal-defense-fund-proposal-to-sushi-dao/
7. https://legalnodes.com/article/wyoming-dao-llc
8. DAO: A Decentralized Governance Layer for the Internet of Value.
9. Ibid.
10. https://legalnodes.com/article/wyoming-dao-llc
11. DAO: A Decentralized Governance Layer for the Internet of Value.
12. https://www.coindesk.com/tech/2023/03/16/arbitrum-to-airdrop-new-token-and-transition-to-dao/
13. https://docs.arbitrum.foundation/airdrop-eligibility-distribution
14. https://coinmarketcap.com/currencies/constitutiondao/

CHAPTER 16 Risks, Regulations, and Taxes

1. https://www.whitehouse.gov/briefing-room/statements-releases/2022/03/09/fact-sheet-president-biden-to-sign-executive-order-on-ensuring-responsible-innovation-in-digital-assets/
2. https://www.reuters.com/article/idUSKBN2HX1OH/
3. https://www.sec.gov/corpfin/framework-investment-contract-analysis-digital-assets.
4. https://cointelegraph.com/news/new-study-says-80-percent-of-icos-conducted-in-2017-were-scams

5. Ibid.
6. The Chainalysis 2024 Crypto Crime Report. Chainalysis.
7. https://www.justice.gov/opa/pr/tornado-cash-founders-charged-money-laundering-and-sanctions-violations
8. The Chainalysis 2024 Crypto Crime Report.
9. Ibid.
10. https://www.justice.gov/usao-sdny/pr/silk-road-dark-web-fraud-defendant-sentenced-following-seizure-and-forfeiture-over-34
11. https://www.wired.com/story/silk-road-auction-bitcoin/
12. The Chainalysis 2024 Crypto Crime Report.
13. https://www.sec.gov/news/press-release/2023-25
14. SEC. press release 2020-338.
15. Ibid.
16. https://www.reuters.com/markets/us/sec-dropping-claims-against-ripple-executives-court-filing-2023-10-19/
17. https://www.esma.europa.eu/esmas-activities/digital-finance-and-innovation/markets-crypto-assets-regulation-mica
18. https://unchainedcrypto.com/what-is-mica/
19. https://tokentax.co/blog/wash-sale-trading-in-crypto
20. Ibid.
21. https://thepointsguy.com/news/tax-on-rewards-ruling/
22. https://www.credit-suisse.com/media/assets/corporate/docs/about-us/research/publications/global-wealth-databook-2022.pdf
23. https://www.sifma.org/resources/research/fact-book/
24. https://cointelegraph.com/news/finding-a-new-home-bitcoin-miners-settling-down-after-china-exodus
25. https://chainbase.com/blog/article/sushi-swap-from-emergence-to-development

CHAPTER 17   Tokenization of Off-Chain Assets

1. https://caia.org/tokenisation
2. https://rallyrd.com/faq/
3. Mattereum.com
4. https://web-assets.bcg.com/1e/a2/5b5f2b7e42dfad2cb3113a291222/on-chain-asset-tokenization.pdf
5. Ibid.
6. Spicevc.com
7. https://www.sifma.org/resources/research/fact-book/
8. https://www.savills.com/impacts/market-trends/the-total-value-of-global-real-estate.html
9. https://www.federalreserve.gov/publications/october-2023-changes-in-us-family-finances-from-2019-to-2022.htm

10. Slavchevska, Vanya, De La O Campos, Ana Paula, Brunelli, Chiara, and Doss, Cheryl. "Beyond Ownership: Women's and Men's Land Rights in Sub-Saharan Africa." *Oxford Development Studies*, 49(1), 2–22, 2021.

11. https://www.bbc.com/news/business-35280945

12. https://consensys.io/blog/can-nfts-crack-royalties-and-give-more-value-to-artists

13. https://tokenist.com/the-first-tokenized-hedge-fund-to-trade-on-an-ats-is-now-available/

14. https://www.coindesk.com/markets/2023/03/09/securities-platform-defyca-to-release-tokenized-private-debt-protocol-on-avalanche/

15. https://www.alchemy.com/top/real-world-asset-dapps

16. https://www.franklintempleton.com/press-releases/news-room/2023/franklin-templeton-money-market-fund-launches-on-polygon-blockchain

CHAPTER 18   Fundamental Valuation Models

1. This chapter is an updated version of author Keith Black's previously published "Cryptocurrencies and Digital Assets: Valuation Models and Due Diligence," Investments and Wealth Monitor, July–August 2022 and "Are Cryptocurrencies the New Dot-Com Bubble," Real Assets Adviser, December 2021.

2. https://internationalbanker.com/history-of-financial-crises/the-dotcombubble-burst-2000/.

3. "Why Do ICOs Fail? Are They Still Worth Investing in 2019–2020?" Appinventiv. (July 16, 2020), https://appinventiv.com/blog/why-icos-fail-and-their-worth-in-2019/.

4. Hougan, M., and D. Lawant. 2021. Cryptoassets: The Guide to Bitcoin, Blockchain, and Cryptocurrency for Investment Professionals. Charlottesville, VA: CFA Institute Research Foundation. https://www.cfainstitute.org/research/foundation/2021/cryptoassets.

5. Burniske, C., and J. Tatar. 2018. *Cryptoassets: The Innovative Investor's Guide to Bitcoin and Beyond*. New York: McGraw Hill.

6. Plan B: Modeling Bitcoin Value with Scarcity (2019a). https://medium.com/@100trillionUSD/modeling-bitcoins-value-with-scarcity-91fa0fc03e25. Plan B: Bitcoin Stock-to-Flow Cross Asset Model (2019b). https://medium.com/@100trillionUSD/bitcoin-stock-to-flow-cross-asset-model-50d260feed12.

7. "Cryptocurrencies and Digital Assets: Valuation Models and Due Diligence."

8. https://www.usv.com/writing/2016/08/fat-protocols/.

9. https://ingoldwetrust.report/the-stock-to-flow-ratio-as-the-most-significant-reason-for-golds-monetary-importance/?lang=en.

10. Plan B: Modeling Bitcoin Value with Scarcity (2019a). https://medium.com/@100trillionUSD/modeling-bitcoins-value-with-scarcity-91fa0fc03e25. Plan B: Bitcoin Stock-to-Flow Cross Asset Model (2019b). https://medium.com/@100trillionUSD/bitcoin-stock-to-flow-cross-asset-model-50d260feed12.

11. Ibid.

12. https://www.dlnews.com/articles/markets/gold-etf-launch-holds-lessons-for-bitcoin-investors/

13. https://cointelegraph.com/news/blackrock-etfs-record-inflow-bitcoin-bullrun
14. Hayes, Adam. "A Cost of Production Model for Bitcoin." SSRN Electronic Journal, 2015.
15. https://www.eia.gov/todayinenergy/detail.php?id=61364
16. https://en.macromicro.me/charts/29435/bitcoin-production-total-cost
17. https://cointelegraph.com/news/bitcoin-miners-can-take-fresh-20-btc-price-hit-before-capitulating-data-shows.
18. Burniske, C., and J. Tatar. 2018. *Cryptoassets: The Innovative Investor's Guide to Bitcoin and Beyond*. New York: McGraw Hill.
19. Fisher, I. 1911. *The Purchasing Power of Money: Its Determination and Relation to Credit Interest and Crises*. New York: Macmillan.
20. Burniske, C., and J. Tatar. 2018. *Cryptoassets*.
21. Peterson, Timothy, (January 22, 2018). Metcalfe's Law as a Model for Bitcoin's Value. *Alternative Investment Analyst Review*, Q2 2018, Vol. 7, No. 2, 9–18. Available at SSRN: https://ssrn.com/abstract=3078248
22. https://valkyrieinvest.com/thought-leadership/valuing-bitcoin-and-ether/
23. https://beincrypto.com/bitcoin-wallets-cross-48-million/

CHAPTER 19   Initial Coin Offerings (ICOs), Security Token Offerings (STOs), and Tokenomics

1. Black, Keith. 2024. "Capital Formation and Crowdfunding." Chapter 9 in the *Emerald Handbook of FinTech*.
2. Angel Capital Association. 2019. "ACA Angel Funders Report."
3. https://wealthpursuits.com/angel-investor-statistics/
4. https://pitchbook.com/news/reports/q3-2023-global-private-market-fundraising-report
5. Burniske, C., and J. Tatar. 2018. *Cryptoassets: The Innovative Investor's Guide to Bitcoin and Beyond*. New York: McGraw Hill.
6. Why do ICOs Fail? Are They Still Worth Investing in 2019–2020? Appinventiv. (July 16, 2020), https://appinventiv.com/blog/why-icos-fail-and-their-worth-in-2019/
7. 101blockchains.com/tokenomics
8. https://www.coindesk.com/policy/2024/04/10/defi-exchange-uniswap-receives-enforcement-notice-from-the-sec/
9. 101blockchains.com/tokenomics
10. Why do ICOs Fail? Are They Still Worth Investing in 2019–2020?
11. Ibid.
12. The ICO market isn't collapsing, it's maturing. Elementus.
13. What is an IDO – Initial DEX Offering? Crypto Potato.
14. Security token offerings: The next phase of financial market evolution? Deloitte.
15. Ibid.
16. Ibid.
17. Ibid.
18. Ibid.

CHAPTER 20 Trading and Technical Analysis

1. Fama, Eugene (1970). "Efficient Capital Markets: A Review of Theory and Empirical Work." *Journal of Finance* 25 (2): 383–417.
2. https://www.spglobal.com/spdji/en/spiva/article/spiva-us/
3. Lo, Andrew W. (2005). "Reconciling Efficient Markets with Behavioral Finance: The Adaptive Markets Hypothesis." *Journal of Investment Consulting* 7 (2): 21–44.
4. "Warren Buffett, Omahan. In Search Of Social Challenges." *Omaha Sunday Journal and Star*. (March 18, 1973).
5. https://www.mlq.ai/what-is-crypto-on-chain-analysis/
6. Binance Academy. *Cryptocurrency Trading*. ebook.
7. Ibid.
8. Ibid.
9. Ibid.
10. Ibid.
11. Ibid.

CHAPTER 21 Investing Directly in Crypto: Wallets, Custody, and Security

1. https://www.coindesk.com/tech/2023/12/27/crypto-users-lost-2b-to-hacks-scams-and-exploits-in-2023-defi-says/
2. https://www.bankrate.com/investing/how-to-recover-lost-bitcoins-and-other-crypto/
3. https://www.cnbc.com/2023/03/16/svb-signature-bank-failures-yellen-says-us-banking-system-is-stable-and-deposits-remain-safe.html
4. Luke 12:48.
5. https://kyc-chain.com/top-25-crypto-custodians-2023-a-comprehensive-guide/
6. Burniske, C., and J. Tatar. 2018. *Cryptoassets: The Innovative Investor's Guide to Bitcoin and Beyond*. New York: McGraw Hill.
7. Narayanan, Arvind, Bonneau, Joseph, Felten, Edward, Miller, Andrew, and Goldfeder, Steven. *Bitcoin and Cryptocurrency Technologies: A Comprehensive Introduction*. Princeton University Press, 2016.
8. https://www.business2community.com/business-pages/winklevoss-twins-net-worth-making-6-billion-from-facebook-to-crypto
9. https://www.business2community.com/business-pages/winklevoss-twins-net-worth-making-6-billion-from-facebook-to-crypto
10. https://www.forbes.com/profile/mark-zuckerberg/?sh=617b28173e06
11. Mezrich, Ben. *Bitcoin Billionaires: A True Story of Genius, Betrayal, and Redemption*. Flatiron Books, 2019.
12. Microsoft: Using multi-factor authentication blocks 99.9% of account hacks. zdnet.com

CHAPTER 22 Derivative Markets: Futures, Options, and Perpetual Swaps

1. Rennison and Pederson. The Volatility Risk Premium. PIMCO 2012.
2. https://www.cboe.com/optionsinstitute/tools/options_calculator/
3. https://www.cmegroup.com/markets/cryptocurrencies/bitcoin/bitcoin.con tractSpecs.html
4. Ibid.
5. https://www.cmegroup.com/media-room/historical-first-trade-dates.html
6. https://www.cmegroup.com/solutions/clearing/financial-and-collateral-management/acceptable-collateral.html
7. https://www.coinglass.com/pro/perpteual-spot-volume
8. https://www.coinglass.com/pro/dashboard/bitcoin
9. https://www.coinglass.com/pro/dashboard/ethereum

CHAPTER 23 Building Portfolios of Stocks, Bonds, Crypto Stocks, and ETFs

1. https://www.ici.org/statistical-report/ret_23_q4
2. https://philanthropynewsdigest.org/news/foundation-assets-rose-100-billion-in-first-half-of-2023-study-finds#:~:text=Total%20assets%20of%20foundations%20in%20the%20United%20States,previous%20three%20quarters%2C%20an%20analysis%20by%20FoundationMark%20finds.
3. https://www.commonfund.org/hubfs/00%20Commonfund.org/03%20 Research%20Center/Press-Releases/2024-0215-NCSE-Press-Release/FY23%20 NCSE%20Press%20Release.pdf#:~:text=The%20688%20ins%EF%BF% BDtu%EF%BF%BDons%20in%20this%20year%E2%80%99s%20 study%20represented,had%20endowments%20that%20were%20%24100% 20million%20or%20less.
4. https://www.ici.org/statistical-report/ret_23_q4
5. https://www.statista.com/statistics/1267499/assets-under-management-of-swfs-worldwide/
6. https://etfs.grayscale.com/gbtc
7. https://ycharts.com/companies/GBTC/discount_or_premium_to_nav
8. https://www.coingecko.com/research/publications/bitcoin-etfs-btc-holdings
9. https://bitwiseinvestments.com/crypto-funds/bitw
10. https://www.coingecko.com/research/publications/bitcoin-etfs-btc-holdings
11. https://www.coingecko.com/research/publications/bitcoin-etfs-btc-holdings
12. https://valkyrieinvest.com/thought-leadership/crypto-miners/
13. https://www.coinwarz.com/mining/bitcoin/hashrate-chart
14. https://www.coingecko.com/research/publications/ethereum-etfs-worldwide
15. "Bitcoin's Role in a Traditional Portfolio." Bitwise. August 2023.

CHAPTER 24 Investing Through Private Equity and Hedge Funds

1. https://cryptofundresearch.com/q4-2023-crypto-fund-report/
2. https://www.mckinsey.com/industries/private-equity-and-principal-investors/our-insights/mckinseys-private-markets-annual-review-2023

3. https://www.reuters.com/markets/us/hedge-fund-assets-reach-43-trillion-q1-says-hfr-2024-04-22/
4. https://cryptofundresearch.com/q4-2023-crypto-fund-report/
5. Ibid.
6. 4th Annual Global Crypto Hedge Fund Report, PWC/AIMA.
7. https://nerdbot.com/2023/11/28/how-arbitrage-is-made-possible-with-kimchi-premium/
8. 5th Annual Global Crypto Hedge Fund Report, PWC/AIMA/CoinShares.
9. https://cryptofundresearch.com/q4-2023-crypto-fund-report/
10. 5th Annual Global Crypto Hedge Fund Report.
11. Ibid.
12. Ibid.
13. 4th Annual Global Crypto Hedge Fund Report, PWC/AIMA.
14. 5th Annual Global Crypto Hedge Fund Report.
15. Ibid.
16. https://www.cbinsights.com/research/top-corporate-venture-capital-investors/
17. https://www.coingecko.com/research/publications/top-crypto-vcs
18. https://www.coindesk.com/business/2024/03/15/binance-spun-off-venture-capital-arm-earlier-this-year-bloomberg/
19. https://eqvista.com/company-valuation/valuation-crypto-assets/simple-agreement-future-tokens/
20. https://www.galaxy.com/insights/research/crypto-and-blockchain-venture-capital-q1-2024/
21. Ibid.
22. Ibid.
23. https://www.rootdata.com/dashboard May 2024.
24. https://www.galaxy.com/insights/research/crypto-and-blockchain-venture-capital-q1-2024/
25. Ibid.
26. Ibid.
27. https://www.rootdata.com/dashboard May 2024.

CHAPTER 25 Due Diligence and Technology Risks: FTX, Terra Luna, Hacks, and Scams

1. https://caia.org/blog/2022/09/12/macro-factors-next-layer-digital-asset-specific-risk-model
2. https://www.coindesk.com/learn/the-fall-of-terra-a-timeline-of-the-meteoric-rise-and-crash-of-ust-and-luna/
3. https://medium.com/@adelgaizo/the-fall-of-the-moon-c7dc6f4b6adc
4. Clements, Ryan. Built to Fail: The Inherent Fragility of Algorithmic Stablecoins (October 28, 2021). 11 Wake Forest L. Rev. Online 131 (October 2021), Available at SSRN: https://ssrn.com/abstract=3952045
5. https://www.coindesk.com/learn/what-is-luna-and-ust-a-guide-to-the-terra-ecosystem/

6. https://www.cnn.com/2023/03/14/tech/viral-bank-run/index.html
7. https://decrypt.co/105416/bankrupt-three-arrows-capital-owes-3-5b-to-creditors-including-2-3b-to-genesis
8. https://www.theblock.co/post/89928/three-arrows-reports-more-than-1-2-billion-position-in-grayscales-gbtc
9. https://cointelegraph.com/news/is-bitcoin-price-really-influenced-by-the-grayscale-gbtc-premium
10. https://cointelegraph.com/news/grayscale-bitcoin-etf-halves-btc-halving
11. https://www.reuters.com/business/archegos-indictment-raises-fresh-questions-over-banks-risk-management-controls-2022-05-02/
12. https://nymag.com/intelligencer/article/three-arrows-capital-kyle-davies-su-zhu-crash.html
13. https://www.cnbc.com/2022/07/17/how-the-fall-of-celsius-dragged-down-crypto-investors.html
14. Ibid.
15. https://decrypt.co/102812/celsius-liquidity-crunch-lido-staked-ethereum-steth
16. https://apnews.com/article/sam-bankman-fried-ftx-cryptocurrency-sentencing-sbf-d7bb1a5e94b4c22039d74dfeab1a2ff1
17. https://cointelegraph.com/news/alameda-research-had-a-65b-secret-line-of-credit-with-ftx-report
18. https://cointelegraph.com/news/sam-bankman-fried-s-alameda-research-troubles-predate-ftx-report
19. https://www.coindesk.com/business/2022/11/02/divisions-in-sam-bankman-frieds-crypto-empire-blur-on-his-trading-titan-alamedas-balance-sheet/
20. https://www.investopedia.com/terms/e/enron.asp
21. https://www.businessinsider.com/ftx-sam-bankman-fried-league-of-legends-investor-pitch-meeting-2022-11
22. https://medium.com/bankless-dao/getting-smart-about-smart-contract-vulnerabilities-32877aabd96
23. https://blaize.tech/article-type/web3-security/9-most-common-smart-contract-vulnerabilities-found-by-blaize/
24. https://cointelegraph.com/news/656m-lost-from-crypto-hacks-scams-and-rug-pulls-in-h12023-report
25. Ibid.
26. Ibid.

About the Author

Keith Black, PhD, CFA, CAIA, FDP, CDAA, is an award-winning author and course designer specializing in making complex topics accessible to audiences of varying sophistication. He currently serves as the managing director of education for RIA Channel, where he designed and co-taught the Nasdaq Advisor Academy course on cryptocurrencies and digital assets.

In his previous role as managing director of content strategy at the CAIA Association, he was a co-author of the second, third, and fourth editions of the level I and II CAIA curriculum on alternative investments.

Dr. Black has also advised foundations, endowments, and pension funds on their asset allocation and manager selection strategies in hedge funds, commodities, and managed futures. Prior experience includes commodities derivatives trading, stock options research and Cboe floor trading, and building quantitative stock selection models for mutual funds and hedge funds.

Dr. Black previously served on the faculty of the Illinois Institute of Technology and currently teaches courses on investment consulting and investing in cryptocurrencies at the University of Massachusetts, Amherst.

He has published 16 refereed journal articles and contributed to 8 books. Dr. Black was named to the *Institutional Investor* magazine's list of "Rising Stars of Hedge Funds."

Dr. Black earned a BA from Whittier College, an MBA from Carnegie Mellon University, and a PhD from the Illinois Institute of Technology. He has earned the Chartered Financial Analyst (CFA) and the Certified Digital Asset Advisor (CDAA) designations and was a member of the inaugural class of both CAIA and FDP Charterholders.

About the Companion Website

If you are an instructor, you have access to the Instructor Companion Site for
Investing in Cryptocurrencies and Digital Assets: A Guide to Understanding Technologies, Business Models, Due Diligence, and Valuation:
www.wiley.com/go/black/cryptocurrencies

This website gives you access to the lecture slides and end-of-chapter questions and answers for each chapter of this text.

You can access the resources in two ways:

- Using the menu at the top, select a chapter. Lecture slides and end-of-chapter questions will be available for each chapter.
- Using the menu at the top, select a resource. This will allow you to access a particular resource section. You will then have the option of selecting resources within the section or going directly to a specific chapter.

Please note that you will receive a prompt to register for the website the first time you attempt to access this material. If you have a Wiley instructor account, then you will only need to sign in using this account. If you do not have a Wiley instructor account, you will receive a prompt to sign up for one.

Index